Parallel
Algorithms for
Matrix
Computations

D1338745

Parallel Algorithms for Matrix Computations

K. A. Gallivan
Michael T. Heath
Esmond Ng
James M. Ortega
Barry W. Peyton
R. J. Plemmons
Charles H. Romine
A. H. Sameh
Robert G. Voigt

siam ®

Philadelphia

Society for Industrial and Applied Mathematics

Library of Congress Cataloging-in-Publication Data

Parallel algorithms for matrix computations / K. A. Gallivan ... [et al.].

     p. cm.

  Includes bibliographical references.

  ISBN 0-89871-260-2

  1. Matrices—Data processing. 2. Algorithms. 3. Parallel processing (Electronic computers) I. Gallivan, K.A. (Kyle A.)

QA188.P367 1990

512.9'434—dc20

90-22017

List of Authors

K. A. Gallivan, Center for Supercomputing Research and Development, University of Illinois, Urbana, IL 61801.

Michael T. Heath, Mathematical Sciences Section, Oak Ridge National Laboratory, P.O. Box 2009, Oak Ridge, TN 37831-8083.

Esmond Ng, Mathematical Sciences Section, Oak Ridge National Laboratory, P.O. Box 2009, Oak Ridge, TN 37831-8083.

James M. Ortega, Applied Mathematics Department, University of Virginia, Charlottesville, VA 22903.

Barry W. Peyton, Mathematical Sciences Section, Oak Ridge National Laboratory, P.O. Box 2009, Oak Ridge, TN 37831-8083.

R. J. Plemmons, Department of Mathematics and Computer Science, Wake Forest University, Winston-Salem, NC 27109.

Charles H. Romine, Mathematical Sciences Section, Oak Ridge National Laboratory, P.O. Box 2009, Oak Ridge, TN 37831-8083.

A. H. Sameh, Center for Supercomputing Research and Development, University of Illinois, Urbana, IL 61801.

Robert G. Voigt, ICASE, NASA Langley Research Center, Hampton, VA 23665.

Preface

This book consists of three papers that collect, describe, or reference an extensive selection of important parallel algorithms for matrix computations. Algorithms for matrix computations are among the most widely used computational tools in science and engineering. They are usually the first such tools to be implemented in any new computing environment. Due to recent trends in the design of computer architectures, the scientific and engineering research community is becoming increasingly dependent upon the development and implementation of efficient parallel algorithms for matrix computations on modern high-performance computers. Architectures considered here include both shared-memory systems and distributed-memory systems, as well as combinations of the two. The volume contains two broad survey papers and an extensive bibliography. The purpose is to provide an overall perspective on parallel algorithms for both dense and sparse matrix computations in solving systems of linear equations, as well as for dense or structured problems arising in least squares computations, eigenvalue and singular-value computations, and rapid elliptic solvers. Major emphasis is given to computational primitives whose efficient execution on parallel and vector computers is essential to attaining high-performance algorithms. Short descriptions of the contents of each of the three papers in this book are provided in the following paragraphs.

The first paper (by Gallivan, Plemmons, and Sameh) contains a general perspective on modern parallel and vector architectures and the way in which they influence algorithm design. The paper also surveys associated algorithms for dense matrix computations. The authors concentrate on approaches to computations that have been used on shared-memory architectures with a modest number of (possibly vector) processors, as well as distributed-memory architectures, such as hypercubes, having a relatively large number of processors. The architectures considered include both commercially available machines and experimental research prototypes. Algorithms for dense or structured matrix computations in direct linear system solvers, direct least squares computations, eigenvalue and singular-value computations, and rapid elliptic solvers are considered. Since the amount of literature in these areas is quite large, an attempt has been made to select representative work.

The second paper (by Heath, Ng, and Peyton) is primarily concerned with parallel algorithms for solving symmetric positive definite sparse linear systems. The main driving force for the development of vector and parallel computers has been scientific and engineering computing, and perhaps the most common problem that arises is that of solving sparse symmetric positive definite linear systems. The authors focus their attention on direct methods of solution, specifically by Cholesky factorization. Parallel algorithms are surveyed for all phases of the solution process for sparse systems, including ordering, symbolic factorization, numeric factorization, and triangular solution.

The final paper (by Ortega, Voigt, and Romine) consists of an extensive bibliography on parallel and vector numerical algorithms. Over 2,000 references, collected by the authors over a period of several years, are provided in this work. Although this is primarily a bibliography on numerical methods, also included are a number of references on machine architecture, programming languages, and other topics of interest to computational scientists and engineers.

The book may serve as a reference guide on modern computational tools for researchers in science and engineering. It should be useful to computer scientists, mathematicians, and engineers who would like to learn more about parallel and vector computations on high-performance computers. The book may also be useful as a graduate text in scientific computing. For instance, many of the algorithms discussed in the first two papers have been treated in courses on scientific computing that have been offered recently at several universities.

R. J. Plemmons
Wake Forest University

Contents

PARALLEL ALGORITHMS FOR DENSE LINEAR ALGEBRA COMPUTATIONS*

K. A. GALLIVAN[†], R. J. PLEMMONS[‡], AND A. H. SAMEH[†]

Abstract. Scientific and engineering research is becoming increasingly dependent upon the development and implementation of efficient parallel algorithms on modern high-performance computers. Numerical linear algebra is an indispensable tool in such research and this paper attempts to collect and describe a selection of some of its more important parallel algorithms. The purpose is to review the current status and to provide an overall perspective of parallel algorithms for solving dense, banded, or block-structured problems arising in the major areas of direct solution of linear systems, least squares computations, eigenvalue and singular value computations, and rapid elliptic solvers. A major emphasis is given here to certain computational primitives whose efficient execution on parallel and vector computers is essential in order to obtain high performance algorithms.

Key words. numerical linear algebra, parallel computation

AMS(MOS) subject classifications. 65-02, 65F05, 65F15, 65F20, 65N20

1. Introduction. Numerical linear algebra algorithms form the most widely-used computational tools in science and engineering. Matrix computations, including the solution of systems of linear equations, least squares problems, and algebraic eigenvalue problems, govern the performance of many applications on vector and parallel computers. With this in mind we have attempted in this paper to collect and describe a selection of what we consider to be some of the more important parallel algorithms in dense matrix computations.

Since the early surveys on parallel numerical algorithms by Miranker [133], Sameh [153], and Heller [91] there has been an explosion of research activities on this topic. Some of this work was surveyed in the 1985 article by Ortega and Voigt [138]. Their main emphasis, however, was on the solution of partial differential equations on vector and parallel computers. We also point to the textbook by Hockney and Jesshope [100] which includes some material on programming linear algebra algorithms on parallel machines. More recently, Ortega, Voigt, and Romine produced an extensive bibliography of parallel and vector numerical algorithms [139]; and Ortega [137] published a textbook containing a discussion of direct and iterative methods for solving linear systems on vector and parallel computers.

Our purpose in the present paper is to provide an overall perspective of parallel algorithms for dense matrix computations in linear system solvers, least squares problems, eigenvalue and singular-value problems, as well as rapid elliptic solvers. In this paper, dense problems are taken to include block tridiagonal matrices in which each block is dense, as well as algorithms for banded matrices which are dense within the band. In particular, we concentrate on approaches to these problems that have been used on available, research and commercial, shared memory multivector architectures

---

* Received by the editors March 6, 1989; accepted for publication (in revised form) October 31, 1989.

† Center for Supercomputing Research and Development, University of Illinois, Urbana, Illinois 61801. This research was supported by the Department of Energy under grant DE-FG02-85ER25001 and the National Science Foundation under grants NSF-MIP-8410110 and NSF-CCR-8717942.

‡ Departments of Computer Science and Mathematics, North Carolina State University, Raleigh, North Carolina 27695-8206. The work of this author was supported by the Air Force Office of Scientific Research under grant AFOSR-88-0285 and by the National Science Foundation under grant DMS-85-21154.

with a modest number of processors and distributed memory architectures such as the hypercube.

Since the amount of literature in these areas is very large we have attempted to select representative work in each. As a result, the topics and the level of detail at which each is treated can not help but be biased by the authors' interest. For example, considerable attention is given here to the discussion and performance analysis of certain computational primitives and algorithms for high performance machines with hierarchical memory systems. Given recent developments in numerical software technology, we believe this is appropriate and timely.

Many important topics relevant to parallel algorithms in numerical linear algebra are not discussed in this survey. Iterative methods for linear systems are not mentioned since the recent text by Ortega [137] contains a fairly comprehensive review of that topic, especially as it relates to the numerical solution of partial differential equations. Parallel algorithms using special techniques for solving generally sparse problems in linear algebra will also not be considered in this particular survey. Although significant results have recently been obtained, the topic is of sufficient complexity and importance to require a separate survey for adequate treatment.

The organization of the rest of this paper is as follows. Section 2 briefly discusses some of the important aspects of the architecture and the way in which they influence algorithm design. Section 3 contains a discussion of the decomposition of algorithms into computational primitives of varying degrees of complexity. Matrix multiplication, blocksize analysis, and triangular system solvers are emphasized. Algorithms for LU and LU-like factorizations on both shared and distributed memory systems are considered in §4. Parallel factorization schemes for block-tridiagonal systems, which arise in numerous application areas, are discussed in detail. Section 5 concerns parallel orthogonal factorization methods on shared and distributed memory systems for solving least squares problems. Recursive least squares computations, on local memory hypercube architectures, are also discussed in terms of applications to computations in control and signal processing. Eigenvalue and singular value problems are considered in §6. Finally, §7 contains a review of parallel techniques for rapid elliptic solvers of importance in the solution of separable elliptic partial differential equations. In particular, recent domain decomposition, block cyclic reduction, and boundary integral domain decomposition schemes are examined.

2. Architectures of interest. To satisfy the steadily increasing demand for computational power by users in science and engineering, supercomputer architects have responded with systems that achieve the required level of performance via progressively complex synergistic effects of the interaction of hardware, system software (e.g., restructuring compilers and operating systems), and system architecture (e.g., multivector processors and multilevel hierarchical memories). Algorithm designers are faced with a large variety of system configurations even within a fairly generic architectural class such as shared memory multivector processors. Furthermore, for any particular system in the architectural class, a CRAY-2 or Cedar [117], the algorithm designer encounters a complex relationship between performance, architectural parameters (cache size, number of processors), and algorithmic parameters (method used, blocksizes). As a result, codes for scientific computing such as numerical linear algebra take the form of a parameterized family of algorithms that can respond to changes within a particular architecture, e.g., changing the size of cluster or global memory on Cedar, or when moving from one member of an architectural family to another, e.g., Cedar to CRAY-2. The latter adaptation may, of course, involve changing the method used completely, say from Gaussian elimination with partial pivoting to a decomposition based on pairwise pivoting.

There are several consequences of such a situation. First, algorithm designers must be sensitive to architecture/algorithm mapping issues and any discussion of parallel numerical algorithms is incomplete if these issues are not addressed. Second, one of the main thrusts of parallel computing research must be to change the situation. That is, if scientific computing is to reap the full benefits of parallel processing, cooperative research involving expertise in the areas of parallel software development (debugging, restructuring compilers, etc.), numerical algorithms, and parallel architectures is required to develop parallel languages and programming environments along with parallel computer systems that mitigate this architectural sensitivity. Such cooperative work is underway at several institutions.

The architecture that first caused a widespread and substantial algorithm redesign activity in numerical computing is the vector processor. Such processors exploit the concept of *pipelining* computations. This technique decomposes operations of interest, e.g., floating point multiplication, into multiple stages and implements a pipelined functional unit that allows multiple instances of the computation to proceed simultaneously — one in each stage of the pipe.[1] Such parallelism is typically very fine-grain and requires the identification in algorithms of large amounts of homogeneous work applied to vector objects. Fortunately, numerical linear algebra is rich in such operations and the vector processor can be used with reasonable success. From the point of view of the functional unit, the basic algorithmic parameter that influences performance is the *vector length*, i.e., the number of elements on which the basic computation is to be performed. Architectural parameters that determine the performance for a particular vector length include cycle time, the number of stages of the pipeline, as well as any other startup costs involved in preparing the functional unit for performing the computations. Various models have been proposed in the literature to characterize the relationship between algorithmic and architectural parameters that determine the performance of vector processors. Perhaps the best known is that of Hockney and Jesshope [100].

The Cyber 205 is a memory-to-memory vector processor that has been successfully used for scientific computation. On every cycle of a vector operation multiple operands are read from memory, each of the functional unit stages operate on a set of vector elements that are moving through the pipe, and an element of the result of the operation is written to memory. Obviously, the influence of the functional unit on algorithmic parameter choices is not the only consideration required. Heavy demands are placed on the memory system in that it must process two reads and a write (along with any other control I/O) in a single cycle. Typically, such demands are met by using a highly interleaved or parallel memory system with $M > 1$ memory modules whose aggregate bandwidth matches or exceeds that demanded by the pipeline. Elements of vectors are then assigned across the memory modules in a simple interleaved form, e.g., $v(i)$ is in module $i \bmod M$, or using more complex skewing schemes [193]. As a result, the reference pattern to the memory modules generated by accessing elements of a vector is crucial in determining the rate at which the memory system can supply data to the processor. The algorithmic parameter that encapsulates this information is the *stride* of vector access. For example, accessing the column of an array stored in column-major order results in a stride of 1 while accessing a row of

---

[1] The details of the architectural tradeoffs involved in a vector processor are somewhat surprisingly subtle and complex. For an excellent discussion of some of them see [174].

the same array requires a stride of *lda* where *lda* is the leading dimension of the array data object.

Not all vector processors are implemented with the three computational memory ports (2 reads/1 write) required by a memory-to-memory processor. The CRAY-1, one CPU of a CRAY-2 and one computational element of an Alliant FX/8 are examples of register-based vector processors that have a single port to memory and, to compensate for the loss in data transfer bandwidth, provide a set of vector registers internal to the processor to store operands and results.[2] Each of the registers can hold a vector of sufficient length to effectively use the pipelined functional units available. The major consequence of this, considered in detail below, is that such processors require careful management of data transfer between memory and register in order to achieve reasonable performance. In particular, care must be taken to reuse a register operand several times before reloading the register or to accumulate as many partial results of successive computations in the same register before storing the values to memory, i.e., reducing the number of loads and stores, respectively.

Some register-based vector processors also use two other techniques to improve performance. The first is the use of parallelism across functional units and ports. Multiple instructions that have no internal resource conflict, e.g., adding two vector registers with the result placed in a third and loading of a fourth register from memory, are executed simultaneously, making as much use of the available resources as possible. This influences kernel design in that careful ordering of assembler level instructions can improve the exploitation of the processor.

The second technique is essentially functional unit parallelism with certain resource dependences managed by the hardware at runtime. The technique is called *chaining* and it allows the result of one operation to be routed into another operation as an operand while both operations are active. For example, on a machine without chaining, loading a vector from memory into a register and adding it to another register would require two distinct nonoverlapped vector operations and therefore two startup periods, etc. Chaining allows the elements of the vector loaded into the first register to be made available, after a small amount of time, for use by the adder before the load is completed. Essentially, it appears as if the vector addition was taking one of its operands directly from memory. For processors that handle chaining of instructions automatically at runtime, careful consideration of the order of instructions used in implementing an algorithm or kernel is required. Some other vector processors, however, make the chaining of functional units and the memory port an explicit part of the vector instruction set. For example, the Alliant FX/8 allows one argument of a vector instruction to be given as an address in memory, thereby chaining the memory port and the appropriate functional units. The best example of this is the workhorse of its instruction set, the triad, which computes $v_1 \leftarrow v_2 + \alpha x$, where v_1 and v_2 are vector registers, α is a scalar, and x is a vector in memory. This instruction explicitly chains the floating point multiplier and adder and the memory port. Such instruction constructs greatly simplify the exploitation of the chaining capabilities of a vector processor at the cost of the loss of a certain amount of flexibility.

While vector processors have been used and can deliver substantial performance for many computations, the quest for even more speed led to the availability and continuing development of MIMD multiprocessors and multivector processors. The processors on such machines are capable of executing arbitrary code segments in

---

[2] Some register-based vector processors also have multiple ports to memory in an attempt to have the best of both worlds, e.g., one CPU of a CRAY X-MP.

parallel and therefore subsume, assuming appropriate overhead levels, the fine-grain parallelism of vector processors. Shared memory architectures have the generic structure shown in Fig. 1(a). They are characterized by the fact that the interconnection network links all of the processors to all of the memory modules, i.e., a *user-controlled* processor can access any element of memory *without* the aid of another *user-controlled* processor. There is no concept of a direct connection between a processor and some subset of the remaining processors, i.e., a connection that does not involve the shared memory modules. Of course, in practice, few shared memory machines strictly adhere to this simple characterization. Many have a small amount of local memory associated with, and only accessible by, each processor. The aggregate size of these local memories is usually relatively insignificant compared to the large shared memory available. As local memory sizes increase, the architecture moves toward the distributed end of the architectural spectrum. Not surprisingly, the ability of the network/memory system to supply data to the multiple processors at a sufficient rate is one of the key components of performance of shared memory architectures. As a result, the organization and proper exploitation of this system must be carefully considered when designing high-performance algorithms.

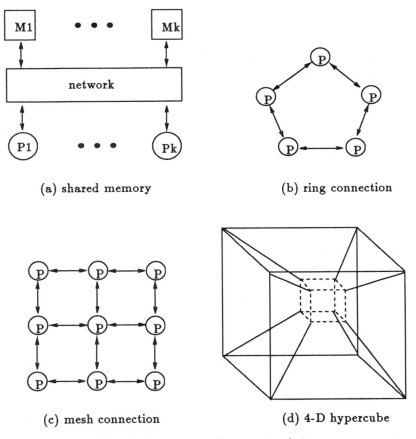

(a) shared memory   (b) ring connection

(c) mesh connection   (d) 4-D hypercube

FIG. 1. *Some memory/processor topologies.*

The generic organization in Fig. 1 shows a highly interleaved or parallel memory system connected to the processors. This connection can take on several forms.

For a small number of processors and memory modules, p, a high-performance bus or crossbar switch can provide complete connectivity and reasonable performance. Unfortunately, such networks quickly become too costly as p increases. For larger systems, it is necessary to build scalable networks out of several smaller completely connected switches such as $(s \times s)$-crossbars. The Ω-network of Lawrie [119] can connect $p = s^k$ processors and memory modules with k network stages. Each stage comprises s^{k-1} $(s \times s)$-crossbars, for a total of $O(p \log_s p)$ switches. As with vector processors, data skewing schemes and access stride manipulation are important in balancing the memory bandwidth achieved with the aggregate computational rate of the processors. Ideally, the two should balance perfectly; in practice, keeping the two within a small multiple is achievable for numerical linear algebra computations via the skewing and stride manipulations or with the introduction of local memory (discussed below). As p increases, however, the latency for each memory access grows as $O(k)$. Fortunately, the addition of architectural features such as data prefetch mechanisms and local memory can provide some mitigation of this problem.

As mentioned above, one of the ways in which the performance of a large shared memory system can be improved is the introduction of local memories or caches with each processor. The idea is similar to the use of registers within vector processors in that data can be kept for reuse in small fast memory private to each processor. If sufficient data locality[3] is present in the computations the processor can proceed at a rate consistent with the data transfer bandwidth of the cache rather than the lower effective bandwidth of the large shared memory due to latency and conflicts. One difference between local memories/caches and vector registers, however, is that registers have a prescribed *shape* and must be used, for the most part, in vector operations; they must contain and be operated on as a vector $v \in \Re^m$ where m is the vector length. On the other hand, local memory or caches can contain, up to a point, arbitrary data objects with no constraint on type or use. These differences can strongly affect the way that these architectural features influence algorithm parameter choices.

Another feature which can significantly influence the performance of an algorithm on a shared memory machine is the architectural support for synchronization of processors. These mechanisms are required for the assignment of parallel work to a processor and enforcing data dependences to ensure correct operation once the assignment is made. The support found on the various multiprocessors varies considerably. Some provide special purpose hardware for controlling small grain tasks on a moderate number of processors and simple TEST-AND-SET[4] synchronization in memory, e.g., the Alliant FX/8. Others provide more complex synchronization processors at the memory module or network level with capabilities such as FETCH-AND-OP or the Zhu–Yew primitives used on Cedar [196]. Finally, there are some which are oriented toward large-grain task parallelism which rely more on system-software-based synchronization mechanisms with relatively large cost to coordinate multiple tasks within a user's job, often at the same time with the tasks of other users.

The discussion above clearly shows that the optimization of algorithms for shared memory multivector architectures involve the consideration of the tradeoffs concern-

---

[3] A computation is said to have high data locality if the ratio of the data elements to the number of operations is small.

[4] The TEST-AND-SET operation allows for the indivisible action of accessing a memory location, testing its value, and setting the location if the test succeeds. It can be used as the basic building block of most synchronization primitives.

ing the influence of architectural features, such as parallelism, load balancing, vector computation, synchronization and parallel or hierarchical memory systems, on the choice of algorithm or kernel organization. Many of these are potentially contradictory. For example, increasing data locality by reorganizing the order of computations can directly conflict with the attempt to increase the vector length of other computations. The modeling and tradeoff analysis of these features will be discussed in detail below for selected topics.

Many shared memory parallel and multivector processors are commercially available over a wide range of price and performance. These include the Encore, Sequent, Alliant FX series, and supercomputers such as the CRAY X-MP and Y-MP, CRAY-2, and NEC. The Alliant FX/8 possesses most of the interesting architectural features that have influenced linear algebra algorithm design on shared memory processors recently; see the cluster blowup in Fig. 2. It consists of up to eight register-based vector processors or computational elements (CE's), each capable of delivering a peak rate of 11.75 Mflops for calculations using 64-bit data (two operations per cycle) implying a total peak rate of approximately 94 Mflops. The startup times for the vector instructions can reduce this rate significantly. For example, the vector triad instruction $v \leftarrow v + \alpha x$ (the preferred instruction for achieving high performance in many codes) has a maximum performance of 68 Mflops. Each CE has eight 32-element vector registers and eight floating point scalar registers as well as other integer registers. The CE's are connected by a concurrency control bus (used as a synchronization facility). This mechanism allows an iteration of a parallel loop to be assigned to a processor within in time equivalent to a few floating point operations and provides synchronization support from lower iterations to higher iterations with a cost of a few cycles. As a result, the CE's can cooperate efficiently on parallel loops with iterations with a granularity of a small number of floating point operations.

There is only one memory port on each CE, like the CRAY-1 and a single CPU of the CRAY-2, therefore management of the vector registers is crucial. The CE's share the physical memory as well as a write-back cache that allows up to eight simultaneous accesses per cycle. The size of the cache can be configured from 64KB up to 512KB. The cache and the four-way interleaved main memory are connected through the main memory bus. Most of the detailed performance information for shared memory machines given below was obtained on this machine.

Distributed memory architectures can be roughly characterized in a fashion similar to that used above for shared memory. In particular, there are two major factors that distinguish them from shared memory architectures. These are the mode of memory access and the mode of synchronization.

On p-processor distributed memory machines with an aggregate memory size M each user-controlled processor has direct access to its local memory only, typically of size M/p. Accessing any other memory location requires the active participation of another user-controlled processor. As a result of this idea of direct interaction between processors to exchange data, distributed memory architectures are often identified by the topology of the connections between processors. Figure 1 illustrates three popular connection schemes. The ring topology (b) uses a linear nearest–neighbor bidirectional connection, essentially a linear array with a wrap-around connection between the first and last processor, while the mesh connection (c) provides two-dimensional nearest neighbor connections (wrap-around meshes are also used extensively). Both of these simple topologies work quite well for many numerical linear algebra algorithms. In particular, several algorithms are presented below for ring architectures. The hypercube connection is perhaps the most discussed distributed memory topology recently. A four-dimensional cube is illustrated in (d). The connection patterns are, as the name implies, local connections in an arbitrarily dimensioned space. In general, a k-dimensional cube has 2^k processors (vertices) each of which is connected to k other processors. It can be constructed from two $(k-1)$-dimensional cubes by simply connecting corresponding vertices. As a result of this construction, the nodes have a very natural binary numbering scheme based on a Gray code. This construction also demonstrates one of the basic scalability problems of the hypercube in that the number of connections for a particular processor grows as the size of the cube increases as opposed to the constant local connection complexity of the simpler mesh and ring topologies. Many of the more common topologies, such as rings and meshes, can be embedded into a hypercube of appropriate dimension. In fact, many of the hypercube algorithms published use the cube as if it were one of the simpler topologies. Commercially available hypercubes include those by Ametek, Intel, and NCUBE.

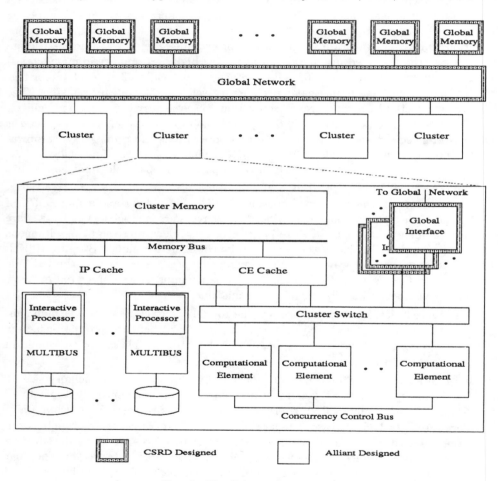

FIG. 2. *The Cedar multiprocessor.*

Synchronization on a distributed memory architecture, due to the memory accessing paradigm, is accomplished via a *data flow* mechanism rather than the indivisible update used in a large shared memory system. Computations can proceed on a processor when due to its position in its local code the processor decides a computation is to be performed *and* all of the memory transactions involving operands for the computation in remote memory modules are complete. (These transactions are the interaction between the processors associated with the local memory and the remote memory modules mentioned above.) Clearly, since the synchronization is so enmeshed in the control and execution of interprocessor communication, the major algorithmic reorganization that can alter the efficiency of the synchronization on distributed memory machines is the partitioning of the computations (or similarly the data) so as to reduce the synchronization overhead required.

As we would expect, the algorithm/architecture mapping questions for a distributed memory machine change appreciably from those of shared memory. Since the machines tend to have more, but less powerful, processors, a key aspect of algorithm organization is the exposure of large amounts of parallelism. Once this is accomplished the major task is the partitioning of the data and the computations onto the processors. This partitioning must address several tradeoffs.

To reduce total execution time, a suitable balance must be achieved between the amount of communication required and efficient spreading of the parallel computations across the machine. One indicator of the efficient partitioning of the computations and data is the relationship between the load balance across processors and the amount of communication between processors. Typically, although not necessarily, a more balanced load produces a more parallel execution of the computations, ignoring for a moment delays due to communication. On the other hand, dispersing the computations over many processors may increase the amount of communication required and thereby negate the benefit of parallelism.

The property of data locality, which was very significant for shared memory machines in the management of registers and hierarchical memory systems, is also very important for some distributed memory machines in achieving the desired balance. Ideally, we would like to partition the data and computations across the processors and memory modules in such a way that a small amount of data is exchanged between processors at each stage of an algorithm, followed by the use of the received data in operations on many local data. As a result the cost of communication is completely amortized over the subsequent computations that make use of the data. If the partitioning of the computations and data also results in a balanced computational load the algorithm proceeds near the aggregate computational rate of the machine. This is, of course, identical to the hierarchical memory problem of amortizing a fetch of a data operand from the farthest level of memory by combining it with several operands in the nearest. Therefore many of the discussions to follow concerning the data-transfer-to-operations ratios that are motivated by shared hierarchical memory considerations are often directly applicable to the distributed memory case, although, as is shown below, there is often a tradeoff between data locality and the amount of exploitable parallelism.

Of course, there is a spectrum of architectures and a particular machine tends to have characteristics of both shared and distributed memory architectures. For these hybrid architectures efficient algorithms often involve a combination of techniques used to achieve high performance on the two extremes. An example of such an architecture that is used in this paper to facilitate the discussion of these algorithms is the Cedar system being built at the University of Illinois Center for Supercomputing Research and Development (see Fig. 2). It consists of clusters of vector processors connected to a large interleaved shared global memory — access to which can be accelerated by data prefetching hardware. At this level it looks much like a conventional shared memory processor. However, each cluster is, in turn, a shared memory multivector processor, a slightly modified Alliant FX/8, whose cluster memory is accessible only by its CE's. The size of the cluster memory is fairly large and therefore the aggregate makes up a considerable distributed memory system. Consequently, the Cedar machine is characterized by its hierarchical organization in both memory and processing capabilities. The memory hierarchy consists of: vector registers private to each vector processor; cache and cluster memory shared by the processors within a cluster; and global memory shared by all processors in the system. Three levels of parallelism are also available: vectorization at the individual processor level, concurrency within each cluster, and global concurrency across clusters. Control and synchronization mechanisms between clusters are supported at two levels of granularity. The larger consists of large-grain tasks and multitasking synchronization primitives such as event waiting and posting similar to CRAY large-grain primitives. These primitives are relatively high cost in that they affect the state of the task from the point of view of the operating system, e.g., a task waiting for a task-level event is marked as blocked from execution and removed from the pool of tasks considered by the operating system when allocating computational resources. The second and lower-cost control mechanism is the SDOALL loop (for spread DOALL) which provides a self-scheduling loop structure whose iterations are grabbed and executed at the cluster level by *helper* tasks created at the initiation of the user's main task. Each iteration can then use the smaller grain parallelism and vectorization available within the cluster upon which it is executing. The medium grain SDOALL loop is ideal for moderately tight intercluster communication such as that required at the highest level of control in multicluster primitives with BLAS-like functionality that can be used in iterations such as the hybrid factorization routine presented in §4. Hardware support for synchronization between clusters on a much tighter level than the task events is supplied by synchronization processors, one per global memory module, which implements the Zhu–Yew synchronization primitives [196].

3. Computational primitives.

3.1. Motivation. The development of high-performance codes for a range of architectures is greatly simplified if the algorithms under consideration can be decomposed into computational primitives of varying degrees of complexity. As new architectures emerge, primitives with the appropriate functionality which exploit the novel architectural features are chosen and used to develop new forms of the algorithms. Over the years, such a strategy has been applied successfully to the development of dense linear algebra codes. These algorithms can be expressed in terms of computational primitives ranging from operations on matrix elements to those involving submatrices. As the pursuit of high performance has increased the complexity of computer architectures, the need to exploit this richness of decomposition has been reflected in the evolution of the Basic Linear Algebra Subroutines (BLAS).

The investigation of dense matrix algorithms in terms of decomposition into lower-level primitives such as the three levels of the BLAS has several advantages. First, for many presently available machines the computational granularity represented by single instances of the BLAS primitives from one of the levels or multiple instances executing simultaneously is sufficient for investigating the relative strengths and weaknesses of the architecture with respect to dense matrix computations. Consequently, since the primitive's computational complexity is manageable, it is possible to probe at an architecture/software level which is free of spurious software considerations such as ways of tricking a restructuring compiler/code generator combination into producing the code we want. Thus, allowing meaningful conclusions to be reached about the most effective way to use a new machine.[5] Second, it aids in the identification of directions in language and restructuring technologies that would help in the implementation of high-performance scientific computing software. For example, matrix-manipulation constructs are already included in many proprietary extensions to Fortran due to the need for higher-level constructs to achieve high performance on some machines. Third, detailed knowledge of the efficient mapping of primitives to different architectures provides a way of thinking about algorithm design that facilitates the rapid generation of new versions of an algorithm by the direct manipulation of its algebraic formulation. (See the discussion of triangular system solvers below for a simple example.) Fourth, exposing the weaknesses of an architecture for the execution of basic primitives provides direction for architectural development. Finally, it simplifies the design of numerical software for nonexpert users. This typically occurs through the use of *total* primitives, i.e., primitives which hide all of the architectural details crucial to performance from the user. Code is designed in terms of a sequential series of calls to primitives which use all of the resources of the machine in the best way to achieve high performance. When such a strategy is possible a certain amount of performance portability is achieved as well. Unfortunately, many important architectures do not lend themselves to total primitives. Even in this case, however, the hiding of parts of the architecture via *partial* primitives is similarly beneficial. A user need only deal with managing the interaction of the partial primitives which may or may not execute simultaneously.

In this section, computational primitives from each level of the BLAS hierarchy are discussed and analyses of their efficiency on the architectures of interest in this paper are presented in various degrees of detail. Based on the discussion in §2 which indicates that the investigation of data locality is of great importance for both shared and distributed memory machines, special attention is given to identifying the strengths and weaknesses of each primitive in this regard and its relationship to the amount of exploitable parallelism.

3.2. Architecture/algorithm analysis methodology. The design of efficient computational primitives and algorithms that exploit them requires an understanding of the behavior of the algorithm/primitive performance as a function of certain system parameters (cache size, number of processors, etc.). It is particularly crucial that the analysis of this behavior identifies any contradictory trends that require tradeoff consideration, and the limits of performance improvement possible via a particular technique such as blocking. Additionally, preferences within a set of primitives can be identified by such an analysis, e.g., on certain architectures a rank-1 BLAS2 primitive does not perform as well as a matrix-vector multiplication. Ideally, the analysis should also yield insight into techniques a compiler could use to automatically restructure code to improve performance, e.g., on hierarchical memory systems [63], [75]. In this paper we are mostly concerned with analyses that concern the effects of hierarchical (registers, cache or local memory, global memory) or distributed memory systems.

As indicated earlier, the consideration of data locality and its relationship to the exploitable parallelism in an algorithm is a key activity in developing high-performance algorithms for both hierarchical shared memory and distributed memory

---

[5] Very loosely speaking this is usually the assembler level, i.e., the level at which the user has direct control over performance-critical algorithm/architecture tradeoffs.

architectures. In this section, we point out some performance modeling efforts concerning these tradeoffs that have appeared in the literature and present a summary of the techniques used on hierarchical shared memory architectures to produce some of the results discussed in later sections.

Several papers have appeared recently which discuss modeling the influence of a hierarchical memory on numerical algorithms, e.g., [3], [76], [99], [101]. Earlier work on virtual memory systems also discusses similar issues, e.g., the work of McKellar and Coffman [131], and Trivedi [185], [186]. In fact, the work of Trivedi performs many of the analyses for virtual memory systems that were later needed for both BLAS2 and BLAS3 such as the effect of blocking, loop orderings in the LU factorization, and prefetching. The details and assumptions for the hierarchical memory case, however, differ enough to require the further investigation that has taken place. Of particular interest here are studies by the groups at the University of Illinois on shared memory multivector processors (the Cedar Project) [9], [66], [67], [105] and at the California Institute of Technology on hypercubes (the Caltech Concurrent Computation Program) [59]–[61]. In these studies performance analyses were developed to express the influence of the blocksizes, used in both the matrix multiplication primitives and the block algorithms built from them, on performance in terms of architectural parameters.

Gallivan, Jalby, Meier, and Sameh [67], [105] proposed the use of a decoupling methodology to analyze in terms of certain architectural parameters the trends in the relationship between the performance and the blocksizes used when implementing BLAS3 primitives and block algorithms on a shared memory multivector processor. In particular, they considered an architecture comprising a moderate number (p) of vector processors that share a small fast cache or local memory and a larger slower global memory. (The analysis is easily altered for the private cache or local memory case.) An example of such an architecture is the Alliant FX/8. In their methodology, two time components, whose sum is the total time for the algorithm, are analyzed separately. A region in the parameter space, i.e., the space of possible blocksize choices, that provides near-optimal behavior is produced for each time component. The intersection of these two regions yields a set of blocksizes that should give near-optimal performance for the time function as a whole.

The first component considered is called the *arithmetic time* and is denoted T_a. This time represents the raw computational speed of the algorithm and is derived by ignoring the hierarchical nature of the memory system: it is the time required by the algorithm given that the cache is infinitely large. The second component of the time function considered is the degradation of the raw computational speed of the algorithm due to the use of a cache of size CS and a slower main memory. This component is called the *data loading overhead* and is denoted Δ_l. The components T_a and Δ_l are respectively proportional to the number of arithmetic operations and data transfers, from memory to cache, required by the algorithm; therefore, the total time for the algorithm is

$$(1) \qquad T = T_a + \Delta_l = n_a \tau_a + n_l \tau_l,$$

where n_a and n_l are the number of operations and data transfers, and τ_a and τ_l are the associated proportionality constants or the "average" times for an operation and data load. *Note that no assumptions have been made concerning the overlap (or lack thereof) of computation and the loading of data in order to write T as a sum of these two terms.* The effect of such overlapping is seen through a reduction in

τ_l. This overlap effect can cause τ_l to vary from zero, for machines which have a perfect prefetch capability from memory to cache, to t_l, where t_l is the amount of time it takes to transfer a single data element, for machines which must fetch data on demand sequentially from memory to cache.

The analysis of T_a considers the performance of the algorithm with respect to the architectural parameters of the multiple vector processors and the register-cache hierarchy under the assumption of an infinite cache. For some machines, the register-cache hierarchy is significant enough to require another application of the decoupling methodology with the added constraint of the *shape* of the registers. Typically, however, the analysis involves questions similar to those discussed concerning the BLAS2 below.

Rather than considering Δ_l directly, the second portion of the analysis attempts a more modest goal. The data loading overhead can be analyzed so as to produce a region in the parameter space where the relative cost of the data loading Δ_l/T_a is small. This analysis is accomplished by expressing Δ_l/T_a in terms of two ratios: a *cache-miss* ratio and a *cost* ratio. Specifically,

$$(2) \qquad \frac{\Delta_l}{T_a} = \lambda\mu$$

where $\mu = n_l/n_a$ is the cache-miss ratio and $\lambda = \tau_l/\tau_a$ is the cost ratio. For the purposes of qualitative analysis, λ can be bounded under various assumptions (average case, worst case, etc.) and trends in the behavior of the primitive or algorithm derived in terms of architectural parameters via the consideration of the behavior of the cache-miss ratio μ as a function of the algorithm's blocksizes.

The utility of the results of the decoupling form of analysis depends upon the fact that the intersection of the near-optimal regions for each term is not empty or at least that the arithmetic time does not become unacceptably large when using parameter values in the region where small relative costs for data loading are achieved. For some algorithms this is not true; reducing the arithmetic time may directly conflict with reducing the relative cost of data loading. In some cases, a technique known as *multilevel blocking* can mitigate these conflicts [67]. In other cases, more machine-specific tradeoff studies must be performed. These studies typically involve probing the interaction of data motion to and from the various levels of memory and the underlying hardware to identify effective tradeoffs [64], [65].

On distributed memory machines, analyses in the spirit of the decoupling methodology can be performed. Fox, Otto, and Hey [59], [61] analyzed the efficiency of the *broadcast-multiply-roll* matrix multiplication algorithm and other numerical linear algebra algorithms on hypercubes in terms of similar parameters. In particular, they expressed efficiency in terms of the number of matrix elements per node (blocksize), the number of processors and a cost ratio t_{comm}/t_{flop} which gives the relative cost of communication to computation. Johnsson and Ho [110] presented a detailed analysis of matrix multiplication on a hypercube with special attention to the complexity of the *communication primitives* required and the associated data partitioning.

3.3. First and second-level BLAS. The first level of the BLAS comprises vector-vector operations such as dotproducts, $\alpha \leftarrow x^T y$, and vector triads (SAXPY), $y \leftarrow y \pm \alpha x$ [121]. This level was used to implement the numerical linear algebra package LINPACK [38]. These primitives possess a simple one-dimensional parallelism especially suitable for vector processors with sufficient memory bandwidth to tolerate the high ratio of memory references to operations; $\mu \approx \frac{3}{2}$ for the triad and $\mu \approx 1$

for the dotproduct. The superiority of the dotproduct is due to the fact that it is a reduction operation that writes a scalar result after accumulating it in a register. The triad, on the other hand, produces a vector result and must therefore write n elements to memory in addition to reading the $2n$ elements of the operands. For vector processors, performance tuning is limited to adjusting the vector length and stride of access. On multivector processors, both primitives are easily decomposed into several smaller versions of themselves for parallel execution. For the triad, $\mu \approx \frac{3}{2} + \frac{p}{2n}$, note that the fetch of α becomes more significant, and $\mu \approx 1 + \frac{p}{n}$ for the dotproduct, where p is the number of processors. As the number of processors increases to a maximum of n, the preference for the dotproduct over the triad is reversed. For $p = n$ the triad requires $O(1)$ time with $\mu \approx 2$ while the dotproduct requires $O(\log n)$ with $\mu \approx 2$. Such a reversal often occurs when considering large numbers of processors relative to the dimension of the primitive. The dependences graph of the reduction operation and its properties that produced a small μ for a limited number of processors scale very poorly as p increases and translate directly into a relative increase in the amount of memory traffic required on a shared memory architecture and interprocessor communication on a distributed memory machine. (For a distributed memory machine, whether or not the reversal of preference occurs can depend strongly on the initial partitioning of the data.)

The advent of architectures with more than a few processors and high-performance register-based vector processors with limited processor-memory bandwidth such as the CRAY-1 exposed the limitations of the first level of the BLAS. New implementations of dense numerical linear algebra algorithms were developed which paid particular attention to vector register management and an emphasis on matrix-vector primitives resulted [24], [56]. This problem was later analyzed in a more systematic way in [42] and resulted in the definition of the extended BLAS or BLAS2 [40]. Architectures with a more substantial number of processors were also more efficiently used since matrix-vector operations consist essentially of multiple BLAS1 primitives that can be executed in parallel — roughly speaking they possess two-dimensional parallelism. The second level of the BLAS includes computations involving $O(n^2)$ operations such as a matrix-vector multiplication, $y \leftarrow y \pm Ax$, and a rank-1 update, $A \leftarrow A \pm xy^T$. Note that these primitives subsume the triad and dotproduct BLAS1 primitives and become those primitives in the limit as one of the dimensions of A tends to 1. These primitives improve data locality in the sense that the number of memory references per operation can be reduced by accumulating the results of several vector operations in a vector register before writing to memory as in matrix-vector multiplication or by keeping in registers operands common to successive vector operations as in a rank-1 update. The two techniques, however, do not result in similar improvements in data locality. In general, it is preferable to write algorithms for register-based multivector processors in terms of matrix-vector multiplications rather than rank-1 updates.

To see this, consider first the efficiency of implementing the two BLAS2 primitives as a set of BLAS1 primitives each of the order of the matrix. (For the rank-1 it is only possible to use the triad; the matrix-vector multiplication allows a choice of primitives.) If the matrix dimensions n_1 and n_2 are larger than the register size[6] of any of the processors there is no possibility of efficient register reuse and the value of μ remains at the disappointing BLAS1 level. For problems where either n_1 or

---

[6] The term register size does not necessarily mean the vector length of a single vector register. It can also refer to the aggregate size of all of the vector registers used in a processor in a given implementation of the primitive.

n_2 is smaller than the register size, however, it is possible to reuse the registers in such a way that both primitives achieve their theoretical minimum values of μ; $\mu = 1 + 1/2n_1 + 1/2n_2$ for the rank-1 update and $\mu = 1/2 + 1/2n_1 + 1/n_2$ for the matrix-vector product. For the small rank-1, this local optimal is achieved by reading the small vector into vector register once and reusing it to form a triad with each row or column of the matrix in turn. As a result, each element of the matrix and the two vectors are loaded into the processor exactly once and the elements of the matrix are written exactly once — the optimal data transfer behavior for a rank-1 update. For the matrix-vector product, the technique depends upon whether n_1 or n_2 is the small dimension. If it is n_2 then a technique similar to the rank-1 update is used. The vector x is loaded into a register once. Each row of A is read in turn and used in an inner product calculation with x in the register, and the result is then added to the appropriate element of y and written back to memory. Every data element is read and written the minimum number of times. If the small dimension is n_1 then a slightly different technique is used. The result of the operation, y, is accumulated in a vector register, thereby suppressing the writes back to memory of partial sums.

As long as n_1 or n_2 do not get very small, which implies that the primitives are degenerating into a first level primitive, the values are an improvement compared to their limiting first level primitives. Of course, the rank-1 update still has a value of μ similar to the dotproduct BLAS1 primitive, but it has the advantage of more exploitable parallelism. If these results could be maintained for arbitrary n_1 and n_2, the superiority of the BLAS2 on register-based multivector processors would be established.

To show that this is indeed possible, we will exploit the richness of structure present in linear algebra computations and partition the primitives into smaller versions of themselves. This is accomplished by partitioning A into $k_1 k_2$ submatrices $A_{ij} \in \Re^{m_1 \times m_2}$, where it is assumed for simplicity that $n_i = k_i m_i$ with k_i and m_i integers, and partitioning x and y conformally. The blocksizes which determine the partitioning are chosen so that the smaller instances of the primitives are locally optimal with respect to their values of μ.

The rank-1 update is thus reduced to $k_1 k_2$ independent small rank-1 updates. The resulting global μ value for the entire rank-1 update is $\mu = 1 + 1/2m_1 + 1/2m_2$. Now consider its behavior as p, the number of register-based vector processors used, increases. For small and moderate p, one of the blocksizes, say m_1, could be taken equal to the corresponding dimension of the matrix, n_1 (the choice of m_1 or m_2 simply depends upon the shape of the matrix and the exact number of processors). It follows that $\mu = 1 + 1/2r + 1/2n_2$ where r is the register length. As p increases further, a true two-dimensional partitioning must be used. So we set $p = k_1 k_2$ which balances the computational load and the amount of data required by each processor. Since the register size determines the largest vector object we can work with and extra transfers to and from registers translate directly into additional time, we make $m_1^{-1} + m_2^{-1}$ as small as possible under the constraint that either $m_1 \leq r$ or $m_2 \leq r$, depending on the implementation chosen for the register-based smaller rank-1 update. Consequently,

$$\mu = 1 + \frac{p}{2n_1 n_2}(m_1 + m_2)$$

and the algorithm requires $O(m_1 m_2)$ time. At the limit of available parallelism, $p = n_1 n_2$ and the rank-1 update requires $O(1)$ time with $\mu = 2$. This is the same as the best BLAS1 primitive. This is not surprising since in the limit each processor is doing essentially the same scalar computation as the BLAS1 triad. The only difference is that in the BLAS2 case there is much more exploitable parallelism. Note also that at some point while increasing the number of processors the vector length used by each processor will fall below the breakeven point for the use of the vector capability of the processor, and the switch should be made to scalar mode.

A similar decomposition technique can be used for the matrix-vector product primitive $y \leftarrow y \pm Ax$. The matrix is partitioned into submatrices $A_{ij} \in \Re^{m_1 \times m_2}$ and partitioning x and y conformally. The resulting algorithm is

> do $i = 1, k_1$
> > $y_i \leftarrow y_i + A_{i1}x_1 + \cdots + A_{ik_2}x_{k_2}$
>
> end do

All of the basic computations $z \leftarrow z + A_{ij}x_j$ can proceed in parallel with a fan-in dependence graph required on the update of the y_i if $k_2 > 1$. As before, for a small to moderate number of processors one of the m_i can be set to the register length and the other to the remaining dimension of A. If $i = 1$ then no synchronization is required since $k_2 = n_2$ and the loop can execute in parallel. The resulting global μ is

$$\mu = \frac{1}{2} + \frac{1}{2r} + \frac{1}{n_2},$$

where r is the vector length. If $i = 2$

$$\mu = \frac{1}{2} + \frac{1}{2n_1} + \frac{1}{r}.$$

In the latter case, k_1 is equal to 1 and synchronization is required. However, since the number of processors is assumed small the partial sums from local matrix-vector products can be accumulated in a vector of length n_1 private to each processor (not necessarily a register). After all processors are finished accumulating their partial sums, a simple fan-in of the results can be done. The time required is $O(m_1 m_2)$. Note that on a moderate number of processors the matrix-vector primitive is twice as efficient as the rank-1 primitive of the same size. Consequently, when implementing algorithms with BLAS2 primitives on a register-based multivector architecture with a moderate number of processors, a matrix-vector product-based algorithm will significantly outperform the same algorithm based on a rank-1 update.

As with the rank-1 update it is possible to derive an estimate of the time and the value of μ for the case where a two-dimensional partitioning is used with $p = k_1 k_2$. In this case, not only must the transfers be computed for the small matrix-vector products performed by each of the processors, but also the transfers associated with the k_1 independent fan-in trees which sum together the partial sums into the final values of y_i for $1 \leq i \leq k_1$. The time required is $O(m_1 m_2) + O(m_1 \log_2 k_2)$ with

$$\mu = \frac{1}{2} + \frac{p}{n_1 n_2} \left[m_1 + \frac{m_2}{2} \right].$$

As with all of the other primitives, when p is as large as possible, in this case $p = n_1 n_2$, the value of μ increases to approximately 2. Due to the reduction nature of the matrix-vector product, its time has a lower bound of $O(\log n_2)$.

The results above demonstrate several important points about first- and second-level BLAS primitives. The most important is that for register-based multivector processors with a moderate number of processors, there can be a significant difference between the performance of a given algorithm when implemented in terms of the four primitives discussed above. This performance order is given from worse to best in terms of decreasing values of μ. The triad with $\mu \approx \frac{3}{2}$ does far too many spurious data transfers to be of use on a processor with a single port to memory. The dotproduct improves the ratio to $\mu \approx 1$ but not all processors have high-performance capabilities. The BLAS2 rank-1 update primitive also has $\mu \approx 1$ but it does not depend upon efficient reduction operations on vector registers being available on a processor and its extra dimension of parallelism makes it more flexible than the previous primitives. By far, however, the preferred primitive for such an architecture is the matrix-vector product due to its superior register management.

The second observation from the results above is how the preferences can reverse when the architecture used is radically altered. In this case we considered increasing the number of register-based vector processors available to the maximum needed. It was shown that in the limit all have similar register-memory transfer behavior and the nonreduction operations have a distinct advantage *if it is assumed that the data and computations have been partitioned ideally.* This last point is crucial. Our discussions implicitly assumed a shared memory architecture when increasing the number of processors. While the results do hold for certain distributed memory architectures, they can be very sensitive to the assumptions concerning initial data partioning. If for some reason the data had been partitioned in a different way the trends need not be the same.

3.4. Third-level BLAS.

3.4.1. Motivation. The highest level of the BLAS is motivated by the use of memory hierarchies. On such systems, only the lowest level of the hierarchy (or in some cases the two lowest, e.g., registers and cache) are able to supply data at the computational bandwidth of the processors. Hence, data locality must be exploited to allow computations to involve mostly data located in the lowest levels. This allows the cost of the data transfer between levels to be amortized over several operations performed at the computational bandwidth of the processors. This problem of data reuse in the design of algorithms has been studied since the beginning of scientific computing. Early machines, which had small physical memories, required the use of secondary storage such as tape or disk to hold all of the data for a problem. Similar considerations were also needed on later machines with paged virtual memory systems. The *block* algorithms developed for such architectures relied on transferring large submatrices between different levels of storage, with prepaging in some cases, and localizing operations to achieve acceptable performance.

Of course, the resulting matrix-matrix primitives could have been used in algorithms for the machines which motivated the BLAS2. Indeed, as Calahan points out [23], the use of matrix-matrix modules was considered when developing algorithms for the CRAY-1. The hierarchy, however, was not distinct enough to achieve a significant advantage over BLAS2 primitives. The introduction of the CRAY X-MP and its additional memory ports delayed even further the move to the next level of the BLAS. It was finally caused by the availability of high-performance architectures which rely on the use of a hierarchical memory system and with more profound performance consequences when not used correctly. Agarwal and Gustavson designed matrix multiplication primitives and block algorithms for solving linear systems to exploit the cache memory on the IBM 3090 in the latter part of 1984. These evolved into the algorithms contained in ESSL, first released in the middle of 1985, for the IBM 3090 with vector processing capabilities [1], [84], [130], and more recently for the multi-processor version of the architecture [2]. A numerical linear algebra library based on block methods was developed and its performance analyzed in terms of architectural parameters in 1985 and early 1986 for a single cluster of the Cedar machine, the multivector processor Alliant FX/8 [9], [105], [156]. At approximately the same time, Calahan developed block LU factorization algorithms for one CPU of the CRAY-2 [23]. In 1985, Bischof and Van Loan developed the use of block Householder reflectors in computing the QR factorization and presented results on an FPS-164/MAX [16].

The development of these routines and numerical linear algebra libraries clearly demonstrated that a third level of primitives, or BLAS3, based on matrix-matrix computations was required to achieve high performance on the emerging architectures. Such primitives achieve a significant improvement in data locality, i.e., the data locality is no longer effectively independent of problem size as it is for the first two levels of the BLAS. Third-level primitives perform $O(n^3)$ operations on $O(n^2)$ data, and they increase the parallelism available by yet another dimension by essentially consisting of multiple independent BLAS2 primitives.

Since the reawakening of interest in block methods for linear algebra, many papers have appeared in the literature considering the topic on various machines, e.g., [5], [44], [149]. The techniques have become so accepted that some manufacturers now provide high-performance libraries which contain block methods and matrix-matrix primitives. Some, such as Alliant, provide matrix multiplication intrinsics in their concurrent/vector processing extensions to Fortran. In 1987, an effort began to standardize for Fortran 77 the BLAS3 primitives and block methods for numerical linear algebra [35], [37], [39].

3.4.2. Some algorithms. The most basic BLAS3 primitive is a simple matrix operation of the form

$$(3) \qquad\qquad C \leftarrow C + AB,$$

where C, A, and B are $n_1 \times n_3$, $n_1 \times n_2$, and $n_2 \times n_3$ matrices, respectively. Clearly, this primitive subsumes the rank-1 update, ($n_2 = 1$), and matrix-vector multiplication, ($n_3 = 1$), BLAS2 primitives. In block algorithms, it is most often used as a rank-ω update ($n_2 = \omega \ll n_1, n_3$) or a matrix multiplied by several vectors ($n_3 = \omega \ll n_1, n_2$). The analysis of the parallel complexity of such a computation has been the subject of much study. In this section we give a brief summary of some generic algorithms and mention some implementations on various machines that have appeared recently in the literature.

The basic scalar computation can be expressed as

$$
\begin{aligned}
&\text{do } r = 1, n_3 \\
&\qquad \text{do } s = 1, n_1 \\
&\qquad\qquad \text{do } t = 1, n_2 \\
&\qquad\qquad\qquad c_{s,r} = c_{s,r} + a_{s,t} b_{t,r} \\
&\qquad\qquad \text{end do} \\
&\qquad \text{end do} \\
&\text{end do}
\end{aligned}
$$

where $c_{s,r}$, $a_{s,t}$, and $b_{t,r}$ denote the elements of C, A respectively B.

There are three basic generic approaches to performing these computations which correspond to different choices of orderings of the loops. They are called the *inner, middle*, and *outer* product methods due to the fundamental kernels used and correspond to the following code segments:

inner_product:
$$\text{do } r = 1, n_3$$
$$\text{do } s = 1, n_1$$
$$c_{s,r} = c_{s,r} + inner\_prod(a_{s,*}, b_{*,r})$$
$$\text{end do}$$
$$\text{end do}$$

middle_product:
$$\text{do } r = 1, n_3$$
$$c_{*,r} = c_{*,r} + Ab_{*,r}$$
$$\text{end do}$$

and

outer_product:
$$\text{do } t = 1, n_2$$
$$C = C + a_{*,t} b_{t,*}^T$$
$$\text{end do}.$$

Each has its advantages and disadvantages for various problem shapes and architectures. All have immediate generalizations involving submatrices. These issues are discussed in the literature, e.g., [100], [137], in several places and will not be repeated here. We do note, however, that for register-based vector and multivector processors with one port to memory, the middle product algorithm facilitates the efficient use of the vector registers and data bandwidth to cache of each processor, and exploits the chaining of the multiplier, adder, and data fetch available on many systems. This is accomplished by performing, possibly in parallel, multiple matrix-vector products — the preferred BLAS2 primitive for vector register management. When the vector processors are such that register-register operations are significantly faster than chained operations from local memory or cache, a more sophisticated two-level generalization of the blocking strategy discussed below can be used to achieve high performance.

Madsen, Rodrigue, and Karush considered, for use on the CDC STAR-100 vector processor, a slightly more exotic matrix multiplication based on storing and manipulating the diagonals of matrices [127]. Their motivation was mitigating the performance degradation of the algorithms above for banded matrices and the difficulties in accessing the transpose of a matrix on some machines.

The BLAS3 primitive implemented for a single cluster of the Cedar machine [66], [67], [105] and applicable to machines with a moderate number of reasonably coupled multivector processors with a shared cache implements a block version of the basic matrix multiplication loops. It proceeds by partitioning the matrices C, A, and B into submatrices C_{ij}, A_{ik}, and B_{kj} whose dimensions are $m_1 \times m_3$, $m_1 \times m_2$, and $m_2 \times m_3$, respectively. The basic loop is of the form
$$\text{do } i = 1, k_1$$
$$\text{do } k = 1, k_2$$
$$\text{do } j = 1, k_3$$

$$C_{ij} = C_{ij} + A_{ik} * B_{kj}$$
$$\text{end do}$$
$$\text{end do}$$

$$\text{end do}$$

where $n_1 = k_1 m_1$, $n_2 = k_2 m_2$, and $n_3 = k_3 m_3$, and k_1, k_2, and k_3 are assumed to be positive integers for simplicity.

The block operations $C_{ij} = C_{ij} + A_{ik} * B_{kj}$ possess a large amount of concurrent and vectorizable computations, so the algorithm proceeds by dedicating the full resources of the p vector processors to each of the block operations in turn. The kernel block multiplication can be computed by any of the basic concurrent/vector algorithms. As noted above the middle product algorithm which performs several multiplications of A_{ik} and columns of B_{kj} in parallel is well suited for register-based architectures like the Alliant FX/8, hence it is assumed in the anaiysis below.

There are, of course, several possible orderings of the block loops and several other kernels that can be used for the block operations.[7] If, for example, the processors are not tightly coupled enough parallelism can moved to the block level. This can also be useful in the case of private caches or local memories for each processor. As is shown below this particular ordering (or one trivially related to it) is appropriate for use in the block algorithms discussed in later sections. However, when developing a robust BLAS3 library, kernels for the block operations which differ from those discussed below and alternate orderings must be analyzed so that selection of the appropriate form of the routine can be done at runtime based on the *shape* of the problem. This is especially important for cases with extreme shapes, e.g., guaranteeing smooth performance characteristics as the shapes become BLAS2-like.

Clearly, if the number of processors are increased to $p = n_1 n_2 n_3$ the inner product form of the algorithm can generate the result in $O(\log_2 n_2)$ time. For a shared memory machine, such an approach would place tremendous strain on a highly interleaved or parallel memory systems. As mentioned earlier, one way that such strain is mitigated is by assigning elements of structured variables to the memory banks in such a way as to minimize the chance of conflicts when accessing certain subsections of the data. For the inner product algorithm it is particularly important that the row and columns of matrices be accessible in a conflict free manner. One of the easiest memory module mapping strategies that achieves this goal dates back to the ILLIAC IV ([114], [115], also see [116]). The technique is called the *skewed storage scheme*. In it the elements of each row of a matrix are assigned in an interleaved fashion across the memory modules. However, when assigning the first element of a row it is placed in the memory module that is skewed by one from the module that contained the first element of the previous row. Any row or column of a matrix can now be accessed in a conflict free fashion. Matrix multiplication algorithms for the distributed memory ILLIAC IV were developed based on this scheme which can be easily adapted to the shared memory situation.

If we are willing to sacrifice some numerical stability, fast schemes which use less than $O(n^3)$ operations can be used to multiply two matrices. In [95], Higham has analyzed this loss of stability for Strassen's method [175] and concluded that it does not preclude the effective use of the method as a BLAS3 kernel. Recently, Bailey has

---

[7] The $i-j-k$ ordering of the block loops, for example, produces distinctly different blocksizes and shapes [105]. Its use can be motivated by the desire to keep a block of C in cache while accumulating its final value. This implies that a block of A must reside in the cache simultaneously thereby altering the optimal shapes.

considered the use of Strassen's method to multiply matrices on the CRAY-2 [7]. The increased performance compared to CRAY's MXM library routine is achieved via the reduced operation count implicit in the method and the careful use of local memory via an algorithm due to Calahan. Speedups as high as 2.01 are reported compared to CRAY's library routine on a single CPU. Bailey also notes that the algorithm is very amenable to use on multiple CPU's of the CRAY-2 although no such results are presented.

The *broadcast-multiply-roll* algorithm for matrix multiplication described and analyzed by Fox et al. is representative of distributed memory algorithms [59]–[61]. (For other distributed memory algorithms see [78], [129], [135].) Consider the calculation of $C \leftarrow C + AB$ where A, B, $C \in \Re^{n \times n}$. Assume the processors are connected as a two-dimensional wrap-around mesh and the square subblock with index (i, j) of each matrix starts out in the memory of the processor correspondingly indexed. The algorithm consists of $\sqrt{n}$ steps each of which consists of broadcast, multiply, and roll phases. In particular, on step i ($i = 0, \cdots, \sqrt{n} - 1$) the processor in each row owning $A_{j,(j+i) \bmod \sqrt{n}}$ broadcasts it to the rest of the processors in the row which store it in a local work array T. Each processor then multiplies T by the subblock of B presently in its memory and adds it to the subblock of C that it owns. The final phase of each step consists of rolling the matrix B up one row in the mesh with appropriate wrap-around at the ends of the mesh. In other words, each processor transmits the subblock of B it has in its memory to the processor in the same column of the mesh but one row up. The repetition of this three-phase step $\sqrt{n}$ times corresponds to the number of steps required to let each subblock of B return to its original processor.

Finally, Johnsson and Ho have considered the implementation of matrix multiplication on a hypercube [110]. In this work they consider the implementation of the computational primitive in terms of *communication* primitives some of which implicitly perform computations as the data move through the cube. As a result, users can write their algorithms as a sequence of calls to these data motion primitives in a fashion similar to the method advocated with respect to the computational primitives discussed above.

3.4.3. Blocksize analysis. In this section we summarize the application of the decoupling methodology to the matrix multiplication algorithm for the single cluster of the Cedar machine described above. Recall that the block level loops were

> do $i = 1, k_1$
> > do $k = 1, k_2$
> > > do $j = 1, k_3$
> > > > $C_{ij} = C_{ij} + A_{ik} * B_{kj}$
> > > end do
> > end do
> end do

where $n_1 = k_1 m_1$, $n_2 = k_2 m_2$, and $n_3 = k_3 m_3$, and k_1, k_2, and k_3 are assumed to be positive integers. Each block operation $C_{ij} = C_{ij} + A_{ik} * B_{kj}$ uses the resources of the p vector processors by performing matrix-vector products in parallel.

Values of m_1, m_2, and m_3 which yield near-optimal values of the arithmetic time for the kernel can be determined by an analysis similar to those presented above for the BLAS2. The essential tradeoffs require balancing the parallel and vector processing capabilities and the bandwidth restrictions due to the single port to memory on each processor. For the Alliant FX/8, the values of m_1, m_2, and m_3 chosen according to the preceding reasoning are: $m_1 = 32k$ or is large; $m_2 \geq 16$ to 32 depending on the overhead surrounding the accumulation; and $m_3 = 8k$ or is large.

The reduction of the data loading overhead reduces to a simple constrained minimization problem. Since the submatrices A_{ik} are associated with the inner loop, it is assumed that each A_{ik} is loaded once and kept in cache for the duration of the j loop. Similarly, it is assumed that each of the C_{ij} and B_{kj} are loaded into cache repeatedly. Note that the conservative approach is taken in that no distinction is made between reads and writes in that λ is set under the pessimistic assumption that anything loaded has to be written back whether or not it was updated. Some cases where this distinction becomes important are discussed below.

It is easily seen by considering the number of transfers required that the cache-miss ratio, μ, is given by

$$(4) \qquad\qquad \mu = \frac{1}{2m_1} + \frac{1}{2m_2} + \frac{1}{2n_3}.$$

The theoretical minimum, given an infinite cache, is

$$\mu = \frac{1}{2n_1} + \frac{1}{2n_2} + \frac{1}{2n_3}.$$

Constraints for the optimization of the terms involving m_1 and m_2 are generated by determining what amount of data must fit into cache at any given time and requiring that this quantity be bounded by the cache size CS. The final set of constraints come from the fact that the submatrices cannot be larger than the matrices being multiplied. Therefore, the minimization of the number of loads performed by the BLAS3 primitive is equivalent to the solution of the minimization problem

$$(5) \qquad\qquad \min \rho(m_1, m_2) = m_1^{-1} + m_2^{-1}$$

$$\text{subject to} \quad m_2(m_1 + p) \leq CS$$
$$1 \leq m_1 \leq n_1$$
$$1 \leq m_2 \leq n_2,$$

where CS is the cache size and p is the number of processors. The constraints trace a rectangle and an hyperbola in the (m_1, m_2)-plane.

The solution to the minimization problem separates the (n_1, n_2) plane into four distinct regions; two of which are of interest for the rank-ω update and matrix-times-ω-vectors primitives, and general large dense matrix multiplication (see [67] for details). These can be summarized as:

1. The value of m_3 is arbitrary and taken to be n_3.
2. If $n_2(n_1 + p) > CS$ and $n_2 \leq CS(\sqrt{CS} + p)^{-1}$

$$m_1 = \frac{CS}{n_2} - p \quad \text{and} \quad m_2 = n_2.$$

3. If $n_2(n_1 + p) > CS$, $n_1 > \sqrt{CS}$, and $n_2 > CS(\sqrt{CS} + p)^{-1}$

$$m_1 = \sqrt{CS} \quad \text{and} \quad m_2 = \frac{CS}{\sqrt{CS} + p}.$$

Note that since the near-optimal region for the arithmetic time component was unbounded in the positive direction, there is a nontrivial intersection between it and the near-optimal region for the data loading component. This implies that, except for some boundary cases where n_1, n_2, and/or n_3 become small, the decoupling methodology does yield a strategy which can be used to choose near-optimal blocksizes for BLAS3 primitives. (The troublesome boundary cases can be handled by altering the block-loop ordering or choosing a different form of the block multiplication kernel.)

For the rank-ω primitive this results in a partitioning of the form

$$(6) \qquad \begin{pmatrix} C_1 \\ \vdots \\ C_k \end{pmatrix} \leftarrow \begin{pmatrix} C_1 \\ \vdots \\ C_k \end{pmatrix} \pm \begin{pmatrix} A_1 \\ \vdots \\ A_k \end{pmatrix} B,$$

where the blocksizes are given by the case above with $n_2 = \omega$ and small. Note that the block loops simplify to

```
do i = 1, k
        C_i = C_i + A_i * B
end do
```

and parallelism at the block-loop level becomes trivially exploitable when necessary. Also note that each block of the matrix C is read and written exactly once implying that this blocking maintains the minimum number of writes back to main memory.

For large dense matrix multiplication and for the matrix-times-ω-vectors primitive the partitioning is

$$(7) \qquad \begin{pmatrix} C_1 \\ \vdots \\ C_k \end{pmatrix} \leftarrow \begin{pmatrix} C_1 \\ \vdots \\ C_k \end{pmatrix} \pm \begin{pmatrix} A_{11} & \cdots & A_{1m} \\ \vdots & \ddots & \vdots \\ A_{k1} & \cdots & A_{km} \end{pmatrix} \begin{pmatrix} B_1 \\ \vdots \\ B_m \end{pmatrix},$$

and the block loops reduce to

```
do i = 1, k
        do j = 1, m
                C_i = C_i + A_ij * B_j
        end do
end do.
```

Once again block parallelism is obviously exploitable when needed. Note however that the blocks of C are written to several times. In general, these writes are not significant since the blocksizes have been chosen to reduce the significance of all transfers (including these writes) to a negligible level. The i-j-k block loop ordering can be used and analyzed in a similar fashion if it is desirable to accumulate a block of C in local memory. The blocksizes that result are, of course, different from the one shown above (see [105]).

The key observation with respect to the behavior of μ for BLAS3 primitives is that it decreases hyperbolically as a function of m_1 and m_2. (This assumes this particular block loop ordering but similar statements can be made about the others.)

It follows that the relative cost of transferring data decreases rapidly and reaches a global minimum of the form

$$(8) \qquad \lambda\mu = \frac{\lambda}{\sqrt{CS}} + \frac{p\lambda}{2CS} + \frac{\lambda}{2n_3}.$$

Therefore, assuming that n_3 is much larger than $\sqrt{CS}$ (large dense matrix multiplication), data loading overhead can be reduced to $O(1/\sqrt{CS})$. This limit on the cache-miss ratio reduction due to blocking is consistent with the bound derived in Hong and Kung [101]. For BLAS3 primitives where one of the dimensions is smaller than the others, with value denoted ω, the data loading overhead is a satisfactory $O(1/\omega)$.

The hyperbolic nature of the data loading overhead implies that reasonable performance can be achieved without increasing the blocksizes to the near-optimal values given above. Of course, exactly how large m_1 and m_2 must be in order to reduce the data loading overhead to an acceptable amount depends on the cost ratio λ of the machine under consideration. The existence of a lower bound on the cache-miss ratio achievable by blocking does, however, have implications with respect to the blocksizes used in block versions of linear algebra algorithms.

The expression for the data loading overhead based on (2) and (4) is also of the correct form for matrix multiplication primitives blocked for register usage in that hyperbolic behavior is also seen. The actual optimization process must be altered. The use of registers imposes shape constraints on blocksize choices and it is often more convenient not to decouple the two components of time. For the most part, however, the conclusions stated here still hold.

For hypercubes, the analysis of Fox, Otto, and Hey [61] derives a result in the same spirit as (8). They show that the efficiency (speedup divided by the number of processors) of the *broadcast-multiply-roll* matrix multiplication algorithms is

$$\epsilon \sim \frac{1}{1 - (c/\sqrt{n})t_{comm}/t_{flop}}$$

where t_{comm}, t_{flop}, and n are the cost for communication of data, cost of a floating point operation, and the number of matrix elements stored locally in each processor (hence bounded by the local memory size). The constant c is 1 for the square subblock decomposition but is $\sqrt{p}/2$ for the row decomposition, where p is the number of processors, indicating the superiority of square blocks for this type of matrix multiplication algorithm.

3.4.4. Preferred BLAS3 primitives. The preceding analysis also allows the issue of superiority of one BLAS3 primitive compared to the others to be addressed. Consider the comparison of the rank-ω primitive to the primitive which multiplies a matrix by ω vectors. If $\omega = 1$ this is the BLAS2 comparison discussed earlier and for the shared memory multivector processor analyzed above the matrix-vector multiplication primitive should be superior. On the other hand, if $\omega = n$, the two primitives are identical and no preference should be predicted by the analysis. Hence, the analysis should result in a preference which is parameterized by ω with end conditions consistent with these two observations.

To make such a comparison we will restrict ourselves to the multivector shared hierarchical memory case considered above and to four partitionings of the primitives which exploit the knowledge that ω is small compared to the other dimensions of the matrices involved (denoted h and l below). Such a strategy was proposed in [105] and has been demonstrated effective on the Alliant FX/8. We will also distinguish between elements which are only read from memory into cache and those which require reading and writing. This allows us to be more precise than the conservative bounding of the cost of data transfer presented above. Also note that this affects the value of the cost ratio λ in that it need not be as large as required above.

The partitioning of the rank-ω update used is of the form given above in (6) but the values of the blocksizes are altered to reflect the more accurate analysis obtained by differentiating between reads and writes. (The qualitative conclusions of the previous analysis do not change.) Three different partitionings for the primitive which multiplies a matrix by ω vectors are analyzed. Each is appropriate under various assumptions about the architecture and shape of the problem.

It is assumed that the primitives make use of code to perform the basic block operations which has been optimized for register-cache transfer and is able to maintain efficient use of the lowest levels of the hierarchy as the shape of the problem changes, i.e., the arithmetic time T_a has been parameterized according to ω and the code adjusted accordingly. In this case, the source of differences in the performance of the two primitives is the amount of data transfer required between cache and main memory which is given by the ratio μ. Below we derive and compare the value of μ for each of the four implementations of the primitives.

The rank-ω update computes $C \leftarrow C \pm AB$ where $C \in \Re^{h \times l}$, $A \in \Re^{h \times \omega}$, and $B \in \Re^{\omega \times l}$. The partitioning used is shown in (6) where $C_i \in \Re^{m \times l}$, $A_i \in \Re^{m \times \omega}$, $km = h$, and m is the blocksize which must be determined. Note that we have used the knowledge of the analysis above to fix two blocksizes at ω and l. The computations requires $2hl\omega$ operations and the block loops are of the form

$$\begin{aligned} &\text{do } i = 1, k \\ &\qquad C_i = C_i + A_i * B \\ &\text{end do.} \end{aligned}$$

The primitive requires $hl + h\omega + kl\omega$ loads from memory and hl writes back to memory. This partitioning/primitive combination is denoted *Form-1*.

The second primitive also computes $C \leftarrow C \pm AB$. In this case, however, $C \in \Re^{h \times \omega}$, $A \in \Re^{h \times l}$, and $B \in \Re^{l \times \omega}$. As noted above, three partitionings are considered. The first two are of the form shown in (7). Both have the block loop form

$$\begin{aligned} &\text{do } i = 1, k \\ &\qquad \text{do } j = 1, m \\ &\qquad\qquad C_i = C_i + A_{ij} * B_j \\ &\qquad \text{end do} \\ &\text{end do.} \end{aligned}$$

They differ in the constraints placed on the blocksizes.

The first version, denoted *Form-2*, results from applying the analysis of the previous section to the i-k-j loop ordering of the original triply nested loop form of the matrix multiplication primitive. One of the blocksizes is fixed at ω. Specifically, the partitioning is such that $A_i \in \Re^{m_1 \times m_2}$, $k_1 m_1 = h$, $k_2 m_2 = l$, and C_i and B_i are dimensioned conformally. The blocksizes m_1 and m_2 are determined under the simplified constraint of $m_1 m_2 \leq CS$. Form-2 requires $hl + hl\omega(m_1^{-1} + m_2^{-1})$ loads and

$k_2 h\omega$ writes to memory.

The second version, denoted *Form*-3, results from analyzing the i-j-k loop ordering of the original triply nested loop form of the matrix multiplication primitive as in [105]. As before, one of the blocksizes is fixed at ω. The partitioning is such that $A_i \in \Re^{m_1 \times m_2}$, $k_1 m_1 = h$, $k_2 m_2 = l$, and C_i and B_i are dimensioned conformally. The blocksizes m_1 and m_2 are determined under the constraint of $m_1(m_2 + \omega) \leq CS$. This constraint is generated by requiring the accumulation in cache of a block C_i which implies that a C_i and the A_{ij} contributing to the product must fit in cache simultaneously. In [105] it is shown that this partitioning sets m_2 to the value τ where τ is determined via the analysis of register-cache transfer cost. This simplifies the minimization problem and leaves only m_1 to be determined. Form-3 requires $hl + h\omega + hl\omega m_1^{-1}$ loads $h\omega$ writes to memory. Additionally, it requires $(k_2 - 1)h\omega$ writes to cache due to the local accumulation of C_i.

TABLE 1
Comparison of the four forms of the BLAS3 primitives.

Form	μ	μ_{opt}	$\mu_{opt}(\sqrt{CS})$	Blocksizes
1	$\frac{1}{2m} + \frac{1}{\omega} + \frac{1}{2l}$	$\frac{1}{\omega} + \frac{\omega}{2CS} + \frac{1}{2l}$	$\frac{3}{2\sqrt{CS}} + \frac{1}{2l}$	$m = CS/\omega$
2	$\frac{1}{2\omega} + \frac{1}{2m_1} + \frac{1}{2m_2}$	$\frac{1}{2\omega} + \frac{\sqrt{2}}{\sqrt{CS}}$	$\frac{2\sqrt{2}+1}{2\sqrt{CS}}$	$m_1 = \sqrt{CS}/2$ $m_2 = \sqrt{2CS}$
3	$\frac{1}{2\omega} + \frac{1}{2m_1} + \frac{1}{l}$	$\frac{1}{2\omega} + \frac{\omega}{2CS} + \frac{1}{l} + \frac{\tau}{2CS}$	$\frac{1}{\sqrt{CS}} + \frac{1}{l} + \frac{\tau}{2CS}$	$m_1 = \frac{CS}{\omega+\tau}$
4	$\frac{1}{2\omega} + \frac{1}{2h} + \frac{1}{2m}$	$\frac{1}{2\omega} + \frac{\omega}{CS} + \frac{1}{2h}$	$\frac{3}{2\sqrt{CS}} + \frac{1}{2h}$	$m = CS/\omega$

The third version, denoted *Form*-4, applies the i-k-j ordering to the transpose of the matrix multiplication to determine blocksizes. This form is valuable for certain architecture/shape combinations. The resulting partitioning is of the form

$$(9) \qquad C \leftarrow C \pm \begin{pmatrix} A_1 & \cdots & A_k \end{pmatrix} \begin{pmatrix} B_1 \\ \vdots \\ B_k \end{pmatrix},$$

where $A_i \in \Re^{h \times m}$, $B_i \in \Re^{m \times \omega}$ and $km = l$. The constraint $m\omega \leq CS$ is applied. Form-4 requires $hl + l\omega + 2kh\omega$ loads and $kh\omega$ writes to memory. The block loops simplify to

```
do i = 1, k
        C = C + A_i * B_i
end do.
```

Note that if parallelism across the blocks is used this form requires synchronization (which is typically done on a subblock level).

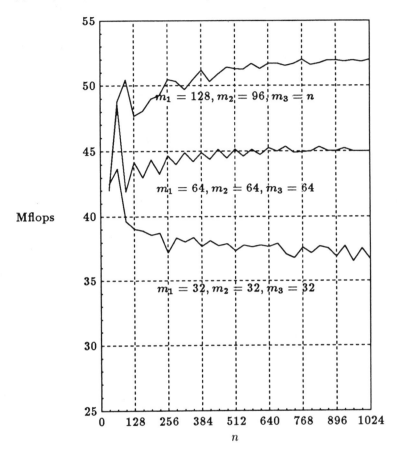

FIG. 3. *Performance of square matrix multiplication on an Alliant* FX/8.

Table 1 lists the results of analyzing each of the four forms presented above. The generic form of μ is given in terms of the dimensions of the problem and the blocksizes used as well as its optimal value. Since the results of the analysis of the primitives given above and the analysis of the block methods which use them indicate that $\omega = \sqrt{CS}$ represents a limit point on performance improvement the optimal μ evaluated there is also given. Finally, the value of the blocksizes which give the optimal data loading cost are also listed. The values show clearly the well-known inferiority of the rank-ω by a factor of 2 when ω is near 1, i.e., in the *near-BLAS2* regime. However, as ω increases, the fact that one is up to a factor of two more than the other (though this multiple rapidly reduces as well) quickly becomes irrelevant since the relative cost of data transfer to computational work has become an insignificant performance consideration. As a result, given these partitionings and an architecture satisfying the assumptions of the analysis, we would not expect significant performance differences between the two primitives when ω and the size of the matrices are large enough. Such observations have been verified on an Alliant FX/8. Consequently, one would not expect the performance of the block algorithms that use the two BLAS3 primitives, e.g., a block LU algorithm, to be significantly different for sufficiently large problems [8]. It would also be expected that the trend in preference for non-reduction types of computations as the number of processors or the cost of processor synchronization increases seen with BLAS2 primitives carry over to the BLAS3.

3.4.5. Experimental results. The performance benefits of using BLAS3 primitives and carefully selecting blocksizes in their implementation has been demonstrated in the literature. In this section, we report briefly on experimental results on the Alliant FX/8. The experiments were performed executing the particular kernel many times and averaging to arrive at an estimate of the time spent in a single instance of the kernel. This technique was used to minimize the experimental error present on the Alliant when measuring a piece of code of short duration. As a consequence of this technique, the curves have two distinct parts. The first is characterized by a peak of high performance. This is the region where the kernel operates on a problem which fits in cache. The performance rate in this region gives some idea of the arithmetic component of the time function. It is interesting to compare this peak to the rest of the curve which corresponds to the kernel operating on a problem whose data is initially in main memory. When the asymptotic performance in the second region is close to the peak in cache the number of loads is being managed effectively.

Figure 3 illustrates the effect of blocksize on the performance of the BLAS3 primitive $C \leftarrow C - AB$ where all three matrices are square and of order n. The blocksizes used for each curve are from low to high performance : $m_1 = 32$, $m_2 = 32$, and $m_3 = 32$; $m_1 = 64$, $m_2 = 64$, and $m_3 = 64$; and $m_1 = 128$, $m_2 = 96$, and $m_3 = n$. It is clear from the asymptotic performance of the top curve that a significant portion of peak performance can be achieved by choosing the correct blocksizes. In this case an asymptotic rate of just below 52 Mflops is achieved on a machine with a peak rate, including vector startup, of 68 Mflops.

Figures 4 and 5 show the performance of various rank-k updates. The parameters m_2 and m_3 are taken as k and n as recommended by the analysis of the BLAS3 primitive. The parameter m_1 is taken to be 96 and 128 in the two figures, respectively. This parameter is kept constant for each figure to allow a fair comparison between the performances of the various kernels. Further, the BLAS3 analysis recommends $m_1 = (CS/k) - p$. In fact, for the values of k considered here, if $m_1 \geq 96$ then the term in the expression for the number of loads for the rank-k kernel which involves m_1 is not significant compared to the term involving m_2.

These curves clearly show that increasing k yields increased performance and a significant portion of the effective peak computational rate is achievable. Also note that as k increases the difference in performance of two successive rank-k kernels diminishes. Indeed, the $k = 96$ curve was not included in Fig. 4 since it delivers performance virtually identical to the $k = 64$ kernel.

It is instructive to compare the performance of the rank-k kernel to typical BLAS and BLAS2 kernels. The BLAS kernels $\alpha \leftarrow x^T y$ and $y \leftarrow y \pm \alpha x$ achieve 11 Mflops and 7 Mflops, respectively, with their arguments in main memory. The BLAS2 matrix-vector product kernel achieves 18 to 20 Mflops.

3.5. Triangular system solvers. Solving triangular systems of linear equations, whether dense or sparse, is encountered in numerous applications. Even though the solution process consumes substantially less time than the associated factoriza-

---

[8] As is discussed later, when the ratio of the blocksize to the problem, ω/n, is small other tradeoffs must be considered in the performance of block algorithms.

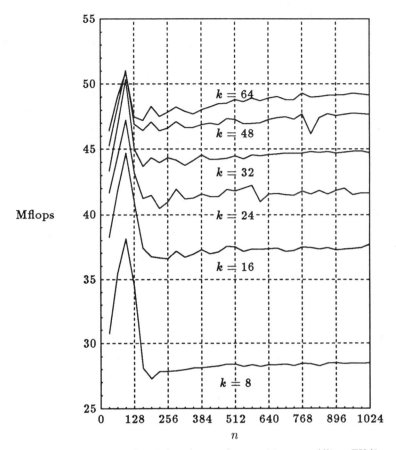

FIG. 4. *Performance of rank-k update with $m_1 = 96$ on an Alliant FX/8.*

tion stage, we often wish to solve these triangular systems repeatedly with different right-hand sides but with the same triangular matrix. Hence, it is vital to solve them as efficiently as possible on the architecture at hand.

There are two classical sequential algorithms for solving a lower triangular system $Lx = f$, where $L = [\lambda_{ij}]$, $f = [\phi_i]$, $x = [\xi_i]$ and $i, j = 1, 2, \cdots, n$. They differ in the fact that one is oriented towards rows, and the other columns. These algorithms are:

Row_oriented :
$$\xi_1 = \phi_1/\lambda_{11}$$
$$\text{do } i = 2, n$$
$$\qquad \text{do } j = 1, i - 1$$
$$\qquad\qquad \phi_i = \phi_i - \lambda_{ij}\xi_j$$
$$\qquad \text{enddo}$$
$$\qquad \xi_i = \phi_i/\lambda_{ii}$$
$$\text{enddo}$$

and

Column_oriented :

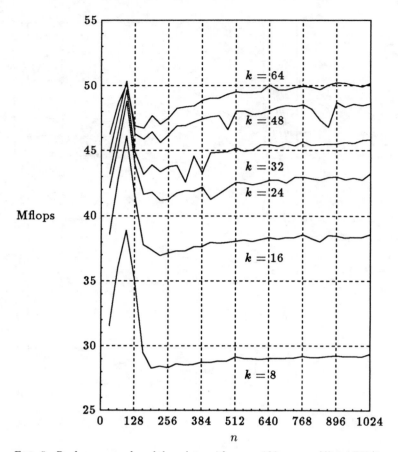

FIG. 5. *Performance of rank-k update with $m_1 = 128$ on an Alliant FX/8.*

$$\begin{aligned}
&\text{do } j = 1, n-1 \\
&\quad\quad \xi_j = \phi_j / \lambda_{jj} \\
&\quad\quad \text{do } i = j+1, n \\
&\quad\quad\quad\quad \phi_i = \phi_i - \lambda_{ij}\xi_j \\
&\quad\quad \text{end do} \\
&\text{end do} \\
&\xi_n = \phi_n / \lambda_{nn}
\end{aligned}$$

As is shown below, these two algorithms are the basis for many adaptations suitable for various vector and parallel architectures.

3.5.1. Shared-memory triangular system solvers.

The inner loops of the row- and column-oriented versions vectorize trivially to yield algorithms based respectively on the BLAS operations of SAXPY and DOTPRODUCT. We refer to these algorithms as the row-sweep or forward-sweep, and the column-sweep [116].

Each step of the row-sweep algorithm requires less data motion than the corresponding step in the column-sweep algorithm; the DOTPRODUCT primitive reads two vectors and produces a scalar while the SAXPY reads two vectors and writes a third back to memory. If the vector processor has adequate bandwidth then, theoretically at least, this should not be an important distinction. In practice, however, the reduced data traffic of the DOTPRODUCT may be preferable. (This assumes, of course, that the implementation of the DOTPRODUCT is not particularly expensive.[9]) The row-sweep algorithm can suffer from the fact that it accesses rows of the matrix. This can be remedied by storing the transpose of the lower triangular matrix, although in some cases this may not be an option, e.g., when the data placement has been determined by some other portion of the algorithm of which the triangular solve is a component.

For register-based vector processors with limited bandwidth to memory such as the CRAY-1 or a single processor of the Alliant FX/8 each of which has a single port to memory, the performance degradation due to excessive register transfers of the vector algorithms described above can be severe. Block forms of the algorithms must be considered. Let $L^{(0)} = L$, $f^{(0)} = f$, and let each of $L^{(j)}$, $x^{(j)}$, and $f^{(j)}$ be of order $(n - j\nu)$, $j = 0, \cdots, \frac{n}{\nu} - 1$ where

$$L^{(j)} = \begin{pmatrix} L_{11}^{(j)} & 0 \\ L_{21}^{(j)} & L_{22}^{(j)} \end{pmatrix}, x^{(j)} = \begin{pmatrix} x_1^{(j)} \\ x_2^{(j)} \end{pmatrix}, f^{(j)} = \begin{pmatrix} f_1^{(j)} \\ f_2^{(j)} \end{pmatrix}$$

with $L_{11}^{(j)}$, $x_1^{(j)}$, and $f_1^{(j)}$ being each of order ν (we assume that ν divides n), and $L^{(j+1)} = L_{22}^{(j)}$. The block column-sweep algorithm may then be described as:

B_Col_Sweep :

    $p = \frac{n}{\nu}$
    do $j = 0, p - 2$
        solve $L_{11}^{(j)} x_1^{(j)} = f_1^{(j)}$ via Col_Sweep or Row_Sweep
        $f^{(j+1)} = f_2^{(j)} - L_{21}^{(j)} x_1^{(j)}$
    end do
    solve $L^{(p-1)} x^{(p-1)} = f^{(p-1)}$ via Col_Sweep or Row_Sweep.

Note that this blocking allows the registers to be used efficiently. The matrix-vector product which updates the right-hand side vector is blocked in the fashion described above to allow the accumulation in a vector register of the result of ν vector operations before writing the register to memory rather than the one write per two reads of the triads in the nonblocked column-sweep. Similarly, the column-sweep algorithm can accumulate the solution to the triangular system $L_{11}^{(j)} x_1^{(j)} = f_1^{(j)}$ in vector registers resulting in a data flow between registers and memory identical to that of a $\nu \times \nu$ block of the matrix-vector product with the exception that the vector length reduces by one for each of the ν operations.

A block row-sweep algorithm can also be derived which reduces the amount of register-memory traffic even further. Using the notation above, partition L so that each block row is of the form $[C_i, L_i, 0]$ where $C_i \in \Re^{\nu \times (i-1)\nu}$ and $L_i \in \Re^{\nu \times \nu}$. Let $x = (x_1^T, \cdots, x_p^T)^T, x^{(j)} = (x_1^T, \cdots, x_j^T)^T$, and $f = (f_1^T, \cdots, f_p^T)^T$, where $x_i, f_i \in \Re^\nu$. The block algorithm is:

B_Row_Sweep :

---

[9] On some machines this is not necessarily a good assumption. The Alliant FX/8 has a considerable increase in the startup cost of the dotproduct compared to that of the triad instruction. Similarly, CRAY machines implement the dotproduct in a two-stage process. The first accumulates 64 partial sums in a vector register and the second reduces these sums to a scalar. The first phase has the memory reference pattern mentioned above but the second is memory intensive and its cost can be significant for smaller vectors.

$$\textit{Proc. 1} \qquad\qquad \textit{Proc. 2}$$

$$\textit{solve } L_{11}x_1 = f_1 \qquad\qquad -$$
$$f_2 \leftarrow f_2 - L_{21}x_1 \qquad\qquad -$$

$$f_3 \leftarrow f_3 - L_{31}x_1 \qquad \textit{solve } L_{22}x_2 = f_2$$

$$f_4 \leftarrow f_4 - L_{41}x_1 \qquad f_3 \leftarrow f_3 - L_{32}x_2$$

$$\textit{solve } L_{33}x_3 = f_3 \qquad f_4 \leftarrow f_4 - L_{42}x_2$$

$$f_4 \leftarrow f_4 - L_{43}x_3 \qquad\qquad -$$
$$\textit{solve } L_{44}x_4 = f_4 \qquad\qquad -$$

FIG. 6. *Two processor* DO-ACROSS *synchronization pattern.*

$p = \frac{n}{\nu}$

solve $L_1 x_1 = b_1$ via Col_Sweep or Row_Sweep

do $j = 2, p$

        $f_j = f_j - C_j x^{(j-1)}$

        solve $L_j x_j = f_j$ via Col_Sweep or Row_Sweep

end do.

This algorithm requires only one or two vector writes per block row computation depending upon whether or not the result of the matrix-vector product is left in registers for the triangular-solve primitive to use. This algorithm is characterized by the use of short and wide matrix-vector operations rather than the tall and narrow shapes of the block column-sweep. It is, of course, quite straightforward to combine the two approaches to use a more consistent shape throughout the algorithm.

Another triangular solver, which is also suited for both shared and distributed memory multiprocessors, is that based on the DO-ACROSS notion. For example, in the above sequential form of the column-oriented algorithm, the main point of a DO-ACROSS is that computing each ξ_j need not wait for the completion of the whole inner iteration $i = j + 1, \cdots, n$. In fact, one processor may compute ξ_j soon after another processor has computed $\phi_j := \phi_j - \lambda_{j,j-1}\xi_{j-1}$. To minimize the synchronization overhead in a DO-ACROSS and efficiently use registers or local memory, the computation is performed by blocks. For example, if $L = [L_{pq}]$, $x = \{x_p\}$, $f = \{f_p\}$, and $p, q = 1, \cdots, 4$, where each block is of order $n/4$, then the DO-ACROSS on two processors may be illustrated as shown in Fig. 6. Vectorization can be exploited in each of the calculations shown if each processor has vector capabilities. The particular parallel schedule used in the DO-ACROSS approach is, of course, highly dependent on the efficiency of the synchronization mechanisms provided on the multiprocessor of interest.

All of the methods presented thus far in this section can be viewed as reorganizations of the task graph in Fig. 7. The row-oriented algorithm executes each row in turn starting from the top and tasks within each row from left to right. The column-oriented, on the other hand, executes each column in turn starting from the left and tasks within a column from the top to bottom. The row and column sweeps

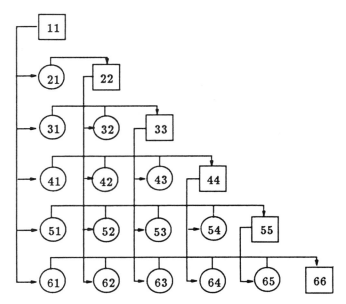

FIG. 7. *Triangular system solution dependence graph.*

on a vector machine merely vectorize the tasks within a row or column, respectively. Block versions of the algorithm interpret each node as corresponding to computations involving a submatrix rather than a single element. Careful consideration of the task graph, however, reveals certain limitations of all methods based upon it. Suppose that each node represents the operation on a submatrix of order m and $n = km$. The dependence graph implies that the maximum number of processors that can ever be active at the same time is $k - 1$. Further, the dependence graph has a critical path with $O(k)$ length which establishes a fundamental limit to the speed at which these algorithms can solve a triangular system. To go faster we need a new dependence graph which relates the solution x to the data L and f.

The new dependence graph can be generated from recognizing the algebraic characterization of the column- and row-sweep algorithms. The algorithms can be easily described algebraically in terms of elementary unit lower triangular matrices. For example, assuming without loss of generality that $\lambda_{ii} = 1$, it follows that

$$L = \prod_{i=1}^{n-1} N_i^{-1} = \prod_{j=2}^{n} M_j^{-1},$$

where $N_i = I - l_i e_i^T$, $M_j = I - e_j v_j^T$, l_i is the vector corresponding to column i in L with the 1 on the diagonal removed and v_j is similarly constructed from row j of L. It is easy to see from the algebraic structure of N_i and M_j that multiplying them by a vector corresponds to the computational primitives of a triad and dotproduct, respectively. It follows immediately that the column-sweep and row-sweep algorithms are specified algebraically by (here with $n = 8$):

$$(N_7(N_6(N_5(N_4(N_3(N_2(N_1 f)))))))$$

and

$$(M_8(M_7(M_6(M_5(M_4(M_3(M_2 f)))))))).$$

The grouping of computations makes clear the source of the $O(n)$ critical path in the dependence graph. Also a simple application of associativity can generate two algorithms that have a much shorter critical path. Specifically, the column-sweep expression can be transformed into

$$(((N_7 N_6)(N_5 N_4))((N_3 N_2)(N_1 f))).$$

Note the logarithmic nature of the critical path. The algorithm specified is called the *product form* and is due to Sameh and Brent [159]. Instead of performing the product $(N_{n-1} \cdots N_2 N_1)f$ in $(n-1)$ stages, we may form it in $O(\log_2 n)$ stages. It can be shown by careful consideration of the structure of the matrices at each stage that the critical path has a length of $k^2/2 + 3k/2$ floating point operations where $k = \log_2 n$. Such an improvement is not without cost, however. The algorithm requires approximately $n^3/10 + O(n^2)$ operations and $n^3/68 + O(n^2)$ processors. It is therefore typically not appropriate for an architecture with a limited number of processors such as those of interest here. For a discussion of the numerical stability of this algorithm see [187].

Note that thus far we have assumed only one right-hand side vector. The BLAS3 primitive triangular solver assumes that multiple right-hand side vectors and solutions are required. This, of course, provides the necessary data locality for high performance on a hierarchical memory system. The generalization of the algorithms above are straightforward and the blocksizes (the number and order of right-hand sides solved in a stage of the algorithm) can be analyzed in a fashion similar to the matrix multiplication primitives.

For banded lower triangular systems in which the bandwidth m (the number of subdiagonals with nonzero entries) is small, column-sweep algorithms are ineffective on vector or parallel computers. Consider such a system $Lx = f$, where L is partitioned as a block-bidiagonal matrix with diagonal submatrices L_i and subdiagonal submatrices R_{i-1}, $i = 1, \cdots, n/m$, where L_i and R_{i-1} are lower and upper triangular, respectively. Premultiplying both sides of $Lx = f$ by $D = \text{diag}(L_i^{-1})$ we obtain the system $L^{(0)}x = f^{(0)}$ where $L^{(0)}$ is block bidiagonal with identities of order m on the diagonal and matrices $G_j^{(0)} = L_{j+1}^{-1} R_j$ on the subdiagonal, and $f^{(0)} = Df$. Note that we do not invert the L_j's, but obtain $f^{(0)}$ and $G_i^{(0)}$ by solving triangular systems using one of the above parallel algorithms. We repeat the process by multiplying both sides of $L^{(0)}x = f^{(0)}$ by $D^{(0)} = \text{diag}((L_i^{(0)})^{-1})$ where

$$(L_i^{(0)})^{-1} = \begin{pmatrix} I_m & 0 \\ -G_{2i-1}^{(0)} & I_m \end{pmatrix}.$$

Now $L^{(1)} = D^{(0)} L^{(0)}$ and $f^{(1)} = D^{(0)} f^{(0)}$ are obtained by simple multiplication. Eventually, $L^{(\log(n/m))} = I_n$ and $f^{(\log(n/m))} = x$. The required number of arithmetic operations is $O(m^2 n \log(n/2m))$ resulting in a redundancy of $O(m \log(n/2m))$, e.g., see [159]. Given $m^2 n/2 + O(mn)$ processor, however, those operations can be completed in $O(\log m \log n)$ time.

This algorithm offers opportunities for both vector and parallel computers. At the first stage we have n/m triangular systems to solve, each of order m, for $(m + 1)$ right-hand sides except for the first system which has only one right-hand side. In the subsequent stages we have several matrix-matrix and matrix-vector multiplications, with the last stage consisting of only one matrix-vector multiplication, in which the matrix is of order $(n/2 \times m)$.

An alternative scheme, introduced by Chen, Kuck, and Sameh [27], may be described as follows. Let the banded lower triangular matrix L be partitioned as

$$
\begin{pmatrix}
L_1 & & & & \\
\tilde{R}_2 & L_2 & & & \\
& \tilde{R}_3 & L_3 & & \\
& & \ddots & \ddots & \\
& & & \tilde{R}_p & L_p
\end{pmatrix},
$$

where

$$
\tilde{R}_j = \begin{pmatrix} 0 & R_j \\ 0 & 0 \end{pmatrix}
$$

and each L_i is of order $(n/p) >> m$ and each R_i is upper triangular of order m. If the right-hand side f and the solution x are partitioned accordingly, then after solving the triangular systems

$$
L_1 x_1 = f_1
$$

and

$$
L_i \left[U_i, g_i \right] = \left[\begin{pmatrix} R_i \\ 0 \end{pmatrix}, f_i \right]
$$

the original system is reduced to $\tilde{L}x = g$ in which $\tilde{L}$ is of the form

$$
\begin{pmatrix}
I_{n/p} & & & & \\
\tilde{U}_2 & I_{n/p} & & & \\
& \tilde{U}_3 & I_{n/p} & & \\
& & \ddots & \ddots & \\
& & & \tilde{U}_p & I_{n/p}
\end{pmatrix},
$$

where

$$
\tilde{U}_j = \begin{pmatrix} 0 & U_j \end{pmatrix}.
$$

Let

$$
U_i = \begin{bmatrix} V_i \\ W_i \end{bmatrix}, \quad x_i = \begin{bmatrix} y_i \\ z_i \end{bmatrix}, \quad g_i = \begin{bmatrix} h_i \\ r_i \end{bmatrix},
$$

in which W_i is a matrix of order m and r_i, z_i are vectors of m elements each. Thus, solving the above system reduces to solving a smaller triangular system of order mp,

$$
\begin{pmatrix}
I_m & & & \\
W_2 & I_m & & \\
& \ddots & \ddots & \\
& & W_p & I_m
\end{pmatrix}
\begin{pmatrix} z_1 \\ z_2 \\ \vdots \\ z_p \end{pmatrix}
=
\begin{pmatrix} r_1 \\ r_2 \\ \vdots \\ r_p \end{pmatrix}.
$$

After solving this system by the previous parallel scheme, for example, we can retrieve the rest of the elements of the solution vector x by obvious matrix-vector multiplications. The algorithm requires approximately $4m^2 n$ operations which, given $\tilde{p} = mp$ processors, can be completed in time $2\tilde{p}^{-1} m^2 n + 3\tilde{p}^{-1} mn + O(m^2)$. See [189] for a discussion of the performance of this algorithm applied to lower bidiagonal systems and the attendant numerical stability properties.

3.5.2. Distributed-memory triangular system solvers. A large number of papers have appeared for handling triangular systems on distributed memory architectures (mainly rings and hypercubes), e.g., see Sameh [158], Romine and Ortega [151], Heath and Romine [89], Li and Coleman [122] and Eisenstat et al. [53]. Most are variations on the basic algorithms above adapted to exploit the distributed nature of the architectures. For such architectures, it is necessary to distinguish whether a given triangular matrix L is stored across the individual processor memories by rows or by columns. For example, suppose that the matrix $[L, f]$ is stored by rows, then the above column-sweep algorithm becomes:

Row_Storage :
    do j = 1 , n
            if j is one of my row indices then
                $\xi_j = \phi_j / \lambda_{jj}$
            communicate(broadcast, fan-out) ξ_j to each processor
            do i = j + 1 , n
                if i is one of my row indices then
                    $\phi_i = \phi_i - \xi_j \lambda_{ij}$
            enddo
    enddo.

Note first that the computations in the inner loop can be executed in parallel, and that on a hypercube with $p = 2^\nu$ processors, the fan-out communication can be accomplished in ν stages. If the lower triangular matrix L is stored by columns then the column-sweep algorithm will cause excessive interprocessor communication. A less communication intensive column storage oriented algorithm has been suggested in [150] and [151]. Such an algorithm is based upon the classical sequential *Row_sweep* algorithm shown above.

In implementing the column storage algorithm on an Intel iPSC hypercube, for example, information is gathered into one processor from all others via a fan-in operation $fan\_in(\tau, i)$. Such an operation enables the processor whose memory contains column i to receive the sum of all the τ's over all processors. The parallel column storage algorithm can be described as follows:

Col_Storage :
    do i = 1 , n
            $\tau = 0$
            do j = 1 , i - 1
                if j is one of my column indices then
                    $\tau = \tau + \xi_j \lambda_{ij}$
            enddo
            $\eta = fan\_in(\tau, i)$
            if i is one of my column indices then
                $\xi_i = (\phi_i - \eta) / \lambda_{ii}$
    enddo.

Here, during stage i of the algorithm, the pseudo-routine $fan\_in(\tau, i)$ collects and sums the partial inner products τ from each processor, leaving the result η in the processor containing column i. Further modifications to the basic row- and column-oriented triangular solvers on distributed memory systems have been studied in [122], there a communication scheme which allows for ring embedding into a hypercube is emphasized. In addition, the study in [53] has improved upon the cyclic type algorithms in [89].

4. LU factorization algorithms. The goal of the LU decomposition is to factor an $n \times n$-matrix A into a lower triangular matrix L and an upper triangular matrix U. This factorization is certainly one of the most used of all numerical linear computations. The classical LU factorization [83] can be expressed in terms any of the three levels of the BLAS, and techniques needed to achieve high performance for both shared and distributed memory systems have been considered in great detail in the literature. In this section we review some of these techniques for the LU and LU-like factorizations for dense and block tridiagonal linear systems.

4.1. Shared-memory algorithms for dense systems. In this subsection we consider some of the approaches used in the literature for implementing the LU factorization of a matrix $A \in \Re^{n \times n}$ on shared-memory multivector processors such as the CRAY-2, CRAY X-MP, and Alliant FX/8. To simplify the discussion of the effects of hierarchical memory organization, we move directly to the block versions of the algorithms. Throughout the discussion ω denotes the blocksize used and the more familiar BLAS2-based versions of the algorithms can be derived by setting $\omega = 1$. Four different organizations of the computation of the classical LU factorization without pivoting are presented with emphasis on identifying the computational primitives involved in each. The addition of partial pivoting is then considered and a block generalization of the LU factorization (L and U being block triangular) is presented for use with diagonally dominant matrices. Finally, the results of an analysis of the architecture/algorithm mapping of this latter algorithm for a multivector processor with a hierarchical memory are also examined along with performance results from the literature.

4.1.1. The algorithms. The are several ways to organize the computations for calculating the LU factorization of a matrix. These reorganizations are typically listed in terms of the ordering of the nested loops that define the standard computation. The essential differences between the various forms are: the set of computational primitives required, the distribution of work among the primitives, and the size and shape of the subproblems upon which the primitives operate. Since architectural characteristics can favor one primitive over another, the choice of computational organization can be crucial in achieving high performance. Of course, this choice in turn depends on a careful analysis of the architecture/primitive mapping.

Systematic comparisons of the reorganizations have appeared in various contexts in the literature. Trivedi considered them in the context of virtual memory systems in combination with other performance enhancement techniques [185], [186]. Dongarra, Gustavson, and Karp [42] and more recently Ortega [137] compare the orderings for vector machines such as the CRAY-1 where the key problem is the efficient exploitation of the register-based organization of the processor and the single port to memory. Ortega has also considered the problem on highly parallel computers [137]. Papers have also appeared that are concerned with comparing the reorderings given a particular machine/compiler/library combination, e.g., see [162]. In general, most of the conclusions reached in these papers can be easily understood and parameterized by analyses of the computational primitives and the algorithms in the spirit of those in the previous section and below.

4.1.1.1. Version 1. *Version* 1 of the algorithm assumes that at step i the LU factorization of the leading principal submatrix of dimension $(i - 1)\omega$, $A_{i-1} =$

$L_{i-1}U_{i-1}$, is available. The next ω rows of L and ω columns of U are computed during step i to produce the factorization of the leading principal submatrix of order $i\omega$. Clearly, after $k = n/\omega$ such steps the factorization $LU = A$ results.

The basic step of the algorithm can be deduced by considering the following partitioning of the factorization of the matrix $A_i \in \Re^{i\omega \times i\omega}$:

$$A_i = \begin{pmatrix} A_{i-1} & C \\ B^T & H \end{pmatrix} = \begin{pmatrix} L_{i-1} & 0 \\ M^T & L_2 \end{pmatrix} \begin{pmatrix} U_{i-1} & G \\ 0 & U_2 \end{pmatrix},$$

where H is a square matrix of order ω and the rest of the blocks are dimensioned conformally. The basic step of the algorithm consists of four phases:

    (i) Solve for G: $C \leftarrow L_{i-1}G = C$.
    (ii) Solve for M: $B \leftarrow U_{i-1}^T M = B$.
    (iii) Update: $H \leftarrow H - M^T G$.
    (iv) Factor $H \leftarrow L_2 U_2 = H$.

(The arrow is used to represent the portion of the array which is overwritten by the new information obtained in each phase.) Clearly, repeating this step on successively larger submatrices will produce the factorization of $A \in \Re^{n \times n}$.

In each step, solving the triangular system requires $2\omega h^2$ operations, the update of H requires $2h\omega^2$ and the factorization requires $O(\omega^3)$, where $h = (i - 1)\omega$. Early stages of the algorithm are dominated by the factorization primitive. The later stages, where most of the work is done, is dominated by solving triangular systems with ω right-hand side vectors. This dominance is particularly pronounced when the BLAS2 ($\omega = 1$) version of the algorithm is used. Note also that when $\omega = 1$ the use of the triangular solver allows efficient use of the vector registers on vector processors like the CRAY-1 or a single CE of the Alliant FX/8 which have single ports to memory.

4.1.1.2. Version 2. *Version 2* of the algorithm assumes that the first $\xi = (i - 1)\omega$ columns of L and ξ rows of U are known at the start of step i, and that the transformations necessary to compute this information have been applied to the submatrix $A^i \in \Re^{n-\xi \times n-\xi}$ in the lower right-hand corner of A that has yet to be reduced. The algorithm proceeds by producing the next ω columns and rows of L and U, respectively, and computing A^{i+1}. This is a straightforward block generalization of the standard rank-1-based Gaussian elimination algorithm.

Assume that the factorization of the matrix $A^i \in \Re^{n-\xi \times n-\xi}$ is partitioned as follows:

$$A^i = \begin{pmatrix} A_{11} & A_{12} \\ A_{21} & A_{22} \end{pmatrix} = \begin{pmatrix} L_{11} & 0 \\ L_{21} & I \end{pmatrix} \begin{pmatrix} U_{11} & U_{12} \\ 0 & A^{i+1} \end{pmatrix},$$

where A_{11} is square and of order ω and the other submatrices are dimensioned conformally. L_{11}, L_{21} and U_{12} are the desired ω columns and rows of L and U and identity defines A^{i+1}.

The basic step of the algorithm consists of:

    (i) Factor: $A_{11} \leftarrow L_{11}U_{11} = A_{11}$.
    (ii) Solve for L_{21}: $A_{21} \leftarrow U_{11}^T L_{21}^T = A_{21}^T$.
    (iii) Solve for U_{12}: $A_{12} \leftarrow L_{11}U_{12} = A_{12}$.
    (iv) Update: $A_{22} \leftarrow A_{22} - L_{21}U_{12}$.

Clearly, the updated A_{22} is A^{i+1} and the algorithm proceeds by repeating the above four phases.

This version of the algorithm is dominated by the rank-ω update of the submatrix $A_{22} \in \Re^{(n-i\omega) \times (n-i\omega)}$. Note that the triangular systems that must be solved are of order ω with many right-hand sides as opposed to the large systems which are solved in Version 1. As in Version 1 the factorization primitive operates on systems of order ω. As is well known and obvious from the analysis of the previous section, the BLAS2 version, based on the rank-1 update, is not the preferred form for register-based vector or multivector processors with a single port to memory due to poor register usage.

4.1.1.3. Version 3. *Version* 3 of the algorithm can be viewed as a hybrid of the first two versions. Like Version 2, it is assumed that the first $(i-1)\omega$ columns of L and rows of U are known at the start of step i. It also assumes, like Version 1, that the transformations that produced these known columns and rows must be applied elements of A which are to be transformed into the next ω columns and rows of L and U. As a result, Version 3 does not update the remainder of the matrix at every step.

Consider the factorization:

$$A = \left(\begin{array}{cc} A_{11} & A_{12} \\ A_{21} & A_{22} \end{array} \right) = \left(\begin{array}{cc} L_{11} & 0 \\ L_{21} & L_{22} \end{array} \right) \left(\begin{array}{cc} U_{11} & U_{12} \\ 0 & U_{22} \end{array} \right),$$

where A_{11} is a square matrix of order $(i-1)\omega$ and the rest are partitioned conformally. By our assumptions, L_{11}, L_{21}, U_{11}, and U_{12} are known and the first ω columns of L_{22} and the first ω rows of U_{22} are to be computed. Since Version 3 assumes that none of the update $A_{22} \leftarrow A_{22} - L_{21}U_{12}$ has occurred in the first $i-1$ steps of the algorithm, the first part of step i is to perform the update to the portion upon which the desired columns of L_{22} and rows of U_{22} depend. This is then followed by the calculation of the columns and rows.

To derive the form of the computations, suppose the update of A_{22} and its subsequent factorization are partitioned

$$A_{22} \leftarrow \left(\begin{array}{cc} H & C^T \\ B & \tilde{A}_{22} \end{array} \right) = \left(\begin{array}{cc} \hat{H} & \hat{C}^T \\ \hat{B} & \hat{A}_{22} \end{array} \right) - L_{21}U_{12}$$

and

$$\left(\begin{array}{cc} H & C^T \\ B & \tilde{A}_{22} \end{array} \right) = \left(\begin{array}{cc} \tilde{L}_{11} & 0 \\ \tilde{L}_{21} & \tilde{L}_{22} \end{array} \right) \left(\begin{array}{cc} \tilde{U}_{11} & \tilde{U}_{12} \\ 0 & \tilde{U}_{22} \end{array} \right),$$

where H and $\hat{H}$ are square matrices of order ω and the other submatrices are dimensioned conformally. Step i then has two major phases: Calculate H, B, and C; and calculate $\tilde{L}_{11}$, $\tilde{L}_{21}$, $\tilde{U}_{11}$, and $\tilde{U}_{12}$. As a result, at the end of stage i, the first $i\omega$ rows and columns of the triangular factors of A are known.

Let $L_{21} = [M_1^T, M_2^T]^T$ and $U_{12} = [M_3, M_4]$, where M_1 and M_3 consist of the first ω rows and columns of the respective matrices. The first phase of step i computes

(i) $[H^T, B^T]^T \leftarrow [H^T, B^T]^T = [\hat{H}^T, \hat{B}^T]^T - L_{21}M_3$.
(ii) $C \leftarrow C^T = \hat{C}^T - M_1M_4$.

In the second phase, the first ω rows and columns of the factorization of the updated A_{22} are then given by:

(i) Factor: $H \leftarrow \tilde{L}_{11}\tilde{U}_{11} = H$.
(ii) Solve for $\tilde{L}_{21}$: $B \leftarrow \tilde{U}_{11}^T\tilde{L}_{21}^T = B^T$.

(iii) Solve for $\tilde{U}_{12}$: $C \leftarrow \tilde{L}_{11}\tilde{U}_{12} = C^T$.

The work in this version of the algorithm is split between a matrix multiplication primitive, a triangular solver, and a factorization primitive; the latter two of which are applied to systems of order ω. Note, however, that the matrix multiplication primitive is applied to a problem which has the shape of a large matrix applied to ω vectors (or the transpose of such a problem). Hence, for $\omega = 1$ this version of the algorithm becomes a form which uses the preferred BLAS2 primitive — matrix-vector multiplication. Although, as noted above, when ω is nontrivial the preference for this block form over Version 2 does not necessarily follow.

4.1.1.4. Version 4. *Version* 4 of the algorithm assumes that at the beginning of step i the first $(i-1)\omega$ columns of L and U are known. Step i computes the next ω columns of the two triangular factors. Consider the factorization

$$A = \begin{pmatrix} A_{11} & A_{12} \\ A_{21} & A_{22} \end{pmatrix} = \begin{pmatrix} L_{11} & 0 \\ L_{21} & L_{22} \end{pmatrix} \begin{pmatrix} U_{11} & U_{12} \\ 0 & U_{22} \end{pmatrix},$$

where A_{11} is a square matrix of order $(i-1)\omega$ and the rest are partitioned conformally. By our assumptions, L_{11}, L_{21}, and U_{11} are known.

Let L_ω, U_ω, and A_ω be the matrices of dimension $n \times \omega$ formed of the first ω columns of $[0, L_{22}^T]^T$, $[U_{12}^T, U_{22}^T]^T$, and $[A_{12}^T, A_{22}^T]^T$, respectively. (These are also columns $(i-1)\omega + 1$ through $i\omega$ of L, U, and A.) Consider the partitioning

$$L_\omega = \begin{pmatrix} 0 \\ \tilde{L} \\ G \end{pmatrix}, \quad U_\omega = \begin{pmatrix} M \\ \tilde{U} \\ 0 \end{pmatrix}, \quad A_\omega = \begin{pmatrix} \tilde{A}_1 \\ \tilde{A}_2 \\ \tilde{A}_3 \end{pmatrix},$$

where $\tilde{L}$, $\tilde{U}$, and $\tilde{A}_2$ are square matrices of order ω with $\tilde{L}$ and $\tilde{U}$ lower and upper triangular respectively.

Step i calculates L_ω and U_ω by applying all of the transformations from steps 1 to $i-1$ to A_ω and then factoring a rectangular matrix. Specifically, step i comprises the computations:

(i) Solve for M: $\tilde{A}_1 \leftarrow L_{11}M = \tilde{A}_1$.
(ii) Update: $[\tilde{A}_2^T, \tilde{A}_3^T]^T \leftarrow [\tilde{A}_2^T, \tilde{A}_3^T]^T - L_{21}M$.
(iii) Factor: $\tilde{A}_2 \leftarrow \tilde{L}\tilde{U} = \tilde{A}_2$.
(iv) Solve for G: $\tilde{A}_3 \leftarrow \tilde{U}^T G^T = \tilde{A}_3^T$.

This version of the algorithm requires the solution of a large triangular system with ω right-hand sides as well as a small triangular system of order ω with many right-hand sides. The factorization kernel operates on a system of order ω. As with Version 3 the matrix multiplication primitive operates on a problem with the shape of a large matrix times ω vectors and the factorization of a system of order ω and the same observations apply. This version also has the feature that it works exclusively with columns of A which can be advantageous in some Fortran and virtual memory environments.

4.1.1.5. Partial pivoting. Partial pivoting can be easily added to Versions 2, 3, and 4 of the algorithm. Step i of each of the versions requires the LU factorization of a rectangular matrix $M \in \Re^{h \times \omega}$, where $h = n - (i-1)\omega$. Specifically, step i computes

$$M = \begin{pmatrix} M_1 \\ M_2 \end{pmatrix} = \begin{pmatrix} \hat{L}_{11} \\ \hat{L}_{21} \end{pmatrix} \hat{U}_{11},$$

where $\hat{L}_{11}$ and $\hat{U}_{11}$ are, respectively, lower and upper triangular matrices of order ω. In the versions above without pivoting, this calculation could be split into two pieces: the factorization of a system of order ω, $\hat{L}_{11}\hat{U}_{11} = M_1$; and the solution of a triangular system of order ω with $h - \omega$ right-hand sides. (These computations are: (i) and (ii) in Version 2; (i) and (ii) of the second phase of Version 3; and (iii) and (iv) of Version 4.) When partial pivoting is added to the versions of the algorithm these computations at each step cannot be separated and are replaced by a single primitive which produces the factorization of a rectangular matrix with permuted rows, i.e.,

$$PM = P \begin{pmatrix} M_1 \\ M_2 \end{pmatrix} = \begin{pmatrix} \hat{L}_{11} \\ \hat{L}_{21} \end{pmatrix} \hat{U}_{11},$$

where P is a permutation matrix. This primitive is usually cast as a BLAS2 version of one of the versions above. Note, however, a fundamental difference compared to the nonpivoting versions. The ability to split the factorization of the tall matrix into smaller BLAS3-based components in the latter case has benefits with respect to hierarchical memory usage, since ω is usually taken so that such systems fit in cache or local memory, see [23], [67]. In the case of pivoting, these operations are performed via BLAS2 primitives repeatedly updating a matrix which can not be kept locally. As a result, the arithmetic component of time and the data transfer overhead both increase. In fact, a conflict between their reductions occurs. This situation is similar to that seen in the block version of Modified Gram Schmidt and Version 5 of the factorization algorithm, both discussed below along with a solution. (Although in the latter case, the source of difficulties is slightly different.)

The information contained in the permutations associated with each step, P_i, can be applied in various ways. For example, the permutation can be applied immediately to the transformations of the previous steps, which are stored in the elements of the array A to the left of the active area for step i, and to the elements of the array A which have yet to reach their final form, which, of course, appear to the right of the active area for step i. The application to either portion of the matrix may also be delayed. The update of the elements of the array which have yet to reach their final form could be delayed by maintaining a global permutation matrix which is then applied to only the elements required for the next step. Similarly, the application to the transformations from steps 1 through $i - 1$ could be suppressed and the P_i could be kept separately and applied incrementally in a modified forward and backward substitution routine.

4.1.1.6. Version 5. A block generalization. In some cases it is possible to use a block generalization of the classical LU factorization in which L and U are lower and upper block triangular matrices, respectively. The use of such a block generalization is most appropriate when considering systems which do not require pivoting for stability, e.g., diagonally dominant or symmetric positive definite. This algorithm decomposes A into a lower block triangular matrix L_ω and an upper block triangular matrix U_ω with blocks of the size ω by ω (it is assumed for simplicity that $n = k\omega$, $k > 1$). Assume that A is diagonally dominant and consider the factorization:

$$A = \begin{pmatrix} A_{11} & A_{12} \\ A_{21} & A_{22} \end{pmatrix} = \begin{pmatrix} I & 0 \\ L_{21} & I \end{pmatrix} \begin{pmatrix} A_{11} & A_{12} \\ 0 & B \end{pmatrix},$$

where A_{11} is a square matrix of order ω. The block LU algorithm is given by:

    (i) $A_{11} \leftarrow A_{11}^{-1}$
    (ii) $A_{21} \leftarrow L_{21} = A_{21}A_{11}$
    (iii) $A_{22} \leftarrow B = A_{22} - L_{21}A_{12}$
    (iv) Proceed recursively on the matrix B.

Statements (i) and (ii) can be implemented in several ways. Since A is assumed to be diagonally dominant, explicit inversion of the diagonal blocks can be done either via the Gauss–Jordan algorithm [143] or an LU decomposition without pivoting. In the latter case, the computations in step (i) above are replaced by solving two triangular systems of order ω with many right-hand sides. (Due to parallel processing, the Gauss–Jordan scheme, historically frowned upon, has recently been the subject of renewed interest. See [34] for a discussion of its application, with appropriate modifications, to general nonsymmetric systems of equations.)

If the Gauss–Jordan kernel is used, as is assumed below, the block LU algorithm is more expensive by a factor of approximately $(1 + 2/k^2)$ than the classical LU factorization which requires about $2n^3/3$ operations. In this form, the above block algorithm uses three primitives: a Gauss–Jordan inversion (or LU decomposition), $A \leftarrow AB$, and a rank-ω update.

Note that when $\omega = 1$ this form of the algorithm becomes the BLAS2 version based on rank-1 updates. As with Versions 1–4, which produce the classical LU factorization, the computations of Version 5 can be reorganized so that different combinations of BLAS3 primitives and different *shapes* of submatrices are used. For example, the main BLAS3 primitive can be changed from a rank-ω update into a matrix multiplying ω row or column vectors. As noted above, the importance of such a reorganization depends highly on the architecture in question.

4.1.2. Performance analysis.
Gallivan et al. have applied the decoupling methodology to Version 5 [67]. Their results demonstrate many of the performance trends observed in the literature for the various forms of block methods. A summary of the important points follows.

There are two general aspects of the block LU decomposition through which the blocksize $\omega = n/k$ influences the arithmetic time: the number of redundant operations (applicable when the Gauss–Jordan approach is used); and the relationship, as a function of ω, between the performance of each of the primitives and the distribution of work among the primitives. The redundancy factor of $(1 + 2/k^2)$ and the fact that the number of operations performed in the Gauss–Jordan primitive is an increasing function of ω cause the arithmetic time component to prefer smaller blocksizes for small and moderately sized systems. For those systems, increasing ω and therefore decreasing k clearly exacerbates the two problems noted above to such a degree that the effect is dominant compared to the reduction in data transfer overhead gained by increasing the blocksize. As the order of the system increases, however, these effects become secondary to data transfer considerations.

The data transfer overhead of the algorithm is most conveniently analyzed by writing the algorithm's cache-miss ratio as the weighted average of the cache-miss ratios of the various instances of each primitive. The weights are the ratio of the number of operations in the particular instance of the primitive to the total number of operations required. In practice, some of the local cache-miss ratios are zero due to the interaction between the instances of the primitives; this occurs when the remaining part of the matrix to be decomposed approaches the size of the cache and later instances of primitives find an increasing proportion of their data left in cache by earlier instances. In [67] the results are derived using the conservative assumption of no interaction between instances of primitives. Note that without a model of the data transfer properties of the primitives such an analysis at the algorithmic level is impossible. This does not imply that blocksizes cannot be set effectively based on observed performance data of the primitives for various shapes and sizes of problems. Such a *black box* tuning approach is quite useful in practice, but it does not provide any *explanation* as to why the performance is as observed. This can only be done by considering the architecture/algorithm mapping of the primitives and the implications of combining them in the manner specified by the particular version of the factorization algorithm used.

The behavior on the interval $1 \leq \omega \leq \sqrt{CS}$, where CS denotes cache size, roughly separates into three regimes. For small values of ω, i.e., $\omega \leq 16$, the cache-miss ratio is of the form:

$$\mu \approx \frac{1}{2\omega} \, \gamma_R + \eta_1,$$

where η_1 is proportional to $1/n$ and γ_R is a function of ω which is bounded by a small constant. This result is expected since the computations are dominated by the rank-ω update which achieves a similar cache-miss ratio. In particular, it is clear that the data locality of a BLAS2 version, $\omega = 1$, is very poor. In the middle of the interval of interest the cache-miss ratio is of the form:

$$\mu \approx \frac{1}{\omega} \, \gamma_R + \eta_2,$$

where η_2 is proportional to $1/n$. Finally, when $\omega \approx \sqrt{CS}$, the cache-miss ratio is

$$\mu \approx \frac{1}{\sqrt{CS}} \gamma_R + \eta_3,$$

where η_3 is proportional to $1/n$. The ratio μ becomes a rapidly increasing function once ω exceeds $\sqrt{CS}$ until it reaches, at the point $\omega = n$, the cache-miss ratio of the algorithm of a BLAS2-based version of the Gauss–Jordan algorithm which has a value of approximately $\frac{1}{4}$. The exact point where this transition to rapidly increasing occurs is dependent on the implementation of the Gauss–Jordan primitive, but, any decrease in μ between $\omega = \sqrt{CS}$ and the transition point is typically insignificant.

4.1.3. Experimental results. The various versions of the algorithms have appeared in different contexts in the literature. Here we list some representative papers and then consider in more detail the performance of Version 5 and its relationship to the trends predicted via the blocksize analysis presented above.

The column-oriented BLAS2 form of Version 4 was used by Fong and Jordan on the CRAY-1 [56]. The results of using a BLAS2 form of Version 3 on the CRAY-1 and one CPU of a CRAY X-MP were given by Dongarra and Eisenstat in [41]. Dongarra and Hewitt discuss the use of a rank-3-based approach on four CPU's of a CRAY X-MP [45]. Calahan demonstrated the power of the block form of Version 3 (with and without pivoting) on the hierarchical memory system of one CPU of a CRAY-2. Agarwal and Gustavson have extended their work which led to single CPU block algorithms for the IBM 3090 by considering parallel forms of the BLAS3 primitives and *LU* factorization on an IBM ES/3090 model 600S [2]. In particular, they discuss the use of parallel block methods in a multitasking environment where the user is not necessarily guaranteed control of all (or any fixed subset) of the six processors in the system. Radicati, Robert, and Sguazzero have presented the results of a rank-k-based code on an IBM 3090 multivector processor for one to six processors [149]. The block form of Version 4 was also considered in a virtual memory setting by Du Croz et al. in [50] and used as a model of a block LU factorization in the BLAS3 standard proposal by Dongarra et al. [39]. Finally, Dayde and Duff have compared the performance of the different organizations of the block computations on a CRAY-2, ETA-10P, and IBM 3090-200/VF.

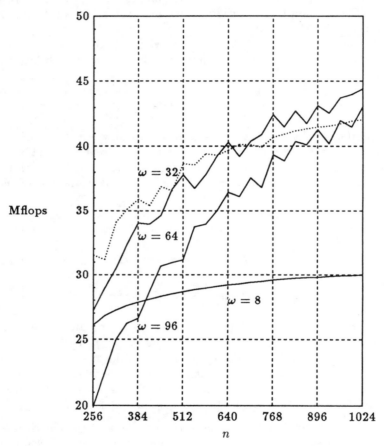

FIG. 8. *Performance of block LU on an Alliant* FX/8.

The performance trends for Version 5 predicted via the decoupling analysis summarized above have been verified in [67]. Figure 8 illustrates the performance of the block LU algorithm for diagonally dominant matrices for various blocksizes on an Alliant FX/8 [67]. The performance was computed using the nonblock version operation count. The actual rate is, therefore, higher for the block methods.

The curves in Fig. 8 clearly show the trends predicted by the analysis above. The significant improvement over BLAS2-based routines by a small amount of blocking can be seen in the performance of the $\omega = 8$ curve and comparing it to the 7 to 10 Mflops possible via a BLAS2-based Version 2 code or the 15 to 17 Mflops of a BLAS2-based

Version 3 code. As expected, for any fixed order of the system, performance improves as ω is increased until an optimal is reached. For small systems, increasing beyond this value causes performance degradation due to the conflict between reducing μ and efficiently distributing work among the primitives. For larger systems, the conflict reduces and performance is maintained until ω exceeds $\sqrt{CS}$.

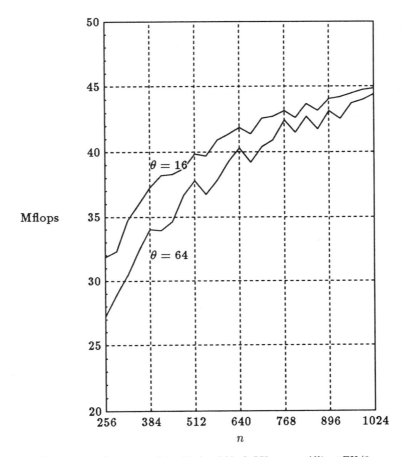

FIG. 9. *Performance of double-level block LU on an Alliant* FX/8.

The conflict between arithmetic time and data loading overhead minimization which produces the shifting of the preferred blocksize as a function of n can be mitigated somewhat by using a double-level blocking [67]. This conflict has been deliberately exacerbated in these experiments by using a Fortran implementation of the Gauss–Jordan primitive and assembler coded BLAS3 routines.

There are two basic approaches to double-level blocking: *inner-to-outer* and *outer-to-inner*. Both require a pair of blocksizes (θ, ω). The outer-to-inner approach replaces the operation of the Gauss–Jordan primitive on a system of order ω with a block LU factorization using the *inner* blocksize θ. The inner-to-outer approach begins with a block LU factorization with blocksize θ which is determined largely by the arithmetic time analysis and which is typically smaller than the single-level load analysis would recommend. Several rank-θ updates are then grouped together into a rank-ω in order to improve the data loading overhead. The decoupling methodology can be used to show that these techniques do mitigate the conflict between reducing the arithmetic time component and the data loading overhead (see [67] for details). Figure 9 demonstrates that the use of inner-to-outer form of double-level blocking can indeed improve performance. Note that that double-level version yields performance higher than all of the single-level implementations of Fig. 8 over the entire interval.

4.2. Distributed-memory algorithms. Our objective here is to describe the effects that the data-storage and pivoting schemes have on the efficiency of the LU factorization of a dense matrix $A = (\alpha_{ij})$ on distributed memory systems. The related parallel Cholesky schemes will not be discussed in this section; for an example, see Heath [88]. We also describe some LU-like factorization schemes that are useful on distributed memory and hybrid architectures.

4.2.1. LU factorization. A number of papers have appeared in recent years describing various parallel LU factorization schemes on such architectures, e.g., see Ipsen, Saad, and Schultz [104], Chu and George [28], Geist and Heath [77], [78], and Geist and Romine [79]. We will concentrate here only on the work of Geist and Romine.

Consider the two basic storage schemes: storage of A by rows and by columns. The row storage case is considered first. Adopting the terminology of Geist and Romine [79], we refer to the following scheme as RSRP, *Row Storage with Row Pivoting*.

RSRP:
each processor executes the following,
do $k = 0, n - 1$
      determine row pivot
      update permutation vector
      if (I own pivot row)
              fan-out(broadcast) pivot row
      else
              receive pivot row
      for (all rows $i > k$ that I own)
              $\lambda_{ik} = \alpha_{ik}/\alpha_{kk}$
              do $j = k + 1, n - 1$
                     $\alpha_{ij} = \alpha_{ij} - \lambda_{ik}\alpha_{kj}$
              enddo
enddo.

In most of the early work, row storage for the coefficient matrix was chosen principally because no efficient parallel algorithms were then known to exist for the subsequent forward and backward sweeps if the coefficient matrix were to be stored by columns. But, as discussed earlier, recent triangular solvers for distributed memory multiprocessors have removed the main reason for preferring row storage. Next, the *Column Storage with Row Pivoting* (CSRP) scheme is given by:

CSRP:
each processor executes the following
do $k = 0, n - 1$
      if (I own column k)

determine pivot row
interchange
do $i = k + 1, n - 1$
$$\lambda_{ik} = \alpha_{ik}/\alpha_{kk}$$
broadcast the column just computed and pivot index

else

receive the column just computed and pivot index
interchange
for (all columns $j > k$ that I own)
do $i = k + 1, n - 1$
$$\alpha_{ij} = \alpha_{ij} - \lambda_{ik}\alpha_{kj}$$
enddo

enddo.

A modification of RSRP, which we refer to as RSCP, *Row Storage with Column Pivoting*, consists of searching the current pivot row for the element with maximum modulus, and then exchanging columns to bring this element to the diagonal. The RSCP algorithm can be readily seen as nothing more than the dual of algorithm CSRP. Geist and Heath [78] indicate that both RSCP and CSRP yield essentially identical speedup on an Intel iPSC hypercube. In fact, Geist and Heath conclude that, in the absence of such techniques as loop unrolling, *LU* factorization with partial pivoting is most efficient when pipelining is used to mask the cost of pivoting. In particular, the two schemes that can most easily be pipelined are: pivoting by interchanging rows when the matrix is distributed across the processors by columns (algorithm CSRP), and pivoting by interchanging columns when the matrix is distributed across the processors by rows (algorithm RSCP).

4.2.2. Pairwise pivoting. Gaussian elimination with pairwise pivoting is an alternative to *LU* factorization which is attractive on a variety of distributed memory architectures including systolic arrays since it introduces parallelism into the pivoting strategy.[10] Such a pivoting strategy dates back to Wilkinson's work on Gaussian elimination using the ACE computer with its limited amount of memory [62]. The main idea is rather simple. If $u^T = [\mu_1, \cdots, \mu_n]$ and $v^T = [\nu_1, \cdots, \nu_n]$ are two row vectors, then we can choose a stabilized elementary transformation

$$S = \begin{pmatrix} 1 & 0 \\ \alpha & 1 \end{pmatrix} P$$

so as to annihilate either μ_1 or ν_1, whichever is smaller in magnitude. Here, P is either the identity of order 2 or (e_2, e_1) so that

$$S \begin{pmatrix} u^T \\ v^T \end{pmatrix} = \begin{pmatrix} \tilde{\mu}_1 & \tilde{\mu}_2 & \cdots & \tilde{\mu}_n \\ 0 & \tilde{\nu}_2 & \cdots & \tilde{\nu}_n \end{pmatrix}.$$

One of the many possible annihilation schemes for reducing a nonsingular matrix A of order n to upper triangular form is illustrated in Fig. 10 for $n = 8$. (The elements marked with i can all be eliminated simultaneously on step i.)

Such a triangularization scheme requires $2n - 3$ *stages* in which each stage consists of a maximum of $\lfloor n/2 \rfloor$ independent stabilized transformations. It is ideally suited

---

[10] Pairwise pivoting can also be useful on shared memory machines to break the bottleneck caused by partial pivoting discussed earlier.

$$\begin{pmatrix}
* \\
1 & * \\
2 & 3 & * \\
3 & 4 & 5 & * \\
4 & 5 & 6 & 7 & * \\
5 & 6 & 7 & 8 & 9 & * \\
6 & 7 & 8 & 9 & 10 & 11 & * \\
7 & 8 & 9 & 10 & 11 & 12 & 13
\end{pmatrix}$$

FIG. 10. *Annihilation scheme for n = 8.*

for a ring of processors [157] or other systolic arrays [80]. Note, however, that it does not produce an LU factorization of the matrix. L is replaced by a product of matrices in which each one can be readily inverted. One possible drawback of this pivoting strategy is that the upper bound on the growth factor is the square of that of partial pivoting [168], [169]. Our extensive numerical experiments indicate that, as is the case with partial pivoting, such growth is rarely encountered in practice. In that sense, our experience contradicts some conclusions of Trefethan and Schreiber [184] indicating that some further work is required to reconcile this seeming inconsistency.

The above annihilation scheme was originally motivated by a parallel Givens reduction introduced in [161] and now used extensively in applications such as signal processing for recursive least squares computations. This parallel Givens reduction was later generalized for a ring of processors [158].

4.2.3. A hybrid scheme. In order to design factorization schemes for multicluster machines, such as Cedar, in which each cluster is a parallel computer with tightly coupled processors, we must combine the strategies outlined above for both shared and distributed memory models. Breaking the problem among the clusters so as to minimize intercluster communication while maintaining load balancing is an issue faced by users of distributed memory architectures. Cedar's advantage is the existence of a shared global memory.

The shared memory block LU algorithm and the BLAS3 primitives, discussed above, are concerned with achieving high performance on an architecture like a single Cedar cluster. While these algorithms and kernels form an invaluable building block for algorithms on the Cedar system and the conclusions of the analysis are applicable over a fairly wide range of multivector architectures, care must be taken not to generalize these conclusions too far. For example, on a single Cedar cluster (and similar architectures) routines for many of the basic linear algebra tasks encountered in practice can be designed as a series of calls to BLAS3 kernels and BLAS2-implemented algorithms thereby masking all of the architectural considerations of parallelism, vectorization, and communication. This method of algorithm design, however, cannot be generalized to all hierarchical shared memory machines. One of the main reasons for this is the fact that an algorithm designed via this method may have problems with an inappropriate choice of task granularity and the resulting excessive communication requirements. The need to introduce double-level blocking forms of the algorithm indicated the onset of such a problem on a Cedar cluster: the attempt to spread the BLAS2-implemented kernel across the processors in a cluster introduced serious limitations on the performance of the block algorithm. When this problem becomes extreme, other forms of the algorithm must be used which typically involve reorganizing the block computations to more efficiently map the algorithm to the architecture via tasks of coarser granularity with more attention focused on minimizing the required communication. Typically this involves some notion of *pipelining* (possibly multidimensional) at the block level, e.g., see [14], [157].

An example of such a situation is the solution of a dense linear system using more than one cluster of Cedar (possibly a subset of the total number available). In this case the algorithm design must take into account that intercluster communication is rather costly. There are several possible designs for such an algorithm. One of the most straightforward is based on the outer-to-inner double-level block form presented above. The block computations can be pipelined across clusters using the necessary Cedar synchronization primitives. A second possibility uses the control structure of the pipelined Givens factorization on a ring of processors described in [158]. A block of rows rather than a single row is communicated between processors and the row rotation is replaced with a block Gaussian elimination procedure. The remainder of this section discusses another algorithm, due to Sameh [157], for solving dense linear systems on a multiple cluster architecture which requires a relatively small amount of intercluster communication. For simplicity a four-cluster Cedar is assumed.

Let A, a nonsingular matrix of order n, be partitioned as

$$A^T = (A_1^T, A_2^T, A_3^T, A_4^T)$$

where A_i resides in the ith cluster memory. The algorithm consists of two major stages. In the first stage, using a block-LU scheme with partial pivoting, each A_i is factored into the form

$$P_i A_i = L_i U_i$$

for $i = 1, 2, 3, 4$ where P_i is a permutation, L_i is unit lower triangular, and U_i is upper trapezoidal.

Assuming, without loss of generality, that each U_i has a nonsingular upper triangular part, the factorization of A may be completed in the second stage which consists of $3n/4$ computational waves pipelined across the four clusters. These computational waves comprise three groups of $n/4$ waves. During the kth group the latest values for the rows of U_k are used by clusters $k+1$ to 4 in a pipelined fashion to further reduce their segments of the decomposition. It should be noted that cluster k is idle during the kth group of waves and the remainder of the algorithm since the other clusters will update the rows of U_k that it has produced and placed in global memory. (For example, cluster 1 only performs the initial reduction of A_1 and is then released for other tasks within the application code of which solving the system is a part or the tasks of other users since Cedar is a multiuser system.) The first group of $n/4$ computational waves which use the rows of U_1 produced by cluster 1 is described below. The pattern of the remaining two groups follows trivially.

Wave 1. Let $U_k \equiv [\mu_{i,j}^k]$. The first row of U_1 is transmitted via the global memory to cluster 2 where it is used, with pairwise pivoting, to annihilate the first element of the (possibly new due to pairwise pivoting) first row of U_2, $\mu_{1,1}^2$. The updated first row of U_1 is then transmitted to cluster 3 so as to annihilate $\mu_{1,1}^3$ and then to cluster 4 where $\mu_{1,1}^4$ is eliminated with the final version of the first row of U_1 residing in global memory.

As soon as $\mu_{1,1}^k$ is annihilated in cluster k, $k = 2, 3, 4$, the nonzero portion of U_k is a $n/4 \times (n-1)$ upper Hessenberg matrix, e.g., for $n = 24$ it is of the form

$$
\begin{pmatrix}
x & x & x & x & x & x & \cdots & x \\
x & x & x & x & x & x & \cdots & x \\
  & x & x & x & x & x & \cdots & x \\
  &   & x & x & x & x & \cdots & x \\
  &   &   & x & x & x & \cdots & x \\
  &   &   &   & x & x & \cdots & x
\end{pmatrix}.
$$

The cluster then proceeds to reduce U_k to upper trapezoidal form through a pipelined Gaussian elimination process using pairwise pivoting.

Waves $2 \leq j \leq n/4$. Similar to the first wave, the jth row of U_1 is transmitted to clusters 2, 3, and 4 to annihilate $\mu_{1,j}^2$, $\mu_{1,j}^3$, and $\mu_{1,j}^4$, respectively. After these annihilations occur, each cluster reduces U_k, which at this point is upper Hessenberg, to upper trapezoidal form.

Note that after this first group of computational waves U_1 is in its final form in global memory. The matrix U_2 is in its penultimate form since it will only change due to the pairwise pivoting done by clusters 3 and 4 in the second group of computational waves. This implies that cluster 2 is now available for other work. The second and third computational groups proceed in the same way as the first did with each cluster fetching the appropriate row from the source matrix, U_2 followed by U_3, transforming U_k to upper Hessenberg form and then reducing it back to an upper trapezoidal matrix. This basic form of the algorithm possesses many levels of communication and computation granularity and can be modified to improve utilization of a multicluster architecture. For example, if the whole Cedar machine were devoted to such a dense solver, simple interleaving of block rows of A would enhance load balancing among the clusters.

4.3. Block tridiagonal linear systems. Block tridiagonal systems arise in numerous applications — one example being the numerical handling of elliptic partial differential equations via finite element discretization. Often, solving such linear systems constitutes the major computational task. Hence, efficient algorithms for solving these systems on vector and parallel computers are of importance. Using block versions of Gaussian elimination for block tridiagonal systems seems a natural extension of the efficient dense solvers discussed above. Some of the early work may be found in [191] and the survey by Heller [90]. A more recent study of block Gaussian elimination on the Alliant FX/8 for solving such systems [11] indicates the importance of efficient dense solvers and the underlying BLAS3 as components for block tridiagonal solvers.

If the size of the blocks is small, i.e., a narrow-banded system, such forms of Gaussian elimination offer little potential vectorization and parallelization. Similar to the above discussions for banded triangular systems, a partitioning scheme, referred to as the *spike* algorithm below, for handling tridiagonal systems on vector or parallel computers was introduced in [161], where Givens reductions were used to handle the diagonal blocks. Later, Wang [192] considered the simpler problem of diagonally dominant systems and gave essentially the same form of the algorithm modified to use Gaussian elimination (made possible by the assumption of diagonal dominance) and a different method for the elimination of the *spikes*. Several studies have generalized this partitioning scheme to narrow-banded systems, e.g., see [46], [47], [120], [132] and the recent book by Ortega [137].

The main idea of this partitioning scheme may be outlined as follows. Let the linear system under consideration be denoted by $Ax = f$, where A is a banded diagonally dominant matrix of order n. It is assumed that the number of superdiagonals $m \ll n$ is equal to the number of subdiagonals and that, for simplicity of presentation, $n = pq$. On a sequential machine such a system would be solved via Gaussian elimination, see [38] for example. The algorithm described below assumes p CPU's of a CRAY X-MP or CRAY-2, or a Cedar system with p clusters. Here, for the sake of illustration, p is taken to be 4.

Let the matrix A be partitioned into the block-tridiagonal form with block row $[C_i, A_i, B_i]$ and conformally x and f, e.g.,

$$\begin{pmatrix} A_1 & B_1 & 0 & 0 \\ C_2 & A_2 & B_2 & 0 \\ 0 & C_3 & A_3 & B_3 \\ 0 & 0 & C_4 & A_4 \end{pmatrix} \begin{pmatrix} x_1 \\ x_2 \\ x_3 \\ x_4 \end{pmatrix} = \begin{pmatrix} f_1 \\ f_2 \\ f_3 \\ f_4 \end{pmatrix},$$

where each A_i, $1 \le i \le p$, is a banded matrix of order $q = n/p$ and bandwidth $2m + 1$ (same as A),

$$B_i = \begin{pmatrix} 0 & 0 \\ \hat{B}_i & 0 \end{pmatrix}$$

and

$$C_{i+1} = \begin{pmatrix} 0 & \hat{C}_{i+1} \\ 0 & 0 \end{pmatrix},$$

$1 \le i \le p - 1$, in which $\hat{B}_i$ and $\hat{C}_{i+1}$ are lower and upper triangular matrices, respectively, each of order m.

The algorithm consists of three stages.

Stage 1. If both sides of $Ax = f$ were premultiplied by $\mathrm{diag}(A_1^{-1}, A_2^{-1}, \cdots, A_p^{-1})$ we obtain a system of the form

$$\begin{pmatrix} I_q & E_1 & 0 & 0 \\ F_2 & I_q & E_2 & 0 \\ 0 & F_3 & I_q & E_3 \\ 0 & 0 & F_4 & I_q \end{pmatrix} \begin{pmatrix} x_1 \\ x_2 \\ x_3 \\ x_4 \end{pmatrix} = \begin{pmatrix} g_1 \\ g_2 \\ g_3 \\ g_4 \end{pmatrix},$$

where

$$E_i = (\hat{E}_i, 0), \qquad F_i = (0, \hat{F}_i),$$

in which $\hat{E}_i$ and $\hat{F}_i$ are matrices of m columns given by

$$\hat{E}_i = A_i^{-1} \begin{pmatrix} 0 \\ \hat{B}_i \end{pmatrix}$$

and

$$\hat{F}_i = A_i^{-1} \begin{pmatrix} \hat{C}_i \\ 0 \end{pmatrix}$$

and will, in general, be full.

In stage 1, $\hat{E}_i$, $\hat{F}_i$, and g_i are obtained by solving the associated linear systems. In each cluster $2 \le k \le 4$ we solve $2m + 1$ linear systems of the form $A_k v = r$, while clusters 1 and 4 each solves $m + 1$ linear systems of the same form. Note that no intercluster communication is needed.

The method of solution used on each cluster (Alliant FX/8) for these 4 systems with multiple right-hand sides, varies with m. For $m < 8$ a variant of the spike algorithm is used. For $8 \le m \le 16$ (approximately), block cyclic reduction is the most effective and for larger m a block Gaussian elimination is recommended [11].

Stage 2. Let $\hat{E}_i$ and $\hat{F}_i$ be partitioned, in turn, as follows

$$\hat{F}_i = \begin{pmatrix} P_i \\ M_i \\ Q_i \end{pmatrix}, \qquad \hat{E}_i = \begin{pmatrix} S_i \\ N_i \\ T_i \end{pmatrix},$$

where P_i, Q_i, S_i, and $T_i \in \Re^{m \times m}$. Also, let g_i and x_i be conformally partitioned:

$$g_i = \begin{pmatrix} h_{2i-2} \\ w_i \\ h_{2i-1} \end{pmatrix}, \qquad x_i = \begin{pmatrix} y_{2i-2} \\ z_i \\ y_{2i-1} \end{pmatrix}.$$

The structure of the resulting partitioned system is such that the unknown vectors y_j, $1 \le j \le 6$ (each of order m) are disjoint from the rest of the unknowns. In other words, the m equations above and the m equations below each of the 3 partitioning lines form an independent system of order $6m$, which is referred to as the *reduced system* $Ky = h$,

$$\begin{pmatrix} I_m & T_1 & & & & \\ P_2 & I_m & & S_2 & & \\ Q_2 & & I_m & T_2 & & \\ & & P_3 & I_m & & S_3 \\ & & Q_3 & & I_m & T_3 \\ & & & & P_4 & I_m \end{pmatrix} \begin{pmatrix} y_1 \\ y_2 \\ y_3 \\ y_4 \\ y_5 \\ y_6 \end{pmatrix} = \begin{pmatrix} h_1 \\ h_2 \\ h_3 \\ h_4 \\ h_5 \\ h_6 \end{pmatrix}.$$

Since A is diagonally dominant, it can be shown that the reduced system is also diagonally dominant and hence there are a number of options available for solving it. Typically, it is small enough to be sent to a single Cedar cluster and solved with an appropriate algorithm.

When it is large enough to warrant a multicluster approach the reduced-system approach could be applied again. Note, however, that the bandwidth of the system has doubled compared to the original system. Block-column permutations can reduce the bandwidth back to its original value but this destroys diagonal dominance and pivoting will usually be required to solve the permuted reduced system. It is also possible to use all of the clusters to solve the reduced system via an iterative technique such as Orthomin(k) [47].

Finally, if the original linear system is *sufficiently* diagonally dominant, we can ignore the matrices Q_i and S_i as $\|S_i\|_\infty$ and $\|Q_i\|_\infty$ are much smaller than $\|T_i\|_\infty$ and $\|P_i\|_\infty$, respectively. This results in a block-diagonal reduced system in which each block is of the form

$$\begin{pmatrix} I_m & T_k \\ P_{k+1} & I_m \end{pmatrix}$$

for $1 \leq k \leq 3$.

Stage 3. Once the y_i's are obtained, the rest of the components of the solution vector of the original system may be retrieved as follows:

$$z_k = w_k - M_k \; y_{2k-3} - N_k \; y_{2k},$$

for $1 \leq k \leq 4$,

$$y_0 = h_0 - S_1 y_2,$$

and

$$y_7 = h_7 - Q_4 \; y_5.$$

Provided that the y_i's are stored in the global memory, this stage requires no inter-cluster communication.

In addition to reporting on the performance results for this algorithm on the Alliant FX/8, [11] also reports on the performance achieved on four CPU's of a CRAY X-MP/416. Using four partitions on a system of order 16384 with blocksize 32, a speedup relative to itself of 3.8 was achieved indicating an efficient use of the micro-tasking capabilities and memory system of the machine. The speedup compared to a block LU algorithm on one CPU was approximately 2.

There are several modifications and reorganizations possible of the spike algorithm for solving banded systems discussed above. These can be used to alter the form of the algorithm to more efficiently map to a variety of shared memory architectures. For one such alternative see [155]. Also, if the system is symmetric positive definite, Dongarra and Johnsson [46] have discussed how the algorithm can be modified to obtain a reduced system that is symmetric positive definite as well.

An analysis of the parallel and numerical aspects of a two-sided Gaussian elimination for solving tridiagonal systems has been given recently by van der Vorst [188].

The work by Johnsson [108], [109] is representative of organization of concurrent algorithms for solving tridiagonal and narrow banded systems on distributed memory machines with various connection topologies, e.g., two-dimensional arrays, shuffle-exchange networks and boolean cubes. Fox et al. have also considered the problem of banded systems on hypercubes. In [60], they provide a detailed performance analysis of the problem.

5. Least squares. In solving the linear least squares problem:

$$(10) \qquad \qquad \min \|f - Ax\|_2,$$

where A is an $m \times n$ matrix of rank n, $(m \geq n)$, it is often necessary to obtain the factorization,

$$(11) \qquad \qquad QA = \begin{pmatrix} R \\ 0 \end{pmatrix},$$

in which Q is an orthogonal matrix and R is a nonsingular upper triangular matrix of order n. Such a factorization may be realized on multiprocessors via plane rotations, see [48], [158], and [161], elementary reflectors, see [16] and [158], or the Modified Gram–Schmidt algorithm, see [9]. (Although the latter algorithm is more commonly associated with the calculation of an orthogonal basis of the range of A.)

In the section concerning shared memory multiprocessors, block versions of Householder reduction and the modified Gram–Schmidt algorithm are presented, as well as a pipelined Givens reduction for updating matrix factorization. For distributed memory multiprocessors, organization of Givens and Householder reductions on a ring of processors convey the main ideas needed for implementation on hypercubes and locally connected distributed memory architectures.

5.1. Shared-memory algorithms.

5.1.1. A block Householder reduction. If $A \equiv A_1 = [a_1^{(1)}, a_2^{(1)}, \cdots, a_n^{(1)}]$, then it is possible to generate elementary reflectors $P_k = I - \alpha_k u_k u_k^T$, $k = 1, \cdots, n$, such that forming $P_k A_k$ produces the kth row of R and the $(m - k) \times (n - k)$ matrix $A_{k+1} = [a_{k+1}^{(k+1)}, \cdots, a_n^{(k+1)}]$ by annihilating all but the first element in $a_k^{(k)}$. The two basic tasks in such a procedure are [170]: (i) generation of the reflector P_k such that $P_k a_k^{(k)} = (\rho_{kk}, 0, \cdots, 0)^T$, $k = 1, 2, \cdots, n$; and (ii) updating the remaining $(n - k)$ columns, $P_k a_j^{(k)} = (\rho_{kj}, a_j^{(k+1)T})^T$, $j = k + 1, \cdots, n$. On a parallel computer, reflector P_{k+1} may be generated even before task (ii) for stage k is finished. While an organization that allows such an overlap is well suited for some shared memory machines and for a distributed memory multiprocessor such as a ring of processors, e.g., see [158], it does not offer the data locality needed in a hierarchical shared memory system such as that of an Alliant FX/8.

A block scheme proposed by Bischof and Van Loan [16], see also the related papers [15], [19], [36], [146], [163], offers such data locality. This scheme depends on the fact that the product of k elementary reflectors $Q_k = (P_k, \cdots, P_2, P_1)$, where $P_i = I_m - w_i w_i^T$, can be expressed as a rank-k update of the identity of order m, i.e.,

$$Q_k = I_m - V_k U_k^T,$$

where $V_1 = U_1 = w_1$, $V_j = (P_j V_{j-1}, w_j)$ and $U_j = (U_{j-1}, u_j)$, for $j = 2, \cdots, k$.

The block algorithm may be described as follows. Let the $m \times n$ matrix $(m \geq n)$ whose orthogonal factorization is desired be given by

$$A = [A_1, B],$$

where A is of rank n, and A_1 consists of the first k columns of A. Next, proceed with the usual Householder reduction scheme by generating the k elementary reflectors P_1 through P_k such that

$$(P_k \cdots P_2 P_1) A_1 = \begin{pmatrix} R_1 \\ 0 \end{pmatrix},$$

where R_1 is upper triangular of order k without modifying the matrix B. If we accumulate the product $Q_k = P_k \cdots P_1 = I - V_k U_k^T$ as each P_i is generated, the matrix B is updated via

$$B \leftarrow (I - V_k U_k^T) B$$

which relies on the high efficiency of one of the most important kernels in BLAS3, that of a rank-k update. The process is then repeated on the modified B with another *well-chosen* block size, and so on until the factorization is completed. It may also be desirable to accumulate the various Q_k's, one per block, to obtain the orthogonal matrix, Q, that triangularizes A.

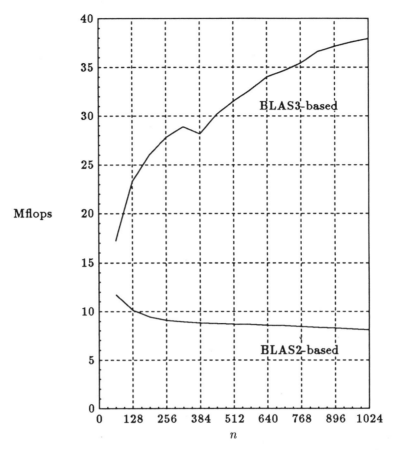

FIG. 11. *Performance of block Householder algorithm on an Alliant* FX/8.

It was shown in [16] that this block algorithm is as numerically stable as the classical Householder scheme. The block scheme, however, requires roughly $(1 + 2/p)$ times the arithmetic operations needed by the classical sequential scheme, where $p = n/k$ is the number of blocks (assuming a uniform block size throughout the factorization). Bischof and Van Loan report the performance of the block algorithm at 18 Mflops for large square matrices ($n = 1000$) on an FPS-164/MAX with a single MAX board and note that an optimized LINPACK QR running on an FPS-164 without MAX boards would achieve approximately 6 Mflops. An example, of the performance achieved by a BLAS3 implementation of the block Householder algorithm (PQRDC) compared to a BLAS2 version (DQRDC) on an Alliant FX/8, [85], is shown in Fig. 11. The performance shown is computed using the nonblock algorithm operation count.

Most recently, Schreiber and Van Loan have considered a more efficient storage scheme for the product of Householder matrices [164]. They describe the *compact WY* representation of the orthogonal matrix Q which is of the form

$$Q = I + YTY^T,$$

where $Y \in \Re^{m \times n}$ is a lower trapezoidal matrix and $T \in \Re^{n \times n}$ is a upper triangular matrix. The representation requires only mn storage locations and can be computed in a stable fashion.

5.1.2. A block-modified Gram–Schmidt algorithm.

The goal of this algorithm is to factor an $m \times n$ matrix A of maximal rank into an orthonormal $m \times n$ matrix Q and an upper triangular R of order n where $m > n$ and A is of maximal rank. Let A be partitioned into two blocks A_1 and B where A_1 consists of ω columns of order m, with Q and R partitioned accordingly:

$$(A_1, B) = (Q_1, P) \begin{pmatrix} R_{11} & R_{12} \\ 0 & R_{22} \end{pmatrix}.$$

The algorithm is given by:

(i) $A_1 = Q_1 R_{11}$,
(ii) $R_{12} = Q_1^T B$,
(iii) $B_1 = B - Q_1 R_{12}$.
(iv) Apply the algorithm recursively to produce $B_1 = P R_{22}$.

If $n = k\omega$, step (i) is performed k times and steps (ii) and (iii) are each performed $k - 1$ times.

Three primitives are needed for the jth step of the algorithm: a QR decomposition (assumed here to be a modified Gram–Schmidt routine — MGS); a matrix multiplication AB; and a rank-ω update of the form $C \leftarrow C - AB$. The primitives allow for ideal decomposition for execution on a limited processor shared memory architecture. The BLAS2 version of the modified Gram–Schmidt algorithm is obtained when $\omega = 1$ or $\omega = n$, and a double-level blocking version of the algorithm is derived in a straightforward manner by recursively calling the single-level block algorithm to perform the QR factorization of the $m \times \omega$ matrix A_1.

Jalby and Philippe have considered the stability of this block algorithm [106] and Gallivan et al. have analyzed the performance as a function of blocksize [67]. Below, a summary of this blocksize analysis is presented along with experimental results on an Alliant FX/8 of single and double-level versions of the algorithm.

The analysis is more complex than that of the block LU algorithm for diagonally dominant matrices discussed above, but the conclusions are similar. This increase in complexity is due to the need to apply a BLAS2-based MGS primitive to an $m \times \omega$ matrix at every step of the algorithm. As with the block version of the LU factorization with partial pivoting, this portion of each step makes poor use of the cache and increases the amount of work done in less efficient BLAS2 primitives. The analysis of the arithmetic time component clearly shows that the potential need for double-level blocking is more acute for this algorithm than for the diagonally dominant block LU factorization on problems of corresponding size.

The behavior of the algorithm with respect to the number of data loads can be discussed most effectively by considering approximations of the cache-miss ratios. For the interval $1 \leq \omega \leq l \approx CS/m$ the cache-miss ratio is

$$\mu \approx \frac{1}{2\omega} + \eta_1,$$

where η_1 is proportional to $1/n$, which achieves its minimum value $m/(2CS)$ at $\omega = l$. Under certain conditions the cache-miss ratio continues to decrease on the interval

$l \leq \omega \leq n$ where it has the form

$$\mu \approx \frac{1}{2\omega}\left(1 - \frac{\gamma}{n}\right) + \frac{\omega}{2}\left(\frac{1}{n} + \frac{1}{CS}\right) + \eta_2,$$

where η_2 is proportional to $1/n$, which reaches its minimum at a point less than $\sqrt{CS}$ and increases thereafter, as expected. (See [67] for details.) When $\omega = n$ the cache-miss ratio for the second interval is $1/2$ corresponding to the degeneration from a BLAS3 method to a BLAS2 method. The composite cache-miss ratio function over both intervals behaves like a hyperbola before reaching its minimum; therefore the cache-miss ratio does not decline as rapidly in latter parts of the interval as it does near the beginning.

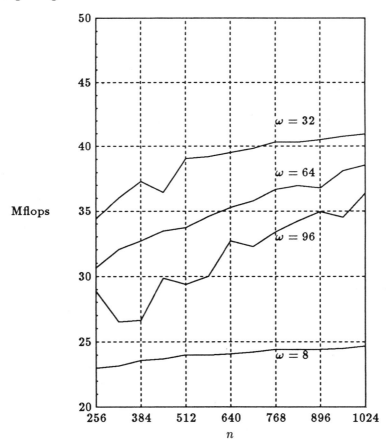

FIG. 12. *Performance of one-level block MGS on an Alliant* FX/8.

A load analysis of the double-level algorithm shows that double-level blocking either reduces or preserves the cache-miss ratio of the single-level version while improving the performance with respect to the arithmetic component of time.

Figures 12 and 13 illustrate, respectively, the results of experiments run on an Alliant FX/8, using single-level and double-level versions of the algorithm applied to square matrices. The cache size on this particular machine is $16K$ double precision words.

For the range of n, the order of the matrix, shown in Fig. 12, the single-level optimal blocksize due to the data loading analysis starts at $\omega = 64$, decreases to $\omega = 21$ for $n = 768$, and then increases to $\omega = 28$ at $n = 1024$. Analysis of the arithmetic time component recommends the use of a blocksize between $\omega = 16$ and $\omega = 32$. Therefore, due to the hyperbolic nature of μ and the arithmetic time component analysis it is expected that the performance of the algorithm should increase until $\omega \approx 32$. The degradation in performance as ω increases beyond this point to, say $\omega = 64$ or 96, should be fairly significant for small and moderately sized systems due to the rather large portion of the operations performed by the BLAS2 MGS primitive.

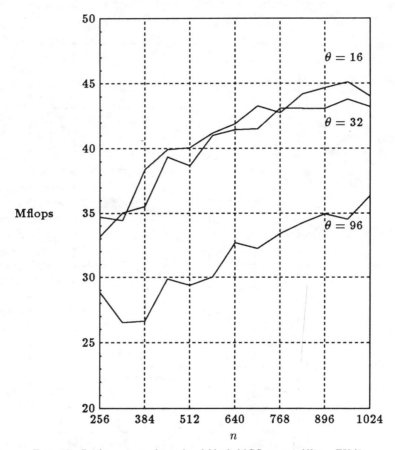

FIG. 13. *Performance of two-level block MGS on an Alliant* FX/8.

The results of the experiments confirm the trends predicted by the theory. The version using $\omega = 32$ is clearly superior. The performance for $\omega = 8$ is uniformly dismal across the entire interval since the blocksize is too small for both data loading overhead and arithmetic time considerations. Note that as n increases the gap in performance between the $\omega = 32$ version and the larger blocksize versions narrows. This is due to both arithmetic time considerations as well as data loading. As noted above, for small systems, the distribution of operations reduces the performance of the larger blocksize version; but, as n increases, this effect decreases in importance. (Note that this narrowing trend is much slower than that observed for the block LU

algorithm. This is due to the fact that the fraction of the total operations performed in the slow primitive is ω/n for the block Gram–Schmidt algorithm and only ω^2/n^2 for the block LU.) Further, for larger systems, the optimal blocksize for data loading is an increasing function of n; therefore, the difference in performance between the three larger blocksizes must decrease.

Figure 13 shows the increase in performance which results from double-level blocking. Since the blocksize indicated by arithmetic time component considerations is between 16 and 32 these two values were used as the inner blocksize θ. For $\theta = 16$ the predicted outer blocksize ranges from $\omega = 64$ up to $\omega = 128$; for $\theta = 32$ the range is $\omega = 90$ to $\omega = 181$. (Recall that the double-level outer blocksize is influenced by the cache size only by virtue of the fact that $\sqrt{CS}$ is used as a maximum cutoff point.) For these experiments the outer blocksize of $\omega = 96$ was used for two reasons. First, it is a reasonable compromise for the preferred outer blocksize given the two values of θ. Second, the corresponding single-level version of the algorithm, i.e., $(\theta, \omega) = (96, 96)$, did not yield high-performance and a large improvement due to altering θ would illustrate the power of double-level blocking. (To emphasize this point the curve with $(\theta, \omega) = (96, 96)$ is included.) The curves clearly demonstrate that double-level blocking can improve the performance of the algorithm significantly. (See [67] for details.)

5.1.3. Pipelined Givens rotations.

While the pipelined implementation of Givens rotations is traditionally restricted to distributed memory and systolic type architectures, e.g., [80], it has been successful on shared memory machines in some settings. In [48] a version of the algorithm was implemented on the HEP and compared to parallel methods based on Householder transformations. Rather than using the standard row-oriented synchronization pattern, the triangular matrix R was partitioned into a number of segments which could span row boundaries. Synchronization of the update of the various segments was enforced via the HEP's *full-empty* mechanism. The resulting pipelined Givens algorithm was shown to be superior to the Householder based approaches.

Gallivan and Jalby have implemented a version of the traditional systolic algorithm (see [80]) adapted to efficiently exploit the vector registers and cache of the Alliant FX/8. The significant improvement in performance of a structural mechanics code due to Berry and Plemmons, which uses weighted least squares methods to solve stiffness equations, is detailed in [10] (see also [144], [145]).

The hybrid scheme for LU factorization discussed earlier for cluster-based shared memory architectures converts easily to a rotation-based orthogonal factorization, see [157]. Chu and George have considered a variation of this scheme for shared memory architectures [31]. The difference is due to the fact that Sameh exploited the hybrid nature of the clustered memory and kept most of the matrix stored in a distributed fashion while pipelining between clusters the rows used to eliminate elements of the matrix. Chu and George's version keep these rows local to the processors and move the rows with elements to be eliminated between processors.

5.2. Distributed memory multiprocessors.

5.2.1. Orthogonal factorization.

Our purpose in this section is to survey parallel algorithms for solving (10) on distributed memory systems. In particular, we discuss some algorithms for the orthogonal factorization of A. Several schemes have been proposed in the past for the orthogonal factorization of matrices on distributed memory systems. Many of them deal with systolic arrays and require the use of $O(n^2)$

Proc. 1	Proc. 2	Proc. 3
1	–	–
21	–	–
31	2	–
41	32	–
51	42	3
61	52	43
71	62	53
4	72	63
54	–	73
64	5	–
74	65	–
–	75	6
–	–	76

FIG. 14. *Givens reduction on a three processor ring.*

processors, where n is the number of columns of the matrix. For instance, Ahmed, Delosme, and Morph [4], Bojanczyk, Brent, and Kung [17], and Gentleman and Kung [80] all consider Givens reduction and require a triangular array of $O(n^2)$ processors, while Luk [125] uses a mesh connected array of $O(n^2)$ processors. Sameh [158], on the other hand, considers both Givens and Householder reduction on a ring of processors in which the number of processors is independent of the problem size. Each processor possesses a local memory with one processor only handling the input and output. Figure 14 shows the organization of Givens reduction on three processors for a rectangular matrix of seven rows and five columns on such a ring. Each column depicts the operations taking place in each processor. An entry ij, $j < i$, indicates the rotation of rows i and j so as to annihilate the ith element of row j.

Recall that the classical Householder reduction may be described as follows. Let $a_j^{(k)}$ denote the jth column of A_k, where $A_{k+1} = Q_k A_k$ in which $Q_k = \text{diag}(I_k, P_k)$. Here, A_k is upper triangular in its first $(k-1)$ rows and columns with P_k being the elementary reflector of order $(m - k + 1)$ that annihilates all the elements below the diagonal of the kth column of A_k. Then Householder reduction on the same matrix and ring architecture as above may be organized as shown in Fig. 15. Here, a P_k alone indicates generation of the kth elementary reflector.

Modi and Clarke [134] have suggested a greedy algorithm for Givens reduction and the equivalent ordering of the rotations, but do not consider a specific architecture or communication pattern. Cosnard, Muller, and Robert [32] have shown that the greedy algorithm is optimal in the number of timesteps required. Theoretical studies and comparisons of such algorithms for Givens reduction have been given by Pothen, Somesh, and Vemulapati [148] and by Elden [54]. We now briefly survey some of these algorithms that have been implemented on current commercially available distributed memory multiprocessors.

In chronological order, we begin with the work of Chamberlain and Powell [25]. In this study the coefficient matrix A is stored by rows across the processors in the usual wrap fashion and most of the rotations involve rows within one processor in a type of *divide-and-conquer* scheme. However, it is necessary to carry out rotations

$$\textit{Proc. 1} \quad \textit{Proc. 2} \quad \textit{Proc. 3}$$

$$P_1$$
$$P_1 a_2^{(1)}$$
$$P_1 a_3^{(1)} \qquad P_2$$
$$P_1 a_4^{(1)} \qquad P_2 a_3^{(2)}$$
$$P_1 a_5^{(1)} \qquad P_2 a_4^{(2)}$$
$$P_2 a_5^{(2)} \qquad P_3$$
$$P_3 a_4^{(3)}$$
$$P_4 \qquad \qquad P_3 a_5^{(3)}$$
$$P_4 a_5^{(4)}$$
$$P_5$$

FIG. 15. *Householder reflectors on a three processor ring.*

involving rows in different processors, which they call *merges*. They describe two ways of implementing the merges and compare them in terms of load balance and communication overhead. Numerical tests were made on an Intel iPSC hypercube with 32 processors based on 80287 floating point coprocessors to illustrate the practicality of their algorithms. The schemes used here are very similar the basic approach suggested originally by Golub, Plemmons, and Sameh [81] and developed further in [145]. We note that Katholi and Suter [112] have also adopted this approach in developing an orthogonal factorization algorithm for shared memory systems, and have performed tests on a 30 processor Sequent Balance computer.

Chu and George [30] have also suggested and implemented algorithms for performing the orthogonal factorization of a dense rectangular matrix on a hypercube multiprocessor. Their recommended scheme involves the embedding of a two-dimensional grid in the hypercube network, and their analysis of the algorithm determines how the aspect ratio of the embedded processor grid should be chosen in order to minimize the execution time or storage usage. Another feature of the algorithm is that redundant computations are incorporated into a communication scheme which takes full advantage of the hypercube connection topology; the data is always exchanged between neighboring processors. Extensive computational experiments which are reported by the authors on a 64-processor Intel hypercube support their theoretical performance analysis results.

Finally in this section we mention two studies which directly compare the results of implementations of Givens rotations with Householder transformations on local memory systems. Pothen and Raghavan [147] have compared the earlier work of Pothen, Somesh, and Vemulapati [148] on a modified version of a greedy Givens scheme with a standard row-oriented version of Householder transformations. Their tests seem to indicate that Givens reduction is superior on such an architecture. Kim, Agrawal, and Plemmons [113], however, have developed and tested a row-block version of the Householder transformation scheme which is based upon the *divide-and-conquer* approach suggested by Golub, Plemmons, and Sameh [81] (see also [29]). The tests by Kim, Agrawal, and Plemmons on a 64-processor Intel hypercube clearly favor their modified Householder transformation scheme.

5.2.2. Recursive least squares. In *recursive least squares* (RLS) it is required to recalculate the least squares solution vector x when observations (i.e., equations) are successively added to or deleted from (10) without resorting to complete refactorization of the matrix A. For example, in many applications information continues to arrive and must be incorporated into the solution x. This is called *updating*. Alternatively, it is sometimes important to delete old observations and have their effects excised from x. This is called *downdating*. Applications of RLS updating and downdating include robust regression in statistics, modification of the Hessian matrix in certain optimization schemes, and in estimation methods in adaptive signal processing and control.

There are two main approaches to solving RLS problems; the *information matrix method* based on modifying the triangular matrix R in (11), and the *covariance matrix method* based instead on modifying the inverse R^{-1}. In theory, the information matrix method is based on modifying the normal equations matrix $A^T A$, while the covariance matrix method is based on modifying the *covariance matrix*

$$P = (A^T A)^{-1}.$$

The covariance matrix P measures the expected errors in the least squares solution x to (10). The Cholesky factor R^{-1} for P is readily available in control and signal processing applications.

Various algorithms for modifying R in the information matrix approach due to updating or downdating have been implemented on a 64-node Intel hypercube by Henkel, Heath, and Plemmons [92]. They make use of either plane rotations or hyperbolic type rotations.

The process of modifying least squares computations by updating the covariance matrix P has been used in control and signal processing for some time in the context of linear sequential filtering. We begin with estimates for $P = R^{-1}R^{-T}$ and x, and update R^{-1} to $\tilde{R}^{-1}$ and x to $\tilde{x}$ at each recursive timestep. Recently Pan and Plemmons [140] have described the following parallel scheme.

Algorithm (*Covariance Updating*). Given the current least squares estimate vector x, the current factor $L \equiv R^{-T}$ of $P = (A^T A)^{-1}$ and the observation $y^T x = \sigma$ being added, the algorithm computes the updated factor $\tilde{L} \equiv \tilde{R}^{-1}$ of $\tilde{P}$ and the updated least squares estimate vector $\tilde{x}$ as follows:

1. Form the matrix vector product

$$(12) \qquad\qquad\qquad a = Ly.$$

2. Choose plane rotations Q_i, to form

$$(13) \qquad\qquad Q_m \cdots Q_1 \begin{bmatrix} -a \\ 1 \end{bmatrix} = \begin{bmatrix} 0 \\ \delta \end{bmatrix}, \quad \delta = \sqrt{1 + \|a\|_2^2},$$

and update L

$$(14) \qquad\qquad Q_m \cdots Q_1 \begin{bmatrix} L \\ 0^T \end{bmatrix} = \begin{bmatrix} \tilde{L} \\ u^T \end{bmatrix}.$$

3. Form

$$(15) \qquad\qquad \tilde{x} = x - \frac{1}{\delta} u(\sigma - y^T x).$$

As the recursive least squares computation proceeds, $\tilde{L}$ replaces L, $\tilde{x}$ replaces x, a new equation is added, and the process returns to step 1. An efficient parallel implementation of this algorithm on the hypercube distributed-memory system making use of bidirectional data exchanges and some redundant computation is given in [93]. Steps 1 and 3 are highly parallelizable and effective implementation details of step 2 on a hypercube are given in [93].

Table 2 shows the speedup and efficiency on an iPSC/2 hypercube (4 MB of memory for each processor) for a single phase of the algorithm on a test problem of size $n = 1024$. One complete recursive update is performed. Here, the speedup is given by,

$$\text{speedup} = \frac{\text{time on 1 processor}}{\text{time on } p \text{ processors}},$$

with the corresponding efficiency,

$$\text{efficiency} = \frac{\text{speedup}}{p}.$$

An alternative hypercube implementation of the RLS scheme of Pan and Plemmons [140] has been given by Chu and George [31].

TABLE 2
Speedup and efficiency on the iPSC/2 *for a problem of size* $n = 1024$.

Number of Processors p	Speedup	Efficiency
1	1	1
4	3.90	0.98
16	15.06	0.94
64	48.60	0.76

6. Eigenvalue and singular value problems.

6.1. Eigenvalue problems. Solving the algebraic eigenvalue problem, either standard $Ax = \lambda x$, or generalized $Ax = \lambda Bx$, is an important and potentially time-consuming task in numerous applications. In this brief review, only the dense case is considered for both the symmetric and nonsymmetric problems. Most of the parallel algorithms developed for the dense eigenvalue problem have been aimed at the standard problem. Algorithms for handling the generalized eigenvalue problem on shared or distributed memory multiprocessors are very similar to those used on sequential machines. Reduction of the symmetric generalized eigenvalue problem to the standard form is achieved by a Cholesky factorization of the symmetric positive definite matrix B which is well-conditioned in most applications. This reduction process can be made efficient on shared memory multiprocessors, for example, by adopting a block Cholesky scheme similar to the block LU decomposition discussed earlier to obtain the Cholesky factor L of B and to explicitly form the matrix $L^{-1}AL^{-T}$ using the appropriate BLAS3. For the nonsymmetric generalized eigenvalue problems where the matrix B is known to be often extremely ill-conditioned in many applications, there is no adequate substitute to Moler and Stewart's QZ-scheme [136]. On a shared memory multiprocessor, the most efficient stage is the initial one of reducing B to the upper triangular form. Dispensing thus with the generalized eigenvalue problems, the remainder of the section will be divided between procedures that depend on reduction to a condensed form, and Jacobi or Jacobi-like schemes for both the symmetric and nonsymmetric standard eigenvalue problems.

6.1.1. Reduction to a condensed form.

We start with the nonsymmetric case. For the standard problem the first step, after balancing, is the reduction to upper Hessenberg form via orthogonal similarity transformations. These usually consist of elementary reflectors which could yield high computational rates on vector machines provided appropriate BLAS2 kernels are used. On parallel computers with hierarchical memories, block versions of the classical scheme, e.g., see [16], [44], [86], yield higher performance than BLAS2-based versions. Such block schemes are similar to those discussed above for orthogonal factorization, and their use does not sacrifice numerical stability. Block sizes can be as small as 2 for certain architectures. For the sake of illustration we present a simplified scheme for this block reduction to the upper Hessenberg form, where we assume that the matrix A is of order n where $n = k\nu + 2$.

$$
\begin{aligned}
&\text{do } j = 1, k \\
&\qquad \text{do } i = (j\text{-}1)\nu + 1, j\nu \\
&\qquad\qquad \text{Obtain an elementary reflector } P_i = I - w_i w_i^T \\
&\qquad\qquad \text{such that } P_i \text{ annihilates the last } n - i - 1 \\
&\qquad\qquad \text{elements of the } i\text{th column of } A \\
&\qquad\qquad \text{Construct:} \\
&\qquad\qquad U_i = (U_{i-1}, w_i) \\
&\qquad\qquad V_i = (P_i V_{i-1}, w_i) \\
&\qquad\qquad Y_i = (Y_{i-1}, A w_i) \\
&\qquad\qquad z_i = V_i^T e_{i+1} \\
&\qquad\qquad \text{if } i = j\nu \text{ go to 10} \\
&\qquad\qquad a_{i+1} = (I - V_i U_i^T)(a_{i+1} - Y_i z_i) \\
&\qquad \text{enddo} \\
&10 \qquad\quad A(j\nu + 1 : n) = (I - V_{j\nu} U_{j\nu}^T)(A(j\nu + 1 : n) - Y_{j\nu} Z_{j\nu}) \\
&\text{enddo.}
\end{aligned}
$$

Here, Z_m consists of the last $(n - m)$ rows of V_m. This block scheme requires more arithmetic operations than the classical algorithm using elementary reflectors by a factor of roughly $1 + 1/k$. Performance of the block scheme on the Alliant FX/8 is shown in Fig. 16 [86]. The performance shown is based on the operation count of the nonblock algorithm.

The next stage is that of obtaining the eigenvalues of the resulting upper Hessenberg matrix via the QR-algorithm with an implicit shifting strategy. This algorithm consists mainly of chasing a bulge represented by a square matrix of order 3 whose diagonal lies along the subdiagonal of the upper Hessenberg matrix. This in turn affects only 3 rows and columns of the Hessenberg matrix, leaving little that can be gained from vectorization, and to a lesser extent, parallelization. Stewart has considered the implementation of this basic iteration on a linear array of processors [172]. More recently, a block implementation with multiple QR shifts was proposed by Bai and Demmel [6] which yields some advantage for vector machines such as the Convex C-1 and Cyber 205.

If we are seeking all of the eigenvectors as well, the performance of the algorithm is enhanced since the additional work required consists of computations that are amenable to vector and/or parallel processing; that of updating the orthogonal matrix used to reduce the original matrix to Hessenberg form.

Similarly, the most common method for handling the standard dense symmetric eigenvalue problem consists of first reducing the symmetric matrix to the tridiagonal form via elementary reflectors followed by handling the tridiagonal eigenvalue problem. Such reduction can be achieved by a minor modification of the above block reduction to the Hessenberg form. On 1 CPU of a CRAY X-MP, with an 8.5 *ns* clock, a BLAS2 implementation of Householder tridiagonalization using rank-2 updates (see [43]) yields a computational rate of roughly 200 Mflops for matrices of order 1000 (see Fig. 17 [87]. The performance of Eispack's TRED2 is also presented in the figure for comparison. Figure 18 shows a comparison of the performance of this BLAS3-based block reduction with a BLAS2-based reduction on the Alliant FX/8 [86]. As before, the performance is computed based on the nonblock version operation count.

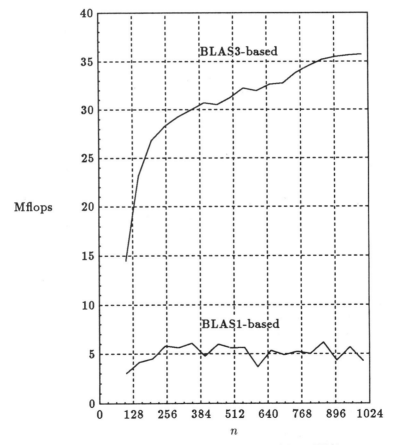

FIG. 16. *Reduction to Hessenberg form on Alliant* FX/8.

Once the tridiagonal matrix is obtained two approaches have been used, on sequential machines, for obtaining its eigenvalues and eigenvectors. If all the eigenvalues are required a QR-based method is used. The classical procedure is inherently sequential, offering nothing in the form of vectorization or parallelism. Recently, Dongarra and Sorensen [49], adapted an alternative due to Cuppen [33] for the use on multiprocessors. This algorithm obtains all the eigenvalues and eigenvectors of the symmetric tridiagonal matrix.

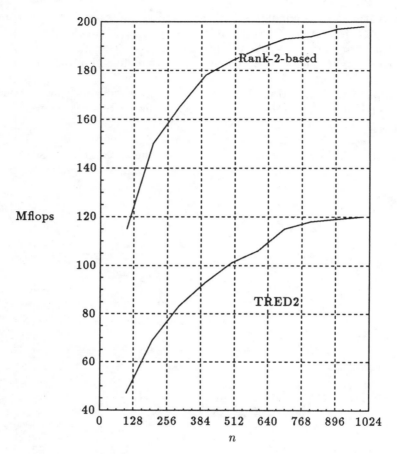

FIG. 17. *Reduction to tridiagonal form on* CRAY X-MP (1 CPU).

In its simplest form, the main idea of the algorithm may be outlined as follows. Let $T = (\beta_i, \alpha_i, \beta_{i+1})$ be the symmetric tridiagonal matrix under consideration, where we assume that none of its off-diagonal elements β_i vanishes. Assuming that it is of order $2m$, it can be written as,

$$T = \begin{pmatrix} T_1 + \tau e_m e_m^T & \beta e_m e_1^T \\ \beta e_1 e_m^T & T_2 + \tau e_1 e_1^T \end{pmatrix},$$

where each T_i is tridiagonal of order m, τ is a "carefully" chosen scalar, and e_i is the ith column of the identity of order m. This in turn can be written as,

$$T = \mathrm{diag}(T_1, T_2) + \gamma v v^T$$

in which the scalar γ and the column vector v can be readily derived. Now, we have two tasks: namely obtaining the spectral decomposition of T_1 and T_2, i.e., $T_i = Q_i D_i Q_i^T$, $i = 1, 2$, where Q_i is an orthogonal matrix of order m and D_i is diagonal. Thus, if $Q = \mathrm{diag}(Q_1, Q_2)$ and $D = \mathrm{diag}(D_1, D_2)$, then T is orthogonally similar to a rank-1 perturbation of a diagonal matrix, i.e.,

$$QTQ^T = D + \rho zz^T,$$

where ρ and z are trivially obtained from γ and z. The eigenvalues of T are thus the roots of

$$\phi(\lambda) = 1 + \rho z^T (D - \lambda I)^{-1} z$$

and its eigenvectors are given by,

$$u_i = \tau (D - \lambda_i I)^{-1} z,$$

where $\tau = \|D - \lambda_i I\|_2$.

This module may be used recursively to produce a parallel counterpart to Cuppen's algorithm [33] as demonstrated in [49]. For example, if the tridiagonal matrix T is of order $2^k m$, then the algorithm will consist of obtaining the spectral decomposition of 2^k tridiagonal matrices each of order m, followed by k stages in which stage j consists of applying the above module simultaneously to 2^{k-j} pairs of tridiagonal matrices in which each is of order $2^{j-1}m$.

If eigenvalues only (or all those lying in a given interval) or selected eigenpairs are desired, then a bisection-inverse iteration combination is used, e.g., see Wilkinson and Reinsch [195] or Parlett [141]. Such a combination has been adapted for the Illiac IV parallel computer, e.g., see [118] and [102], and later for the Alliant FX/8, see [123]. This modification depends on a multisectioning strategy in which the interval containing the desired eigenvalues is divided into $(p-1)$ subintervals where p is the number of processors. Using the Sturm sequence property we can simultaneously determine the number of eigenvalues contained in each of the $(p-1)$ subintervals. This is accomplished by having each processor evaluate the well-known linear recurrence leading to the determinant of the tridiagonal matrix $T - \mu I$ or the corresponding nonlinear recurrence so as to avoid over- or underflow, e.g., see [141]. This process is repeated until all the eigenvalues, or clusters of computationally coincident eigenvalues, are separated. This "isolation" stage is followed by the "extraction" stage where the separated eigenvalues are evaluated using a root finder which is a hybrid of pure bisection and the combination of bisection and the secant methods, namely the ZEROIN procedure due to Brent and Dekker, see [58]. If eigenvectors are desired, then the final stage consists of a combination of inverse iteration and orthogonalization for those vectors corresponding to poorly separated eigenvalues.

This scheme proved to be the most effective on the Alliant FX/8 for obtaining all or few of the eigenvalues only. Compared to its execution time on one CE, it achieves a speedup of 7.9 on eight CE's, and is more than four times faster than Eispack's TQL1, e.g., see [167] or [195], for the tridiagonal matrix [-1,2,-1] of order 500 with the same achievable accuracy for the eigenvalues. Even if all the eigenpairs of the above tridiagonal matrix are required, this multisectioning scheme is more than 13 times faster than the best BLAS2-based version of Eispack's TQL2, 27 times faster than Eispack's pair Bisect and Tinvit, and five times faster than its nearest competitor, parallel Cuppen's procedure [49], with the same accuracy in the computed eigenpairs. For matrices with clusters of poorly separated eigenvalues, however, the multisectioning algorithm may not be competitive if all the eigenpairs are required with high accuracy. For example, for the well-known Wilkinson matrices W_{127}^+, e.g.,

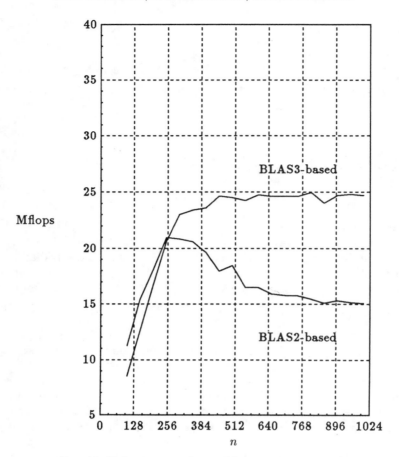

FIG. 18. *Reduction to tridiagonal form on Alliant* FX/8.

see [194], which have pairs of very close eigenvalues, the multisectioning method requires roughly twice the time required by the parallel Cuppen's procedure in order to achieve the same accuracy for all the eigenpairs.

Further studies by Simon [166] demonstrate the robustness of the above multisectioning strategy compared to other bisection-inverse iteration combinations proposed in [8]. Also, comparisons between the above multisectioning scheme and parallel Cuppen's algorithm have been given by Ipsen and Jessup on hypercubes [103] indicating the effectiveness of multisectioning on distributed memory multiprocessors for cases in which the eigenvalues are not pathologically clustered.

6.1.2. Jacobi and Jacobi-like schemes. An alternative to reduction to a condensed form is that of using one of the Jacobi schemes for obtaining all the eigenvalues or all the eigenvalues and eigenvectors. Work on such parallel procedures dates back to the Illiac IV distributed memory parallel computer, e.g., see [152]. Algorithms for handling the two-sided Jacobi scheme for the symmetric problem, which are presented in that work, exploit the fact that independent rotations can be applied simultaneously. Furthermore, several ordering schemes of these independent rotations are presented that minimize the number of orthogonal transformations (i.e., direct sum of rotations) within each sweep. Much more work has been done since on this parallel two-sided

Jacobi scheme for the symmetric eigenvalue problem. These have been motivated primarily by the emergence of systolic arrays, e.g., see Brent and Luk [18]. A most important byproduct of such investigation of parallel Jacobi schemes is a result due to Luk and Park [126], where they show the equivalence of various parallel Jacobi orderings to the classical sequential cyclic by row ordering for which Forsythe and Henrici [57] proved convergence of the method.

Also, in [152] a Jacobi-like algorithm for solving the nonsymmetric eigenvalue problem due to Eberlein [51], has been modified for parallel computations, primarily for the Illiac IV. More recent related parallel schemes, aimed at distributed memory multiprocessors as well, have been developed by Stewart [171] and Eberlein [52] for the Schur decomposition of nonsymmetric matrices.

Unlike the two-sided Jacobi scheme, for the symmetric eigenvalue problem, the one-sided Jacobi scheme due to Hestenes [94] requires only accessing of the columns of the matrix under consideration. This feature makes it more suitable for shared memory multiprocessors with hierarchical organization such as the Alliant FX/8. This procedure may be described as follows. Given a symmetric nonsingular matrix A of order n and columns a_i, $1 \le i \le n$, obtain through an iterative process an orthogonal matrix V such that

$$AV = S$$

where S has orthogonal columns within a given tolerance. The orthogonal matrix V is constructed as the product of plane rotations in which each is chosen to orthogonalize a pair of columns,

$$(a_i, a_j) \begin{pmatrix} c & -s \\ s & c \end{pmatrix} = (\tilde{a}_i, \tilde{a}_j)$$

where $i < j$, so that $\tilde{a}_i^T \tilde{a}_j = 0$ and $\|\tilde{a}_i\|_2 > \|\tilde{a}_j\|_2$. This is accomplished as follows, if

$$\beta > 0$$
$$c = \sqrt{(\beta + \gamma)/2\gamma}$$
$$s = \alpha/(2\gamma c)$$

otherwise,

$$s = \sqrt{(\gamma - \beta)/2\gamma}$$
$$c = \alpha/(2\gamma s)$$

Here, $\alpha = 2a_i^T a_j$, $\beta = \|a_i\|_2^2 - \|a_j\|_2^2$, and $\gamma = \sqrt{\alpha^2 + \beta^2}$. Several schemes can be used to select the order of the plane rotations. Shown below is the pattern for one sweep for a matrix of order $n = 8$ an annihilation scheme related to those recommended in [152],

$$
\begin{array}{ccccccccc}
* & 7 & 6 & 5 & 4 & 3 & 2 & 1 \\
  & * & 5 & 4 & 3 & 2 & 1 & 8 \\
  &   & * & 3 & 2 & 1 & 8 & 7 \\
  &   &   & * & 1 & 8 & 7 & 6 \\
  &   &   &   & * & 7 & 6 & 5 \\
  &   &   &   &   & * & 5 & 4 \\
  &   &   &   &   &   & * & 3 \\
  &   &   &   &   &   &   & *
\end{array}
$$

where each sweep consists of n orthogonal transformations each being the direct sum of no more than $\lfloor n/2 \rfloor$ independent plane rotations. An integer $k = 8$, for example, denotes that the column pairs (2,8), (3,7), (4,6) can be orthogonalized simultaneously by 3 independent rotations. After convergence of this iterative process, usually in a few sweeps, the matrix V yields a set of approximate eigenvectors from which the eigenvalues may be obtained via Rayleigh quotients. If the matrix A is positive-definite, however, then its eigenvalues are taken as the 2-norms of the columns of S. Note that if A is not known to be nonsingular, we treat the eigenvalue problem $\tilde{A}x = (\lambda + \alpha)x$, where $\tilde{A} = A + \alpha I$, with α being the smallest number chosen such that $\tilde{A}$ is positive definite. On an Alliant FX/8, this Jacobi scheme is faster than algorithms that depend on tridiagonalization, with the same size residuals, for matrices of size less than 150 or for matrices that have few clusters of almost coincident eigenvalues.

Finally, a block generalization of the two-sided Jacobi scheme has been considered by Van Loan [190] and Bischof [13] for distributed memory multiprocessors. The convergence of cyclic block Jacobi methods has been discussed by Shroff and Schreiber [165].

6.2. Singular-value problems. Several algorithms have been developed for obtaining the singular-value decomposition on vector and parallel computers. The most robust of these schemes are those that rely first on reducing the matrix to the bidiagonal form, i.e., by using the sequential algorithm due to Golub and Reinsch [82]. The most obvious implementation of the reduction to the bidiagonal form on a parallel or vector computer follows the strategy suggested by Chan [26]. The matrix is first reduced to the upper triangular form via the block Householder reduction, suggested in the previous section, leading to the achievement of high performance. This is then followed by the chasing of zeros via rotation of rows and columns to yield a bidiagonal matrix. The application of the subsequent plane rotations has to proceed sequentially but some benefit due to vectorization can still be realized.

Once the bidiagonal matrix is obtained a generalization of Cuppen's algorithm (e.g., see [107]) may be used to obtain all the singular values and vectors. Similarly, a generalization of the multisectioning algorithm may be used to obtain selected singular values and vectors.

Luk has used the one-sided Jacobi scheme to obtain the singular-value decomposition on the Illiac IV [124] and block variations of Jacobi's method have been attempted by Bischof on IBM's LCAP system [13].

For tall and narrow matrices with certain distributions of clusters of singular values and/or extreme rank deficiencies, Jacobi schemes may also be used to efficiently obtain the singular-value decomposition of the upper triangular matrix resulting from the orthogonal factorization via block Householder transformations. The same one-sided Jacobi scheme discussed above has proved to be most effective on the hierarchical memory system of the Alliant FX/8. Such a procedure results in a performance that is superior to the best vectorized version of Eispack's or LINPACK routines which are based on the algorithm in [82]. Experiments showed that the block-Householder reduction and the one-sided Jacobi scheme combination is up to five times faster, on the Alliant FX/8, than the best BLAS2-version of LINPACK's routine for matrices of order 16000×128 [12].

7. Rapid elliptic solvers. In this section, we review parallel schemes for rapid elliptic solvers. We start with the classical Matrix Decomposition (MD), and Block-Cyclic Reduction (BCR) schemes for separable elliptic P.D.E.'s on regular domains. This is followed by a Boundary Integral-based Domain Decomposition method for handling the Laplace equation on irregular domains that consist of regular domains; examples of such domains are the right-angle or T-shapes.

Efficient direct methods for solving the finite-difference approximation of the Poisson equation on the unit square have been developed by Buneman [20], Hockney [96], [97], and Buzbee, Golub, and Nielson [22]. The most effective sequential algorithm combines the block cyclic reduction and Fourier analysis schemes. This is Hockney's $FACR(l)$ algorithm [97]. Excellent reviews of these methods on sequential machines have been given by Swarztrauber [177] and Temperton [182], [183]. In [177] it is shown that the asymptotic operation count for $FACR(l)$ on an $n \times n$ grid is $O(n^2 \log_2 \log_2 n)$, and is achieved when the number l of the block cyclic reduction steps preceding Fourier analysis is taken approximately as $(\log_2 \log_2 n)$. Using only cyclic reduction, or Fourier analysis, to solve the problem on a sequential machine would require $O(n^2 \log_2 n)$ arithmetic operations.

Buzbee [21] observed that Fourier analysis, or the matrix decomposition Poisson solver (MD-Poisson solver), is ideally suited for parallel computation. It consists of performing a set of independent sine transforms, and solving a set of independent tridiagonal systems. On a parallel computer consisting of n^2 processors, with an arbitrarily powerful interconnection network, the MD-Poisson solver for the two-dimensional case requires $O(\log_2 n)$ parallel arithmetic steps [160]. It can be shown, [142] and [173], that a perfect shuffle interconnection network is sufficient to keep the communication cost to a minimum. Ericksen [55] considered the implementation of $FACR(l)$, [97], and $CORF$, [22], on the ILLIAC IV; and Hockney [98] compared the performance of $FACR(l)$ on the CRAY-1, Cyber-205, and the ICL-DAP.

7.1. A domain decomposition MD-scheme.

We consider first the MD-algorithm for solving the 5-point finite difference approximation of the Poisson equation on the unit square with a uniform $n \times n$ grid, where for the sake of illustration we consider only Dirichlet boundary conditions. The multiprocessor version algorithm presented below can be readily modified to accommodate Neumann and periodic boundary conditions.

Using natural ordering of the grid points, we obtain the well-known linear system of order n^2:

$$
\begin{pmatrix}
T & -I & & & \\
-I & T & -I & & \\
& \ddots & \ddots & \ddots & \\
& & -I & T & -I \\
& & & -I & T
\end{pmatrix}
\begin{pmatrix}
u_1 \\
u_2 \\
\vdots \\
u_{n-1} \\
u_n
\end{pmatrix}
=
\begin{pmatrix}
f_1 \\
f_2 \\
\vdots \\
v_{n-1} \\
v_n
\end{pmatrix},
$$

where $T = [-1, 4, -1]$ is a tridiagonal matrix of order n.

This parallel MD-scheme consists of 3 stages [154]:

Stage 1. Each cluster j, $1 \le j \le 4$ (a four cluster Cedar is assumed), forms the subvectors $f_{(j-1)q+1}$, $f_{(j-1)q+2}, \cdots, f_{jq}$ of the right-hand side, where $q = n/4$. Next each cluster j obtains $\hat{g}_j^T = (g_{(j-1)q+1}^T, \cdots, g_{jq}^T)$, where $g_k = Qf_k$, in which $Q = [(2/[n+1])^{1/2} \sin(lm\pi/[n+1])]$, $l, m = 1, 2, \cdots, n$, is the eigenvector matrix of T. This amounts to performing in each cluster q sine transforms each of length n. Now we have the system

$$
\begin{pmatrix}
M & E & & \\
E^T & M & E & \\
& E^T & M & E \\
& & E^T & M
\end{pmatrix}
\begin{pmatrix}
\hat{v}_1 \\
\hat{v}_2 \\
\hat{v}_3 \\
\hat{v}_4
\end{pmatrix}
=
\begin{pmatrix}
\hat{g}_1 \\
\hat{g}_2 \\
\hat{g}_3 \\
\hat{g}_4
\end{pmatrix},
$$

where each cluster memory contains one block row. Here, $\hat{v}_j^T = (v_{(j-1)q+1}^T, \cdots, v_{jq}^T)$ with $v_k = Qu_k$, $M = [-I_n, \Lambda, -I_n]$ is a block tridiagonal matrix of order qn, and

$$
E = \begin{pmatrix} 0 & 0 \\ -I_n & 0 \end{pmatrix}.
$$

This system, in turn, may be reduced to,

$$
\begin{pmatrix}
I_{qn} & F & & \\
G & I_{qn} & F & \\
& G & I_{qn} & F \\
& & G & I_{qn}
\end{pmatrix}
\begin{pmatrix}
\hat{v}_1 \\
\hat{v}_2 \\
\hat{v}_3 \\
\hat{v}_4
\end{pmatrix}
=
\begin{pmatrix}
\hat{h}_1 \\
\hat{h}_2 \\
\hat{h}_3 \\
\hat{h}_4
\end{pmatrix},
$$

where $\hat{h}_j^T = (h_{(j-1)q+1}^T, \cdots, h_{jq}^T)$, F and G are given by: $M\hat{h}_j = \hat{g}_j$, $1 \le j \le 4$, $MF = E$, and $MG = E^T$. Observing that M consists of n independent tridiagonal matrices $T_k = [-1, \lambda_k, -1]$ each of order q, where $\lambda_k = 4 - 2\cos(k\pi/[n+1])$, $k = 1, 2, \cdots, n$, the right-hand side of the above system is obtained by solving in each cluster j the n independent systems

$$
T_k r_k = s_k,
$$

for $k = 1, 2, \cdots, n$, where $\hat{e}_i^T s_k = e_k^T g_{(j-1)q+i}$, and $\hat{e}_i^T r_k = e_k^T h_{(j-1)q+i}$, for $i = 1, 2, \cdots, q$, and $1 \le j \le 4$. Here, $\hat{e}_i$ and e_i are the ith columns of I_q and I_n, respectively.

The matrices F and G can be similarly obtained by solving, in each cluster j, the independent systems $T_k c_k = \hat{e}_1$, and $T_k d_k = \hat{e}_q$, for $k = 1, 2, \cdots, n$. Since T_k is a Toeplitz matrix, however, we have $c_k = J d_k$, where $J = [\hat{e}_q, \cdots, \hat{e}_1]$, see [111] for example. As a result, in order to obtain F and G we need only solve in each cluster the n systems $T_k d_k = \hat{e}_q$, $k = 1, 2, \cdots, n$. Hence, F and G are of the form,

$$
F = \begin{pmatrix} \Gamma_q & 0 \\ \vdots & \vdots \\ \Gamma_1 & 0 \end{pmatrix},
$$

and

$$
G = \begin{pmatrix} 0 & \Gamma_1 \\ \vdots & \vdots \\ 0 & \Gamma_q \end{pmatrix},
$$

where $\Gamma_i = -\text{diag}(\gamma_i^{(1)}, \cdots, \gamma_i^{(n)})$, in which $\gamma_i^{(k)} = \hat{e}_i^T c_k$, for $i = 1, 2, \cdots, q$, and $k = 1, 2, \cdots, n$.

Stage 2. From the structure of (7.1) it is seen that the three pairs of n equations above and below each partition are completely decoupled from the rest of the n^2

equations [161]. This reduced system, of order $6n$, consists of interlocking blocks of the form:

$$\begin{pmatrix} I_n & \Gamma_1 & 0 & 0 & & \\ \Gamma_1 & I_n & 0 & \Gamma_q & & \\ \Gamma_q & 0 & I_n & \Gamma_1 & 0 & 0 \\ & & \Gamma_1 & I_n & 0 & \Gamma_q \\ & & \Gamma_q & 0 & I_n & \Gamma_1 \\ & & & & \Gamma_1 & I_n \end{pmatrix}$$

This system, in turn, comprises n independent pentadiagonal systems each of order 6, which can be solved in a very short time.

Stage 3. Now, that the subvectors v_{kq}, v_{kq+1}, $k = 1, 2, 3$, are available, each cluster j obtains

$$v_{(j-1)q+i} = h_{(j-1)q+i} - (\Gamma_i v_{(j-1)q} + \Gamma_{q-i+1} v_{jq+1})$$

for $i = 2, 3, \cdots, q - 1$, where $v_0 = v_{4q+1} = 0$. Finally, each cluster j retrieves the q subvectors $u_{(j-1)q+i} = Q v_{(j-1)q+i}$, for $i = 1, 2, \cdots, q$, of the solution via q sine transforms, each of length n.

Note that one of the key computational kernels in this algorithm is the calculation of multiple sine transformations. In order to design an efficient version of this kernel it is necessary to perform an analysis of the influence of the memory hierarchy similar to that presented above for the block LU algorithm. Such an analysis is contained in [74].

7.2. A modified block cyclic reduction. The discretization of the separable elliptic equation

$$(16) \qquad a(x)\frac{\partial^2 u}{\partial x^2} + b(x)\frac{\partial u}{\partial x} + c(x)u + \frac{\partial^2 u}{\partial y^2} \;=\; f(x, y)$$

with Dirichlet boundary conditions and a five-point stencil on a naturally ordered $n \times m$ grid defined on a rectangular region leads to a system of the form $\mathcal{A}u = f$. In this case $\mathcal{A}$ is the n block tridiagonal matrix $\text{diag}[-I, A, -I]$, where A, I are respectively tridiagonal and identity matrices of order m. Block cyclic reduction (BCR) dates back to the work of Hockney and was presented in [22] in its stabilized form due to Buneman. The work in [176], [178], [180] resulted in the development of FISHPAK, a package based on BCR for the solution of (16) and extensions thereof. BCR is a rapid elliptic solver (RES) having sequential computational complexity $O(nm \log n)$. Assuming that $n = 2^k - 1$, the idea of the method for reduction steps $r = 1, \cdots, k-1$ is to combine the current $2^{k-r+1} - 1$ vectors into $2^{k-r} - 1$ ones, and then solve a system of the form

$$p_{2^{r-1}}(A)X = Y$$

where $Y \in \Re^{m \times (2^{k-r}-1)}$ and $p_{2^{r-1}}(A)$ is a Chebyshev polynomial of degree 2^{r-1} in A. Since its roots $\lambda_i^{(r-1)}$ are known, it can be written in product form, where each factor is tridiagonal. Hence the system to be solved becomes

$$(17) \qquad \prod_{i=1}^{2^{r-1}} (A - \lambda_i^{(r-1)} I)[x_1| \cdots |x_{2^{k-r}-1}] = [y_1| \cdots |y_{2^{k-r}-1}].$$

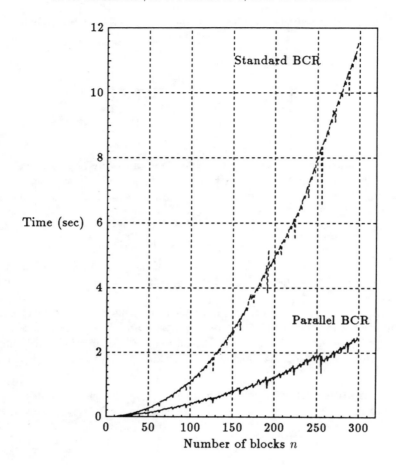

FIG. 19. *Parallel and standard* BCR *on* $n \times n$ *grid on Alliant* FX/8.

Clearly as r increases, the effectiveness of a parallel or vector machine to handle (17) decreases rapidly.

A parallel version of BCR was recently discovered [70], [181]. In summary, the method is based in expressing the matrix rational function $[p_{2^{r-1}}(A)]^{-1}$ as a partial fraction, i.e., as a linear combination of the 2^{r-1} components $(A - \lambda_i^{(r-1)} I)^{-1}$

$$(18) \qquad [x_1| \cdots |x_{2^{k-r}-1}] = \sum_{i=1}^{2^{r-1}} \alpha_i^{(r-1)} (A - \lambda_i^{(r-1)} I)^{-1} [y_1| \cdots |y_{2^{k-r}-1}].$$

Coefficients $\alpha_i^{(r-1)}$ are equal to $1/(p'_{2^{r-1}}(\lambda_i^{(r-1)}))$ and can be derived analytically. Figure 19 shows the performance of the parallel and standard BCR on the Alliant FX/8.

For a discussion of parallel BCR on distributed memory machines see [73], [179]. Partial fraction decomposition can also be applied to the parallel solution of parabolic equations. See [71], [72] for details.

7.3. Boundary integral domain decomposition. A new method (BIDD) was recently proposed for the solution of Laplace's equation [68], [69]. The method is characterized by the decoupling of the problem into independent subproblems on sub-domains. An approximation $\hat{u}$ to the solution u is sought as a finite linear combination of N fundamental solutions [128] $\phi_j(z) = -\frac{1}{2\pi} \log |z - w_j|$ of $\nabla^2 u = 0$:

$$(19) \qquad \hat{u}(z) = \sum_{j=1}^{N} \sigma_j \phi_j(z)$$

For a given set of N points w_j lying outside the domain, $\sigma \in \Re^N$ is computed to minimize $\|g - G\sigma\|_\rho$ for some norm ρ. $G \in \Re^{\nu \times N}$ is the influence matrix consisting of fundamental solutions based at w_j for each boundary point. $g \in \Re^\nu$ consists of boundary values for u. Once σ has been computed, the solution at any μ points on the domain is $\hat{u} = H\sigma$, with $H \in \Re^{\mu \times N}$ being the influence matrix for the μ points. Choosing these μ points to be subdomain boundary points, we can compute the solution by applying the elliptic solvers most suitable for each subdomain.

REFERENCES

[1] *IBM Engineering and Scientific Subroutine Library Guide and Reference*, IBM, 1986.

[2] R. AGARWAL AND F. GUSTAVSON, *A parallel implementation of matrix multiplication and LU factorization on the IBM 3090*, in Aspects of Computation on Asynchronous Parallel Processors, M. H. Wright, ed., North-Holland, Amsterdam, 1989, pp. 217–221.

[3] A. AGGARWAL, B. ALPERN, A. CHANDRA, AND M. SNIR, *A model for hierarchical memory*, in Proc. 19th ACM Symp. Theory of Computing, 1987, pp. 305–314.

[4] H. AHMED, J. DELOSME, AND M. MORPH, *Highly concurrent computing structures for matrix arithmetic and signal processing*, Computing, 15 (1982), pp. 65–82.

[5] J. ARMSTRONG, *Algorithm and performance notes for block LU factorization*, in Proc. Intl. Conf. Par. Processing, D. Bailey, ed., IEEE Computer Society Press, 1988, pp. 161–164.

[6] Z. BAI AND J. DEMMEL, *On a block implementation of Hessenberg multishift QR iterations*, Tech. Rep., Courant Institute of Mathematical Sciences, New York University, New York, 1988.

[7] D. BAILEY, *Extra high speed matrix multiplication on the CRAY-2*, SIAM J. Sci. Statist. Comput., 9 (1988), pp. 603–607.

[8] H. BERNSTEIN AND M. GOLDSTEIN, *Optimizing Givens' algorithm for multiprocessors*, SIAM J. Sci. Statist. Comput., 9 (1988), pp. 601–602.

[9] M. BERRY, K. GALLIVAN, W. HARROD, W. JALBY, S. LO, U. MEIER, B. PHILIPPE, AND A. SAMEH, *Parallel numerical algorithms on the Cedar system*, in CONPAR 86, Lecture Notes in Computer Science, W. Handler et al., eds., Springer-Verlag, Berlin, 1986.

[10] M. BERRY AND R. PLEMMONS, *Algorithms and experiments for structural mechanics on high performance architectures*, Comput. Methods Appl. Mech. Engrg., 64 (1987), pp. 487–507.

[11] M. BERRY AND A. SAMEH, *Multiprocessor schemes for solving block tridiagonal linear systems*, Intl. J. Supercomputer Appl., 2 (1988), pp. 37–57.

[12] ———, *Parallel algorithms for the singular value and dense symmetric eigenvalue problems*, Tech. Rep. CSRD Rept. 761, Center for Supercomputing Research and Development, University of Illinois, Urbana, IL, 1988.

[13] C. BISCHOF, *Computing the singular value decomposition on a distributed system of vector processors*, Tech. Rep. TR86-798, Dept. of Computer Science, Cornell University, Ithaca, NY, 1986.

[14] ———, *A pipelined block QR decomposition algorithm*, in Proc. of Third SIAM Conf. on Par. Processing for Scientific Computing, G. Rodrigue, ed., Society for Industrial and Applied Mathmatics, Philadelphia, 1988.

[15] ———, *QR factorization algorithms for coarse-grained distributed systems*, Tech. Rep. TR 88-939, Dept. of Computer Science, Cornell University, Ithaca, NY, 1988.

[16] C. BISCHOF AND C. VAN LOAN, *The WY representation for products of Householder matrices*, SIAM J. Sci. Statist. Comput., 8 (1987), pp. s2–s13.

[17] A. BOJANCZYK, R. BRENT, AND H. KUNG, *Numerically stable solution of dense systems of linear equations using mesh-connected processors*, SIAM J. Sci. Statist. Comput., 5 (1984), pp. 95–104.

[18] R. BRENT AND F. LUK, *The solution of singular-value and symmetric eigenvalue problems on multiprocessor arrays*, SIAM J. Sci. Statist. Comput., 6 (1985), pp. 69–84.

[19] O. BRONLUND AND T. L. JOHNSEN, *QR-factorization of partitioned matrices*, Comput. Methods Appl. Mech. Engrg., 3 (1974), pp. 153–172.

[20] O. BUNEMAN, *A compact non-iterative Poisson solver*, Tech. Rep. Report 294, Stanford University Institute for Plasma Research, Stanford, CA, 1969.

[21] B. BUZBEE, *A fast Poisson solver amenable to parallel computation*, IEEE Trans. Comput., C-22 (1973), pp. 793–796.

[22] B. BUZBEE, G. GOLUB, AND C. NIELSON, *On direct methods for solving Poisson's equation*, SIAM J. Numer. Anal., 7 (1970), pp. 627–656.

[23] D. CALAHAN, *Block-oriented local-memory-based linear equation solution on the* CRAY-2: *uniprocessor algorithms*, in Proc. Intl. Conf. Par. Processing, IEEE Computer Society Press, New York, 1986, pp. 375–378.

[24] D. CALAHAN, W. AMES, AND E. SESEK, *A collection of equation solving codes for the* CRAY-1, Tech. Rep. SEL 133, University of Michigan, Ann Arbor, MI, 1979.

[25] R. CHAMBERLAIN AND M. POWELL, *QR factorization for linear least squares on the hypercube*, Tech. Rep. CCS 86/10, Chr. Michelsen Institute, Bergen, Norway, 1986.

[26] T. CHAN, *An improved algorithm for computing the singular value decomposition*, ACM Trans. Math. Software, 8 (1982), pp. 72–83.

[27] S. CHEN, D. KUCK, AND A. SAMEH, *Practical parallel band triangular system solvers*, ACM Trans. Math. Software, 4 (1978), pp. 270–277.

[28] E. CHU AND A. GEORGE, *Gaussian elimination with partial pivoting and load balancing on a multiprocessor*, Parallel Comput., 5 (1987), pp. 65–74.

[29] ———, *A balanced submatrix merging algorithm for multiprocessor architectures*, Tech. Rep. CS-88-45, Faculty of Mathematics, University of Waterloo, Waterloo, Canada, 1988.

[30] ———, *QR factorization of a dense matrix on a hypercube multiprocessor*, Tech. Rep. ORNL/TM-10691, Oak Ridge National Lab., Oak Ridge, TN, 1988.

[31] ———, *Updating and downdating the inverse of a Cholesky factor on a hypercube multiprocessor*, Tech. Rep. CS-88-46, Dept. of Computer Science, University of Waterloo, Waterloo, Canada, 1988.

[32] M. COSNARD, J. MULLER, AND Y. ROBERT, *Parallel QR decomposition of a rectangular matrix*, Numer. Math., 48 (1986), pp. 239–249.

[33] J. CUPPEN, *A divide and conquer method for the symmetric tridiagonal eigenproblem*, Numer. Math., 36 (1981), pp. 177–195.

[34] T. DEKKER AND W. HOFFMAN, *Rehabilitation of the Gauss-Jordan algorithm*, Tech. Rep. TR86-28, Dept. of Mathematics, University of Amsterdam, Amsterdam, 1986.

[35] J. DEMMEL, J. DONGARRA, J. D. CROZ, A. GREENBAUM, S. HAMMARLING, AND D. SORENSEN, *Prospectus for the development of a linear algebra library for high-performance computers*, Tech. Rep. TM-97, Mathematics and Computer Science Div., Argonne National Laboratory, Argonne, IL, 1987.

[36] G. DIETRICH, *A new formulation of the hypermatrix Householder-QR decomposition*, Comput. Methods Appl. Mech. Engrg., 9 (1976), pp. 273–280.

[37] J. DONGARRA, *Workshop on the Level 3 BLAS*, Tech. Rep. TM-89, Mathematics and Computer Science Div., Argonne National Laboratory, Argonne, IL, 1987.

[38] J. DONGARRA, J. BUNCH, C. MOLER, AND G. W. STEWART, *LINPACK User's Guide*, Society for Industrial and Applied Mathematics, Philadelphia, 1979.

[39] J. DONGARRA, J. D. CROZ, I. DUFF, AND S. HAMMARLING, *A proposal for a set of Level 3 basic linear algebra subprograms*, Tech. Rep. TM-88, Mathematics and Computer Science Div., Argonne National Laboratory, Argonne, IL, 1987.

[40] J. DONGARRA, J. D. CROZ, S. HAMMARLING, AND R. HANSON, *A proposal for an extended set of Fortran basic linear algebra subprograms*, Tech. Rep. TM-41, Mathematics and Computer Science Div., Argonne National Laboratory, Argonne, IL, 1984.

[41] J. DONGARRA AND S. EISENSTAT, *Squeezing the most out of an algorithm in CRAY Fortran*, ACM Trans. Math. Software, 10 (1984), pp. 219–230.

[42] J. DONGARRA, F. GUSTAVSON, AND A. KARP, *Implementing linear algebra algorithms for dense matrices on a vector pipeline machine*, SIAM Rev., 26 (1984), pp. 91–112.

[43] J. DONGARRA, S. HAMMARLING, AND L. KAUFMAN, *Squeezing the most out of eigenvalue solvers on high-performance computers*, Tech. Rep. TM-46, Mathematics and Computer Science Div., Argonne National Laboratory, Argonne, IL, 1985.

[44] J. DONGARRA, S. HAMMARLING, AND D. SORENSEN, *Block reduction of matrices to condensed form for eigenvalue computations*, Tech. Rep. TM-99, Mathematics and Computer Science Div., Argonne National Laboratory, Argonne, IL, 1987.

[45] J. DONGARRA AND T. HEWITT, *Implementing dense linear algebra algorithms using multitasking on the CRAY X-MP/4*, SIAM J. Sci. Statist. Comput., 7 (1986), pp. 347–350.

[46] J. DONGARRA AND L. JOHNSSON, *Solving banded systems on a parallel processor*, Parallel Comput., 5 (1987), pp. 219–246.

[47] J. DONGARRA AND A. SAMEH, *On some parallel banded system solvers*, Parallel Comput., 1 (1984), pp. 223–235.

[48] J. DONGARRA, A. SAMEH, AND D. SORENSEN, *Implementation of some concurrent algorithms for matrix factorization*, Parallel Comput., 3 (1986), pp. 25–34.

[49] J. DONGARRA AND D. SORENSEN, *A fully parallel algorithm for the symmetric eigenvalue problem*, SIAM J. Sci. Statist. Comput., 8 (1987), pp. s139–s154.

[50] J. DU CROZ, S. NUGENT, J. REID, AND D. TAYLOR, *Solving large full sets of linear equations in a paged virtual store*, ACM Trans. Math. Software, 7 (1981), pp. 527–536.

[51] P. EBERLEIN, *A Jacobi-like method for the automatic computation of eigenvalues and eigenvectors of an arbitrary matrix*, J. Soc. Indust. Appl. Math., 10 (1962), pp. 74–88.

[52] ———, *On the Schur decomposition of a matrix for parallel computation*, IEEE Trans. Comput., C-36 (1987), pp. 167–174.

[53] S. EISENSTAT, M. HEATH, C. HENKEL, AND C. ROMINE, *Modified cyclic algorithms for solving triangular systems on distributed memory multiprocessors*, SIAM J. Sci. Statist. Comput., 9 (1988), pp. 589–600.

[54] L. ELDEN, *A parallel QR decomposition algorithm*, Tech. Rep. Lith-MAT-R-1988-02, Linkoping University, Linkoping, Sweden, 1987.

[55] J. ERICKSEN, *Iterative and direct methods for solving Poisson's equation and their adaptability to Illiac IV*, Tech. Rep. CAC Doc. 60, Center for Advanced Computations, University of Illinois, Urbana, IL, 1972.

[56] K. FONG AND T. JORDAN, *Some linear algebra algorithms and their performance on CRAY-1*, Tech. Rep. LA-6774, Los Alamos National Laboratory, Los Alamos, NM, 1977.

[57] G. FORSYTHE AND P. HENRICI, *The cyclic Jacobi method for computing the principal values of a complex matrix*, Trans. Amer. Math. Soc., 94 (1960), pp. 1–23.

[58] G. FORSYTHE, M. MALCOLM, AND C. MOLER, *Computer Methods for Mathematical Computations*, Prentice-Hall, Englewood Cliffs, NJ, 1977.

[59] G. FOX, *Domain decomposition in distributed and shared memory environments*, in Lecture Notes in Comput. Sci. 297: Proc. 1987 Intl. Conf. Supercomputing, Springer-Verlag, Berlin, 1987, pp. 1042–1073.

[60] G. FOX, M. JOHNSON, G. LYZENGA, S. OTTO, J. SALMON, AND D. WALKER, *Solving Problems on Concurrent Processors*, Vol. 1, Prentice-Hall, Englewood Cliffs, NJ, 1988.

[61] G. FOX, S. OTTO, AND A. HEY, *Matrix algorithms on a hypercube I: matrix multiplication*, Parallel Comput., 4 (1987), pp. 17–31.

[62] L. FOX, E. GOODWIN, J. MICHEL, F. OLVER, AND J. WILKINSON, *Modern Computing Methods*, First edition, Philosophical Library, New York, 1961.

[63] K. GALLIVAN, D. GANNON, AND W. JALBY, *Strategies for cache and local memory management by global program transformation*, J. Parallel Dist. Computing, 5 (1988), pp. 587–616.

[64] K. GALLIVAN, D. GANNON, W. JALBY, A. MALONY, AND H. WIJSHOFF, *Behavioral characterization of multiprocessor memory systems*, in Proc. 1989 ACM SIGMETRICS Conf. on Measuring and Modeling Computer Systems, ACM Press, New York, 1989, pp. 79–89.

[65] K. GALLIVAN, W. JALBY, A. MALONY, AND H. WIJSHOFF, *Performance prediction of loop constructs on multiprocessor hierarchical memory systems*, in Proc. 1989 Intl. Conf. Supercomputing, ACM Press, New York, 1989, pp. 433–442.

[66] K. GALLIVAN, W. JALBY, AND U. MEIER, *The use of BLAS3 in linear algebra on a parallel processor with a hierarchical memory*, SIAM J. Sci. Statist. Comput., 8 (1987), pp. 1079–1084.

[67] K. GALLIVAN, W. JALBY, U. MEIER, AND A. SAMEH, *Impact of hierarchical memory systems on linear algebra algorithm design*, Intl. J. Supercomputer Appl., 2 (1988), pp. 12–48. Presented at the Level 3 BLAS Workshop, Argonne National Laboratory, January 1987.

[68] E. GALLOPOULOS AND D. LEE, *Boundary integral domain decomposition on hierarchical memory multiprocessor*, in Proc. 1988 Intl. Conf. Supercomputing, ACM Press, New York, 1988, pp. 488–499.

[69] ———, *Fast Laplace solver by boundary integral-based domain decomposition*, in Proc. of

Third SIAM Conf. on Par. Processing for Scientific Computing, G. Rodrigue, ed., Society for Industrial and Applied Mathematics, Philadelphia, 1988.

[70] E. GALLOPOULOS AND Y. SAAD, *Parallel block cyclic reduction algorithm for the fast solution of elliptic equations*, Parallel Comput., 10 (1989), pp. 143–160. Also presented at 1987 Int'l. Conf. on Supercomputing, Athens, Greece.

[71] ———, *Efficient parallel solution of parabolic equations: explicit methods*, Tech. Rep., Center for Supercomputing Research and Development, University of Illinois, Urbana, IL, June 1989. To be presented at the Fourth SIAM Conf. Parallel Processing for Scientific Computing.

[72] ———, *Efficient parallel solution of parabolic equations: implicit methods*, Tech. Rep., Center for Supercomputing Research and Development, University of Illinois, Urbana, IL, June 1989. To be presented at the Fourth SIAM Conf. Parallel Processing for Scientific Computing.

[73] ———, *Some fast elliptic solvers for parallel architectures and their complexities*, Int'l. J. High Speed Comput., 1 (May 1989), pp. 113–141.

[74] D. GANNON AND W. JALBY, *The influence of memory hierarchy on algorithm organization: programming FFTs on a vector multiprocessor*, in The Characteristics of Parallel Algorithms, L. Jamieson, D. Gannon, and R. Douglass, eds., MIT Press, Cambridge, 1987, pp. 277–301.

[75] D. GANNON, W. JALBY, AND K. GALLIVAN, *On the problem of optimizing data transfers for complex memory systems*, in Proc. 1988 Intl. Conf. Supercomputing, ACM Press, New York, 1988, pp. 238–253.

[76] D. GANNON AND J. VAN ROSENDALE, *On the impact of communication complexity on the design of parallel numerical algorithms*, IEEE Trans. Comput., C-33 (1984), pp. 1180–1195.

[77] A. GEIST AND M. HEATH, *Parallel Cholesky factorization on a hypercube multiprocessor*, Tech. Rep. ORNL-6190, Oak Ridge National Laboratory, Oak Ridge, TN, 1985.

[78] ———, *Matrix factorization on a hypercube*, in Hypercube Multiprocessors 1986, M. T. Heath, ed., Society for Industrial and Applied Mathematics, Philadelphia, 1986, pp. 161–180.

[79] A. GEIST AND C. ROMINE, *LU factorization algorithms on distributed memory multiprocessor architectures*, SIAM J. Sci. Statist. Comput., 9 (1988), pp. 639–649.

[80] W. GENTLEMAN AND H. T. KUNG, *Matrix triangularization by systolic arrays*, in Proc. SPIE 298, Real Time Signal Processing, San Diego, CA, 1981, pp. 19–26.

[81] G. GOLUB, R. PLEMMONS, AND A. SAMEH, *Parallel block schemes for large-scale least squares computations*, in High Speed Computing, Scientific Applications and Algorithm Design, R. Wilhelmson, ed., University of Illinois Press, Urbana, IL., 1988, pp. 180–195.

[82] G. GOLUB AND C. REINSCH, *Singular value decomposition and least squares solutions*, Numer. Math., 14 (1970), pp. 403–420.

[83] G. GOLUB AND C. VAN LOAN, *Matrix Computations*, The Johns Hopkins University Press, Baltimore, 1983.

[84] F. GUSTAVSON, private communication.

[85] W. HARROD, *Programming with the BLAS*, in The Characteristics of Parallel Algorithms, L. Jamieson, D. Gannon, and R. Douglass, eds., MIT Press, Cambridge, 1987, pp. 253–276.

[86] ———, *A block scheme for reduction to condensed form*, Tech. Rep. CSRD Rept. 696, Center for Supercomputing Research and Development, University of Illinois, Argonne, IL, 1988.

[87] P. HARTEN, private communication.

[88] M. HEATH, *Parallel Cholesky factorization in message passing multiprocessor environments*, Tech. Rep. ORNL-6150, Oak Ridge National Lab., Oak Ridge, TN, 1985.

[89] M. HEATH AND C. ROMINE, *Parallel solution of triangular systems on distributed memory multiprocessors*, SIAM J. Sci. Statist. Comput., 9 (1988), pp. 558–588.

[90] D. HELLER, *Some aspects of the cyclic reduction algorithm for block tridiagonal linear systems*, SIAM J. Numer. Anal., 13 (1976), pp. 484–496.

[91] ———, *A survey of parallel algorithms for numerical linear algebra*, SIAM Rev., 20 (1978), pp. 740–777.

[92] C. HENKEL, M. HEATH, AND R. PLEMMONS, *Cholesky downdating on a hypercube*, in Hypercube Multiprocessors 1988, G. Fox, ed., ACM Press, New York, 1988, pp. 1592–1598.

[93] C. HENKEL AND R. PLEMMONS, *Recursive least squares on a hypercube multiprocessor using the covariance factorization*, Tech. Rep., Dept. Computer Science, North Carolina State University, Raleigh, NC, 1988. SIAM J. Sci. Statist. Comput., 11 (1990), to appear.

[94] M. HESTENES, *Inversion of matrices by biorthogonalization and related results*, J. Soc. In-

dust. Appl. Math., 6 (1958), pp. 51–90.

[95] N. HIGHAM, *Exploiting fast matrix multiplication with the Level 3 BLAS*, Tech. Rep. TR 89-984, Dept. of Computer Science, Cornell University, Ithaca, NY, 1989.

[96] R. HOCKNEY, *A fast direct solution of Poisson's equation using Fourier analysis*, JACM, 12 (1965), pp. 95–113.

[97] ———, *The potential calculation and some applications*, Methods Comput. Phys., 9 (1970), pp. 135–211.

[98] ———, *Optimizing the FACR(l) Poisson solver on parallel computers*, in Proc. Intl. Conf. Par. Processing, IEEE Computer Society Press, New York, 1982.

[99] ———, *Problem related performance parameters for supercomputers*, in Performance Evaluation of Supercomputers, J. Martin, ed., Elsevier Science Publishers B.V., Amsterdam, 1988, pp. 215–235.

[100] R. HOCKNEY AND C. JESSHOPE, *Parallel Computers*, First edition, Adam Hilger, Bristol, 1981.

[101] J. HONG AND H. T. KUNG, *I/O complexity: the red-blue pebble game*, in Proc. 13th ACM Symp. Theory of Computing, 1981, pp. 326–333.

[102] H. HUANG, *A parallel algorithm for symmetric tridiagonal eigenvalue problems*, Tech. Rep. CAC Doc. 109, Center for Advanced Computation, University of Illinois, Urbana, IL, 1974.

[103] I. IPSEN AND E. JESSUP, *Solving the symmetric tridiagonal eigenvalue problem on the hypercube*, Tech. Rep. RR-548, Dept. of Computer Science, Yale University, New Haven, CT, 1987.

[104] I. IPSEN, Y. SAAD, AND M. SCHULTZ, *Complexity of dense linear system solution on a multiprocessor ring*, Linear Algebra Appl., 77 (1986), pp. 205–239.

[105] W. JALBY AND U. MEIER, *Optimizing matrix operations on a parallel mulitprocessor with a hierarchical memory system*, in Proc. Intl. Conf. Par. Processing, IEEE Computer Society Press, New York, 1986, pp. 429–432.

[106] W. JALBY AND B. PHILIPPE, *Loss of orthogonality in a Gram-Schmidt process*, Tech. Rep., IRISA, Rennes, France, 1987.

[107] E. JESSUP AND D. SORENSEN, *A parallel algorithm for computing the singular value decomposition of a matrix*, Tech. Rep. TM-102, Mathematics and Computer Science Div., Argonne National Laboratory, Argonne, IL, 1987.

[108] L. JOHNSSON, *Solving narrow banded systems on ensemble architectures*, ACM Trans. Math. Software, 11 (1985), pp. 271–288.

[109] ———, *Solving tridiagonal systems on ensemble architectures*, SIAM J. Sci. Statist. Comput., 8 (1987), pp. 354–392.

[110] L. JOHNSSON AND C. T. HO, *Algorithms for multiplying matrices of arbitrary shapes using shared memory primitives on Boolean cubes*, Tech. Rep. YALEU/DCS/TR-569, Dept. Computer Science, Yale University, New Haven, 1987.

[111] T. KAILATH, A. VIEIRA, AND M. MORF, *Inversion of Toeplitz operators, innovations and orthogonal polynomials*, SIAM Rev., 20 (1978), pp. 106–119.

[112] C. KATHOLI AND B. SUTER, *QR factorization of a rectangular matrix*, Tech. Rep. TR88-07, University of Alabama at Birmingham, Birmingham, AL, 1988.

[113] S. KIM, D. AGRAWAL, AND R. PLEMMONS, *Recursive least squares filtering for signal processing on distributed memory multiprocessors*, Tech. Rep., Dept. of Computer Science, North Carolina State University, Raleigh, NC, 1988. Inter. J. Parallel Proc. (1990), to appear.

[114] M. KNOWLES, B. OKAWA, Y. MURAOKA, AND R. WILHELMSON, *Matrix operations on ILLIAC IV*, Tech. Rep. ILLIAC IV Doc. 118, Dept. of Computer Science, University of Illinois, Urbana, IL, 1967.

[115] D. KUCK, *ILLIAC IV software and application programming*, IEEE Trans. Comput., C-17 (1968), pp. 758–770.

[116] ———, *The Structure of Computers and Computations*, Vol. 1, John Wiley, New York, 1978.

[117] D. KUCK, E. DAVIDSON, D. LAWRIE, AND A. SAMEH, *Parallel supercomputing today and the Cedar approach*, Science, 231 (1986), pp. 967–974.

[118] D. KUCK AND A. SAMEH, *Parallel computations of eigenvalues of real matrices*, in Proc. IFIP Congress 1971, North-Holland, Amsterdam, 1972, pp. 1266–1272.

[119] D. LAWRIE, *Access and alignment of data in an array processor*, IEEE Trans. Comput., C-24 (1975), pp. 1145–1155.

[120] D. LAWRIE AND A. SAMEH, *The computations and communication complexity of a parallel banded system solver*, ACM Trans Math. Software, 10 (1984), pp. 185–195.

[121] C. LAWSON, R. HANSON, D. KINCAID, AND F. KROGH, *Basic linear algebra subprograms*

for Fortran use, ACM Trans. Math. Software, 5 (1979), pp. 308–323.

[122] G. LI AND T. COLEMAN, A parallel triangular solver on a distributed memory multiprocessor, SIAM J. Sci. Statist. Comput., 9 (1988), pp. 485–502.

[123] S. LO, B. PHILIPPE, AND A. SAMEH, A multiprocessor algorithm for the symmetric tridiagonal eigenvalue problem, SIAM J. Sci. Statist. Comput., 8 (1987), pp. s155–s165.

[124] F. LUK, Computing the singular value decomposition on the Illiac IV, ACM Trans. Math. Software, 6 (1980), pp. 524–539.

[125] ———, A rotation method for computing the QR decomposition, SIAM J. Sci. Statist. Comput., 7 (1987), pp. 452–549.

[126] F. LUK AND H. PARK, A proof of convergence for two parallel Jacobi SVD algorithms, 1987. IEEE Trans. Comput., to appear.

[127] N. MADSEN, G. RODRIGUE, AND J. KARUSH, Matrix multiplication by diagonals on a vector/parallel processor, Inform. Process. Lett., 5 (1976), pp. 41–45.

[128] R. MATHON AND R. JOHNSTON, The approximate solution of elliptic boundary-value problems by fundamental solutions, SIAM J. Numer. Anal., 14 (1977), pp. 638–650.

[129] O. MCBRYAN AND E. VAN DE VELDE, Hypercube algorithms and implementations, SIAM J. Sci. Statist. Comput., 8 (1987), pp. s227–s287.

[130] J. MCCOMB AND S. SCHMIDT, Engineering and scientific library for the IBM 3090 vector facility, IBM Systems Journal, 27 (1988), pp. 404–415.

[131] A. MCKELLAR AND E. COFFMAN JR., Organizing matrices and matrix operations for paged memory systems, Comm. ACM, 12 (1969), pp. 153–165.

[132] U. MEIER, A parallel partition method for solving banded systems of linear equations, Parallel Comput., 2 (1985), pp. 33–43.

[133] W. MIRANKER, A survey of parallelism in numerical analysis, SIAM Rev., 13 (1971), pp. 524–547.

[134] J. MODI AND M. CLARKE, An alternative Givens ordering, Numer. Math., 43 (1984), pp. 83–90.

[135] C. MOLER, Matrix computations on distributed memory multiprocessors, in Hypercube Multiprocessors 1986, M. T. Heath, ed., Society for Industrial and Applied Mathematics, Philadelphia, 1986, pp. 181–195.

[136] C. MOLER AND G. W. STEWART, An algorithm for generalized matrix eigenvalue problems, SIAM J. Numer. Anal., 10 (1973), pp. 241–256.

[137] J. ORTEGA, Introduction to Parallel and Vector Solution of Linear Systems, Plenum, New York, 1988.

[138] J. ORTEGA AND R. VOIGT, Solution of partial differential equations on vector and parallel computers, SIAM Rev., 27 (1985), pp. 149–240.

[139] J. ORTEGA, R. VOIGT, AND C. ROMINE, A bibliography on parallel and vector numerical algorithms, Tech. Rep. ORNL/TM-10998, Oak Ridge National Laboratory, Oak Ridge, TN, 1989.

[140] C. PAN AND R. PLEMMONS, Least squares modifications with inverse factorizations: parallel implications, Tech. Rep., Dept. of Computer Science, North Carolina State University, Raleigh, NC, 1987. Comput. Appl. Math., to appear.

[141] B. PARLETT, The Symmetric Eigenvalue Problem, Prentice-Hall, Englewood Cliffs, NJ, 1980.

[142] M. PEASE, An adaption of the fast Fourier transform for parallel processing, JACM, 15 (1968), pp. 252–264.

[143] G. PETERS AND J. WILKINSON, On the stability of Gauss-Jordan elimination with pivoting, Comm. ACM, 18 (1975), pp. 20–24.

[144] R. PLEMMONS, A parallel block scheme applied to computations in structural analysis, SIAM J. Algebraic Discrete Methods, 7 (1986), pp. 337–347.

[145] R. PLEMMONS AND R. WHITE, Substructuring methods for computing the nullspace of equilibrium matrices, Tech. Rep., Center for Research in Sci. Comp., North Carolina State University, Raleigh, NC, 1988.

[146] R. PLEMMONS AND S. WRIGHT, An efficient parallel scheme for minimizing a sum of Euclidean norms, Linear Algebra Appl., 121 (1989), pp. 71–85.

[147] A. POTHEN AND P. RAGHAVAN, Orthogonal factorization on a distributed memory multiprocessor, Tech. Rep. CS-87-24, Pennsylvania State University, Computer Science Dept., University Park, PA, 1987.

[148] A. POTHEN, J. SOMESH, AND U. VEMULAPATI, Orthogonal factorization on a distributed memory multiprocessor, in Hypercube Multiprocessors 1987, M. T. Heath, ed., Society for Industrial and Applied Mathematics, Philadelphia, 1987, pp. 587–596.

[149] G. RADICATI, Y. ROBERT, AND P. SGUAZZERO, Dense linear systems Fortran solvers on the IBM 3090 vector multiprocessor, Parallel Comput., 8 (1988), pp. 377–384.

[150] C. ROMINE, *The parallel solution of triangular systems on a hypercube*, in Hypercube Multiprocessors 1987, M. T. Heath, ed., Society for Industrial and Applied Mathematics, Philadelphia, 1987, pp. 552–559.

[151] C. ROMINE AND J. ORTEGA, *Parallel solution of triangular systems of equations*, Parallel Comput., 6 (1988), pp. 109–114.

[152] A. SAMEH, *On Jacobi and Jacobi-like algorithms for a parallel computer*, Math. Comp., 25 (1971), pp. 579–590.

[153] ———, *Numerical parallel algorithms – a survey*, in High Speed Computer and Algorithm Organization, D. Kuck, D. Lawrie, and A. Sameh, eds., Academic Press, New York, 1977, pp. 207–228.

[154] ———, *A fast Poisson solver for multiprocessors*, in Elliptic Problem Solvers II, G. Birkhoff and A. Schoenstadt, eds., Academic Press, New York, 1984, pp. 175–186.

[155] ———, *On two numerical algorithms for multiprocessors*, in High Speed Computation, J. Kowalik, ed., Springer-Verlag, Berlin, 1984, pp. 311–328.

[156] ———, *Numerical algorithms on the Cedar system*, presented at Second SIAM Conference on Parallel Processing, 1985.

[157] ———, *On some parallel algorithms on a ring of processors*, Comput. Phys. Comm., 37 (1985), pp. 159–166.

[158] ———, *Solving the linear least squares problem on a linear array of processors*, in Algorithmically-Specialized Parallel Computers, Academic Press, West Lafayette, IN, 1985, pp. 191–200. Proc. 1982 Purdue Univ. Workshop.

[159] A. SAMEH AND R. BRENT, *Solving triangular systems on a parallel computer*, SIAM J. Numer. Anal., 14 (1977), pp. 1101–1113.

[160] A. SAMEH, S. CHEN, AND D. KUCK, *Parallel Poisson and biharmonic solvers*, Computing, 17 (1976), pp. 219–230.

[161] A. SAMEH AND D. KUCK, *On stable parallel linear systems solvers*, JACM, 25 (1978), pp. 81–91.

[162] H. SAMUKAWA, *Programming style on the IBM vector facility considering both performance and flexibility*, IBM Systems Journal, 27 (1988), pp. 453–474.

[163] R. SCHREIBER AND B. PARLETT, *Block reflectors: theory and computation*, SIAM J. Numer. Anal., 25 (1988), pp. 189–205.

[164] R. SCHREIBER AND C. VAN LOAN, *A storage-efficient WY representation for products of Householder transformations*, SIAM J. Sci. Statist. Comput., 10 (1989), pp. 53–57.

[165] G. SHROFF AND R. SCHREIBER, *On the convergence of the cyclic Jacobi method for parallel block orderings*, Tech. Rep. 88-11, Dept. of Computer Science, Rensselaer Polytechnic Institute, Troy, NY, 1988.

[166] H. SIMON, *Bisection is not optimal on vector processors*, SIAM J. Sci. Statist. Comput., 10 (1989), pp. 205–209.

[167] B. SMITH, J. BOYLE, Y. IKEBE, V. KLEMA, AND C. MOLER, *Matrix Eigensystem Routines: EISPACK Guide*, Second edition, Springer-Verlag, Berlin, 1976.

[168] D. SORENSEN, *Analysis of pairwise pivoting in Gaussian elimination*, IEEE Trans. Comput., C-34 (1985), pp. 274–278.

[169] J. STERN, *A fast Gaussian elimination scheme and automated roundoff error analysis for SIME machines*, Master's thesis, Dept. of Computer Science, University of Illinois, Urbana, IL, 1979.

[170] G. W. STEWART, *Introduction to Matrix Computations*, Academic Press, New York, 1973.

[171] ———, *A Jacobi-like algorithm for computing the Schur decomposition of a nonhermitian matrix*, SIAM J. Sci. Statist. Comput., 6 (1985), pp. 853–864.

[172] ———, *A parallel implementation of the QR-algorithm*, Parallel Comput., 5 (1987), pp. 187–196.

[173] H. STONE, *Parallel processing with the perfect shuffle*, IEEE Trans. Comput., C-20 (1971), pp. 153–161.

[174] H. S. STONE, *High-Performance Computer Architecture*, First edition, Addison-Wesley, Reading, 1987.

[175] V. STRASSEN, *Gaussian elimination is not optimal*, Numer. Math., 13 (1969), pp. 354–356.

[176] P. SWARZTRAUBER, *A direct method for the discrete solution of separable elliptic equations*, SIAM J. Numer. Anal., 11 (1974), pp. 1136–1150.

[177] ———, *The methods of cyclic reduction, Fourier analysis and the FACR algorithm for the discrete solution of Poisson's equation on a rectangle*, SIAM Rev., 19 (1977), pp. 490–501.

[178] P. SWARZTRAUBER AND R. SWEET, *Algorithm 541: efficient Fortran subprograms for the solution of separable elliptic partial differential equations*, ACM Trans. Math. Software, 5 (1979), pp. 352–364.

[179] ———, *Vector and parallel methods for the direct solution of Poisson's equation*, J. Comput. Appl. Math., 27 (1989), pp. 241–263.

[180] R. SWEET, *A cyclic reduction algorithm for solving block tridiagonal systems of arbitrary dimension*, SIAM J. Numer. Anal., 14 (1977), pp. 707–720.

[181] ———, *A parallel and vector variant of the cyclic reduction algorithm*, SIAM J. Sci. Statist. Comput., 9 (1988), pp. 761–765.

[182] C. TEMPERTON, *Direct methods for the solution of the discrete Poisson equation: some comparisons*, J. Comput. Phys., 31 (1979), pp. 1–20.

[183] ———, *On the FACR(l) algorithm for the discrete Poisson equation*, J. Comput. Phys., 34 (1980), pp. 314–329.

[184] L. TREFETHAN AND R. SCHREIBER, *Average-case stability of Gaussian elimination*, Tech. Rep. RUU-CS-84-7, Dept. of Mathematics, MIT, Cambridge, MA, 1988.

[185] K. TRIVEDI, *Prepaging and applications to structured array problems*, Tech. Rep. UIUCDCS-R-74-662, Dept. of Computer Science, University of Illinois, Urbana, IL, 1974.

[186] ———, *On the paging performance of array algorithms*, IEEE Trans. Comput., C-26 (1977), pp. 938–947.

[187] N. TSAO, *On the accuracy of solving triangular systems in parallel*, Tech. Rep. ICOMP-88-19, NASA Lewis Research Center, Cleveland, OH, 1988.

[188] H. VAN DER VORST, *Analysis of a parallel solution method for tridiagonal linear systems*, Parallel Comput., 5 (1987), pp. 303–311.

[189] H. VAN DER VORST AND K. DEKKER, *Vectorization of linear recurrence relations*, SIAM J. Sci. Statist. Comput., 10 (1989), pp. 27–35.

[190] C. VAN LOAN, *The block Jacobi method for computing the singular value decomposition*, Tech. Rep. TR85-680, Dept. of Computer Science, Cornell University, Ithaca, NY, 1985.

[191] R. VOIGT, *The influence of vector computer architecture on numerical algorithms*, in High Speed Computer and Algorithm Organization, D. Kuck, D. Lawrie, and A. Sameh, eds., Academic Press, New York, 1977, pp. 229–244.

[192] H. WANG, *A parallel method for tridiagonal equations*, ACM Trans. Math. Software, 7 (1981), pp. 170–183.

[193] H. A. G. WIJSHOFF, *Data Organization in Parallel Computers*, Kluwer, Boston, 1989.

[194] J. WILKINSON, *The Algebraic Eigenvalue Problem*, Clarendon Press, Oxford, 1965.

[195] J. WILKINSON AND C. REINSCH, *Handbook for Automatic Computation: Linear Algebra*, Vol. 2, Springer-Verlag, Berlin, 1971.

[196] C. Q. ZHU AND P. C. YEW, *A scheme to enforce data dependences on large multiprocessor systems*, IEEE Trans. Soft. Engrg., SE-13 (1987), pp. 726–739.

PARALLEL ALGORITHMS FOR SPARSE LINEAR SYSTEMS

MICHAEL T. HEATH*, ESMOND NG* AND BARRY W. PEYTON*

Abstract. In this paper we survey recent progress in the development of parallel algorithms for solving sparse linear systems on computer architectures having multiple processors. We focus our attention on direct methods for solving sparse symmetric positive definite systems, specifically by Cholesky factorization. We survey recent progress on parallel algorithms for all phases of the solution process, including ordering, symbolic factorization, numeric factorization, and triangular solution.

Key Words. parallel algorithms, sparse linear systems, Cholesky factorization

AMS(MOS) subject classifications. 65F,65W

1. Introduction. Dense matrix computations are of such central importance in scientific computing that they are usually among the first algorithms implemented in any new computing environment. The need for high performance on common operations such as matrix multiplication and solving systems of linear equations has had a strong influence on the design of many architectures, compilers, etc., and such computations have become standard benchmarks for evaluating the performance of new computer systems. A survey of parallel algorithms for dense matrix computations is given in [34]. Sparse matrix computations are equally as important and pervasive, but both their performance and their influence on computer system design have tended to lag those of their dense matrix counterparts. In a sense this relative lack of attention and success is not surprising: sparse matrix computations involve more complex algorithms, sophisticated data structures, and irregular memory reference patterns, making efficient implementations on novel architectures substantially more difficult to achieve than for dense matrix computations. One could plausibly argue, however, that the greater complexity and irregularity of sparse matrix computations make them much more realistic representatives of typical scientific computations, and therefore even more useful as design targets and benchmark criteria than the dense matrix computations that have usually played this role.

Despite the difficulty and relative neglect of sparse matrix computations on advanced computer architectures, there have been some notable successes in attaining very high performance (e.g., [14]), and the needs of sparse matrix computations have had some effect on computer design (e.g., the inclusion of scatter/gather instructions on some vector supercomputers). Nevertheless, it is ironic that sparse matrix computations contain more inherent parallelism than the corresponding dense matrix computations (in a sense to be discussed below), yet typically show significantly lower efficiency on today's parallel architectures. In this paper we will examine the reasons for this state of affairs, reviewing the major issues and progress to date in sparse matrix computations on parallel computer architectures. In addition to surveying the literature in this area, we will try to sketch the conceptual framework in which this work has taken place. To keep the scope of the article within reasonable bounds, we will focus our attention on the solution of sparse symmetric positive definite linear systems by Cholesky factorization. There has, of course, also been progress

* Mathematical Sciences Section, Oak Ridge National Laboratory, P.O. Box 2009, Oak Ridge, Tennessee 37831-8083. This research was supported by the Applied Mathematical Sciences Research Program, Office of Energy Research, U.S. Department of Energy under contract DE-AC05-84OR21400 with Martin Marietta Energy Systems Inc.

on parallel algorithms for other matrix problems (e.g., nonsymmetric linear systems, least squares, eigenvalues), other factorizations (e.g., LU and QR), and other basic approaches (e.g., iterative methods), but a comprehensive treatment of all of these topics would easily require an entire book. Our discussion of sparse Cholesky factorization illustrates some of the major issues that also arise in other parallel sparse matrix factorizations as well, but there are many additional issues associated with parallel iterative algorithms or parallel sparse eigenvalue algorithms that we do not specifically address.

An outline of the paper is as follows. First, we will sketch briefly some necessary background material on serial algorithms for solving sparse symmetric positive definite linear systems. For a much more complete treatment, the reader should consult [25] or [47]. We then survey the progress to date in developing parallel implementations for each of the major phases of the solution process. We will see that the same graph theoretic tools originally developed for analyzing sequential sparse matrix algorithms also play a critical role in understanding parallel algorithms as well. We conclude with some observations on future research directions.

2. Background. Consider a system of linear equations

$$Ax = b,$$

where A is an $n \times n$ symmetric positive definite matrix, b is a known vector, and x is the unknown solution vector to be computed. One way to solve the linear system is first to compute the Cholesky factorization

$$A = LL^T,$$

where the Cholesky factor L is a lower triangular matrix with positive diagonal elements. Then the solution vector x can be computed by successive forward and back substitutions to solve the triangular systems

$$Ly = b, \quad L^T x = y.$$

If A is a sparse matrix, meaning that most of its entries are zero, then during the course of the factorization some entries that are initially zero in the lower triangle of A may become nonzero entries in L. These entries of L are known as *fill* or *fill-in*. Usually, however, many zero entries in the lower triangle of A remain zero in L. For efficient use of computer memory and processing time, it is desirable for the amount of fill to be small, and to store and operate on only the nonzero entries of A and L.

It is well known that row or column interchanges are not required to maintain numerical stability in the factorization process when A is positive definite. Furthermore, when roundoff errors are ignored, a given linear system yields the same solution regardless of the particular order in which the equations and unknowns are numbered. This freedom in choosing the ordering can be exploited to enhance the preservation of sparsity in the Cholesky factorization process. More precisely, let P be any permutation matrix. Since PAP^T is also a symmetric positive definite matrix, we can choose P based solely on sparsity considerations. That is, we can often choose P so that the Cholesky factor $\bar{L}$ of PAP^T has less fill than L. The permuted system is equally useful for solving the original linear system, with the triangular solution phase simply becoming

$$\bar{L}y = Pb, \quad \bar{L}^T z = y, \quad x = P^T z.$$

Unfortunately, finding a permutation P that minimizes fill is a very difficult combinatorial problem (an NP-complete problem) [107]. Thus, a great deal of research effort has been devoted to developing good heuristics for limiting fill in sparse Cholesky factorization, including the nested dissection algorithm [39,45] and the minimum degree algorithm [48,70,98]. Limiting fill is also the primary motivation for a number of methods based on reducing the bandwidth or profile of A. These band-oriented methods have been less successful, however, than the more general sparse ordering techniques, and as we shall see, they are at an even greater disadvantage in a parallel context.

Since pivoting is not required in the factorization process, once the ordering is known, the precise locations of all fill entries in L can be predicted in advance[1], so that a data structure can be set up to accommodate L before any numeric computation begins. This data structure need not be modified during subsequent computations, which is a distinct advantage in terms of efficiency. The process by which the nonzero structure of L is determined in advance is called "symbolic factorization." Thus, the direct solution of $Ax = b$ consists of the following sequence of four distinct steps:

1. *Ordering*: Find a good ordering P for A; that is, determine a permutation matrix P so that the Cholesky factor L of PAP^T suffers little fill.
2. *Symbolic Factorization*: Determine the structure of L and set up a data structure in which to store A and compute the nonzero entries of L.
3. *Numeric Factorization*: Insert the nonzeros of A into the data structure and compute the Cholesky factor L of PAP^T.
4. *Triangular Solution*: Solve $Ly = Pb$ and $L^T z = y$, and then set $x = P^T z$.

Note that the first two steps are entirely symbolic, involving no floating-point computation. Several software packages [17,27,29] for serial computers use this basic approach to solve sparse symmetric positive definite linear systems. We now briefly discuss algorithms and methods for performing each of these steps on sequential machines.

2.1. Ordering. As one might expect from the combinatorial nature of the ordering problem for sparse factorization, graph theory has proved to be an extremely helpful tool in modeling the symbolic or structural aspects of sparse elimination algorithms. The use of a graph theoretic model dates to the early work of Parter [91] and Rose [97], and has now come to permeate the subject. The graph of an $n \times n$ symmetric matrix A, denoted by $G(A)$, is a labelled undirected graph having n vertices (or nodes), with an edge between two vertices i and j if the corresponding entry a_{ij} is nonzero in the matrix. The structural effect of Gaussian elimination on the matrix is then easily described in terms of the corresponding graph. The fill introduced into the matrix as a result of eliminating a variable adds fill edges to the corresponding graph precisely so that the neighbors of the eliminated vertex become a clique. This fact suggests that fill can be limited, or at least postponed, by eliminating first those vertices having fewest neighbors (i.e., vertices of lowest degree). The elimination or factorization process can thus be modeled by a sequence of graphs, each having one less vertex than the previous graph but possibly gaining edges, until only one vertex remains. We will also have occasion to refer to the *filled graph*, $F(A)$, which is the graph of A with all fill edges added (i.e., there is an edge between two vertices i and j of $F(A)$, with $i > j$, if $\ell_{ij} \neq 0$ in the Cholesky factor matrix L).

---

[1] We assume that exact cancellation never occurs, and thus *fill* refers to the *structural nonzeros* of L, i.e., every location of the factor that is occupied by a nonzero entry at some point in the factorization.

The foregoing discussion provides the basis for the minimum degree algorithm, which is the most successful and widely applicable heuristic developed to date for limiting fill in sparse Cholesky factorization. At each step of the elimination process, this simple heuristic selects as the next node to be eliminated a node of minimum degree in the current elimination graph. Despite its simplicity, the minimum degree algorithm produces reasonably good orderings over a remarkably broad range of problem classes. Another strength is its efficiency: as a result of a number of refinements over several years, current implementations are extremely efficient on most problems. George and Liu [48] review a series of enhancements to implementations of the minimum degree algorithm and demonstrate the consequent reductions in ordering time.

As might be expected from the "greedy" nature of the algorithm, however, several weaknesses of the minimum degree ordering heuristic are well documented in the literature. Experiments in both [24] and [48] illustrate the sensitivity of the quality of minimum degree orderings to the way ties are broken when there is more than one node of minimum degree from which to choose. Attempts to make the selection more intelligent or less myopic, however, have proven to be computationally expensive. No tie-breaking scheme proposed to date is both effective and efficient, though some interesting results using deficiency (the number of fill edges created by the elimination step) to break ties are reported in [15]. Berman and Schnitger [13] show that for a model problem there exists a minimum degree tie-breaking scheme for which the time and space complexity of the factorization is worse than that of known asymptotically optimal orderings. To summarize, minimum degree is, on balance, an effective and efficient ordering heuristic, but its success is not well understood, and no robust and efficient way is known for dealing with the wide variability in the quality of the orderings it produces.

Another effective algorithm for limiting fill in Cholesky factorization is nested dissection, which is based on a divide-and-conquer paradigm. Let S be a set of nodes (called a separator) whose removal, along with all edges incident on nodes in S, divides the graph into at least two remaining pieces. If the matrix is reordered so that the variables in each piece are numbered contiguously and the variables in the separator are numbered last, then the matrix will have a bordered block diagonal nonzero pattern. More importantly, elimination of a node within one of the pieces cannot introduce fill into any of the other pieces; fill is restricted to the diagonal blocks and the border [47,99]. This idea can be applied recursively, breaking the pieces into smaller and smaller pieces with successive sets of separators, giving a nested sequence of dissections of the graph. The effectiveness of nested dissection in limiting fill is highly dependent on the size of the separators used to split the graph. For highly regular, planar problems (e.g., two-dimensional finite difference or finite element grids), suitably small separators can usually be found [68,69]. For problems in dimensions higher than two, or for highly irregular problems with less localized connectivity, nested dissection is much less effective. Nevertheless, nested dissection is important not only for its practical usefulness on suitable problems, but also for its asymptotically optimal fill properties for certain model problems, which serves as a kind of theoretical benchmark for the quality of orderings [39,60].

2.2. Symbolic Factorization. A naive approach to symbolic factorization is simply to carry out Cholesky factorization on the structure of A symbolically. However, such an algorithm would then have the same time complexity as the numeric factorization itself (i.e., it would require the same number of symbolic operations as the number of floating-point operations required by the numeric factorization). With a little care, the complexity of symbolic factorization can be reduced to $O(\eta(L))$, where $\eta(L)$ denotes the number of nonzeros in L, as follows.

For a given sparse matrix M, define

$$Struct(M_{i*}) := \{k < i \mid m_{ik} \neq 0\}$$

and

$$Struct(M_{*j}) := \{k > j \mid m_{kj} \neq 0\}.$$

In other words, $Struct(M_{i*})$ is the sparsity structure of row i of the strict lower triangle of M, and $Struct(M_{*j})$ is the sparsity structure of column j of the strict lower triangle of M. For a given lower triangular Cholesky factor matrix L, define the function p as follows:

$$p(j) := \begin{cases} \min\{i \in Struct(L_{*j})\}, & \text{if } Struct(L_{*j}) \neq \emptyset, \\ j, & \text{otherwise.} \end{cases}$$

Thus, when there is at least one off-diagonal nonzero in column j of L, $p(j)$ is the row index of the first off-diagonal nonzero in that column. It is easy to show that

$$Struct(L_{*j}) \subseteq Struct(L_{*,p(j)}) \cup \{p(j)\}.$$

Moreover, it can be shown that the structure of column j of L can be characterized as follows [47]:

$$Struct(L_{*j}) := Struct(A_{*j}) \cup \left(\bigcup_{i<j} \{Struct(L_{*i}) \mid p(i) = j\} \right) - \{j\}.$$

That is, the structure of column j of L is given by the structure of the lower triangular portion of column j of A, together with the structure of each column of L whose first off-diagonal nonzero is in row j. This characterization leads directly to an algorithm for performing the symbolic factorization, shown in Figure 1, in which the sets R_j are used to record the columns of L whose structures will affect that of column j of L.

> **for** $j := 1$ **to** n **do**
> $\quad R_j := \emptyset$
> **for** $j := 1$ **to** n **do**
> $\quad S := Struct(A_{*j})$
> $\quad$ **for** $i \in R_j$ **do**
> $\quad\quad S := S \cup Struct(L_{*i}) - \{j\}$
> $\quad Struct(L_{*j}) := S$
> $\quad$ **if** $Struct(L_{*j}) \neq \emptyset$ **then**
> $\quad\quad p(j) := \min\{i \in Struct(L_{*j})\}$
> $\quad\quad R_{p(j)} := R_{p(j)} \cup \{j\}$

FIG. 1. *Symbolic factorization algorithm.*

This simple symbolic factorization algorithm is already very efficient, with time and space complexity $O(\eta(L))$, but it is subject to further refinement. For example, if R_j contains only one column, say i, and $Struct(A_{*j}) \subseteq Struct(L_{*i})$, then clearly $Struct(L_{*j}) = Struct(L_{*i}) - \{j\}$. This shortcut can be used to speed up the symbolic factorization algorithm and to reduce the storage requirements using a technique known as "subscript compression" [104]. In fact, these conditions are often satisfied when j is relatively large, as the columns tend to become more dense toward the end of the factorization. An efficient implementation of the symbolic factorization algorithm is presented in [47]. With its low complexity and an efficient implementation, the symbolic factorization step usually requires less computation than any of the other three steps in solving a symmetric positive definite system by Cholesky factorization.

Once the structure of L is known, a compact data structure is set up to accommodate all of its nonzero entries. Since only the nonzero entries of the matrix are stored, additional indexing information must be stored to indicate the locations of the nonzeros. Although this integer overhead potentially rivals the space requirements for the nonzeros themselves, in practice the subscript compression technique mentioned above greatly reduces this overhead storage [46].

2.3. Numeric Factorization. In its simplest form, Gaussian elimination on a dense matrix A can be described as a triple nested loop around the single statement

$$a_{ij} = a_{ij} - (a_{ik}a_{kj})/a_{kk}.$$

The loop indices i, j, and k can be nested in any order, each with a different pattern of memory access. This freedom can be exploited to take better advantage of particular architectural features of a given machine (cache, virtual memory, vectorization, etc.) [21]. Specializing to Cholesky factorization, where symmetry is exploited so that only the lower triangle of the matrix is accessed, we see that there are three basic types of algorithms, depending on which of the three indices is placed in the outer loop:

1. *Row-Cholesky*: Taking i in the outer loop, successive rows of L are computed one by one, with the inner loops solving a triangular system for each new row in terms of the previously computed rows.
2. *Column-Cholesky*: Taking j in the outer loop, successive columns of L are computed one by one, with the inner loops computing a matrix-vector product that gives the effect of previously computed columns on the column currently being computed.
3. *Submatrix-Cholesky*: Taking k in the outer loop, successive columns of L are computed one by one, with the inner loops applying the current column as a rank-1 update to the remaining partially-reduced submatrix.

These three families of algorithms have markedly different memory reference patterns in terms of which parts of the matrix are accessed and modified at each stage of the factorization (see Figure 2), and each has its advantages and disadvantages in a given context. For sparse Cholesky factorization, row-Cholesky is seldom used because of the difficulty in designing a compact row-oriented data structure for storing the nonzeros of L that can also be accessed efficiently in the numerical factorization phase [71]. Efficient implementation of sparse row-Cholesky is even more difficult on vector and parallel architectures since it is difficult to vectorize or parallelize sparse triangular solutions (see discussions in Sections 2.4 and 3.5). We will therefore concentrate our attention on the two column-oriented methods, column-Cholesky and submatrix-Cholesky.

In column-oriented Cholesky factorization algorithms, there are two fundamental types of subtasks:

1. $cmod(j, k)$: modification of column j by column k, $k < j$,

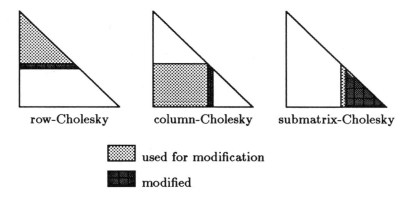

row-Cholesky   column-Cholesky   submatrix-Cholesky

used for modification

modified

FIG. 2. *Three forms of Cholesky factorization.*

2. $cdiv(j)$: division of column j by a scalar.

These sparse matrix operations correspond to **saxpy** and **sscal** in the terminology of the BLAS [64] for dense linear algebra, but we use different notation to emphasize that we are dealing with their sparse counterparts. In terms of these basic operations, high-level descriptions of the column-Cholesky and submatrix-Cholesky algorithms are given in Figures 3 and 4.

> **for** $j = 1$ **to** n **do**
>   **for** $k \in Struct(L_{j*})$ **do**
> $cmod(j, k)$
> $cdiv(j)$

FIG. 3. *Sparse column-Cholesky factorization algorithm.*

> **for** $k = 1$ **to** n **do**
> $cdiv(k)$
>   **for** $j \in Struct(L_{*k})$ **do**
> $cmod(j, k)$

FIG. 4. *Sparse submatrix-Cholesky factorization algorithm.*

In column-Cholesky, column j of A remains unchanged until the index of the outer loop takes on that particular value. At that point the algorithm updates column j with a nonzero multiple of each column $k < j$ of L for which $\ell_{jk} \neq 0$. After all column modifications have been applied to column j, the diagonal entry ℓ_{jj} is computed and used to scale the completely updated column to obtain the remaining nonzero entries of L_{*j}. Column-Cholesky is sometimes said to be a "left-looking" algorithm, since at each stage it accesses needed columns to the left of the current column in the matrix. It can also be viewed as a "demand-driven" algorithm, since the inner products that affect a given column are not accumulated until actually needed to modify and complete that column. It is also sometimes referred to as a "fan-in" algorithm, since the basic operation is to combine the effects of multiple previous columns on a single subsequent column. The column-Cholesky algorithm is the most commonly used method in commercially available sparse matrix packages [17,27,29].

In submatrix-Cholesky, as soon as column k is completed, its effects on all subsequent columns are computed immediately. Thus, submatrix-Cholesky is sometimes said to be a "right-looking" algorithm, since at each stage columns to the right of the current column are modified. It can also be viewed as a "data-driven" algorithm, since each new column is used as soon as it is completed to make all modifications to all the subsequent columns it affects. It is also sometimes referred to as a "fan-out" algorithm, since the basic operation is for a single column to affect multiple subsequent columns. We will see that these characterizations of the column-Cholesky and submatrix-Cholesky algorithms have important implications for parallel implementations.

Having stated the "pure" column- and submatrix-Cholesky algorithms, we note that many variations and hybrid implementations of these schemes are possible, which essentially amount to different ways of amalgamating partial results. For example, frontal methods [61], and their generalizations to multifrontal methods [28], are essentially variations on submatrix-Cholesky. But while the $cmod(j, k)$ updating operations are computed in the order shown in Figure 4, they are not applied directly to the column j being updated. Instead they are accumulated and passed on through a succession of update matrices until finally they are incorporated into the target column. The reason for this approach is that in the frontal method most of the matrix is kept out of core on auxiliary storage, with only a relatively small "frontal" matrix representing currently "active" columns kept in main memory. Similarly, the out-of-core version of the multifrontal method can be implemented so that only a few small "frontal" matrices are kept in main memory. To minimize I/O traffic, access to inactive portions of the matrix, both columns already completed and columns yet unreduced, must be kept to a minimum. For further details on multifrontal methods, see [28] or [78].

One of the main motivations for frontal and multifrontal methods is that the frontal matrices can be treated as dense, and therefore one can take advantage of vectorization more readily on hardware that supports it [3,5,11,19]. Moreover, the localization of memory references in these methods is advantageous in exploiting cache [100] or on machines with virtual memory and paging [76].

Before leaving the general topic of sparse factorization, we introduce two additional concepts that are useful in analyzing and efficiently implementing sparse factorization algorithms. A *supernode* is a set of contiguous columns in the Cholesky factor L that share essentially the same sparsity structure. More specifically, the set of contiguous columns $j, j + 1, \ldots, j + t$ constitutes a supernode if $Struct(L_{*,k}) = Struct(L_{*,k+1}) \cup \{k + 1\}$ for $j \leq k \leq j + t - 1$. A set of supernodes for an example matrix is shown in Figure 5. Columns in the same supernode can be treated as a unit for both computation and storage. Supernodes have long played an important role in enhancing the efficiency of both the minimum degree ordering [50] and the symbolic factorization [104]. More recently, supernodes have been used to organize sparse factorization algorithms around matrix-vector or matrix-matrix operations that reduce memory traffic by making more efficient use of vector registers [5,11] or cache [3,100]. The cited reports document the substantial gains in performance obtained by using these techniques.

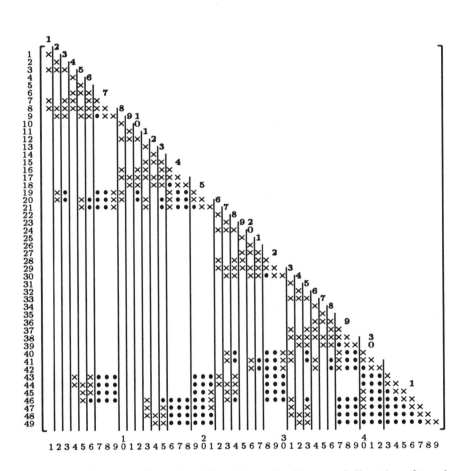

FIG. 5. *Supernodes for 7 × 7 nine-point grid problem ordered by nested dissection. (× and ● refer to nonzeros in A and fill in L, respectively. Numbers over diagonal entries label supernodes.)*

The *elimination tree* $T(A)$ [71,103] associated with the Cholesky factor L of a given matrix A has $\{1, 2, \ldots, n\}$ as its node set, and has an edge between two vertices i and j, with $i > j$, if $i = p(j)$, where p is the function defined in Section 2.2. In this case, node i is said to be the *parent* of node j, and node j is a *child* of node i. Liu [79] discusses the many uses of elimination trees in sparse matrix computations. Among these is their use in managing the frontal and update matrices in the multifrontal method. Another key role is in the analysis of data dependencies that must be observed when factoring the matrix, which has obvious implications for implementing the factorization in parallel. Figure 6 shows the elimination tree for the matrix shown in Figure 5.

Let $T[j]$ denote the subtree of $T(A)$ rooted at node j. It is shown in [71] and [103] that the set of columns/nodes that modify column/node j (namely, the set $Struct(L_{j*})$) is a subset of $T[j]$ denoted by $T_r[j]$. Moreover, $T_r[j]$ is also a subtree of $T(A)$ rooted at node j. For this reason, $T_r[j]$ is called the *row subtree of j*. It follows that column j can be completed only after every column in $T_r[j]$ has been computed. It also follows that the columns that receive updates from column j are ancestors of j in $T(A)$. In other words, the node set $Struct(L_{*j})$ is a subset of the ancestors of j in the tree.

2.4. Triangular Solution. There is relatively little to be said about the triangular solution step. The structure of the forward and back substitution algorithms is more or less dictated by the sparse data structure used to store the triangular Cholesky factor L and by the structure of the elimination tree $T(A)$. Because triangular solution requires many fewer floating-point operations than the factorization step that precedes it, the triangular solution step usually requires only a small fraction of the total time to solve a sparse linear system on conventional sequential computers. These proportions can change, however, with more advanced computer architectures, since it is often more difficult to take full advantage of vector or parallel processors in performing triangular solutions. We will discuss these issues in greater detail in Section 3.5.

3. Parallel Algorithms. In this section we summarize the progress to date in adapting direct methods for the solution of sparse symmetric positive definite linear systems to perform well on the various parallel architectures that have become available in recent years. The most widely available and commercially successful parallel architectures thus far fall into three rough categories: shared-memory MIMD (multiple-instruction, multiple-data stream) architectures typically having 30 or fewer processors, distributed-memory MIMD architectures typically having on the order of 32 to 1024 processors, and SIMD (single-instruction, multiple-data stream) architectures typically having tens of thousands of processors. Some machines have an additional level of parallelism in the form of vector units within each individual processor. Parallel architectures display an enormous variation in the number and power of processors, organization of memory, control mechanisms, and synchronization and communication overhead, so it is not surprising that they demand a comparable range of algorithmic techniques to achieve good efficiency in the various settings. Nevertheless, we will try to concentrate on general principles that are widely applicable, while focusing occasionally on implementation issues that may arise in a more specific context.

In exploiting parallelism to solve any problem, the computational work must be broken into a number of subtasks that can be assigned to separate processors. The most appropriate number and size of these tasks (e.g., a small number of large tasks

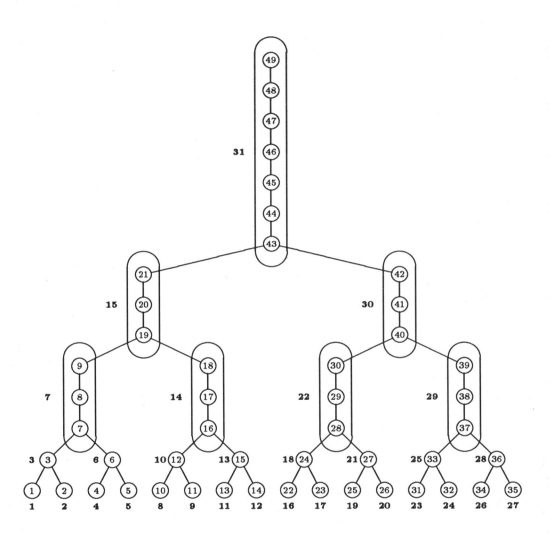

FIG. 6. *Elimination tree for the matrix shown in Figure 5. Ovals enclose supernodes that contain more than one node. Nodes not enclosed by an oval are singleton supernodes. Bold-face numbers label supernodes.*

or a large number of small tasks) depend on the target parallel architecture and the levels at which parallelism naturally occurs in the problem. The term often used to denote the size of computational tasks in a parallel implementation is *granularity*. In sparse factorization, as in most problems, a number of levels of computational granularity can potentially be exploited. Liu [72] uses the elimination tree to analyze the following levels of parallelism in Cholesky factorization:

1. *fine-grain parallelism*, in which each task is a single floating-point operation or *flop*, i.e., multiply-add pair,
2. *medium-grain parallelism*, in which each task is a single *cmod* or *cdiv* column operation,
3. *large-grain parallelism*, in which each task is the completion of all columns in a subtree of the elimination tree.

Here, large-grain parallelism refers to the independent work done in computing columns in disjoint subtrees. Consider two disjoint subtrees $T[j]$ and $T[i]$, where neither root node is a descendent of the other. All work required to compute the columns of $T[j]$ is completely independent of all work required to compute the columns of $T[i]$. For example, in Figure 6 the columns of $T[9]$ (columns 1–9) are completely independent of the columns of $T[18]$ (columns 10–18). This type of parallelism is available only in sparse factorization; it is not available in the dense case. But of course we are not limited to exploiting only parallelism of this nature. There is much more parallelism to be found at the medium-grain level of the individual *cmod* operations. Let j_1 and j_2 be two column indices whose subtrees $T[j_1]$ and $T[j_2]$ are *not* disjoint. Suppose that k_1 and k_2 are indices of columns that must be used to modify columns j_1 and j_2, respectively. Clearly, the updates $cmod(j_1, k_1)$ and $cmod(j_2, k_2)$ can be performed in parallel. This is the primary source of parallelism in the dense case, and it is an extremely important source of parallelism in the sparse case as well.

While we will have a great deal to say about algorithms that employ the first two sources of parallelism, we will have little to say about finer grain parallelism. Fine grain parallelism can be exploited in two distinctly different ways:

1. vectorization of the column operations *cmod* and *cdiv* on vector supercomputers,
2. parallelizing the rank-one update that constitutes a major step of submatrix-Cholesky on an SIMD machine.

Exploiting vectorization requires some changes and refinement of the basic sequential algorithms [3,5,11,19], but it does not require changes as extensive and basic as those required to exploit higher levels of parallelism. Developing parallel sparse submatrix-Cholesky algorithms for SIMD machines presents a more difficult challenge, and research on this topic is still in its infancy [54].

To date, implementation on parallel architectures has caused no fundamental change in the overall high-level approach to solving sparse symmetric positive definite linear systems. On parallel machines the same sequence of four distinct steps is performed: ordering, symbolic factorization, numeric factorization, and triangular solution. However, both shared-memory and distributed-memory MIMD machines require an additional step to be performed: the tasks into which the problem is decomposed must be mapped onto the processors. Obviously, one of the goals in mapping the problem onto the processors is to ensure that the work load is balanced across all processors. Moreover, it is desirable to schedule the problem so that the amount of synchronization and/or communication is low. On shared-memory machines the scheduling problem is relatively easy to deal with: a shared queue of tasks

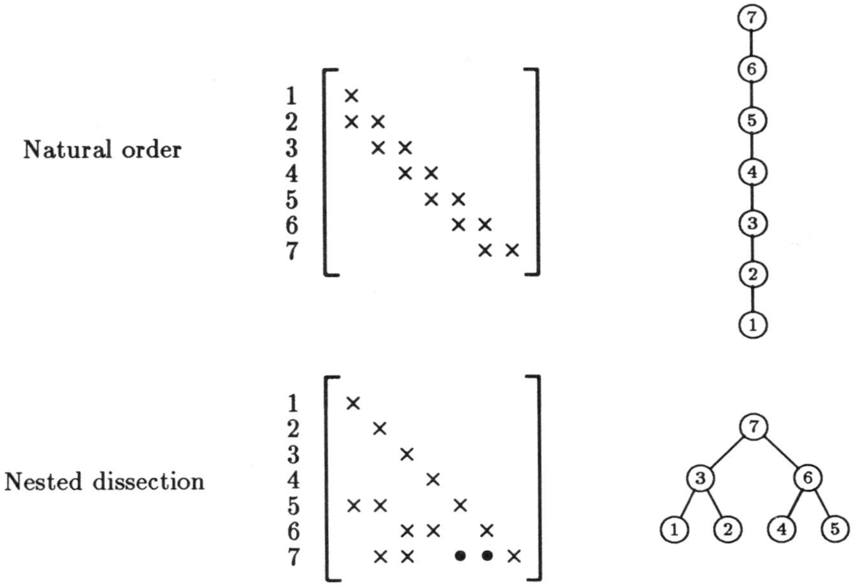

FIG. 7. *Factor matrices and corresponding elimination trees for tridiagonal matrix using natural ordering and nested dissection reordering (even-odd reduction).* × *and* • *refer to original nonzeros and fill nonzeros, respectively.*

can be used to achieve dynamic load balancing. Dynamic load balancing tends to be inefficient on current distributed-memory machines, however, so a static assignment of tasks to processors must be determined in advance.

We now proceed to discuss the progress made in developing parallel algorithms for each of these five steps.

3.1. Ordering. There are two distinct issues associated with the ordering problem in a parallel environment:

1. Determining an ordering appropriate for performing the subsequent factorization efficiently on the parallel architecture in question.
2. Computing the ordering itself *in parallel*.

3.1.1. Orderings for parallel factorization. On sequential or vector machines, while there are sometimes other secondary considerations, the primary goal of reordering the matrix is simply to lower the work and space required for the factorization step. Experience and intuition suggest that the two almost inevitably rise and fall together, so that the goal can be further simplified to lowering fill only. Simply lowering fill, however, may not provide an ordering appropriate for parallel factorization.

Orderings for a tridiagonal system serve to illustrate the point. Let us call the ordering that preserves the tridiagonal structure the *natural ordering*. Under the natural ordering, the matrix incurs no fill during factorization. In fact, both the fill and work are minimized. Nevertheless, the natural ordering is the poorest possible ordering for parallel factorization. First, note that the natural ordering results in an elimination tree that is a *chain* (see Figure 7). Indeed, there is no large-grain (subtree-level parallelism) to exploit. Moreover each column j, $2 \leq j \leq n$, requires a single column modification $cmod(j, j - 1)$ before it can be completed with the $cdiv(j)$ operation, then and only then becoming available for the subsequent column modification $cmod(j + 1, j)$. Thus, there is no medium-grain (column-modification level) parallelism to exploit. There is also no fine-grain parallelism to exploit. Thus, there is no parallelism at all to exploit in the floating-point computation; the floating-point work is strictly sequential. But it is well known that even-odd reduction schemes for these systems, though they introduce more work, also greatly increase the parallelism. These solution schemes are equivalent to reordering the system with a nested dissection ordering (again, see Figure 7). Using the nested dissection ordering, the height of the elimination tree is approximately $\log_2 n$, which is much shorter than the height $n - 1$ obtained using the natural ordering. While the total floating-point work (ignoring square roots) increases by a factor between two and three, parallel completion time using the nested dissection ordering is ideally $O(\log n)$ compared with $O(n)$ using the standard ordering.

This example is an extreme illustration of how inappropriate the goal of fill-reduction can be in the parallel setting. However, there have been no systematic attempts to develop metrics for measuring the quality of parallel orderings. Thus far, most work on the parallel ordering problem has used elimination tree height as the criterion for comparing orderings, with short trees assumed to be superior to taller trees [62,65,77,80], but with little more than intuition as a basis for this choice. For massively parallel SIMD machines, it has been suggested that small elimination tree height may indeed be a suitable goal [54,65]. This contention is based on the assumption of a submatrix-Cholesky parallel factorization algorithm that requires roughly uniform time for the elimination of each column. It remains to be shown that this assumption is in fact realized for sparse problems on available SIMD machines. The assumption is more doubtful on other parallel architectures. Moreover, it is worth noting that the problem of ordering a matrix to minimize its elimination tree height, like the problem of minimizing fill, is a very difficult combinatorial problem [93]. In [77], Liu suggests some more realistic measures of *parallel completion time*, but there is not yet an agreed upon objective function for the parallel ordering problem.

3.1.2. Computing the ordering in parallel. A separate problem is the need to compute the ordering in parallel on the same machine on which the other steps of the solution process are to be performed. The highly sophisticated ordering algorithms discussed earlier, namely minimum degree and nested dissection, are extremely efficient and normally constitute only a small fraction of the total execution time in solving a sparse system on sequential computers. Despite the limited potential for any gain in execution time, however, there is still motivation for adapting these algorithms, or developing new ones, to run on parallel architectures, especially in the case of distributed-memory machines. In particular, a distributed implementation of the ordering step is necessary to take advantage of the large amount of local memory available on such machines in solving very large problems. Otherwise, the ordering step will remain a bottleneck limiting the size of problems that can be solved on distributed-memory parallel architectures. We now consider some of the difficulties in performing the ordering step efficiently in parallel.

The basic minimum degree algorithm has an inherently sequential outer loop, with a single node eliminated at each stage. Multiple elimination of independent nodes of minimum or near-minimum degree [70,92] could potentially be exploited to permit parallel execution. Moreover, the search for nodes of minimum degree and the necessary graph transformations and degree updates could conceivably be spread across multiple processors. However, there are several problems with this approach. First, it is not clear that minimum degree orderings would be particularly appropriate for parallel factorization. For example, applying the basic minimum degree algorithm to the tridiagonal system discussed above produces an elimination tree that is a chain, and thus the resulting elimination tree height would be at least $\lfloor n/2 \rfloor$. Duff et al. [26] contains several suggestions for dealing with this problem, the most promising of which increases the size of the independent sets by allowing all nodes whose degree are within a constant factor α of the current minimum degree, where $1.1 \leq \alpha \leq 1.5$, to be candidates for inclusion in the next independent set. A different approach for computing independent sets for parallel elimination is described in [66]. Second, the highly successful enhancements incorporated into current implementations of the method [48] have resulted in an intricate and extremely efficient algorithm: there is very little work to be partitioned among the processors, and that work is of a highly irregular and somewhat sequential nature. Nevertheless, an algorithm based on this approach has been developed for use on a massively parallel SIMD machine [54]. It is possible that such an approach could also be reasonably effective on some shared-memory MIMD machines, but we know of no such implementations. It is doubtful, however, that this approach would have acceptable efficiency on distributed-memory MIMD machines, and we are not aware of any attempt to produce such an implementation. It is ironic that much of the research on parallel algorithms for sparse factorization has been performed on the latter class of machines, yet it is on this class of machines that the ordering problem seems most difficult to address.

The standard nested dissection ordering heuristic [45] would appear to offer much greater opportunity for an effective parallel implementation. The divide-and-conquer paradigm introduces a natural source of parallelism, both in computing the ordering and in subsequently using it for the factorization step, due to the independence of the successive pieces into which the graph is split. Unfortunately, there are also difficulties with this approach. First, the nested dissection heuristic (based on the generation of level structures) is effective in reducing fill for a much more restricted class of problems than minimum degree. Second, the divide-and-conquer approach provides only a logarithmic potential speedup, with relatively little parallelism in the first few levels of the dissection. Third, for a distributed-memory implementation there is something of a bootstrapping problem: in order to utilize all of the local memory and simultaneously minimize interprocessor communication costs, the original graph should be distributed across the processors in some intelligent way *before* the dissection process is begun. Finally, nested dissection is similar to minimum degree in that it enjoys a very efficient sequential implementation, and its primary subtask (generating a level structure via breadth-first search) is inherently serial.

To summarize this discussion, it is evident that the problem of computing effective parallel orderings *in parallel* is very difficult and remains largely untouched by research efforts to date. We focus our attention in the remainder of this section on the effectiveness of various ordering strategies in facilitating the subsequent parallel factorization, with little regard for whether the ordering can itself be computed effectively in parallel.

3.1.3. Parallel ordering algorithms. We now turn our attention to the problem of ordering for parallel factorization and/or executing the ordering algorithms on the target parallel machine. As noted above, these problems are very difficult to deal with, and much work remains to be done before mature, reliable algorithms and software become available.

Tree restructuring for parallel elimination. One approach to generating low-fill orderings that are suitable for parallel sparse factorization is to decouple the reduction of fill and enhancement of parallelism into separate phases. First a standard ordering technique, such as minimum degree, is applied to produce a low-fill ordering for the matrix, then based on this initial ordering an *equivalent* reordering is produced that is more suitable for parallel factorization. By "equivalent" we mean an ordering that generates the same fill edges but may substantially restructure the elimination tree. Thus, an equivalent ordering is simply a different perfect elimination ordering for the filled graph $F(A)$ that models the sparsity structure of L determined by the initial fill-reducing ordering. The effectiveness of this approach depends in part on whether there is in fact a good parallel ordering within the class of orderings equivalent to the initial low-fill ordering. The tridiagonal example cited earlier demonstrates that there may be no such ordering. On the other hand, since some of the parallelism in sparse factorization is due specifically to sparsity, low-fill would seem to enhance potential parallelism rather than suppress it. Very little is known, however, about the conditions under which good equivalent parallel orderings might exist for realistic classes of problems.

Implementation of the equivalent ordering approach requires an initial fill-reducing ordering, a mechanism for restructuring the elimination tree, and a computable criterion for determining when a given reordering will in fact reduce the subsequent parallel factorization time. In [77], Liu uses tree rotations [73] to find equivalent orderings that reduce elimination tree height, where the initial ordering used is a minimum degree ordering. He reports substantial reductions for a number of test problems. In the same report, Liu proves that the Jess and Kees algorithm [62] produces an equivalent ordering whose associated elimination tree height is *minimum* among all equivalent orderings. In [80] Liu and Mirzaian present a practical $O(\eta(L))$ implementation of the Jess and Kees algorithm. Tests comparing Liu's tree rotations heuristic with their implementation of the Jess and Kees algorithm showed that the heuristic almost always produces a minimum-height tree. This interesting phenomenon is not fully understood. Their timings showed the tree rotations heuristic to be far more efficient than their implementation of the Jess and Kees algorithm. In [67] a more efficient implementation of the Jess and Kees algorithm is presented. Roughly speaking, the latter implementation is linear in the number of compressed subscripts used to represent the structure of L. Tests of this implementation indicate that a Jess and Kees ordering can usually be obtained in roughly the same amount of time as an ordering using the tree rotations heuristic.

Of course, the height of the elimination tree may not be a very accurate indicator of the actual parallel factorization time. Moreover, elimination trees produced by minimum degree orderings typically have height already close to the minimum, so that the potential gain from restructuring may be quite small. Perhaps the primary problem with this approach is that it fails to get at the heart of the problem. Our intuition based on limited experience is that equivalent orderings have the capacity to modify only relatively minor features of the parallelism possessed by the initial fill-reducing ordering. Thus, this approach may be able to fine-tune an ordering for use in parallel factorization, but the key question of how much parallelism might be available in the original underlying problem goes unanswered.

Nested dissection and graph partitioning heuristics. Given the natural divide-and-conquer parallelism exhibited by nested dissection, several researchers have explored various implementations of nested dissection in an effort to generate good orderings for parallel factorization. The effectiveness of nested dissection in reducing fill and enhancing parallelism depends on graph partitioning heuristics to find small node separators for the graph. Some of the graph partitioning heuristics employed in fact produce edge separators, which then must be converted into node separators.

The basic scheme in nested dissection is as follows:

1. Use a graph partitioning heuristic to obtain a small edge separator of the graph, or more specifically, a small set of edges whose removal from the graph separates the graph into two vertex sets of roughly equal size.
2. Transform the small edge separator into a small node separator, or more specifically, a small set of nodes whose removal separates the graph into two portions of roughly equal size.
3. Number the nodes of the separator last in the ordering, and recursively apply steps 1 and 2 to the two subgraphs produced in step 2.

We now review some specific implementations of this approach.

Level structures. In [44] the adaptation of an automatic nested dissection algorithm [45] for execution on distributed-memory MIMD machines is discussed. The algorithm first generates a level structure by means of a breadth-first search. The choice of starting node in the search can be crucial; see [45] for details. Then one of the middle levels is chosen as a node separator, subdividing the problem into two or more independents subgraphs, to which the process is applied recursively. This method generates a node separator directly, and therefore omits step 1 from the general scheme given above. An advantage of this method is that it is simple and generally inexpensive to compute. But the automatic nested dissection heuristic is generally not as effective at reducing fill as the minimum degree heuristic, and thus the quality of the ordering is poorer on many, but not all, problems. As with most nested dissection algorithms, the algorithm for finding a separator appears to be inherently sequential. Thus, there is little parallelism to exploit until the ordering algorithm is several levels down into the recursion, where there are adequately many independent subproblems to work on.

Kernighan-Lin. Gilbert and Zmijewski [55] use the Kernighan-Lin heuristic [63] to generate a small edge separator. Associated with an edge separator are *wide* and *narrow* node separators, defined as follows. Let P_1 and P_2 be the two sets of nodes into which the edge separator partitions the graph. Let V_1 contain the nodes in P_1 incident on at least one edge in the separator set, and define $V_2 \subset P_2$ in the same way. The set $V = V_1 \cup V_2$ is the associated wide separator and both V_1 and V_2 are the associated narrow separators. Gilbert and Zmijewski ran tests using both kinds of separators and report ordering times and factorization times on an Intel iPSC/1 hypercube.

Fiduccia-Mattheyses. Lewis and Leiserson [65] use a variant of the Kernighan-Lin heuristic due to Fiduccia-Mattheyses [31] to generate edge separators. They use a greedy heuristic to generate node separators from edge separators. Their heuristic is guaranteed to find a *minimal* node separator among the nodes belonging to $V = V_1 \cup V_2$. In their tests they use elimination tree height to compare the quality of their orderings with those obtained by using tree rotations to reduce the elimination tree height of minimum degree orderings. They report fairly substantial and consistent reductions in tree height for their test problems. However, they did not implement their algorithm on a parallel machine; all their tests were run on an unspecified sequential machine and no timings results were reported.

Spectral separators. Pothen, Simon and Liou [95] study the use of *spectral partitions* [32,33] in the framework described above. To generate an edge separator, they first compute the eigenvector y associated with the smallest positive eigenvalue of the Laplacian matrix associated with the $G(A)$. They use an implementation of the Lanczos algorithm to compute the required eigenvector for general sparse graphs. Then the median entry y_m of y is found, and the vertices in P_1 are taken to be those corresponding to entries y_i of y for which $y_i < y_m$, while the vertices in P_2 are those corresponding to entries y_i of y for which $y_i \geq y_m$. The authors use matching theory for bipartite graphs, in particular the Dulmage-Mendelsohn decomposition, to generate from the edge separator a minimum-cardinality node separator [94]. Thus, their bipartite-matching method for transforming an edge separator into a node separator is optimal in the sense that it minimizes the size of the node separator over all possible node separators that can be obtained from the given edge separator (i.e., over all separators contained in the set of nodes incident on the separator edges). The report cited here does not include statistics for complete nested dissection orderings based on this technique; it includes statistics for the top-level separator only. Since most of the time is spent performing Lanczos iterations, which can be parallelized in a fairly straightforward manner, their method should run efficiently in parallel even in the top few levels of the nested dissection recursion.

A hybrid approach. In [74] and [75] Liu presents a hybrid approach that combines elements of both the minimum degree and nested dissection algorithms. The primary emphasis of the two papers is simply to produce improved fill-reducing orderings, but the application of the method to parallel factorization is noted in both papers. The method proceeds as follows. After a standard minimum degree ordering algorithm is initially applied to the problem, a "middle" separator determined by the minimum degree ordering is chosen. A technique based on matching theory for bipartite graphs is then used to improve (i.e., shrink) this separator. The nodes of the new separator are numbered last in the ordering, and then the process is applied recursively to the subproblems remaining to be ordered.

This method generates a nested dissection ordering (a top-down ordering), but uses a minimum degree ordering (a bottom-up ordering), along with some matching theory, to obtain the separators. Thus, it is a hybrid of two very different ordering techniques. Again, computing the ordering in parallel with this approach appears to be very difficult. However, the timings and ordering statistics reported indicate that it obtains good orderings in a reasonably efficient manner on a sequential machine.

3.2. Task Partitioning and Scheduling.

3.2.1. Shared-memory MIMD machines.
In implementing sparse column-Cholesky on a shared-memory MIMD machine, the problem of partitioning the factorization into tasks for concurrent execution on multiple processors is fairly simple. Each column j corresponds to a task $Tcol(j)$ defined by

$$Tcol(j) := \{cmod(j,k) \mid k \in Struct(L_{j*})\} \cup \{cdiv(j)\}.$$

That is, $Tcol(j)$ consists of all column modifications, as well as the final scaling operation, to be applied to column j. The tasks $Tcol(j)$ are maintained in a queue and doled out to processors as they complete previous tasks. Since all necessary data are globally accessible by all processors, there need be no concern over which specific processor picks up a given task. This approach achieves good load balancing dynamically, an ideal arrangement for the highly irregular task profile usually generated by sparse problems. In short, uniform access to main memory permits the use of dynamic load balancing and a fairly simple restructuring of a sequential sparse Cholesky algorithm to obtain a good parallel algorithm. See Section 3.4.1 and [41,88] for parallel implementations of sparse Cholesky based on these ideas.

Efficient scheduling of the tasks $Tcol(j)$ on shared-memory MIMD machines is also easily accomplished. An ordering of the elimination tree is a *topological* ordering if each node is numbered higher than all of its descendants. Performance usually is not very sensitive to which topological ordering is used to schedule the column tasks, and it is often adequate to use the fill-reducing ordering to schedule the tasks. In this case, the task queue Q is given by:

$$Q := \{Tcol(1), Tcol(2), \ldots, Tcol(n)\}.$$

However, scheduling columns by their height in the elimination tree usually improves performance by reducing synchronization delays, as shown in [88]. The ordering of the elimination tree shown in Figure 8 is particularly appropriate. Scheduling the column tasks in this manner is especially worthwhile, since the overhead required to do so is trivial — a single n-vector computed in $O(n)$ time. A more dynamic queue management strategy is to initialize the queue to contain only the tasks corresponding to the leaf nodes, with additional column tasks appended to the queue after their descendants have been completed.

3.2.2. Distributed-memory MIMD machines.
The situation is much more difficult on distributed-memory MIMD machines, the target architecture for much of the algorithm development for parallel sparse factorization reported in the literature. On these machines, the lack of globally accessible memory means that issues concerned with data locality are dominant considerations. Currently, there is no efficient means of implementing dynamic load balancing on these machines for problems of this type. Thus, a static assignment of tasks to processors is normally employed in this setting, and such a mapping must be determined in advance of the factorization, based on the trade-offs between load balancing and the cost of interprocessor communication.

Elimination trees. As we have seen, the elimination tree contains information on data dependencies among tasks and the corresponding communication requirements. Thus, the elimination tree is an extremely helpful guide in determining an effective assignment of columns (and corresponding tasks) to processors in the distributed-memory case. In attempting to compute the elimination tree, however, we appear to be confronted by a bootstrapping problem: prior to symbolic factorization, we do not yet know the structure of L on which the definition of $T(A)$ is based. Fortunately, $T(A)$ can be generated directly from the structure of A by an extremely efficient algorithm [79]. It is desirable to compute the elimination tree in parallel, but again we face the recurring problem of having very little work to distribute over the processors. For large problems, if a single processor cannot store the adjacency structure of A, then the structure of A must be distributed among the processors, which also requires distributed computation of the elimination tree. In [110], Gilbert and Zmijewski present an algorithm for computing the elimination tree in parallel on a distributed-memory multiprocessor. Roughly speaking, their algorithm proceeds as follows. Each processor uses its portion of the adjacency structure of A to compute a "local" version of the elimination tree. In essence, this "local" tree contains in a compressed form the contribution of each processor's local adjacency list to the final elimination tree. The final phase of the algorithm combines these "local" trees to obtain the final

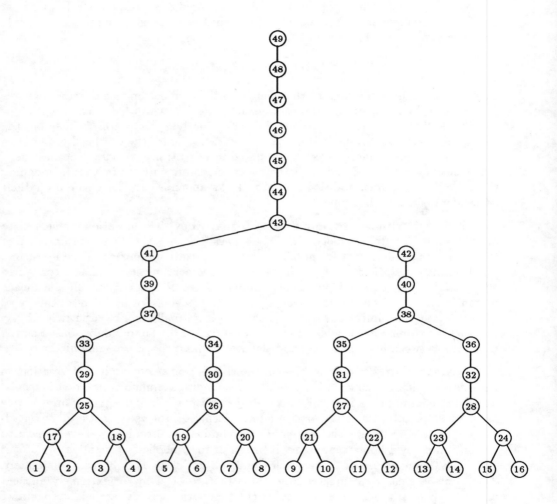

FIG. 8. *A good ordering of column tasks in task queue used by parallel column-Cholesky algorithm for shared-memory MIMD machines.*

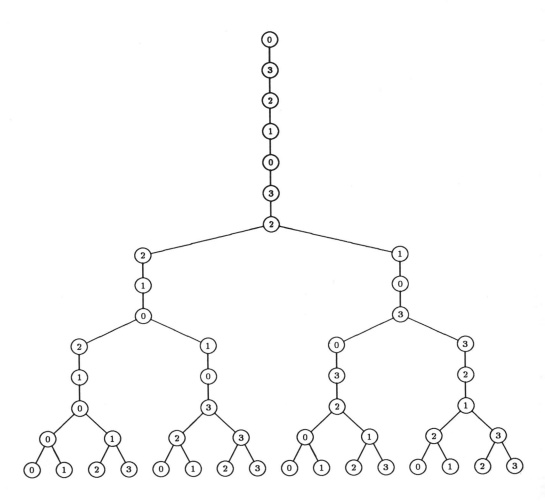

FIG. 9. *A wrap-mapping of the factor columns onto four processors numbered 0, 1, 2, and 3. Nodes belonging to the same separator in the elimination tree are assigned to the processors in wrap fashion.*

elimination tree. All communication associated with the algorithm is restricted to this final "combining" operation. In the experiments reported in [110], the parallel algorithm takes considerably more time than the sequential algorithm, though the differences are not unreasonable.

Mapping the problem onto the processors. After the elimination tree has been generated, the next step is to use it in mapping the columns onto the processors. The primary goals of the mapping are good load balance and low interprocessor communication. These goals can be in conflict, however, especially for highly irregular problems.

In the early work on this problem, successive levels in the elimination tree were wrap-mapped to the processors, as shown in Figure 9. This resulted in good load balancing for the model problem, but it also often results in unnecessarily high message volume. The "subtree-to-subcube" mapping, introduced in [49], does an excellent

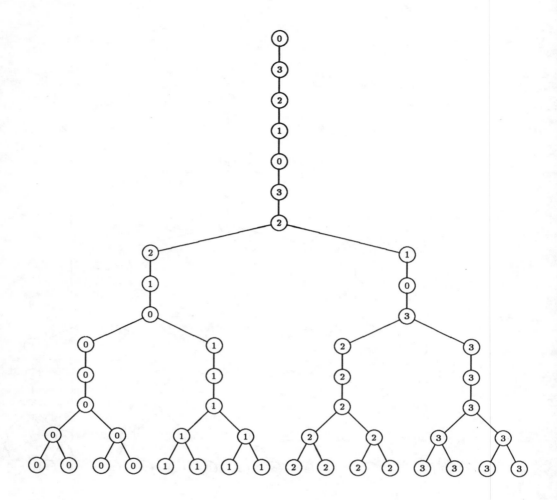

FIG. 10. *Subtree-to-subcube mapping of the columns of the matrix to four processors numbered 0, 1, 2 and 3.*

job of reducing communication while maintaining good load balance for model grid problems and other problems with similar regularity in their structure. Although the use of subcubes is specific to hypercube architectures, a similar processor clustering concept is applicable to most distributed-memory architectures.

The basic idea is quite simple. If P is the number of processors, one selects an appropriate set of P subtrees of the elimination tree, say $T_0, T_1, \ldots, T_{P-1}$, and then assigns the columns corresponding to T_i to processor i ($0 \le i \le P-1$). Where two subtrees merge together into a single subtree, their processor sets are merged together and wrap-mapped onto the nodes/columns of the separator that begins at that point. The root separator is wrap-mapped onto the set of all available processors. Figure 10 shows this mapping for our model problem. George et al. [49] show that for the fan-out distributed factorization algorithm (see Section 3.4.2) applied to model problems defined on $k \times k$ grids, communication volume can be limited to $O(Pk^2)$, which is asymptotically optimal. Gao and Parlett [35] prove the slightly stronger result that the communication volume for each processor is $O(k^2)$, which indicates that the overhead associated with communication is, in some sense, balanced among the processors. Closely related results can be found in two papers by Naik and Patrick [86,87].

It is quite easy and natural to obtain a good "subtree-to-subcube" mapping for elimination trees obtained by applying standard nested dissection orderings to model problems. It is difficult, however, to generalize the subtree-to-subcube mapping to more irregular problems. Progress in that direction is reported in [38] and [101]. However, an adequate understanding of the trade-offs between communication and load balance for more realistic problems will require further study.

3.3. Symbolic Factorization. On a distributed-memory MIMD multiprocessor, it is necessary to compute $Struct(L_{*j})$ for every column j of L and to store $Struct(L_{*j})$ on the processor responsible for computing that column. Thus, a distributed algorithm for computing the symbolic factorization is required. The sequential algorithm for this step is remarkably efficient, and so once again we find ourselves with little work to distribute among the processors, so that good efficiency is difficult to achieve in a parallel implementation.

As we have seen, $Struct(L_{*j})$ depends on $Struct(A_{*j})$ and on $Struct(L_{*k})$ for every k such that $p(k) = j$ (i.e., for every child k of j in the elimination tree). In [42] a column-oriented parallel symbolic factorization algorithm is presented. At any point during the execution of this algorithm, the number of tasks available for parallel execution is limited to the number of leaves in the subtree of the elimination tree induced by nodes whose structures are not yet complete. Limited parallelism, small task sizes, and communication overhead make it difficult to attain good speed-ups. Moreover, the subscript compression technique so critical to the space and time efficiency of the sequential symbolic factorization algorithm can be only partially realized on these machines. For example, let columns j and $j+1$ of L be two columns belonging to the same supernode but assigned to two distinct processors, say p_0 and p_1, respectively. The sequential algorithm exploits the fact that $Struct(L_{*,j+1}) = Struct(L_{*j}) - \{j+1\}$ to save both time and storage, as discussed earlier in Section 2.2. The parallel algorithm, however, must store $Struct(L_{*j})$ on processor p_0 and $Struct(L_{*,j+1})$ on processor p_1. Good mappings typically wrap-map columns belonging to the same supernode. Thus the situation in our illustration is typical — even pervasive; hence parallel symbolic factorization necessarily requires more total work and storage on distributed-memory MIMD multiprocessors, although the *parallel completion* time will usually still be less. The test results reported in [42] confirm that currently only modest speed-ups are attainable.

It is possible to improve parallel symbolic factorization on distributed-memory MIMD multiprocessors if the supernodal structure is known in advance [81]. The key observation is that it is necessary to compute only the structure of the first column of each supernode. Processors holding other columns in that supernode do not have to compute the structures of these columns; all they need to do is to retrieve the structure from the processor that is responsible for computing the structure of the first column.

In [110] Zmijewski and Gilbert present a row-oriented parallel symbolic factorization algorithm that has more potential parallelism, but is more complicated and requires rearrangement of the output into a column-oriented format. Timing results for this algorithm are not presented, but the authors indicate that its cost is high.

However, the problems they experimented with were quite small, so it remains unclear how competitive the algorithm might be on larger problems. In a study [53] that may be applicable on massively parallel machines, Gilbert and Hafsteinsson show that using a shared-memory CRCW (concurrent-read, concurrent-write) PRAM (parallel random access machine) model of computation, there is a parallel algorithm for symbolic factorization that requires $O(\log^2 n)$ time using $\eta(L)$ processors.

3.4. Numeric Factorization. On sequential machines, numeric factorization is typically much more expensive than the other steps in the solution process. As a result, parallel numeric factorization has received considerably more attention than the other steps in the parallel solution process. It is also more amenable to parallelization than the other solution steps, though it is still much more difficult to deal with than dense factorization. Development of reasonably good parallel sparse Cholesky algorithms has taken longer than development of their dense counterparts. The bookkeeping and irregular structure dealt with in the sparse algorithms present a greater challenge to the algorithm developer; consequently, many more issues and difficulties remain to be addressed in future work.

Most of the work has been directed towards the development of parallel algorithms that exploit medium- and large-grain parallelism on shared-memory or distributed-memory MIMD machines. Some exceptions are work on vectorizing sparse Cholesky factorization on powerful vector supercomputers [3,5,11,19], work on fine-grained algorithms for massively parallel SIMD machines [54], and work on systolic-like algorithms for multiprocessor grids [18,106]. We will restrict our discussion to algorithms designed for MIMD machines.

3.4.1. Parallel column-Cholesky for shared-memory machines. Of the three formulations of sparse Cholesky, column-Cholesky is in many ways the simplest to implement. As noted earlier, it has been more commonly used in sparse matrix software packages [17,27,29] than other methods, such as the multifrontal method. It is probably better known to a broader audience than the other methods. George et al. [41] show that the algorithm can be adapted in a straightforward manner to run efficiently in parallel on shared-memory MIMD machines. For all these reasons this algorithm is an ideal place to begin our discussion of parallel sparse Cholesky algorithms.

A parallel algorithm. To facilitate our discussion, we introduce a more detailed version of the column-Cholesky algorithm shown earlier in Figure 3. In particular, we need to indicate how the row structure sets $Struct(L_{j*})$ are generated by the algorithm. The more detailed version of the algorithm shown in Figure 11 requires the following new notation. Let $next(j,k)$, $k \leq j$, be the lowest numbered column greater than j that requires updating by column k. That is, $next(j,k)$ is the row index of the first nonzero in column k after row j. (Note that $next(j,j)$ is merely the parent of j in the elimination tree.) The column index sets S_i $(1 \leq i \leq n)$ are initially empty, but when column j is processed, $S_j = Struct(L_{j*})$, as required. For simplicity and brevity, the algorithm in Figure 11 does not detail how to handle the case when there is no "next" column to be updated. The use of the index sets S_i and other implementation details of the serial algorithm are discussed in [47]. However, we note one particular detail in the implementation. Since each completed column k appears in no more than one set S_i at any time during the algorithm's execution, a single n-vector *link* suffices to maintain each set S_i $(1 \leq i \leq n)$ as a singly-linked list [47].

for $j = 1$ **to** n **do**
$\quad S_j := \emptyset$
for $j = 1$ **to** n **do**
$\quad$ **for** $k \in S_j$ **do**
$\quad\quad cmod(j, k)$
$\quad\quad i := next(j, k)$
$\quad\quad S_i := S_i \cup \{k\}$
$\quad cdiv(j)$
$\quad i := next(j, j)$
$\quad S_i := S_i \cup \{j\}$

FIG. 11. *Sparse column-Cholesky factorization algorithm, showing the computation of row structure sets* $Struct(L_{i*})$ *in the sets* S_i, $1 \leq i \leq n$.

This algorithm can be implemented in parallel on a shared-memory MIMD machine in a fairly straightforward manner [40]. Each column j corresponds to a task

$$Tcol(j) := \{cmod(j, k) \mid k \in Struct(L_{j*})\} \cup \{cdiv(j)\},$$

as discussed in Section 3.2. Initially, the task queue, denoted by Q, contains all column tasks $Tcol(j)$ ordered by some topological ordering of the elimination tree. For ease of notation, we assume that the elimination ordering and the schedule-prescribed ordering are the same, so we have

$$Q := \{Tcol(1), Tcol(2), \ldots, Tcol(n)\}.$$

As the computation proceeds, a processor obtains (and removes) the column task currently at the front of the queue and proceeds to compute that task. After completing the task, the processor obtains from Q another column task to compute, and it continues in this manner, as do all the other processors, until the factorization is complete. This simple "pool of tasks" approach does an excellent job of dynamically balancing the load, even though the column task profile for typical sparse problems is quite irregular. Obviously, access to this queue must be synchronized to ensure that each column task $Tcol(j)$ is executed by one and only one processor. The parallel algorithm also must synchronize access to the n-vector *link* in which the sets S_i ($1 \leq i \leq n$) are maintained. Only one processor at a time can modify this array, and thus the two sequences of instructions that manipulate *link* must be critical sections in the algorithm. A high-level description of the parallel algorithm is given in Figure 12.

Recent improvements. The algorithm in Figure 12 has two significant drawbacks. First, the number of synchronization operations (obtaining and relinquishing a lock) is $O(n + \eta(L))$, which is quite high. Second, since the algorithm does not exploit supernodes, it will not vectorize well on vector supercomputers with multiple processors, natural target machines for the algorithm. The introduction of supernodes into the algorithm deals quite effectively with both problems [88].

The use of supernodes to improve computational rates on vector supercomputers is well documented [3,5,11,19]. The duplicate sparsity structure found in columns within the same supernode enables one to organize the computation around level-2 or level-3 BLAS-like computational kernels. Such block operations reduce memory

$Q := \{Tcol(1), Tcol(2), \ldots, Tcol(n)\}$
for $j = 1$ **to** n **do**
    $S_j := \emptyset$
while $Q \neq \emptyset$ **do**
    pop $Tcol(j)$ from Q
    while column j requires further $cmod$'s **do**
        if $S_j = \emptyset$ **do**
            wait until $S_j \neq \emptyset$
        obtain k from S_j
        $i := next(j, k)$
        lock
        $S_i := S_i \cup \{k\}$
        unlock
        $cmod(j, k)$
    $cdiv(j)$
    $i := next(j, j)$
    lock
    $S_i := S_i \cup \{j\}$
    unlock

FIG. 12. *Parallel sparse column-Cholesky factorization algorithm for shared-memory MIMD machines.*

traffic by retaining and reusing data in cache, vector registers, or whatever limited rapid-access memory resource is provided on the particular machine in question.

In the following discussion, we will let bold-face integers **1**, **2**, ..., **N** stand for the supernodes. Thus, $\mathbf{N} \leq n$ is the number of supernodes. We will also use bold-face capital letters such as **J** and **K** to denote each supernode by its index, and use small letters such as i, j, and k to denote each individual column by its number.

Let **K** be a supernode comprising the set of contiguous columns $\{k, k+1, k+2, \ldots, k+t\}$. Because of the sparsity structure shared by each column of **K**, every column of **K** modifies column j, $j > k+t$, if and only if at least one column of **K** modifies column j. For example, column 40 in supernode **30** in Figure 5 is modified by each column 37, 38, and 39 in the previous supernode, but it is modified by none of the columns 19, 20, and 21 that compose supernode **15**. The block operation used to improve the algorithms in Figures 3 and 12 is a level-2 BLAS-like kernel, $cmod(j, \mathbf{K})$, which modifies column j with a multiple of the appropriate entries of each column $k \in \mathbf{K}$. In particular, the modifications from the columns in **K** can be accumulated as dense **saxpy** operations and no indirect addressing is required until the result is applied to column j. For a column $k + i \in \mathbf{K}$, we let $cmod(k+i, \mathbf{K})$ denote the operation of updating column $k + i$ with every column of **K** numbered earlier than $k + i$. That is, $cmod(k + i, \mathbf{K})$ is given by

$$cmod(k+i, \mathbf{K}) := \{cmod(k+i, k), cmod(k+i, k+1), \ldots, cmod(k+i, k+i-1)\}.$$

For the matrix in Figure 5, $cmod(30, \mathbf{22})$ is given by

$$cmod(30, \mathbf{22}) := \{cmod(30, 28), cmod(30, 29)\}.$$

Since columns k, $k + 1$, ..., $k + i - 1$ in supernode **K** have the same structure below row $k + i - 1$, the modifications to column $k + i$ can again be performed by dense **saxpy** operations, with no indirect addressing required. The next column to be updated by supernode **K** after it has updated column j is denoted by $next(j, \mathbf{K})$, and similarly the first column *outside* supernode **K** requiring modification by the columns of **K** is denoted by $next(\mathbf{K}, \mathbf{K})$. Using this notation, Figures 13 and 14 display supernodal versions of the sequential and parallel column-Cholesky algorithm shown in Figures 11 and 12, respectively.

> **for** $j = 1$ **to** n **do**
> $S_j := \emptyset$
> **for** $\mathbf{J} = 1$ **to** $\mathbf{N}$ **do**
>   **for** $j \in \mathbf{J}$ **do**
>   **for** $\mathbf{K} \in S_j$ **do**
> $cmod(j, \mathbf{K})$
> $i := next(j, \mathbf{K})$
> $S_i := S_i \cup \{\mathbf{K}\}$
> $cmod(j, \mathbf{J})$
> $cdiv(j)$
> $i := next(\mathbf{J}, \mathbf{J})$
> $S_i := S_i \cup \{\mathbf{J}\}$

FIG. 13. *Sequential sparse supernodal column-Cholesky factorization algorithm.*

> $Q := \{Tcol(1), Tcol(2), \ldots, Tcol(n)\}$
> **for** $j = 1$ **to** n **do**
> $S_j := \emptyset$
> **while** $Q \neq \emptyset$ **do**
>   pop $Tcol(j)$ from Q
>   let **J** be the supernode containing column j
>   **while** column j requires further $cmod$'s **do**
>   **if** $S_j = \emptyset$ **do**
>   wait until $S_j \neq \emptyset$
>   obtain **K** from S_j
> $i := next(j, \mathbf{K})$
>   lock
> $S_i := S_i \cup \{\mathbf{K}\}$
>   unlock
> $cmod(j, \mathbf{K})$
> $cmod(j, \mathbf{J})$
> $cdiv(j)$
>   **if** j is the last column of supernode **J** **do**
> $i := next(\mathbf{J}, \mathbf{J})$
>   lock
> $S_i := S_i \cup \{\mathbf{J}\}$
>   unlock

FIG. 14. *Parallel sparse supernodal column-Cholesky factorization algorithm for shared-memory MIMD machines.*

Let $\sigma(L)$ denote the number of subscripts in the supernodal representation of the sparsity structure of L. The use of supernodes reduces the number of synchronization operations to a number proportional to $\sigma(L)$, which is often much less than $\eta(L)$, sometimes by as much as an order of magnitude [46].

3.4.2. Distributed fan-out algorithm. The algorithm introduced in [43], now known as the fan-out algorithm, was the first sparse Cholesky factorization algorithm developed for distributed-memory machines. It is a parallel version of the submatrix-Cholesky factorization algorithm shown in Figure 4. We will denote the k-th task performed by the outer loop of the algorithm by $Tsub(k)$, which is defined by

$$Tsub(k) := \{cdiv(k)\} \cup \{cmod(j,k) \mid j \in Struct(L_{*k})\}.$$

That is, $Tsub(k)$ first obtains L_{*k} by performing the $cdiv(k)$ operation, and then performs all column modifications that use the new column.

Algorithms for distributed-memory machines are usually structured around some prior distribution of the data to the processors. In order to keep the cost of interprocessor communication at acceptable levels, it is essential for the algorithm to make *local* use of *local* data as much as possible. The distributed fan-out, fan-in, and multifrontal algorithms are typical examples of this type of distributed algorithm (the fan-in and multifrontal algorithms will be discussed in the following subsections). These three distributed algorithms are all designed within the following framework.

- All three require assignment of the matrix columns to the processors.
- All three use the column assignment to distribute among the processors the tasks found in the outer loop of one of the serial implementations of sparse Cholesky factorization.

The differences among these algorithms stem from the various formulations of *serial* sparse Cholesky upon which they are based. The fan-in algorithm is based on column-Cholesky; it partitions each task $Tcol(j)$ among the processors. The distributed multifrontal algorithm partitions among the processors the tasks upon which the sequential multifrontal method is based: partial dense submatrix-Cholesky factorization and the assembly operations, both of which are introduced later in the subsection dealing with this algorithm. The fan-out algorithm is based on submatrix-Cholesky; it partitions each task $Tsub(k)$ among the processors.

We now detail how the fan-out algorithm partitions the task $Tsub(k)$ among the processors. Each column L_{*k} is stored on one and only one of P available processors. An n-vector *map* is required to record the distribution of columns to processors: if column k is stored on processor p, then $map[k] := p$. We let $mycols(p)$ denote the set of columns owned by processor p. The fan-out algorithm is a data-driven algorithm, where the data sent from one processor to another are the completed factor columns. The outer loop of the fan-out algorithm constantly checks the message queue for incoming columns. When it receives a column L_{*k}, it uses it to modify every column $j \in mycols(p)$ for which $cmod(j,k)$ is required. In other words, it performs the following set of *cmods*:

$$\{cmod(j,k) \mid j \in Struct(L_{*k}) \cap mycols(p)\}.$$

Indeed, each task $Tsub(k)$ is partitioned among the processors by the partition defined by the column mapping. More precisely, the column partition

$$\{mycols(1), mycols(2), \ldots, mycols(P)\}$$

induces the partition of $Tsub(k)$ into subtasks of the form

$$\{Tsub(k,1), Tsub(k,2), \ldots, Tsub(k,P)\}$$

where

$$Tsub(k,p) := \{cmod(j,k) \mid j \in Struct(L_{*k}) \cap mycols(p)\},$$

with each non-empty task $Tsub(k,p)$ assigned to processor p, the owner of the columns updated by the task.

Of course, many of these tasks will be empty. Only the processors in the set

$$procs(L_{*k}) := \{map[j] \mid j \in Struct(L_{*k})\}$$

require column L_{*k}. When processor $p = map[j]$ has completed all column modifications required by column j, it then performs $cdiv(j)$ and sends it to every processor in $procs(L_{*j})$, where it eventually is used to modify later columns in the matrix. The algorithm is shown in Figure 15.

> **for** $j \in mycols(p)$ **do**
>   **if** j is a leaf node in $T(A)$ **do**
> $cdiv(j)$
>   send L_{*j} to the processors in $procs(L_{*j})$
> $mycols(p) := mycols(p) - \{j\}$
>   **while** $mycols(p) \neq \emptyset$ **do**
>   receive any column of L, say L_{*k}
>   **for** $j \in Struct(L_{*k}) \cap mycols(p)$ **do**
> $cmod(j,k)$
>   **if** column j required no more $cmod$'s **do**
> $cdivj$
>   send L_{*j} to the processors in $procs(L_{*j})$
> $mycols(p) := mycols(p) - \{j\}$

FIG. 15. *Fan-out Cholesky factorization algorithm for processor p of a distributed-memory MIMD machine.*

Historically, the fan-out algorithm was first to be implemented on a distributed-memory machine, but due to several weaknesses it has since been superseded by fan-in algorithms and distributed multifrontal algorithms. The distributed fan-out algorithm incurs greater interprocessor communication costs than the other two methods, both in terms of total number of messages and total message volume. It simply does not exploit a good communication-reducing column mapping, such as the subtree-to-subcube mapping, as effectively as the other methods do. Ashcraft et al. [9] and Zmijewski [109] have independently improved the algorithm by having it send aggregated update columns rather than individual factor columns for columns belonging to a subtree that has been mapped to a single processor. Though the resulting improvement in performance is substantial, it still is insufficient to make the method competitive.

Another problem with the method is the expense of mapping the entries of the updating column k to the corresponding entries of the updated column j when performing $cmod(j,k)$. The set $Struct(L_{*k})$ must accompany the factor column L_{*k} when it is sent to other processors to enable these processors to complete column modifications of the form $cmod(j, k)$. This roughly doubles the communication volume and creates a more complicated message that must be packed by the sending processor and unpacked by the receiving processor. Moreover, each $cmod(j, k)$ requires that both index sets $Struct(L_{*j})$ and $Struct(L_{*k})$ be searched in order to match indices. This results in poor *serial* efficiency. These weaknesses have provoked efforts to develop better distributed factorization algorithms.

   3.4.3. Distributed fan-in algorithm. One of the improved distributed factorization algorithms is the fan-in algorithm, introduced by Ashcraft et al. in [10]. Based on the sparse column-Cholesky algorithm, it distributes each column task $Tcol(j)$ among the processors in a manner similar to the distribution of tasks $Tsub(k)$ in the fan-out algorithm. Viewed in a more general way, the fan-in method is analogous to the standard parallel algorithm for a dot product, in which each processor first *locally* reduces the data *assigned to it* down to a single number, and then participates in a *global* phase during which the processors cooperate in reducing down to a single number the P local reductions generated during the preceding "perfectly parallel" phase. Indeed, the name "fan-in" is taken from the fan-in distributed algorithm for dense triangular solution [58], which computes a series of inner product calculations in precisely this manner. Note that throughout this subsection we freely use the notation introduced in the previous subsection.

   As with the fan-out algorithm, each processor p is responsible for computing $cdiv(j)$ for every column $j \in mycols(p)$. Of course, $cdiv(j)$ cannot be computed until all modifications $cmod(j, k)$, $k \in Struct(L_{j*})$, have been performed. The fan-in algorithm is a demand-driven algorithm, where the data required are aggregated update columns computed by the sending processor *using columns it owns*, and needed by the receiving processor to update a target column. Let $u(j, k)$ denote the scaled column accumulated into the factor column by the $cmod(j, k)$ operation. The outer loop of the algorithm processes every column j of the matrix in ascending order by column number. When processor p processes column j, it aggregates into a single update vector u every update vector $u(j, k)$ for which $k \in mycols(p) \cap Struct(L_{j*})$. Indeed, each task $Tcol(j)$ is partitioned among the processors by the partition of the columns induced by the column mapping. More precisely, the column partition

$$\{mycols(1), mycols(2), \ldots, mycols(P)\}$$

induces the partition of $Tcol(j)$ into subtasks of the form

$$\{Tcol(j, 1), Tcol(j, 2), \ldots, Tcol(j, P)\}$$

where $Tcol(j, p)$ aggregates into a single update vector every update vector $u(j, k)$ for which $k \in Struct(L_{j*}) \cap mycols(p)$, with each *non-null* task $Tcol(j, p)$ assigned to processor p, the owner of the updating columns used by the task.

   After performing $Tcol(j, p)$, if processor p does *not* own column j, then it sends the resulting aggregated update column to processor $q = map[j]$, which will eventually incorporate it into column j. If, on the other hand, processor p does own column j, it must receive and process any aggregated update columns required by column j from other processors before it can complete the $cdiv(j)$ operation. The fan-in algorithm is given in Figure 16.

   It is interesting to note that any column $j \in mycols(p)$ will receive an aggregated update column from every processor in the set

$$procs(L_{j*}) := \{map[k] \mid k \in Struct(L_{j*})\}.$$

for $j := 1$ **to** n **do**
    if $j \in mycols(p)$ **or** $Struct(L_{j*}) \cap mycols(p) \neq \emptyset$ **do**
        $u := 0$
        for $k \in Struct(L_{j*}) \cap mycols(p)$ **do**
            $u := u + u(j, k)$
        if $map[j] \neq p$ **do**
            send u to processor $q = map[j]$
        else
            incorporate u into the factor column j
            while any aggregated update column for column j remains unreceived **do**
                receive in u another aggregated update column for column j
                incorporate u into the factor column j
            $cdiv(j)$

FIG. 16. *Fan-in sparse Cholesky factorization algorithm for processor p of a distributed-memory MIMD machine.*

In contrast, the fan-out algorithm sent the factor column L_{*j} to every processor in the processor set $procs(L_{*j})$. Consider the communication costs incurred by the two algorithms during the computation of columns that constitute a subtree of the elimination tree that has been mapped to a single processor by a subcube-to-subtree mapping. For the fan-in algorithm there will be *no communication* during this portion of the computation, because for every column j in the subtree, $Struct(L_{j*})$ also belongs to the subtree. On the other hand, the fan-out algorithm must send L_{*j} to another processor if there is a column index $k \in Struct(L_{*j})$ for some column j in the subtree, such that $map[k] \neq map[j]$. This observation is an informal indication of why the fan-in algorithm is better than the fan-out algorithm at exploiting a good mapping to reduce interprocessor communication.

A more visual comparison of the communication patterns of the fan-out and fan-in algorithms is given in Figures 17 and 18. These figures illustrate snapshots of the execution of the two algorithms on an Intel iPSC/2 hypercube, with time on the horizontal axis. Processor activity is shown by horizontal lines and interprocessor communication by slanted lines. The horizontal line corresponding to each processor is either solid or blank, depending on whether the processor is busy or idle, respectively. Each message sent between processors is shown by a line drawn from the sending processor at the time of transmission to the receiving processor at the time of reception of the message. The problem being solved is the factorization of a matrix of order 225 derived from a model finite element problem on a 15×15 grid, using a nested dissection ordering and subtree-to-subcube mapping on eight processors. The divide-and-conquer nature of the nested dissection ordering is clearly visible in Figure 18, which also illustrates the ability of the fan-in algorithm, given an appropriate mapping, to exploit this structure to reduce communication. By contrast, the fan-out algorithm shown in Figure 17 exhibits much greater communication traffic as well as a less regular communication pattern, even under the ideal conditions represented here. These diagrams were produced using a package developed at Oak Ridge National Laboratory for visualizing the behavior of parallel algorithms [57].

Compute-ahead fan-in algorithm. In Figure 16, observe that processor p will fall idle if, while receiving aggregated update columns destined for a column $j \in$

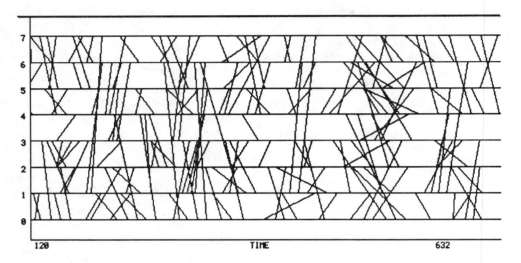

FIG. 17. *Communication pattern of fan-out algorithm for a model problem.*

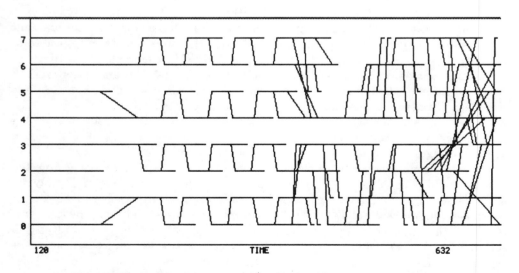

FIG. 18. *Communication pattern of fan-in algorithm for a model problem.*

$mycols(p)$, it has no such updates in its message queue. One straightforward enhancement to the method is to probe the queue for such messages, and when there are none, proceed with useful work on later factor columns. When unable to complete the current column j, the algorithm toggles between performing so-called *compute-ahead* tasks on columns $i > j$, and detecting and processing incoming aggregated updates for the current column j.

There are two types of compute-ahead tasks to be performed on later columns of the factor:

1. For some column $i > j$, aggregate into a work vector the update vector $u(i, k)$ for each completed column $k \in Struct(L_{i*}) \cap mycols(p)$.

2. Receive an aggregated update column for some column $i > j$, and incorporate it into the factor column.

Compute-ahead tasks of the first type have priority over compute-ahead tasks of the second type; that is, compute-ahead tasks of the second type are performed only when the algorithm has exhausted its supply of tasks of the first type.

Compute-ahead aggregating of update columns is limited to target columns $i > j$ that belong to the same supernode as the current column j. This is due primarily to the ease and "naturalness" with which successive aggregate update columns sharing the same sparsity pattern can be computed. Since the aggregate update columns are managed so that they share the same sparsity structure as the target column, no indirect indexing is required to incorporate them into the factor column. Thus, compute-ahead tasks of the second type require merely a receive, followed by a **saxpy**. For details concerning these and other implementation issues, consult [8].

Though supernodes play an important role in organizing the compute-ahead fan-in algorithm, current implementations of both the basic and compute-ahead fan-in algorithms do not exploit supernodes to reduce memory traffic in the inner loops of the computation — one of their key roles in the parallel shared-memory column-Cholesky algorithm. There is no reason why supernodes cannot serve in this role in the fan-in algorithm also. However, it is interesting to note that the potential exploitation of supernodes in distributed-memory algorithms is somewhat limited because good mappings typically distribute the columns of a supernode among several processors.

3.4.4. Parallel multifrontal algorithms.

As noted earlier, multifrontal methods are generalizations of single-front methods. The original motivation for developing frontal methods was for more effective use of auxiliary storage in the out-of-core solution of sparse systems, and more efficient inner-loop computations by avoiding the indirect addressing that is characteristic of general sparse data structures. The fundamental idea in frontal methods is to keep only a relatively small portion of the matrix in main memory at any given time, and to use a full matrix representation for this "active" portion of the matrix, so that computations involving it are more efficient on scalar machines and more readily vectorized on vector machines. Although the data structure for the active matrix is very simple, the overall data management required in frontal methods is quite complicated, involving the assembly of matrix elements, their insertion into the proper location in the full active matrix data structure, and the writing of completed portions of the factor to disk, all of which must account for the fact that the active matrix constitutes a moving "window" through the problem.

The success of frontal methods is dependent on keeping the size of the active matrix small, which in turn depends on the structure of the problem and the ordering used in solving it. In structural analysis, for example, a long thin truss is ideal for a frontal solution technique in that, with an appropriate ordering, a single narrow "front" passes along the length of the truss. If a single front would become unacceptably large, however, then multiple fronts can be employed, leading to multifrontal methods. Of course, the various fronts must eventually merge before the problem can be completed, but the hope is that with an appropriate ordering such mergers can be postponed as late as possible in the computation. The use of multiple fronts seems to suggest an obvious parallel implementation: simply assign a separate front to each processor. As we shall see, however, the situation is not quite so straightforward.

A self-contained presentation of parallel multifrontal algorithms would occupy more space than we can afford in an article of this scope. The difficulties in producing a brief but clear description stem primarily from the complexity of the method: a *sequential* multifrontal code is considerably more complicated than a *sequential* sparse column-Cholesky code. As might be expected, modifying the method to run on MIMD machines is also more difficult and complicated, though it is by no means unmanageable; there have been implementations on both shared-memory [12,22,23,105] and distributed-memory [9,36,82] machines. This section is limited to a brief overview of the literature on the subject and a short discussion of some of the problems that arise in parallel implementations. The reader should consult [28] or [78] for background material on multifrontal methods.

We should also point out that some of the codes and algorithms cited in this section are designed for nonsymmetric linear systems, and at least one includes pivoting for stability. For instance, the work in [22] and [23] is based on the Harwell MA37 code, which solves nonsymmetric systems and pivots for stability. Nevertheless, such codes can be discussed within the framework of this article because they perform a symbolic factorization of the structurally symmetric matrix $A + A^T$, and compute a structurally symmetric numerical factorization of A within the resulting data structure. Therefore, much of the material in [22] and [23] is directly applicable to sparse multifrontal Cholesky factorization.

Background. As noted in Section 2, the multifrontal method is a sophisticated variant of the sparse submatrix-Cholesky factorization algorithm (Figure 4) for which the $cmod(j, k)$ operations are not applied directly to column j of the factor matrix. Instead, each is accumulated and passed on through a succession of update matrices until it is finally incorporated into the target column. The outer loop of the serial multifrontal algorithm processes the supernodes $1, 2, \ldots, N$ in order, completing the columns of each supernode when the supernode is processed. The order in which the supernodes are processed is critical. For reasons discussed below, they are processed in the order in which they are visited by a postorder traversal of a *supernodal elimination tree*. A supernodal elimination tree with 31 supernodes is displayed in Figure 6.

Every supernode K has associated with it a frontal matrix in which the factor and update columns associated with the supernode are computed. The factor and update columns computed within this matrix are stored in a dense matrix format, essentially minimizing the use of indirect addressing — one of the major strengths of the method. The algorithm performs two tasks within this frontal matrix:

1. The *assembly* step inserts the required data into the frontal matrix.
2. After the assembly step, *dense partial submatrix-Cholesky factorization* within the frontal matrix generates the factor and update columns.

We discuss first the partial submatrix-Cholesky factorization step and then the assembly step in more detail.

Suppose that K contains r columns of the matrix, and assume that the assembly step for supernode K's frontal matrix has been completed. The algorithm then computes r major steps of *dense submatrix-Cholesky* factorization within the frontal matrix, after which the first r columns of the frontal matrix contain the r factor columns of $\mathbf{K}$, and the trailing columns in the frontal matrix contain aggregated update columns for later columns of the matrix. These trailing columns constitute the *update* matrix generated by this block elimination step. Henceforth, we will denote this task by $Tsub(\mathbf{K})$. The update matrix is stored and assembled later into the frontal matrix of its "parent supernode" in the elimination tree.

The *assembly* step consists of the following three steps:
1. Zero out the frontal matrix.
2. Insert the required entries of A into the appropriate locations of the matrix.
3. For each "child supernode," obtain its associated update matrix and add each entry to its corresponding entry in the frontal matrix.

Because the supernodes are ordered by a postorder traversal of the elimination tree, the update matrices can be stored efficiently on a stack, limiting both the storage and time required to store them. New update matrices are pushed onto the stack as soon as they are generated, while update matrices for child supernodes are popped off the stack as needed during each assembly step.

Shared-memory MIMD machines. One key problem associated with parallel multifrontal algorithms for shared-memory MIMD multiprocessors is the management of auxiliary storage for the update matrices. The postordering of supernodes used in the sequential algorithm severely limits the parallelism available; in particular, it limits exploitation of the parallelism that exists among the many disjoint subtrees of the elimination tree available in most realistic problems. To create more independent processes, algorithm developers have abandoned the postordering and the stack of update matrices. Instead, they process the supernodes in some order that allows greater exploitation of the large-grained (subtree-level) parallelism, but which complicates management of the working storage for update matrices, increasing both the storage and time required by this part of the algorithm [23,83,105].

In [22] and [23], Duff considered several strategies for dealing with the resulting fragmentation of working storage. Garbage collection to reclaim unused storage requires a critical section that seriously inhibits parallelism. Subdividing the working storage in an effort to localize the garbage collection operations and reduce their negative effect on parallelism proved to be too complicated and ineffective [22]. Breaking up individual update matrices to make better use of free storage was not considered because it would destroy the data locality vital for efficient use of cache — one of the important strengths of the multifrontal method and a key consideration on the Alliant FX/8 [23]. In [23], Duff used the *buddy system* to manage the storage for update matrices. For any given update matrix, the buddy system obtains a free block of storage of length 2^k, where k is the smallest power of two that provides enough contiguous storage locations to hold the matrix. The scheme is guaranteed to waste no more than half the working storage.

We are aware of two other parallel multifrontal codes designed to run on parallel shared-memory MIMD machines. A parallel multifrontal code developed by Lucas [83] for the CRAY 2 allocates subtrees to individual processors and has each processor manage a local stack for its assigned subtree. During the course of the computation, there are eventually more processors than independent subtrees. At that point, the code abandons the use of subtree-level parallelism. Instead, it successively processes the remaining tasks $Tsub(\mathbf{K})$, using CRAY autotasking to partition each task $Tsub(\mathbf{K})$ among *all* the processors. A parallel multifrontal code developed by

Vu [105] for the CRAY Y-MP uses a similar strategy.

A second issue discussed in [23] is partitioning the work among the processors for execution in parallel. Here, we restrict our attention to issues associated with distributing the tasks $Tsub(1)$, $Tsub(2)$, ..., $Tsub(N)$ among the processors. The situation is not as simple as it is for parallel column-Cholesky, where simply dealing out the column tasks $Tcol(j)$, with some care in the scheduling, is very effective in exploiting both subtree- and column-level parallelism (see section 3.4.1). If the multifrontal method distributes indivisible tasks $Tsub(K)$ among the processors in a similar fashion, then, as noted in [22] and [26], parallelism decreases as the computation proceeds toward the root supernode and disappears altogether when the root supernode is reached. Typically, most of the work is performed in the larger frontal matrices associated with supernodes near the root, and thus smaller granularity is required for acceptable performance. That is, the tasks $Tsub(K)$ for supernodes K near the root supernode must be partitioned into smaller tasks and distributed among the processors. In [23], Duff parameterizes his code so that it can spawn tasks of any granularity between two extremes, the largest being the tasks $Tsub(K)$, and the smallest being individual *cmods* and *cdivs*. His results indicate that working with small blocks of columns is most effective. Near the root of the supernodal elimination tree, the algorithms of Lucas [83] and Vu [105] use the autotasking capabilities of their target machines, the CRAY 2 and CRAY Y-MP, to partition the tasks $Tsub(K)$ among the processors.

Distributed-memory MIMD machines. Lucas [82,84] developed the first implementation of the multifrontal method for distributed-memory MIMD machines. Since then, Ashcraft [9] has also developed parallel multifrontal codes for such machines. Lucas's code and the first code developed by Ashcraft implement essentially the same distributed multifrontal algorithm [6,83]. This section contains a brief discussion of a few features of this algorithm. Further enhancements to the algorithm, and a systematic comparison of all the distributed-memory factorization algorithms will appear in [7].

As with other distributed factorization algorithms, each column k of the matrix is assigned to and stored on one processor, $map[k]$. Consider a supernode K and let $map(K)$ denote the set of processors that own at least one column of K or a descendant of a column K in the elimination tree. The key feature of the algorithm is the distribution of *all* the columns of K's frontal matrix among the processors in $map(K)$; that is, both the factor columns and the aggregated update columns generated by the task $Tsub(K)$ are distributed among the processors in $map(K)$.

The processors in $map(K)$ work together to perform the task $Tsub(K)$, i.e., dense submatrix-Cholesky factorization on the first $|K|$ columns of the distributed frontal matrix. The algorithm used to perform this task can be viewed as a straightforward adaptation of the parallel dense submatrix-Cholesky algorithm presented in [37]. When processor $p = map[k] \in map(K)$ completes factor column $k \in K$, it broadcasts L_{*k} to the other processors in $map(K)$. The other processors in $map(K)$ at some point receive L_{*k} and use it to modify every column of the frontal matrix that they own. Thus, this phase of the algorithm is very similar to the fan-out algorithm shown in Figure 15.

Before the task $Tsub(K)$ can be performed, supernode K's distributed frontal matrix must be assembled. Contributions from distributed update matrices for any children of K must be sent to the appropriate processors and scatter-added into the appropriate frontal matrix locations. More precisely, if an update column from a "child" update matrix is located on a different processor than the *corresponding* column of its "parent" frontal matrix, then the aggregated update column must be sent to its "new owner," where it is incorporated into the appropriate column of the frontal matrix.

Both phases of the factorization require interprocessor communication. The factorization phase performs a restricted broadcast of completed factor columns, while the assembly phase moves aggregated update columns from one processor to another. The two forms of communication result in somewhat higher communication cost for the multifrontal algorithm than that incurred by the fan-in algorithm. However, its extra communication overhead is far smaller than that incurred by the pure fan-out algorithm, and preliminary results indicate similar performance for the fan-in and distributed multifrontal algorithms [9].

3.5. Triangular Solution. Unfortunately, there is relatively little to say about parallel algorithms for forward and backward triangular solutions. Data dependencies and a paucity of work to distribute among the processors make it very difficult to achieve high computational rates, even for dense problems. Heath and Romine [58] and Eisenstat et al. [30] have shown that intricate pipelining techniques are required to achieve computational rates as high as 50% efficiency for *large dense problems* on distributed-memory hypercube multiprocessors. Two factors make the situation even more difficult in the sparse case. First, due to preservation of sparsity in the factor matrix, there is usually far less work to distribute among the processors — approximately $\eta(L)$ flops rather than the $n(n-1)/2$ flops available in the dense case. Second, the successful pipelining techniques used in [30,58] appear to require the extremely regular structure of a dense matrix. Loss of this regularity in sparse Cholesky factors increases the difficulty of using these complicated techniques to speed up sparse triangular solution. Generalizing these techniques so that they can be incorporated into a parallel sparse triangular solution algorithm is a possible avenue for future improvement. A step in this direction has been made by Zmijewski [108], who considered the use of cyclic algorithms for solving sparse triangular systems.

These difficulties are mitigated somewhat by the subtree-level parallelism that is available only in the sparse case. Though the parallel algorithms for sparse forward and back triangular solutions contained in [44] exploit this parallelism, they nonetheless performed rather poorly. Other work on parallel sparse triangular solution algorithms [4,56,85,102] has been directed primarily toward use in the preconditioned conjugate gradient algorithm. Some of the work in [4], however, is applicable to complete, as well as incomplete, Cholesky factorizations.

4. Concluding remarks. In this paper, we have provided a summary of parallel algorithms currently available for the four phases in the solution of sparse symmetric positive definite systems. It is clear from the relative length of the discussions that much of this research has been focused on the design and implementation of parallel numerical factorization algorithms. Some of these algorithms have exhibited reasonable speed-up ratios, particularly on shared-memory MIMD multiprocessors. Although there have been attempts in developing parallel algorithms for the other phases, namely ordering, symbolic factorization and triangular solutions, these algorithms have generally been less successful and lacking in efficiency. Much research is needed in those areas. The ordering problem seems particularly problematic in a distributed-memory environment because of the difficulty of partitioning the graph of the matrix among the processors in an intelligent way *before* the ordering is determined.

It may be argued that current sequential algorithms for symbolic factorization and triangular solution are so efficient that perhaps they can be used on one processor in a multiprocessor environment instead of developing parallel versions. This may be true for MIMD multiprocessors with globally shared memory. On MIMD multiprocessors with local memory, there are at least two reasons why parallel algorithms are needed for symbolic factorization and triangular solution, even if these algorithms may be less efficient that their sequential counterparts. First, although symbolic factorization and triangular solution are often the least expensive phases in the solution process on serial machines, they may become the dominant phases as more efficient parallel numerical factorization algorithms are developed. Thus, research on the design of efficient parallel algorithms for symbolic factorization and triangular solution will be necessary eventually. Second, even if they are somewhat inefficient, parallel algorithms are still needed to make use of the large (collectively) local memory available on distributed-memory parallel machines for solving large problems; there may not be enough memory on a single processor to carry out symbolic factorization and/or triangular solution serially. Third, many algorithms require multiple triangular solutions.

Our emphasis in this paper has been on parallel direct methods for solving sparse symmetric positive definite systems. Work has also been done on parallel algorithms for other matrix computations. In the case of direct methods for solving sparse nonsymmetric linear systems, much of the research has been carried out on shared-memory MIMD multiprocessors. Some recent examples can be found in [1,2,3,20,22,23,51,52]. Parallel algorithms for sparse least squares problems are discussed in [16,59,96]. There has been a great deal of research on parallel iterative methods for solving large sparse linear systems as well. For a summary of such work and references to this extensive literature, see the book by Ortega [89]. Many additional references on all aspects of parallel matrix computations can be found in [90].

Acknowledgment. The authors would like to thank Eduardo D'Azevedo, Alan George and Joseph Liu for their suggestions and comments, which have improved the presentation of the material.

REFERENCES

[1] G. ALAGHBAND, *Parallel pivoting combined with parallel reduction and fill-in control*, Parallel Computing, 11 (1989), pp. 201–221.

[2] G. ALAGHBAND AND H. JORDAN, *Multiprocessor sparse L/U decomposition with controlled fill-in*, Tech. Report 85-48, ICASE, NASA Langley Research Center, Hampton, Virginia, 1985.

[3] P. AMESTOY AND I. DUFF, *Vectorization of a multiprocessor multifrontal code*, Internat. J. Supercomp. Appl., 3 (1989), pp. 41–59.

[4] E. ANDERSON AND Y. SAAD, *Solving sparse triangular linear systems on parallel computers*, Internat. J. High Speed Comput., 1 (1989), pp. 73–95.

[5] C. ASHCRAFT, *A vector implementation of the multifrontal method for large sparse, symmetric positive definite linear systems*, Tech. Report ETA-TR-51, Engineering Technology Applications Division, Boeing Computer Services, Seattle, Washington, 1987.

[6] ———. Personal communication, 1990.

[7] ———, *Ph.D. Thesis*. Dept. of Computer Science, Yale University, 1990.

[8] C. ASHCRAFT, S. EISENSTAT, J. LIU, B. PEYTON, AND A. SHERMAN, *A compute-ahead implementation of the fan-in sparse distributed factorization scheme*, Tech. Report ORNL/TM-11496, Oak Ridge National Laboratory, Oak Ridge, TN, 1990.

[9] C. ASHCRAFT, S. EISENSTAT, J. LIU, AND A. SHERMAN, *A comparison of three column-based distributed sparse factorization schemes*, Tech. Report YALEU/DCS/RR-810, Department of Computer Science,Yale University, New Haven, CT, 1990.

[10] C. ASHCRAFT, S. EISENSTAT, AND J. W.-H. LIU, *A fan-in algorithm for distributed sparse numerical factorization*, SIAM J. Sci. Stat. Comput., 11 (1990), pp. 593–599.

[11] C. ASHCRAFT, R. GRIMES, J. LEWIS, B. PEYTON, AND H. SIMON, *Progress in sparse matrix methods for large linear systems on vector supercomputers*, Internat. J. Supercomp. Appl, 1 (1987), pp. 10–30.

[12] R. BENNER, G. MONTRY, AND G. WEIGAND, *Concurrent multifrontal methods: shared memory, cache, and frontwidth issues*, Internat. J. Supercomp. Appl, 1 (1987), pp. 26–44.

[13] P. BERMAN AND G. SCHNITGER, *On the performance of the minimum degree ordering for Gaussian elimination*, SIAM J. Matrix Anal. Appl., 11 (1990), pp. 83–88.

[14] J. BROWNE, J. DONGARRA, A. KARP, K. KENNEDY, AND D. KUCK, *1988 Gordon Bell prize*, IEEE Software, 6 (May 1989), pp. 78–85.

[15] I. CAVERS, *Tiebreaking the minimum degree algorithm for ordering sparse symmetric positive definite matrices*, Master's thesis, Department of Computer Science, University of British Columbia, 1987.

[16] E. CHU AND A. GEORGE, *Sparse orthogonal decomposition on a hypercube multiprocessor*, SIAM J. Matrix Anal. Appl., 11 (1990), pp. 453–465.

[17] E. CHU, A. GEORGE, J. W.-H. LIU, AND E. G.-Y. NG, *User's guide for SPARSPAK-A: Waterloo sparse linear equations package*, Tech. Report CS-84-36, University of Waterloo, Waterloo, Ontario, 1984.

[18] J. CONROY, *Parallel direct solution of sparse linear systems of equations*, Tech. Report TR 1714, Department of Computer Science University of Maryland, College Park, Maryland 20742, 1986.

[19] A. DAVE AND I. DUFF, *Sparse matrix calculations on the Cray-2*, Parallel Computing, 5 (1987), pp. 55–64.

[20] T. DAVIS AND P. YEW, *A nondeterministic parallel algorithm for general unsymmetric sparse LU factorization*, SIAM J. Matrix Anal. Appl., 11 (1990), pp. 383–402.

[21] J. DONGARRA, F. GUSTAVSON, AND A. KARP, *Implementing linear algebra algorithms for dense matrices on a vector pipeline machine*, SIAM Review, 26 (1984), pp. 91–112.

[22] I. DUFF, *Parallel implementation of multifrontal schemes*, Parallel Computing, 3 (1986), pp. 193–204.

[23] ———, *Multiprocessing a sparse matrix code on the Alliant FX/8*, J. Comput. Appl. Math., 27 (1989), pp. 229–239.

[24] I. DUFF, A. ERISMAN, AND J. REID, *On George's nested dissection method*, SIAM J. Numer. Anal., 13 (1976), pp. 686–695.

[25] I. DUFF, A. ERISMAN, AND J. K. REID, *Direct Methods for Sparse Matrices*, Oxford University Press, Oxford, England, 1987.

[26] I. DUFF, N. GOULD, M. LESCRENIER, AND J. K. REID, *The multifrontal method in a parallel environment*, in Advances in Numerical Computation, M. Cox and S. Hammarling, eds., Oxford University Press, 1990. (To appear).

[27] I. DUFF AND J. REID, *MA27 - a set of Fortran subroutines for solving sparse symmetric sets of linear equations*, Tech. Report AERE R 10533, Harwell, 1982.

[28] ———, *The multifrontal solution of indefinite sparse symmetric linear equations*, ACM Trans. Math. Software, 9 (1983), pp. 302–325.

[29] S. EISENSTAT, M. GURSKY, M. SCHULTZ, AND A. H. SHERMAN, *The Yale sparse matrix package I. the symmetric codes*, Internat. J. Numer. Meth. Engrg., 18 (1982), pp. 1145–1151.

[30] S. EISENSTAT, M. HEATH, C. HENKEL, AND C. ROMINE, *Modified cyclic algorithms for solving triangular systems on distributed-memory multiprocessors*, SIAM J. Sci. Stat. Comput., 9 (1988), pp. 589–600.

[31] C. FIDUCCIA AND R. MATTHEYSES, *A linear-time heuristic for improving network partitions*, in Proceedings of the 19th Design Automation Conference, 1982, pp. 175–181.

[32] M. FIEDLER, *Algebraic connectivity of graphs*, Czech. Math. J., 23 (1973), pp. 298–305.

[33] ———, *A property of eigenvectors of non-negative symmetric matrices and its application to graph theory*, Czech. Math. J., 25 (1975), pp. 619–633.

[34] K. GALLIVAN, R. PLEMMONS, AND A. SAMEH, *Parallel algorithms for dense linear algebra computations*, SIAM Review, 32 (1990), pp. 54–135.

[35] F. GAO AND B. PARLETT, *Communication cost of sparse Cholesky factorization on a hypercube*, Tech. Report PAM-436, Center for Pure and Applied Mathematics, University of California, Berkeley, California, 1988.

[36] G. GEIST, *Solving finite element problems with parallel multifrontal schemes*, in Hypercube

Multiprocessors 1987, M. T. Heath, ed., Philadelphia, 1987, SIAM, pp. 656–661.

[37] G. GEIST AND M. HEATH, *Parallel Cholesky factorization on a hypercube multiprocessor*, Tech. Report ORNL-6211, Oak Ridge National Laboratory, Oak Ridge, Tennessee, 1985.

[38] G. GEIST AND E. G.-Y. NG, *Task scheduling for parallel sparse Cholesky factorization*, Internat. J. Parallel Programming, 18 (1989), pp. 291–314.

[39] A. GEORGE, *Nested dissection of a regular finite element mesh*, SIAM J. Numer. Anal., 10 (1973), pp. 345–363.

[40] A. GEORGE, M. HEATH, AND J. W.-H. LIU, *Parallel Cholesky factorization on a shared-memory multiprocessor*, Linear Alg. Appl., 77 (1986), pp. 165–187.

[41] A. GEORGE, M. HEATH, J. W.-H. LIU, AND E. G.-Y. NG, *Solution of sparse positive definite systems on a shared memory multiprocessor*, Internat. J. Parallel Programming, 15 (1986), pp. 309–325.

[42] ———, *Symbolic Cholesky factorization on a local-memory multiprocessor*, Parallel Computing, 5 (1987), pp. 85–95.

[43] ———, *Sparse Cholesky factorization on a local-memory multiprocessor*, SIAM J. Sci. Stat. Comput., 9 (1988), pp. 327–340.

[44] ———, *Solution of sparse positive definite systems on a hypercube*, J. Comp. Appl. Math., 27 (1989), pp. 129–156.

[45] A. GEORGE AND J. W.-H. LIU, *An automatic nested dissection algorithm for irregular finite element problems*, SIAM J. Numer. Anal., 15 (1978), pp. 1053–1069.

[46] ———, *An optimal algorithm for symbolic factorization of symmetric matrices*, SIAM J. Comput., 9 (1980), pp. 583–593.

[47] ———, *Computer Solution of Large Sparse Positive Definite Systems*, Prentice-Hall Inc., Englewood Cliffs, New Jersey, 1981.

[48] ———, *The evolution of the minimum degree ordering algorithm*, SIAM Review, 31 (1989), pp. 1–19.

[49] A. GEORGE, J. W.-H. LIU, AND E. G.-Y. NG, *Communication results for parallel sparse Cholesky factorization on a hypercube*, Parallel Computing, 10 (1989), pp. 287–298.

[50] A. GEORGE AND D. MCINTYRE, *On the application of the minimum degree algorithm to finite element systems*, SIAM J. Numer. Anal., 15 (1978), pp. 90–111.

[51] A. GEORGE AND E. G.-Y. NG, *Parallel sparse Gaussian elimination with partial pivoting*, Annals of Operations Research, 22 (1990), pp. 219–240.

[52] J. GILBERT, *An efficient parallel sparse partial pivoting algorithm*, Tech. Report CMI No. 88/45052-1, Centre for Computer Science, Dept. of Science and Technology, Chr. Michelsen Institute, Bergen, Norway, 1988.

[53] J. GILBERT AND H. HAFSTEINSSON, *Parallel symbolic factorization of sparse linear systems*, Parallel Computing, 14 (1990), pp. 151–162.

[54] J. GILBERT AND R. SCHREIBER, *Highly parallel sparse Cholesky factorization*, Tech. Report CSL-90-7, Xerox Palo Also Research Center, 1990. (Submitted to SIAM J. Sci. Stat. Comput.).

[55] J. GILBERT AND E. ZMIJEWSKI, *A parallel graph partitioning algorithm for a message-passing multiprocessor*, Intern. J. Parallel Programming, 16 (1987), pp. 427–449.

[56] A. GREENBAUM, *Solving sparse triangular linear systems using fortran with extensions on the NYU Ultracomputer prototype*, Tech. Report Tech. Rept. 99, NYU Ultracomputer Note, New York University, April 1986.

[57] M. HEATH, *Visual animation of parallel algorithms for matrix computations*, in Proc. Fifth Distributed Memory Computng Conf., Charleston, SC, 1990. (To appear).

[58] M. HEATH AND C. ROMINE, *Parallel solution of triangular systems on distributed-memory multiprocessors*, SIAM J. Sci. Stat. Comput., 9 (1988), pp. 558–588.

[59] M. HEATH AND D. SORENSEN, *A pipelined Givens method for computing the QR factorization of a sparse matrix*, Linear Alg. Appl., 77 (1986), pp. 189–203.

[60] A. HOFFMAN, M. MARTIN, AND D. ROSE, *Complexity bounds for regular finite difference and finite element grids*, SIAM J. Numer. Anal., 10 (1973), pp. 364–369.

[61] B. IRONS, *A frontal solution program for finite element analysis*, Int. J. Num. Meth. Engng., 2 (1970), pp. 5–32.

[62] J. JESS AND H. KEES, *A data structure for parallel L/U decomposition*, IEEE Trans. Comput., C-31 (1982), pp. 231–239.

[63] B. KERNIGHAN AND S. LIN, *An efficient heuristic procedure for partitioning graphs*, Bell System Technical Journal, 49 (1970), pp. 291–307.

[64] C. LAWSON, R. HANSON, D. KINCAID, AND F. KROGH, *Basic linear algebra subprograms for Fortran usage*, ACM Trans. Math. Software, 5 (1979), pp. 308–371.

[65] C. LEISERSON AND J. LEWIS, *Orderings for parallel sparse symmetric factorization*, in Parallel

Processing for Scientific Computing, G. Rodrigue, ed., Philadelphia, PA, 1989, SIAM, pp. 27–32.

[66] M. Leuze, *Independent set orderings for parallel matrix factorization by Gaussian elimination*, Parallel Computing, 10 (1989), pp. 177–191.

[67] J. Lewis, B. Peyton, and A. Pothen, *A fast algorithm for reordering sparse matrices for parallel factorization*, SIAM J. Sci. Stat. Comput., 10 (1989), pp. 1156–1173.

[68] R. Lipton, D. Rose, and R. Tarjan, *Generalized nested dissection*, SIAM J. Numer. Anal., 16 (1979), pp. 346–358.

[69] R. Lipton and R. Tarjan, *A separator theorem for planar graphs*, SIAM J. Appl. Math., 36 (1979), pp. 177–199.

[70] J. W.-H. Liu, *Modification of the minimum degree algorithm by multiple elimination*, ACM Trans. Math. Software, 11 (1985), pp. 141–153.

[71] ———, *A compact row storage scheme for Cholesky factors using elimination trees*, ACM Trans. Math. Software, 12 (1986), pp. 127–148.

[72] ———, *Computational models and task scheduling for parallel sparse Cholesky factorization*, Parallel Computing, 3 (1986), pp. 327–342.

[73] ———, *Equivalent sparse matrix reordering by elimination tree rotations*, SIAM J. Sci. Stat. Comput., 9 (1988), pp. 424–444.

[74] ———, *A graph partitioning algorithm by node separators*, ACM Trans. Math. Software, 15 (1989), pp. 198–219.

[75] ———, *The minimum degree ordering with constraints*, SIAM J. Sci. Stat. Comput., 10 (1989), pp. 1136–1145.

[76] ———, *The multifrontal method and paging in sparse Cholesky factorization*, ACM Trans. Math. Software, 15 (1989), pp. 310–325.

[77] ———, *Reordering sparse matrices for parallel elimination*, Parallel Computing, 11 (1989), pp. 73–91.

[78] ———, *The multifrontal method for sparse matrix solution: theory and practice*, Tech. Report CS-90-04, Dept. of Computer Science, York University, North York, Ontario, 1990.

[79] ———, *The role of elimination trees in sparse factorization*, SIAM J. Matrix Anal. Appl., 11 (1990), pp. 134–172.

[80] J. W.-H. Liu and A. Mirzaian, *A linear reordering algorithm for parallel pivoting of chordal graphs*, SIAM J. Disc. Math., 2 (1989), pp. 100–107.

[81] J. W.-H. Liu and E. G.-Y. Ng, *A supernodal symbolic Cholesky factorization on a local-memory multiprocessor*. In preparation, 1990.

[82] R. Lucas, *Solving planar systems of equations on distributed-memory multiprocessors*, PhD thesis, Department of electrical engineering, Stanford University, 1987.

[83] ———. Personal communication, 1990.

[84] R. Lucas, W. Blank, and J. Tieman, *A parallel solution method for large sparse systems of equations*, IEEE Trans. Computer Aided Design, CAD-6 (1987), pp. 981–991.

[85] R. Melhem, *Parallel solution of linear systems with striped sparse matrices*, Parallel Computing, 6 (1988), pp. 165–184.

[86] V. Naik and M. Patrick, *Data traffic reduction schemes for sparse Cholesky factorization*, Tech. Report ICASE Report No. 88-14, ICASE, NASA Langley Research Center, Hampton, Virginia, 1988.

[87] ———, *Data traffic reduction schemes for Cholesky factorization on asynchronous multiprocessor systems*, Tech. Report ICASE Report No. 89-40, ICASE, NASA Langley Research Center, Hampton, Virginia, 1989.

[88] E. Ng and B. Peyton, *A supernodal Cholesky factorization algorithm for shared-memory multiprocessors*. In preparation, 1990.

[89] J. Ortega, *Introduction to parallel and vector solution of linear systems*, Plenum Press, New York, 1988.

[90] J. Ortega, R. Voigt, and C. Romine, *A bibliography on parallel and vector numerical algorithms*, Tech. Report ORNL/TM-10998, Oak Ridge National Laboratory, Oak Ridge, TN, 1989.

[91] S. Parter, *The use of linear graphs in Gaussian elimination*, SIAM Review, 3 (1961), pp. 364–369.

[92] F. Peters, *Parallel pivoting algorithms for sparse symmetric matrices*, Parallel Computing, 1 (1984), pp. 99–110.

[93] A. Pothen, *The complexity of optimal elimination trees*, Tech. Report CS-88-16, Department of Computer Science, The Pennsylvania State University, University Park, PA, 1988.

[94] A. Pothen and C.-J. Fan, *Computing the block triangular form of a sparse matrix*, Tech. Report CS-88-51, Department of Computer Science, The Pennsylvania State University,

University Park, PA, 1988. (To appear in ACM Trans. Math. Software).

[95] A. POTHEN, H. SIMON, AND K. LIOU, *Partitioning sparse matrices with eigenvectors of graphs*, SIAM J. Matrix Anal. Appl., 11 (1990), pp. 430–452.

[96] P. RAGHAVAN AND A. POTHEN, *Parallel orthogonal factorization*. SIAM Symposium on Sparse Matrices, Gleneden Beach, Oregon, 1989.

[97] D. ROSE, *Triangulated graphs and the elimination process*, J. Math. Anal. Appl., 32 (1970), pp. 597–609.

[98] ———, *A graph-theoretic study of the numerical solution of sparse positive definite systems of linear equations*, in Graph Theory and Computing, R. C. Read, ed., Academic Press, 1972, pp. 183–217.

[99] D. ROSE, R. TARJAN, AND G. LUEKER, *Algorithmic aspects of vertex elimination on graphs*, SIAM J. Comput., 5 (1976), pp. 266–283.

[100] E. ROTHBERG AND A. GUPTA, *Fast sparse matrix factorization on modern workstations*, Tech. Report STAN-CS-89-1286, Stanford University, Stanford, California, 1989.

[101] P. SADAYAPPAN AND V. VISVANATHAN, *Distributed sparse factorization of circuit matrices via recursive E-tree partitioning*. SIAM Symposium on Sparse Matrices, Gleneden Beach, Oregon, 1989.

[102] J. SALTZ, *Aggregation methods for solving sparse triangular systems on multiprocessors*, SIAM J. Sci. Stat. Comput., 11 (1990), pp. 123–144.

[103] R. SCHREIBER, *A new implementation of sparse Gaussian elimination*, ACM Trans. Math. Software, 8 (1982), pp. 256–276.

[104] A. SHERMAN, *On the efficient solution of sparse systems of linear and nonlinear equations*, PhD thesis, Yale University, 1975.

[105] P. VU. Personal communication, 1990.

[106] P. WORLEY AND R. SCHREIBER, *Nested dissection on a mesh-connected processor array*, in New Computing Environments: Parallel, Vector, and Systolic, A. Wouk, ed., Philadelphia, 1986, SIAM Publications, pp. 8–38.

[107] M. YANNAKAKIS, *Computing the minimum fill-in is NP-complete*, SIAM J. Alg. Disc. Meth., 2 (1981), pp. 77–79.

[108] E. ZMIJEWSKI, *Sparse Cholesky Factorization on a Multiprocessor*, PhD thesis, Department of Computer Science, Cornell University, Ithaca, New York 14853-7501, August 1987.

[109] ———, *Limiting communication in parallel sparse Cholesky factorization*, Tech. Report TRCS89-18, Department of Computer Science, University of California, Santa Barbara, California 93106, 1989.

[110] E. ZMIJEWSKI AND J. GILBERT, *A parallel algorithm for sparse symbolic Cholesky factorization on a multiprocessor*, Parallel Computing, 7 (1988), pp. 199–210.

A BIBLIOGRAPHY ON PARALLEL AND VECTOR NUMERICAL ALGORITHMS

JAMES M. ORTEGA*, ROBERT G. VOIGT† AND CHARLES H. ROMINE‡

Since parallel and vector computation is expanding rapidly, we hope that the references we have collected over the years will be of some value to researchers entering the field. Naturally, any such collection will be incomplete. Our apologies in advance to authors whose works we have missed. For further information about access to an electronic copy of the bibliography, send email to either `romine@msr.epm.ornl.gov` or `rgv@icase.edu`.

Although this is a bibliography on numerical methods, we have included a number of other references on machine architecture, programming languages, and other topics of interest to scientific computing.

Certain conference proceedings and anthologies that have been published in book form we list under the name of the editor (or editors) and then list individual articles with a pointer back to the whole volume; for example, the reference

[225] A. BRANDT [1981]. *Multigrid solvers on parallel computers*, in Schultz[1752], pp. 39–83.

refers to the article by Brandt in the volume listed under [1752] M. SCHULTZ. Note that the cross-reference is by reference number, not by year.

This bibliography was also published in January of 1989 by Oak Ridge National Laboratory as ORNL-TM/10998, and by the Institute for Computer Applications in Science and Engineering as ICASE Interim Report 6.

REFERENCES

[1] H. ABDEL-WAHAB AND T. KAMEDA [1978]. *Scheduling to minimize maximum cumulative cost subject to series-parallel precedence constraints*, Oper. Res., 26, pp. 141–158.

[2] I. ABSAR [1983]. *Vectorization of a penalty function algorithm for well scheduling*, in Gary [700], pp. 361–370.

[3] I. ABU-SHOMAYS [1985]. *Comparison of methods and algorithms for tridiagonal systems and for vectorization of diffusion computation*, in Numrich [1469], pp. 29–56.

[4] W. ABU-SUFAH AND A. MALONY [1986]. *Experimental results for vector processing on the Alliant FX/8*, Tech. Report 539, Center for Supercomputing Research and Development, University of Illinois at Urbana-Champaign, February.

[5] W. ABU-SUFAH AND A. MALONY [1986]. *Vector processing on the Alliant FX/8 multiprocessor*, Proc. 1986 Int. Conf. Par. Proc., pp. 559–566.

[6] T. ADAM, K. CHANDY, AND J. DICKSON [1974]. *A comparison of list schedules for parallel processing systems*, Comm. ACM, 17, pp. 685–690.

[7] G. ADAMS, R. BROWN, AND P. DENNING [1985]. *On evaluating parallel computing systems*, Tech. Report TR-85.3, RIACS, NASA Ames Research Center, May.

* The work of this author was supported in part by the National Aeronautics and Space Administration under NASA Contract No. NAS-1-46-6.

† The work of this author was supported by the National Aeronautics and Space Administration under NASA Contract Nos. NAS1-18107 and NAS1-18605 at the Institute for Computer Applications in Science and Engineering (ICASE), NASA Langley Research Center, Hampton, VA 23665.

‡ The work of this author was supported by the Applied Mathematical Sciences Research Program, Office of Energy Research, U.S. Department of Energy under contract DE-AC05-84OR21400 with Martin Marietta Energy Systems Inc.

[8] G. ADAMS, R. BROWN, AND P. DENNING [1985]. *Report on an evaluation study of data flow computation*, Tech. Report TR-85.2, RIACS, NASA Ames Research Center, April.

[9] L. ADAMS [1982]. *Iterative Algorithms for Large Sparse Linear Systems on Parallel Computers*, PhD dissertation, The University of Virginia, Department of Applied Mathematics and Computer Science. Also published as NASA CR-166027, NASA Langley Research Center.

[10] L. ADAMS [1983]. *An M-step preconditioned conjugate gradient method for parallel computation*, Proc. 1983 Int. Conf. Par. Proc., pp. 36–43.

[11] L. ADAMS [1985]. *M-step preconditioned conjugate gradient methods*, SIAM J. Sci. Statist. Comput., 6, pp. 452–463.

[12] L. ADAMS [1986]. *Reordering computations for parallel execution*, Comm. Appl. Numer. Meth., 2, pp. 263–271.

[13] L. ADAMS AND T. CROCKETT [1984]. *Modeling algorithm execution time on processor arrays*, Computer, 17(7), pp. 38–43.

[14] L. ADAMS AND H. JORDAN [1985]. *Is SOR color-blind?*, SIAM J. Sci. Statist. Comput., 7, pp. 490–506.

[15] L. ADAMS AND E. ONG [1987]. *Additive polynomial preconditioners for parallel computers*, Parallel Computing. To appear.

[16] L. ADAMS AND J. ORTEGA [1982]. *A multi-color SOR method for parallel computation*, Proc. 1982 Int. Conf. Par. Proc., pp. 53–56.

[17] L. ADAMS AND R. VOIGT [1984]. *Design, development and use of the Finite Element Machine*, in Parter [1529], pp. 301–321.

[18] L. ADAMS AND R. VOIGT [1984]. *A methodology for exploiting parallelism in the finite element process*, in Kowalik [1116], pp. 373–392.

[19] N. ADAMS AND O. JOHNSON [1985]. *A vector elastic model for the Cyber 205*, in Numrich [1469], pp. 101–114.

[20] T. AGERWALA AND ARVIND. [1982]. *Data flow systems*, Computer, 15(2), pp. 10–13.

[21] V. AGGARNAL, S. DHALL, J. DIAZ, AND S. LAKSHMIRARAHUN [1985]. *A parallel algorithm for solving large scale sparse linear systems using block pre-conditioned conjugate gradient method on an MIMD machine*, Tech. Report OU-PPI, TR-85-02, Schools of Electrical Engineering and Computer Science, University of Oklahoma, January.

[22] A. AGGARWAL, B. CHAZELLE, L. GUIBAS, C. O'DUNLAING, AND C. YAP [1985]. *Parallel computational geometry*, Proc. IEEE Conference on Fundamentals of Computer Science, pp. 468–477.

[23] D. AGRAWAL, ed. [1986]. *Advanced Computer Architecture*, North-Holland, Amsterdam.

[24] R. AHLBERG AND B. GUSTAFSSON [1984]. *A note on parallel algorithms for partial differential equations*, in Feilmeier et al. [623], pp. 93–98.

[25] H. AHMED, J. DELOSME, AND M. MORF [1982]. *Highly concurrent computing structures for matrix arithmetic and signal processing*, Computer, 15(1), pp. 65–82.

[26] G. ALAGHBAND [1987]. *Parallel pivoting combined with parallel reduction*, Tech. Report 87-75, ICASE, NASA Langley Research Center, Hampton, VA, December.

[27] G. ALAGHBAND [1988]. *Multiprocessor Sparse LU Decomposition with Controlled Fill-in*, PhD dissertation, University of Colorado, Boulder, Department of Electrical and Computer Engineering.

[28] G. ALAGHBAND AND H. JORDAN [1983]. *Parallelization of the MA28 sparse matrix package for the HEP*, Tech. Report CSDG-83-3, Department of Electrical and Computer Engineering, University of Colorado, Boulder.

[29] G. ALAGHBAND AND H. JORDAN [1985]. *Multiprocessor sparse L/U decomposition with controlled fill-in*, Tech. Report 85-48, ICASE, NASA Langley Research Center, Hampton, VA.

[30] G. ALAGHBAND AND H. JORDAN [1986]. *Sparse Gaussian elimination with controlled fill-in on a shared memory multiprocessor*, ECSE Tech. Report 86-1-5, Department of Electrical and Computer Engineering, University of Colorado, Boulder.

[31] T. ALLEN AND G. CYBENKO [1987]. *Recursive binary partitions*, Tech. Report, Department of Computer Science, Tufts University, October.

[32] E. ALLROTH [1984]. *Minimization of the processing time of parallel computers*, Physics Letters, 106A(7), pp. 329–331.

[33] V. ALMEIDA, L. DOWDY, AND M. LEUZE [1988]. *An analytic model for parallel Gaussian elimination on a binary N-cube*, in Fox et al. [651], pp. 1550–1553.

[34] R. ALT [1985]. *Computing roots of polynomials on vector processing machines*, Comm. Appl. Numer. Meth., 1, pp. 299–308.

[35] H. AMANO, T. BOKU, T. KUDOH, AND H. AISO [1985]. *A new version of the sparse ma-*

trix solving machine, Proc. 12th International Symposium on Computer Architecture, pp. 100–107.

[36] G. AMDAHL [1967]. *The validity of the single processor approach to achieving large scale computing capabilities*, AFIPS Conf. Proc., 30, pp. 483–485.

[37] G. AMDAHL [1988]. *Limits of expectation*, Int. J. Supercomputer Appl., 2(1), pp. 88–97.

[38] D. ANDERSON, A. FRY, R. GRUBER, AND A. ROY [1987]. *Gigaflop speed algorithm for the direct solution of large block-tridiagonal systems in 3D physics applications*, Tech. Report UCRL-96034, Lawrence Livermore National Laboratory. Submitted to J. Parallel Comput.

[39] D. ANDERSON, A. FRY, R. GRUBER, AND A. ROY [1987]. *Plasma physics at gigaflops on the CRAY-2*, Third Symposium on Science and Engineering on Cray Supercomputers, Minneapolis, MN.

[40] D. ANDERSON, R. GRUBER, A. FRY, AND A. ROY [1987]. *Parallel cyclic reduction algorithm for the direct solution of large block-tridiagonal systems*, First International Conference Industrial and Applied Math., Paris.

[41] D. ANDERSON, R. GRUBER, AND A. ROY [1987]. *Measurements and estimates of the PAMS plasma equilibrium solver on existing and near-term supercomputers*, Twelfth Conf. on Numerical Simulation of Plasmas, San Francisco, CA. (Paper PM11).

[42] D. ANDERSON, E. HOROWITZ, A. KONIGES, AND M. MCCOY [1986]. *Parallel computing and multitasking*, Comput. Phys. Comm., 43, pp. 69–88.

[43] D. ANDERSON, A. KONIGES, M. MCCOY, AND A. MIRIN [1987]. *A survey of linear systems solvers on the NMFECC system*, American Physical Society Division of Plasma Physics Meeting, San Diego, CA. Paper 6S10.

[44] G. ANDERSON AND E. JENSEN [1975]. *Computer interconnection structures: Taxonomy, characteristics, and examples*, ACM Computing Surveys, 7, pp. 197–213.

[45] J. ANDERSON [1965]. *Program structures for parallel processing*, Comm. ACM, 8, pp. 786–788.

[46] R. ANDERSON, R. GRIMES, R. RIEBMAN, AND H. SIMON [1987]. *Early experience with the SCS-40*, Supercomputer, 22, pp. 26–36.

[47] R. ANDERSON, R. GRIMES, AND H. SIMON [1987]. *Performance comparison of the CRAY X-MP/24 and the CRAY-2*, Tech. Report ETA-TR-57, Boeing Computer Services, July.

[48] F. ANDRE, D. HERMAN, AND J. VARJUS [1985], *Synchronization of Parallel Programs*, MIT Press, Cambridge.

[49] G. ANDREWS AND F. SCHNEIDER [1983]. *Concepts and notations for concurrent programming*, ACM Computing Surveys, 15, pp. 3–43.

[50] M. ANNARATONE, E. ARNOULD, T. GROSS, H. KUNG, M. LAM, AND O. MENZILCIOGLU [1986]. *WARP architecture and implementation*, SPIE Real Time Signal Processing IX.

[51] M. ANNARATONE, E. ARNOULD, T. GROSS, H. KUNG, M. LAM, O. MENZILCIOGLU, AND J. WEBB [1987]. *The Warp computer: Architecture, implementation, and performance*, IEEE Trans. Comput., C-36, pp. 1523–1538.

[52] M. ANWAR AND M. EL TARZI [1985]. *Asynchronous algorithms for Poisson's equation with nonlinear boundary conditions*, Computing, 34, pp. 155–168.

[53] N. ARENSTORF AND H. JORDAN [1987]. *Comparing barrier algorithms*, Tech. Report 87-65, ICASE, NASA Langley Research Center.

[54] J. ARMSTRONG [1987]. *Optimization of Householder transformations part I. Linear least squares*, Proc. 1987 Int. Conf. Par. Proc., pp. 495–498.

[55] W. ARMSTRONG, T. MARSLAND, M. OLAFSSON, AND J. SCHAEFFER [1987]. *Solving equations of motion on a virtual tree machine*, SIAM J. Sci. Statist. Comput., 8, pp. s59–s72.

[56] C. ARNOLD [1982]. *Performance evaluation of three automatic vectorizer packages*, Proc. 1982 Int. Conf. Par. Proc., pp. 235–242.

[57] C. ARNOLD [1983]. *Vector optimization on the CYBER 205*, Proc. 1983 Int. Conf. Par. Proc., pp. 530–536.

[58] C. ARNOLD [1984]. *Machine independent techniques for scientific supercomputing*, Proc. COMPCON 84, IEEE Comp. Sci. Conf., pp. 74–83.

[59] C. ARNOLD, M. PARR, AND M. DEWE [1983]. *An efficient parallel algorithm for the solution of large sparse linear matrix equations*, IEEE Trans. Comput., C-32, pp. 265–273.

[60] D. ARPASI AND E. MILNER [1986]. *Mathematical model partitioning and packing for parallel computer calculation*, Proc. 1986 Int. Conf. Par. Proc., pp. 67–74.

[61] ARVIND AND R. BRYANT [1979]. *Parallel computers for partial differential equations simulation*, Proc. Scientific Computer Information Exchange Meeting, Livermore, CA, pp. 94–102.

[62] ARVIND AND V. KATHAIL [1981]. *A multiple processor data flow machine that supports gen-*

eralized procedures, 8th Annual Sym. Comp. Arch., May, pp. 291–302.

[63] S. ARYA AND D. CALAHAN [1981]. *Optimal scheduling of assembly language kernels for vector processors*, 19th Allerton Conf. on Comm. Control and Computers, University of Illinois at Urbana-Champaign.

[64] C. ASHCRAFT [1985]. *A moving computation front approach for vectorizing ICCG calculations*, Tech. Report GMR-5174, General Motors Research Lab.

[65] C. ASHCRAFT [1985]. *Parallel reduction methods for the solution of banded systems of equations*, Computer Science Tech. Report, General Motors, June.

[66] C. ASHCRAFT [1987]. *Domain decoupled incomplete factorizations*, Applied Mathematics Tech. Report ETA-TR-49, Boeing Computer Services.

[67] C. ASHCRAFT [1987]. *A vector implementation of the multifrontal method for large sparse, symmetric positive definite linear systems*, Applied Mathematics Tech. Report ETA-TR-51, Boeing Computer Services.

[68] C. ASHCRAFT AND R. GRIMES [1987]. *The influence of relaxed supernode partitions on the multifrontal method*, Tech. Report ETA-TR-60, Boeing Computer Services.

[69] C. ASHCRAFT AND R. GRIMES [1988]. *On vectorizing incomplete factorization and SSOR preconditioners*, SIAM J. Sci. Statist. Comput., 9, pp. 122–151.

[70] C. ASHCRAFT, R. GRIMES, J. LEWIS, B. PEYTON, AND H. SIMON [1987]. *Recent progress in sparse matrix methods for large linear systems on vector supercomputers*, Int. J. Supercomputer Appl., 1, pp. 10–30.

[71] C. ASHCRAFT, J. LEWIS, AND B. PEYTON [1987]. *A supernodal implementation of general sparse factorization for vector computers*, Tech. Report ETA-TR-52, Boeing Computer Services.

[72] C. ASHCRAFT, G. SHOOK, AND J. JONES [1986]. *A computational survey of the conjugate gradient preconditioners on the CRAY 1-S*, Tech. Report GMR-5299, General Motors Research Lab.

[73] M. ASHWORTH AND A. LYNE [1988]. *A segmented FFT algorithm for vector computers*, Parallel Computing, 6, pp. 217–224.

[74] S. ASKEW AND F. WALKDEN [1984]. *On the design and implementation of a package for solving a class of partial differential equations*, in Paddon [1512], pp. 107–114.

[75] V. ASRIELI [1985]. *Base language of the programming system of a vector processor*, Computational Processes and Systems, Izdatel'stvo Nauka, Moscow, pp. 73–83.

[76] V. ASRIELI AND P. BORISOV [1985]. *Experience with programming a vector processor for the solution of the Navier-Stokes equations in a three-dimensional region*, Computational Processes and Systems, Izdatel'stvo Nauka, Moscow, pp. 84–90.

[77] W. ATHAS AND C. SEITZ [1988]. *Multicomputers: Message-passing concurrent computers*, Computer, 21(8), pp. 9–24.

[78] J. AVILA AND J. TOMLIN [1979]. *Solution of very large least squares problems by nested dissection on a parallel processor*, Proc. Computer Science and Statistics: Twelfth Annual Symposium on the Interface, J. Gentleman, ed., Waterloo, Ontario, Canada, University of Waterloo, pp. 9–14.

[79] A. AVIZIENIS, M. EVCEGOVAC, T. LANG, P. SYLVAIN, AND A. THOMASIAN [1977]. *An investigation of fault-tolerant architectures for large scale numerical computing*, in Kuck et al. [1133], pp. 159–183.

[80] T. AXELROD [1986]. *Effects of synchronization barriers on multiprocessor performance*, Parallel Computing, 3, pp. 129–140.

[81] O. AXELSSON [1985]. *A survey of vectorizable preconditioning methods for large scale finite element matrix problems*, BIT, 25, pp. 166–187.

[82] O. AXELSSON [1986]. *Analysis of incomplete matrix factorizations as multigrid smoothers for vector and parallel computers*, Appl. Math. & Comp., 19(1-4). (Special Issue, Proceedings of the Second Copper Mountain Conference on Multigrid Methods, Copper Mountain, CO, S. McCormick, ed.)

[83] O. AXELSSON [1988]. *Incomplete block matrix factorization preconditioning methods. The ultimate answer?*, J. Comput. Appl. Math., 12/13, pp. 3–18.

[84] O. AXELSSON AND V. EIJKHOUT [1986]. *A note on the vectorization of scalar recursions*, Parallel Computing, 3, pp. 73–84.

[85] C. AYKANAT, S. DORAIVELU, P. SADAYAPPAN, K. SCHWAN, AND B. WEIDE [1986]. *Parallel computers and finite element analysis*, 1986 ASME Int. Conf. Computers in Engineering, pp. 43–50.

[86] C. AYKANAT AND F. OZGUNER [1987]. *Large grain parallel conjugate gradient algorithms on a hypercube multiprocessor*, Proc. 1987 Int. Conf. Par. Proc., pp. 641–644.

[87] C. AYKANAT, F. OZGUNER, S. MARTIN, AND S. DORAIVELU [1987]. *Parallelization of a finite*

element application program on a hypercube multiprocessor, in Heath [860], pp. 662–673.

[88] R. BABB [1984]. *Parallel processing with large-grain data flow techniques*, Computer, 17(7), pp. 55–61.

[89] R. BABB [1986]. *Parallel processing on the CRAY X-MP with large-grain data flow techniques*, in Fernbach [630], pp. 239–251.

[90] R. BABB, L. STORC, AND R. HIROMOTO [1986]. *Developing a parallel Monte Carlo transport algorithm using large-grain data flow*, Tech. Report LA-UR-86-2080, Los Alamos National Laboratory.

[91] I. BABUSKA AND H. ELMAN [1988]. *Some aspects of parallel implementation of the finite element method on message passing architectures*, Tech. Report CS-TR-2030, Department of Computer Science, University of Maryland.

[92] S. BADEN [1986]. *Dynamic load balancing of a vortex calculation running on multiprocessors*, Tech. Report LBL-22584, Lawrence Berkeley Laboratory, December.

[93] J.-L. BAER [1973]. *A survey of some theoretical aspects of multiprocessing*, ACM Computing Surveys, 5, pp. 31–80.

[94] J.-L. BAER [1977]. *Multiprocessing systems*, IEEE Trans. Comput., C-25, pp. 1271–1277.

[95] J.-L. BAER [1980]. *Supercomputers*, Computer Systems Architecture, Computer Science Press, Los Alamitos, CA.

[96] J.-L. BAER [1984]. *Computer architecture*, Computer, 17(10), pp. 77–87.

[97] D. BAILEY [1987]. *A high performance fast Fourier transform algorithm for the CRAY-2*, J. Supercomputing, 1, pp. 43–60.

[98] D. BAILEY [1988]. *Extra high speed matrix multiplication on the Cray-2*, SIAM J. Sci. Statist. Comput., 8, pp. 603–607.

[99] D. BAILEY, J. CUNY, AND B. MACLEOD [1987]. *Reducing communication overhead: A parallel code optimization*, J. Par. Dist. Comp., 4, pp. 505–520.

[100] E. BAJAJ, W. DYKSEN, C. HOFFMAN, E. HOUSTIS, J. KORB, AND J. RICE [1987]. *Computing about physical objects*, Tech. Report TR-696, Department of Computer Science, Purdue University.

[101] K. BAKER AND L. SCHRAGE [1978]. *Finding an optimal sequence by dynamic programming: An extension to precedence-related tasks*, Oper. Res., 26, pp. 111–120.

[102] W. BALLHAUS [1984]. *Computational aerodynamics and supercomputers*, Proc. COMPCON 84, IEEE Comp. Soc. Conf., pp. 3–14.

[103] I. BAR-ON [1987]. *A practical parallel algorithm for solving band symmetric positive definite systems of linear equations*, ACM Trans. Math. Softw., 13, pp. 323–332.

[104] D. BARKAI AND A. BRANDT [1983]. *Vectorized multigrid Poisson solver for the CDC CYBER 205*, Appl. Math. & Comp., 13(3-4), pp. 215–228. (Special Issue, Proceedings of the First Copper Mountain Conference on Multigrid Methods, Copper Mountain, CO, S. McCormick and U. Trottenberg, eds.).

[105] D. BARKAI, M. CAMPOSTRINI, K. MORIARTY, AND L. RABBI [1987]. *Applications development of the ETA-10*, Comput. Phys. Comm., 46, pp. 13–33.

[106] D. BARKAI AND K. MORIARTY [1986]. *Application development on the CDC Cyber 205*, Comput. Phys. Comm., 40, pp. 159–172.

[107] D. BARKAI AND K. MORIARTY [1986]. *Vectorization of the multigrid method: The two-dimensional Poisson equation*, Tech. Report UMSI 86145, University of Minnesota, September.

[108] D. BARKAI, K. MORIARTY, AND C. REBBI [1984]. *A highly optimized vectorized code for Monte Carlo simulation of SU(3) lattice gauge theories*, Comput. Phys. Comm., 32, pp. 1–9.

[109] D. BARKAI, K. MORIARTY, AND C. REBBI [1984]. *A highly optimized vectorized code for Monte Carlo simulation of SU(3) lattice gauge theories*, Proc. 1984 Int. Conf. Par. Proc., pp. 101–108.

[110] D. BARKAI, K. MORIARTY, AND C. REBBI [1984]. *A modified conjugate gradient solver for very large systems*, in Numrich [1469].

[111] D. BARKAI, K. MORIARTY, AND C. REBBI [1985]. *A modified conjugate gradient solver for very large systems*, Comp. Phys. Comm., 36, pp. 1–8.

[112] D. BARKAI, K. MORIARTY, AND C. REBBI [1985]. *A modified conjugate gradient solver for very large systems*, Proc. 1985 Int. Conf. Par. Proc., pp. 284–290.

[113] J. BARLOW AND I. IPSEN [1987]. *Scaled Givens rotations for the solution of linear least squares problems on systolic arrays*, SIAM J. Sci. Statist. Comput., 8, pp. 716–733.

[114] R. BARLOW AND D. EVANS [1982]. *Synchronous and asynchronous iterative parallel algorithms for linear systems*, Comput. J., 25, pp. 56–60.

[115] R. BARLOW, D. EVANS, AND J. SHANEHCHI [1982]. *Comparative study of the exploitation of*

different levels of parallelism on different parallel architectures, Proc. 1982 Int. Conf. Par. Proc., pp. 34–40.

[116] R. BARLOW, D. EVANS, AND J. SHANEHCHI [1983]. *Parallel multisection applied to the eigenvalue problem*, Comput. J., 6, pp. 6–9.

[117] R. BARLOW, D. EVANS, AND J. SHANEHCHI [1984]. *Sparse matrix vector multiplication on the DAP*, in Paddon [1512], pp. 147–155.

[118] G. BARNES, R. BROWN, M. KATZ, D. KUCK, D. SLOTNICK, AND R. STOKER [1968]. *The Illiac IV computer*, IEEE Trans. Comput., C-17, pp. 746–757.

[119] K. BATCHER [1974]. *STARAN parallel processor system hardware*, AFIPS Conf. Proc. 43, NCC, pp. 405–410.

[120] K. BATCHER [1976]. *The Flip network in STARAN*, Proc. 1976 Int. Conf. Par. Proc., P. H. Enslow, ed., Silver Spring, MD, Institute of Electrical and Electronics Engineers, Inc., pp. 65–71.

[121] K. BATCHER [1979]. *MPP — A Massively Parallel Processor*, Proc. 1979 Int. Conf. Par. Proc., p. 249.

[122] K. BATCHER [1980]. *Design of a Massively Parallel Processor*, IEEE Trans. Comput., C-29, pp. 836–840.

[123] K. BATCHER [1985]. *The Massively Parallel Processor system overview*, in Potter [1584], pp. 142–149.

[124] G. BAUDET [1977]. *Iterative methods for asynchronous multiprocessors*, in Kuck et al. [1133], pp. 309–310.

[125] G. BAUDET [1978]. *Asynchronous iterative methods for multiprocessors*, J. ACM, 25, pp. 226–244.

[126] D. BAXTER, J. SALTZ, M. SCHULTZ, S. EISENSTAT, AND K. CROWLEY [1988]. *An experimental study of methods for parallel preconditioned Krylov methods*, Tech. Report RR-629, Department of Computer Science, Yale University.

[127] G. BEHIE AND P. FORSYTH [1984]. *Incomplete factorization methods for fully implicit simulation of enhanced oil recovery*, SIAM J. Sci. Statist. Comput., 5, pp. 543–561.

[128] M. BEKAKOS AND D. EVANS [1987]. *A rotating and folding algorithm using a two-dimensional "systolic" communication geometry*, Parallel Computing, 4, pp. 221–228.

[129] C. BELL [1985]. *Multis: A new class of multiprocessor computers*, Science, 228, pp. 462–467.

[130] J. BELL AND G. PATTERSON [1987]. *Data organization in large numerical computations*, J. Supercomputing, 1, pp. 105–136.

[131] M. BEN-ARI [1982], *Principles of Concurrent Programming*, Prentice-Hall, Inc., Englewood Cliffs, NJ.

[132] V. BENES [1962]. *Heuristic remarks and mathematical problems regarding the theory of connecting systems*, Bell System Tech. J., 41, pp. 1201–1247.

[133] V. BENES [1965], *Mathematical Theory of Connecting Networks and Telephone Traffic*, Academic Press, New York.

[134] R. BENNER [1986]. *Shared memory, cache, and frontwidth considerations in multifrontal algorithm development*, Tech. Report SAND85-2752, Fluid and Thermal Sciences Department, Sandia National Laboratories, Albuquerque, NM.

[135] R. BENNER AND G. MONTRY [1986]. *Overview of preconditioned conjugate gradient (PCG) methods in concurrent finite element analysis*, Tech. Report SAND-85-2727, Sandia National Laboratory, Albuquerque, NM.

[136] M. BENSON AND P. FREDERICKSON [1987]. *Fast parallel algorithms for the Moore-Penrose pseudo-inverse*, in Heath [860], pp. 597–604.

[137] M. BENSON AND P. FREDERICKSON [1988]. *Fast pseudo-inverse algorithms on hypercubes*, in McCormick [1312].

[138] M. BENSON, J. KRETTMANN, AND M. WRIGHT [1984]. *Parallel algorithms for the solution of certain large sparse linear systems*, Int. J. Comput. Math., 16, pp. 245–260.

[139] P. BENYON [1985]. *Exploiting vector computers for simulation*, Math. Comp. Simul., 27, pp. 121–127.

[140] H. BERENDSEN, W. VAN GUNSTEREN, AND J. POSTMA [1984]. *Molecular dynamics on CRAY, CYBER and DAP*, in Kowalik [1116], pp. 425–438.

[141] M. BERGER AND S. BOKHARI [1985]. *A partitioning strategy for PDE's across multiprocessors*, Proc. 1985 Int. Conf. Par. Proc., pp. 166–170.

[142] M. BERGER AND S. BOKHARI [1987]. *Partitioning strategy for non-uniform problems on multiprocessors*, IEEE Trans. Comput., C-36, pp. 570–580.

[143] M. BERGER, J. OLIGER, AND G. RODRIGUE [1981]. *Predictor-corrector methods for the solution of time dependent parabolic problems on parallel processors*, in Schultz [1752], pp. 197–202.

[144] P. BERGER, P. BROUAYE, AND J. SYRE [1982]. *A mesh coloring method for efficient MIMD processing in finite element problems*, Proc. 1982 Int. Conf. Par. Proc., pp. 41–46.

[145] P. BERGER, M. DAYDE, AND C. FRABOUL [1985]. *Experience in parallelizing numerical algorithms for MIMD architecture use of asynchronous methods*, La Recherche Aerospatiale, 5, pp. 325–340.

[146] D. BERGMARK, J. FRANCIONI, B. HELMINEN, AND D. POPLAWSKI [1987]. *On the performance of the FPS T-series hypercube*, in Heath [860], pp. 193–199.

[147] F. BERMAN AND L. SNYDER [1987]. *On mapping parallel algorithms into parallel architectures*, J. Par. Dist. Comp., 4, pp. 439–458.

[148] L. BERNARD AND F. HELTON [1982]. *A vectorizable eigenvalue solver for sparse matrices*, Comput. Phys. Comm., 25, pp. 73–79.

[149] H. BERNSTEIN AND M. GOLDSTEIN [1986]. *Parallel implementation of bisection for the calculation of eigenvalues of tridiagonal symmetric matrices*, Computing, 37, pp. 85–91.

[150] H. BERNSTEIN AND M. GOLDSTEIN [1988]. *Optimizing Givens' algorithm for multiprocessors*, SIAM J. Sci. Statist. Comput., 8, pp. 601–602.

[151] M. BERRY, K. GALLIVAN, W. HARROD, W. JALBY, S. LO, U. MEIER, B. PHILLIPPE, AND A. SAMEH [1986]. *Parallel algorithms on the Cedar system*, Tech. Report 581, Center for Supercomputing Research and Development, University of Illinois at Urbana-Champaign, October.

[152] M. BERRY AND R. PLEMMONS [1985]. *Computing a banded basis of the null space on the Denelcor HEP multiprocessor*, Contemporary Math., 47, pp. 7–23.

[153] M. BERRY AND R. PLEMMONS [1985]. *Parallel algorithms for finite element structural analysis on the HEP multiprocessor*, Proc. Denelcor Workshop on the HEP, University of Oklahoma, March.

[154] M. BERRY AND R. PLEMMONS [1987]. *Algorithms and experiments for structural mechanics on high performance architectures*, Comput. Meth. Appl. Mech. Engrg., 64, pp. 487–508.

[155] M. BERRY AND A. SAMEH [1986]. *Multiprocessor Jacobi algorithms for dense symmetric eigenvalue and singular value decompositions*, Proc. 1986 Int. Conf. Par. Proc., pp. 433–440.

[156] M. BERRY AND A. SAMEH [1987]. *A multiprocessor scheme for the singular value decomposition*, Tech. Report 690, Center for Supercomputing Research and Development, University of Illinois at Urbana-Champaign, August.

[157] D. BERTSEKAS [1982]. *Distributed dynamic programming*, IEEE Trans. Automat. Control, AC-27, pp. 610–616.

[158] D. BERTSEKAS [1983]. *Distributed asynchronous computation of fixed points*, Math. Programming, 27, pp. 107–120.

[159] M. BERZINS, T. BUCKLEY, AND P. DEW [1984]. *Path Pascal simulation of multiprocessor lattice architectures for numerical computations*, in Paddon [1512], pp. 25–33.

[160] M. BERZINS, T. BUCKLEY, AND P. DEW [1984]. *Systolic matrix iterative algorithms*, in Feilmeier et al. [623], pp. 483–488.

[161] R. BEVILACQUA, B. CODENOTTI, AND F. ROMANI [1988]. *Parallel solution of block tridiagonal linear systems*, Lin. Alg. & Appl., 104, pp. 39–58.

[162] V. BHAVSAR [1981]. *Some parallel algorithms for Monte Carlo solutions of partial differential equations*, Advances in Computer Methods for Partial Differential Equations, vol. 4, R. Vichnevetsky and R. Stepleman, eds., IMACS, New Brunswick, Canada, pp. 135–141.

[163] V. BHAVSAR AND U. GUJAR [1984]. *VLSI algorithms for Monte Carlo solutions of partial differential equations*, in Vichnevetsky and Stepleman [1920], pp. 268–276.

[164] V. BHAVSAR AND J. ISAAC [1987]. *Design and analysis of parallel Monte Carlo algorithms*, SIAM J. Sci. Statist. Comput., 8, pp. s73–s95.

[165] V. BHAVSAR AND V. KANETKAR [1977]. *A multiple microprocessor system (MMPS) for the Monte Carlo solution of partial differential equations*, Advances in Computer Methods for Partial Differential Equations, vol. 2, R. Vichnevetsky, ed., IMACS, New Brunswick, Canada, pp. 205–213.

[166] V. BHAVSAR AND A. PADGAONKAR [1979]. *Effectiveness of some parallel computer architectures for Monte Carlo solution of partial differential equations*, Advances in Computer Methods for Partial Differential Equations, vol. 3, R. Vichnevetsky and R. Stepleman, eds., IMACS, New Brunswick, Canada, pp. 259–264.

[167] V. BHAVSAR, T. TASSOU, E. HUSSEIN, AND K. GALLIVAN [1987]. *Monte Carlo neutron transport on the Alliant FX/8*, Proc. 1987 Int. Conf. Par. Proc., pp. 421–423.

[168] S. BHUTT AND I. IPSEN [1985]. *How to embed trees in hypercubes*, Tech. Report YALEU/DCS/RR-443, Department of Computer Science, Yale University.

[169] L. BHUYAN AND D. AGRAWAL [1984]. *Generalized hybercube and hyberbus structures for a computer network*, IEEE Trans. Comput., 33, pp. 323–333.

[170] D. BINI [1984]. *Parallel solution of certain Toeplitz linear systems*, SIAM J. Comput., 13, pp. 368–476.

[171] S. BIRINGEN [1983]. *A numerical simulation of transition in plane channel flow*, Paper 83-47, AIAA, Reno, NV, January.

[172] S. BIRINGEN [1983]. *Simulation of late transition in plane channel flow*, Proceedings of the Third International Conference on Numerical Methods in Laminar and Turbulent Flow, Seattle WA, August.

[173] G. BIRKHOFF AND A. SCHOENSTADT, eds. [1984]. *Elliptic Problem Solvers II*, Academic Press, Orlando.

[174] L. BIRTA AND O. ABOU-RABIA [1987]. *Parallel block predictor-corrector methods for ODE's*, IEEE Trans. Comput., C-36, pp. 299–311.

[175] C. BISCHOF [1986]. *A parallel ordering for the block Jacobi method on a hypercube architecture*, Tech. Report TR 96-740, Department of Computer Science, Cornell University.

[176] C. BISCHOF [1987]. *The two-sided block Jacobi method on a hypercube*, in Heath [860], pp. 612–618.

[177] C. BISCHOF AND C. VAN LOAN [1986]. *Computing the singular value decomposition on a ring of array processors*, Large Scale Eigenvalue Problems, J. Cullum and R. Willoughby, eds., North-Holland, Amsterdam.

[178] C. BISCHOF AND C. VAN LOAN [1987]. *The WY representation for products of Householder matrices*, SIAM J. Sci. Statist. Comput., 8, pp. s2–s13.

[179] P. BJØRSTAD [1987]. *A large scale, sparse, secondary storage, direct linear equation solver for structural analysis and its implementation on vector and parallel architectures*, Parallel Computing, 5, pp. 3–12.

[180] P. BJØRSTAD AND A. HVIDSTEN [1988]. *Iterative methods for substructured elascticity problems in structural analysis*, in Glowinski et al. [762], pp. 301–312.

[181] P. BJØRSTAD AND O. WIDLUND [1984]. *Solving elliptic problems on regions partitioned into substructures*, in Birkhoff and Schoenstadt [173], pp. 245–255.

[182] P. BJØRSTAD AND O. WIDLUND [1986]. *Iterative methods for the solution of elliptic problems on regions partitioned into substructures*, SIAM J. Numer. Anal., 23, pp. 1097–1121.

[183] E. BLUM [1982]. *Programming parallel numerical algorithms in Ada*, The Relationship between Numerical Computation and Programming Languages, J. K. Reid, ed., North-Holland, Amsterdam, pp. 297–304.

[184] M. BLUMEMFELD [1984]. *Preconditioning conjugate gradient methods on vector computers*, in Feilmeier et al. [623], pp. 107–113.

[185] A. BODE, G. FRITSCH, W. HÄNDLER, W. HENNING, F. HOFMANN, AND J. VOLKERT [1985]. *Multigrid oriented computer architecture*, Proc. 1985 Int. Conf. Par. Proc., pp. 89–95.

[186] J. BOISSEAU, M. ENSELME, D. GUINRAUD, AND P. LEED [1982]. *Potential assessment of a parallel structure for the solution of partial differential equations*, Rech. Aerosp.

[187] A. BOJANCZYK [1984]. *Optimal asynchronous Newton method for the solution of nonlinear equations*, J. ACM, 31, pp. 792–803.

[188] A. BOJANCZYK AND R. BRENT [1985]. *Tridiagonalization of a symmetric matrix on a square array of mesh-connected processors*, J. Par. Dist. Comp., 2, pp. 261–276.

[189] A. BOJANCZYK, R. BRENT, AND H. KUNG [1984]. *Numerically stable solution of dense systems of linear equations using mesh-connected processors*, SIAM J. Sci. Statist. Comput., 5, pp. 95–104.

[190] S. BOKHARI [1979]. *On the mapping problem*, Proc. 1979 Int. Conf. Par. Proc., pp. 239–248.

[191] S. BOKHARI [1981]. *On the mapping problem*, IEEE Trans. Comput., C-30, pp. 207–214.

[192] S. BOKHARI [1984]. *Finding maximum on an array processor with a global bus*, IEEE Trans. Comput., C-33, pp. 133–139.

[193] S. BOKHARI [1988]. *Partitioning problems in parallel, pipelined and distributed computing*, IEEE Trans. Comput., C-37, pp. 48–57.

[194] S. BOKHARI, M. HUSSAINI, J. LAMBIOTTE, AND S. ORSZAG [1982]. *Navier-Stokes solution on the CYBER-203 by a pseudospectral technique*, Second IMAC International Symposium on Parallel Computation, Newark, DE, November 9-11, pp. 305–307.

[195] S. BOKHARI, M. HUSSAINI, AND S. ORSZAG [1982]. *Fast orthogonal derivatives on the STAR*, Comput. Math. Appl., 8, pp. 367–377.

[196] D. BOLEY [1978]. *Vectorization of block relaxation techniques: Some numerical experiments*, Proc. 1978 LASL Workshop on Vector and Parallel Processors, Los Alamos, NM.

[197] D. BOLEY [1984]. *A parallel method for the generalized eigenvalue problem*, Tech. Report 84-21, Department of Computer Science, University of Minnesota, September.

[198] D. BOLEY [1986]. *Solving the generalized eigenvalue problem on a synchronous linear processor array*, Parallel Computing, 3, pp. 153–166.

[199] D. BOLEY, B. BUZBEE, AND S. PARTER [1978]. *On block relaxation techniques*, Tech. Report 1860, Mathematics Research Center, University of Wisconsin.

[200] E. BONDARENKO [1985]. *Paralleling of methods for the modification of matrix factorizations*, Computational Processes and Systems, Izdatel'stvo Nauka, Moscow, pp. 228–264.

[201] L. BONEY AND R. SMITH [1979]. *A vectorization of the Hess-McDonnel-Douglas potential flow program NUED for the STAR-100 computer*, NASA Tech. Report TM-78816, NASA Langley Research Center.

[202] J. BONOMO AND W. DYKSEN [1987]. *Pipelined iterative methods for shared memory machines*, Tech. Report CSD-TR-688, Department of Computer Science, Purdue University.

[203] D. BOOK, ed. [1981]. *Finite Difference Techniques for Vectorized Fluid Dynamics Calculation*, Springer-Verlag, New York, NY.

[204] C. BORGERS AND O. WIDLUND [1987]. *A domain decomposition Laplace solver for internal combustion engine modeling*, Tech. Report 315, Department of Computer Science, New York University.

[205] J. BORIS [1976]. *Flux-corrected transport modules for solving generalized continuity equations*, Tech. Report 3237, Naval Research Laboratory.

[206] J. BORIS [1976]. *Vectorized tridiagonal solvers*, Tech. Report 3048, Naval Research Laboratory.

[207] J. BORIS [1986]. *A vectorized "near neighbors" algorithm of order n using a monotonic logical grid*, J. Comp. Phys., 66, pp. 1–22.

[208] J. BORIS AND N. WINSOR [1982]. *Vectorized computation of reactive flow*, in Rodrigue [1643], pp. 173–215.

[209] A. BORODIN AND I. MUNRO [1975], *Computational Complexity of Algebraic and Numeric Processes*, American Elsevier.

[210] A. BOSSAVIT [1982]. *On the vectorization of algorithms in linear algebra*, Proc. 10th IMACS World Congress on Systems Simulation and Scientific Computation, vol. 1, IMACS, pp. 95–97.

[211] S. BOSTIC [1984]. *Solution of a tridiagonal system of equations on the Finite Element Machine*, NASA Tech. Report TM-85710, NASA Langley Research Center.

[212] S. BOSTIC AND R. FULTON [1985]. *A concurrent processing approach to structural vibration analysis*, 26th AIAA Structures, Structural Dynamics and Materials Conf., Orlando, FL.

[213] S. BOSTIC AND R. FULTON [1987]. *Implementation of the Lanczos method for structural vibration analysis on a parallel computer*, Computers and Structures, 25, pp. 395–404.

[214] A. BOUDOUVIS AND L. SCRIVEN [1985]. *Explicitly vectorized frontal routine for hydrodynamic stability and bifurcation analysis by Galerkin/finite element methods*, in Numrich [1469], pp. 197–213.

[215] W. BOUKNIGHT, S. DENENBERG, D. MCINTYRE, J. RANDALL, A. SAMEH, AND D. SLOTNICK [1972]. *The Illiac IV system*, Proc. IEEE, 60, pp. 369–379.

[216] B. BOWEN AND R. BUHR [1980], *The Logical Design of Multiple-Microprocessor Systems*, Prentice-Hall, Inc., Englewood Cliffs, NJ.

[217] G. BOWGEN AND J. MODI [1985]. *Implementation of QR factorization on the DAP using Householder transformations*, Comput. Phys. Comm., 37, pp. 167–170.

[218] K. BOWLER AND G. PAWLEY [1984]. *Molecular dynamics and Monte Carlo simulations in solid-state and elementary particle physics*, Proc. IEEE, 72, pp. 42–55.

[219] P. BRADLEY, D. DWOYER, AND J. SOUTH [1984]. *Vectorized schemes for conical flow using the artificial density method*, Paper 84-0162, AIAA, January.

[220] P. BRADLEY, P. SIEMERS, AND K. WEILMUENSTER [1982]. *Comparison of shuttle flight pressure data to computational and wind-tunnel results*, Journal of Spacecraft and Rockets, 19, pp. 419–422.

[221] I. BRAILOVSKAYA [1965]. *A difference scheme for numerical solution of the two-dimensional non-stationary Navier-Stokes equations for a compressible gas*, Soviet Physics Doklady, 10, pp. 107–110.

[222] J. BRAMBLE, J. PASCIAK, AND A. SCHATZ [1987]. *The construction of preconditioners for elliptic problems by substructuring*, Math. Comp., 49(179), pp. 1–16.

[223] J. BRANDENBURG AND D. SCOTT [1986]. *Embeddings of communication trees and grids into hypercubes*, iPSC Tech. Report 1, Intel.

[224] A. BRANDT [1977]. *Multigrid adaptive solutions to boundary value problems*, Math. Comp., 31, pp. 333–390.

[225] A. BRANDT [1981]. *Multigrid solvers on parallel computers*, in Schultz [1752], pp. 39–83.

[226] A. BRANDT [1984]. *Local and multi-level parallel processing mill*, Tech. Report, Department of Applied Mathematics, Weizmann Institute, Rehovot, Israel.

[227] A. BRANDT [1988]. *Multilevel computations: Review and recent developments*, in McCormick [1312], pp. 35–63.

[228] W. BRANTLEY, K. MCAULIFFE, AND J. WEISS [1985]. *RP3 processor memory element*, Proc. 1985 Int. Conf. Par. Proc., pp. 782–789.

[229] A. BRASS AND G. PARRLEY [1986]. *Two and three dimensional FFTs on highly parallel computers*, Parallel Computing, 3, pp. 167–184.

[230] R. BRENT AND H. KUNG [1982]. *A systolic VLSI array for integer GCD computation*, Tech. Report TR-CS-82-11, Department of Computer Science, Australian National University, December.

[231] R. BRENT, H. KUNG, AND F. LUK [1983]. *Some linear-time algorithms for systolic arrays*, Proc. IFIP 9th World Computer Congress, Amsterdam, North-Holland, pp. 865–876.

[232] R. BRENT AND F. LUK [1982]. *Computing the Cholesky factorization using a systolic architecture*, Tech. Report TR 82-521, Department of Computer Science, Cornell University, Ithaca, NY, September.

[233] R. BRENT AND F. LUK [1982]. *A systolic architecture for almost linear-time solution of the symmetric eigenvalue problem*, Tech. Report TR-CS-82-10, Department of Computer Science, Australian National University.

[234] R. BRENT AND F. LUK [1982]. *A systolic architecture for the singular value decomposition*, Tech. Report TR-82-522, Department of Computer Science, Cornell University.

[235] R. BRENT AND F. LUK [1983]. *Computing the Cholesky factorization using a systolic architecture*, Proc. 6th Australian Computer Science Conf., Australian Computer Science Communications 5, pp. 295–302.

[236] R. BRENT AND F. LUK [1983]. *A systolic array for the linear time solution of Toeplitz systems of equations*, J. of VLSI and Computer Systems, 1, pp. 1–22.

[237] R. BRENT AND F. LUK [1985]. *The solution of singular-value and symmetric eigenvalue problems on multiprocessors*, SIAM J. Sci. Statist. Comput., 6, pp. 69–84.

[238] R. BRENT, F. LUK, AND C. VAN LOAN [1983]. *Computation of the generalized singular value decomposition using mesh-connected processors*, Proc. SPIE vol. 431: Real Time Signal Processing VI.

[239] R. BRENT, F. LUK, AND C. VAN LOAN [1985]. *Computation of the singular value decomposition using mesh connected processors*, J. of VLSI and Computer Systems, 1, pp. 242–270.

[240] R. BRICKNER, R. HIROMOTO, AND B. WIENKE [1987]. *Parallel iterative transport algorithms and comparative performance on distributed and common memory systems*, Tech. Report LA-UR-87-2163, Los Alamos National Laboratory.

[241] R. BRICKNER AND R. PATERNOSTER [1987]. *Multitasking a two-dimensional (R,Z)-geometry discrete ordinates neutron transport algorithm*, Tech. Report LA-UR-87-2164, Los Alamos National Laboratory.

[242] W. BRIGGS, L. HART, S. MCCORMICK, AND D. QUINLAN [1987]. *Multigrid methods on a hypercube*, in McCormick [1312], pp. 63–83.

[243] W. BRIGGS, L. HART, R. SWEET, AND A. O'GALLAGHER [1987]. *Multiprocessor FFT methods*, SIAM J. Sci. Statist. Comput., 8, pp. s27–s42.

[244] W. BRIGGS AND T. TURNBULL [1988]. *Fast Poisson solvers for MIMD computers*, Parallel Computing, 6, pp. 265–275.

[245] P. BRINCH HANSEN [1973]. *Concurrent programming concepts*, ACM Computing Surveys, 6, pp. 223–245.

[246] P. BRINCH HANSEN [1977], *The Architecture of Concurrent Programs*, Prentice-Hall, Inc., Englewood Cliffs, NJ.

[247] P. BRINCH HANSEN [1978]. *Distributed processes: A concurrent programming concept*, Comm. ACM, 21.

[248] P. BRINCH HANSEN [1979]. *A keynote address on concurrent programming*, Computer, 12(5), pp. 50–56.

[249] L. BROCHARD [1984]. *Communication and control costs of domain decomposition on loosely coupled multiprocessors*, Proc. 7th Int. Conf. Dist. Comp. Syst., Berlin, pp. 200–205.

[250] B. BRODE [1981]. *Precompilation of Fortran programs to facilitate array processing*, Computer, 14(9), pp. 46–51.

[251] E. BROOKS [1984]. *A multitasking kernel for the C and Fortran programming languages*, Tech. Report UCID-20167, Lawrence Livermore National Laboratory, Livermore, CA, September.

[252] E. BROOKS [1985]. *Performance of the Butterfly processor-memory interconnection in a vec-

tor environment, Proc. 1985 Int. Conf. Par. Proc., pp. 21–24.

[253] E. BROOKS [1985]. *The shared memory hypercube*, Tech. Report, Lawrence Livermore National Laboratory, Livermore, CA, March.

[254] E. BROOKS [1987]. *A butterfly processor-memory interconnection for a vector processing environment*, Parallel Computing, 4, pp. 103–110.

[255] E. BROOKS [1988]. *The indirect k-ary n-cube for a vector processing environment*, Parallel Computing, 6, pp. 339–348.

[256] E. BROOKS [1988]. *The shared memory hypercube*, Parallel Computing, 6, pp. 235–246.

[257] G. BROOMELL AND J. HEATH [1983]. *Classification categories and historical development of circuit switching topologies*, ACM Computing Surveys, 15, pp. 95–134.

[258] J. BROWNE [1984]. *Parallel architecture for computer systems*, Physics Today, 37(5), pp. 28–35.

[259] J. BROWNE [1984]. *TRAC: An environment for parallel computing*, Proc. COMPCON 84, IEEE Comp. Soc. Conf., pp. 294–299.

[260] J. BROWNE [1985]. *Formulation and programming of parallel computations: A unified approach*, Proc. 1985 Int. Conf. Par. Proc., pp. 624–631.

[261] J. BROWNE [1986]. *Framework for formulation and analysis of parallel computation structures*, Parallel Computing, 3, pp. 1–10.

[262] R. BRU, M. NEUMANN, AND L. ELSNER [1988]. *Models of parallel chaotic iteration methods*, Lin. Alg. & Appl., 103, pp. 175–192.

[263] J. BRUNO [1984]. *Final report on the feasibility of using the Massively Parallel Processor for large eddy simulations and other computational fluid dynamics applications*, Tech. Report 84.2, RIACS, NASA Ames Research Center, June.

[264] J. BRUNO [1986]. *Report on the feasibility of hypercube concurrent processing systems in computational fluid dynamics*, Tech. Report 86.7, RIACS, NASA Ames Research Center, March.

[265] I. BUCHER [1983]. *The computational speed of supercomputers*, Proc. ACM Sigmetrics Conf. on Measurement and Modeling of Computer Systems, pp. 151–165.

[266] I. BUCHER AND T. JORDAN [1984]. *Linear algebra programs for use on a vector computer with a secondary solid state storage device*, in Vichnevetsky and Stepleman [1920], pp. 546–550.

[267] I. BUCHER AND T. JORDAN [1984]. *Solving very large elliptic problems on a supercomputer with solid state disk*, J. Comp. Phys., 55, pp. 340–345.

[268] P. BUDNIK AND D. KUCK [1971]. *The organization and use of parallel memories*, IEEE Trans. Comput., C-20, pp. 1566–1569.

[269] O. BUNEMAN [1969]. *A compact non-iterative Poisson solver*, Tech. Report 294, Institute for Plasma Research, Stanford University.

[270] P. BUNING AND J. LEVY [1979]. *Vectorization of implicit Navier-Stokes codes on the CRAY-1 computer*, Tech. Report, Department of Aeronautics and Astronautics, Stanford University.

[271] P. BURKE, B. DAVIES, AND D. EDWARDS, eds. [1982]. *Some Research Applications on the CRAY-1 Computer at the Daresbury Laboratory, 1979-81*, Daresbury Laboratory, England.

[272] P. BURKE AND L. DELNES, eds. [1982]. *Proceedings of the International Conference on Vector and Parallel Processors in Computational Science, Chester, England, August, 1981*.

[273] P. BURNS AND D. PRYOR [1987]. *Vectorized Monte Carlo radiative heat transfer simulation of the laser isotope separation process*, Tech. Report 87002, Institute for Scientific Computing, Fort Collins, CO.

[274] BURROUGHS CORP. [1979]. *Final report. NAS facility feasibility study*, Contractor Report NAS2-9897, NASA.

[275] R. BUTLER, E. LUSK, W. McCUNE, AND R. OVERBEEK [1985]. *Parallel logic programming for numeric applications*, MCS Tech. Report, Argonne National Laboratory, Argonne, IL.

[276] T. BUTLER, J. CLOUTMAN, AND J. RAMSHAW [1981]. *Multidimensional numerical simulation of reactive flow in internal combustion engines*, Prog. Energy Combust. Sci., 7, pp. 293–315.

[277] B. BUZBEE [1973]. *A fast Poisson solver amenable to parallel computation*, IEEE Trans. Comput., C-22, pp. 793–796.

[278] B. BUZBEE [1981]. *Implementing techniques for elliptic problems on vector processors*, in Schultz [1752], pp. 85–98.

[279] B. BUZBEE [1983]. *Remarks for the IFIP congress '83 panel on how to obtain high performance for high-speed processors*, Tech. Report LA-UR-83-1392, Los Alamos National

Laboratory.

[280] B. BUZBEE [1983]. *Vectorization of algorithms for solving systems of elliptic difference equations*, in Noor [1450], pp. 81–88.

[281] B. BUZBEE [1984]. *Application of MIMD machines*, Tech. Report LA-UR-84-2004, Los Alamos National Laboratory.

[282] B. BUZBEE [1984]. *Gaining insight from supercomputing*, Proc. IEEE, 72, pp. 19–21.

[283] B. BUZBEE [1985]. *Two parallel formulations of particle-in-cell models*, in Snyder et al. [1808], pp. 223–232.

[284] B. BUZBEE [1986]. *A strategy for vectorization*, Parallel Computing, 3, pp. 187–192.

[285] B. BUZBEE, D. BOLEY, AND S. PARTER [1979]. *Applications of block relaxation*, Proc. 1979 AIME Fifth Symposium on Reservoir Simulation.

[286] B. BUZBEE, R. EWALD, AND J. WORLTON [1982]. *Japanese supercomputer technology*, Science, 218(17), pp. 1189–93.

[287] B. BUZBEE, G. GOLUB, AND J. HOWELL [1977]. *Vectorizations for the CRAY-1 of some methods for solving elliptic difference equations*, in Kuck et al. [1133], pp. 255–271.

[288] B. BUZBEE, G. GOLUB, AND C. NIELSON [1970]. *On direct methods for solving Poisson's equation*, SIAM J. Numer. Anal., 7, pp. 627–656.

[289] B. BUZBEE AND J. MORRISON, eds. [1978]. *Proc. 1978 LASL Workshop on Vector and Parallel Processors*, Los Alamos, NM.

[290] B. BUZBEE AND D. SHARP [1985]. *Perspectives on computing*, Science, 227, pp. 591–597.

[291] B. BUZBEE, J. WORLTON, G. MICHAEL, AND G. RODRIGUE [1980]. *DOE research in utilization of high performance systems*, Tech. Report LA-8609-MS, Los Alamos National Laboratory.

[292] J. CAHOUET [1988]. *On some difficulties occurring in the simulation of incompressible fluid flows by domain decomposition methods*, in Glowinski et al. [762], pp. 313–332.

[293] D. CALAHAN [1973]. *Parallel solution of sparse simultaneous linear equations*, Proceedings of the 11th Allerton Conference on Circuit and System Theory, University of Illinois at Urbana-Champaign, pp. 729–738.

[294] D. CALAHAN [1975]. *Complexity of vectorized solution of two-dimensional finite element grids*, Tech. Report 91, Systems Engineering Laboratory, University of Michigan.

[295] D. CALAHAN [1977]. *Algorithmic and architectural issues related to vector processors*, Proc. Int. Symp. Large Eng. Sys., Pergammon Press.

[296] D. CALAHAN [1979]. *A block-oriented sparse equation solver for the CRAY-1*, Proc. 1979 Int. Conf. Par. Proc., pp. 116–123.

[297] D. CALAHAN [1979]. *Vectorized sparse elimination*, Proc. Sci. Computer Information Exchange Meeting, Livermore, CA.

[298] D. CALAHAN [1980]. *Multi-level vectorized sparse solution of LSI circuits*, Proc. IEEE Conf. on Circuits and Computers, Rye, NY, October, pp. 976–979.

[299] D. CALAHAN [1981]. *Direct solution of linear equations on the CRAY-1*, CRAY Channels, 3, pp. 1–5.

[300] D. CALAHAN [1981]. *Performance of linear algebra codes on the CRAY-1*, SPE Journal, pp. 558–564.

[301] D. CALAHAN [1981]. *Sparse vectorized direct solution of elliptic problems*, in Schultz [1752], pp. 241–245.

[302] D. CALAHAN [1982]. *High performance banded and profile equation-solvers for the CRAY-1: The unsymmetric case*, Tech. Report 160, Systems Engineering Laboratory, University of Michigan.

[303] D. CALAHAN [1982]. *Vectorized direct solvers of 2-D grids*, Proc. 6th Symp. Resevoir Simulation, pp. 489–506.

[304] D. CALAHAN [1983]. *Tasking studies in solving a linear algebra problem on a CRAY-class multiprocessor*, Tech. Report SARL-2, Supercomputer Algorithm Research Laboratory, University of Michigan.

[305] D. CALAHAN [1984]. *Influence of task granularity on vector multiprocessor performance*, Proc. 1984 Int. Conf. Par. Proc., pp. 278–284.

[306] D. CALAHAN [1985]. *Task granularity studies on a many-processor CRAY X-MP*, Parallel Computing, 2, pp. 109–118.

[307] D. CALAHAN [1986]. *Block-oriented, local-memory-based linear equation solution on the CRAY-2: Uniprocessor algorithms*, Proc. 1986 Int. Conf. Par. Proc., pp. 375–378.

[308] D. CALAHAN AND W. AMES [1979]. *Vector processors: Models and applications*, IEEE Trans. Circuits and Syst., CAS-26, pp. 715–776.

[309] D. CALAHAN, W. AMES, AND E. SESEK [1979]. *A collection of equation solving codes for the CRAY-1*, Tech. Report, Systems Engineering Laboratory, University of Michigan.

[310] D. CALAHAN, W. JOY, AND P. ORBITS [1976]. *Preliminary report on results of matrix benchmarks on vector processors*, Tech. Report, Systems Engineering Laboratory, University of Michigan.

[311] P. CAPPELLO [1985]. *A mesh automaton for solving dense linear systems*, Proc. 1985 Int. Conf. Par. Proc., pp. 418–425.

[312] P. CAPPELLO [1987]. *Gaussian elimination on a hypercube automaton*, J. Par. Dist. Comp., 4, pp. 288–308.

[313] C. CARDELMO AND P.-Y. CHEN [1985]. *A new parallel algorithm for solving a complex function $f(z) = 0$*, Proc. 1985 Int. Conf. Par. Proc., pp. 305–310.

[314] G. CAREY [1981]. *High speed processors and implications for algorithms and methods*, Nonlinear Finite Element Analysis — Structural Mechanics, W. Wunderlich, E. Stein, and K. Bathe, eds., Springer-Verlag, Berlin.

[315] G. CAREY [1985]. *Inherent and induced parallelism in finite element computations*, Tech. Report CNA-198, Center for Numerical Analysis, University of Texas at Austin, February.

[316] G. CAREY [1986]. *Parallelism in finite element modeling*, Comm. Appl. Numer. Meth., 2, pp. 281–287.

[317] G. CAREY, E. BARRAGY, R. MCLAY, AND M. SHARMA [1988]. *Element by element vector and parallel computations*, Comm. Appl. Numer. Meth., 4, pp. 299–308.

[318] W. CARLSON AND K. HWANG [1985]. *Algorithmic performance of dataflow multiprocessors*, Computer, 18(12), pp. 30–40.

[319] A. CARROLL AND R. WETHERALD [1967]. *Application of parallel processing to numerical weather prediction*, J. ACM, 14, pp. 591–614.

[320] D. CASASENT [1984]. *Acoustooptic linear algebra processors — Architectures, algorithms and applications*, Proc. IEEE, 72, pp. 831–849.

[321] C. CATHERASOO [1987]. *The vortex method on a hypercube concurrent processor*, in Heath [860], pp. 756–761.

[322] D. CAUGHEY [1983]. *Multigrid calculation of three-dimensional transonic potential flows*, Appl. Math. & Comp., 13(3-4), pp. 241–260. (Special Issue, Proceedings of the First Copper Mountain Conference on Multigrid Methods, Copper Mountain, CO, S. McCormick and U. Trottenberg, eds.).

[323] D. CAUGHEY, P. NEWMAN, AND A. JAMESON [1978]. *Recent experiences with three dimensional transonic potential flow calculations*, NASA Tech. Report TM-78733, NASA Langley Research Center.

[324] R. CHAMBERLAIN [1986]. *Experiences with the Intel iPSC hypercube*, Supercomputer, 16, pp. 24–29.

[325] R. CHAMBERLAIN [1987]. *An alternative view of LU factorization with partial pivoting on a hypercube multiprocessor*, in Heath [860], pp. 569–575.

[326] R. CHAMBERLAIN [1988]. *Gray codes, fast Fourier transforms, and hypercubes*, Parallel Computing, 6, pp. 225–234.

[327] R. CHAMBERLAIN, P. FREDERICKSON, J. LINDHEIM, AND J. PETERSEN [1987]. *A high level library for hypercubes*, in Heath [860], pp. 651–655.

[328] R. CHAMBERLAIN AND M. POWELL [1986]. *QR factorization for linear least squares problems on the hypercube*, Tech. Report CCS 86/10, Department of Science and Technology, Chr. Michelsen Institute, Bergen, Norway.

[329] T. CHAN [1987]. *Analysis of preconditioners for domain decomposition*, SIAM J. Numer. Anal., 27, pp. 382–390.

[330] T. CHAN [1987]. *On the implementation of kernel numerical algorithms for computational fluid dynamics on hypercubes*, in Heath [860], pp. 747–755.

[331] T. CHAN AND T. HOU [1988]. *Domain decomposition preconditioners for general second order elliptic problems*, CAM Report 88-16, Department of Mathematics, UCLA.

[332] T. CHAN AND D. RESASCO [1987]. *A domain-decomposed fast Poisson solver on a rectangle*, SIAM J. Sci. Statist. Comput., 8, pp. s14–s26.

[333] T. CHAN AND D. RESASCO [1987]. *Hypercube implementation of domain decomposed fast Poisson solvers*, in Heath [860], pp. 738–746.

[334] T. CHAN AND D. RESASCO [1988]. *A framework for the analysis and construction of domain decomposition preconditioners*, in Glowinski et al. [762], pp. 217–230.

[335] T. CHAN AND Y. SAAD [1985]. *Multigrid algorithms on the hypercube multiprocessor*, Tech. Report YALEU/DCS/RR-368, Department of Computer Science, Yale University, New Haven, CT, February.

[336] T. CHAN AND Y. SAAD [1986]. *Multigrid algorithms on the hypercube multiprocesor*, IEEE Trans. Comput., C-35, pp. 969–977.

[337] T. CHAN, Y. SAAD, AND M. SCHULTZ [1985]. *Solving elliptic partial differential equations on the hypercube multiprocessor*, Tech. Report YALEU/DCS/RR-373, Department of Computer Science, Yale University, March.

[338] T. CHAN, Y. SAAD, AND M. SCHULTZ [1987]. *Solving elliptic partial differential equations on the hypercube multiprocessor*, Comm. Appl. Numer. Meth., 3, pp. 81–88.

[339] T. CHAN AND R. SCHREIBER [1985]. *Multigrid algorithms on the hypercube multiprocessor*, Tech. Report 368, Department of Computer Science, Yale University.

[340] T. CHAN AND R. SCHREIBER [1985]. *Parallel networks for multigrid algorithms: Architecture and complexity*, SIAM J. Sci. Statist. Comput., 6, pp. 698–711.

[341] T. CHAN AND R. TUMINARO [1987]. *Implementation of multigrid algorithms on hypercubes*, in Heath [860], pp. 730–737.

[342] T. CHAN AND R. TUMINARO [1988]. *Design and implementation of parallel multigrid algorithms*, in McCormick [1312], pp. 101–115.

[343] T. CHAN AND R. TUMINARO [1988]. *Implementation and evaluation of multigrid algorithms on hybercubes*, in McCormick [1312].

[344] T. CHAN AND R. TUMINARO [1988]. *A survey of parallel multigrid algorithms*, CAM Report 87-16, Department of Mathematics, UCLA.

[345] R. CHANDRA [1978]. *Conjugate Gradient Methods for Partial Differential Equations*, PhD dissertation, Yale University, Department of Computer Science.

[346] H. CHANG, S. UTKU, M. SALAMA, AND D. RAPP [1988]. *A parallel Householder tridiagonalization strategem using scattered square decomposition*, Parallel Computing, 6, pp. 297–312.

[347] H. CHANG, S. UTKU, M. SALAMA, AND D. RAPP [1988]. *A parallel Householder tridiagonalization strategem using scattered row decomposition*, I. J. Num. Meth. Eng., 26, pp. 857–874.

[348] S. CHANG [1982]. *Borehole acoustic simulation on vector computers*, in Control Data Corporation [411].

[349] D. CHAPMAN [1979]. *Computational aerodynamics development and outlook*, 17th Aerospace Sciences Meeting. AIAA paper 79-0129.

[350] A. CHARLESWORTH AND J. GUSTAFSON [1986]. *Introducing replicated VLSI to supercomputing: The FPS-164/MAX scientific computer*, Computer, 19(3), pp. 10–23.

[351] Y. CHAUVET [1984]. *Multitasking a vectorized Monte Carlo algorithm on the CRAY X-MP/2*, CRAY Channels, 6(3), pp. 6–9.

[352] D. CHAZAN AND W. MIRANKER [1969]. *Chaotic relaxation*, Lin. Alg. & Appl., 2, pp. 199–222.

[353] D. CHAZAN AND W. MIRANKER [1970]. *A non-gradient and parallel algorithm for unconstrained minimization*, SIAM J. Control, 8, pp. 207–217.

[354] A. CHEN AND C. WU [1984]. *Optimum solution to dense linear systems of equations*, Proc. 1984 Int. Conf. Par. Proc., pp. 417–424.

[355] K. CHEN AND K. IRANI [1980]. *A Jacobi algorithm and its implementation on parallel computers*, Proc. 18th Allerton Conf. on Comm., Cont. and Comp., pp. 564–573.

[356] M. CHEN [1983]. *Space-time Algorithms: Semantics and Methodology*, PhD dissertation, California Institute of Technology.

[357] M. CHEN [1986]. *A design methodology for synthesizing parallel algorithms and architectures*, J. Par. Dist. Comp., 3, pp. 461–491.

[358] M.-Q. CHEN AND S.-P. HAN [1987]. *A parallel quasi-Newton method for partially separable large scale minimization*, Tech. Report 689, Center for Supercomputing Research and Development, University of Illinois at Urbana-Champaign.

[359] M.-S. CHEN AND K. SHIN [1987]. *Processor allocation in an n-cube multiprocessor using Gray codes*, IEEE Trans. Comput., C-36, pp. 1396–1407.

[360] S. CHEN [1975]. *Speedup of Iterative Programs in Multi-Processing Systems*, PhD dissertation, University of Illinois at Urbana-Champaign, Department of Computer Science.

[361] S. CHEN [1982]. *Polynomial Scaling in the Conjugate Gradient Method and Related Topics in Matrix Scaling*, PhD dissertation, Pennsylvania State University, Department of Computer Science.

[362] S. CHEN [1984]. *Large-scale and high-speed multiprocessor system for scientific applications: CRAY X-MP-2 series*, in Kowalik [1116], pp. 59–67.

[363] S. CHEN, J. DONGARRA, AND C. HSUING [1984]. *Multiprocessing linear algebra algorithms on the CRAY X-MP-2: Experiences with small granularity*, J. Par. Dist. Comp., 1, pp. 22–31.

[364] S. CHEN AND D. KUCK [1975]. *Time and parallel processor bounds for linear recurrence systems*, IEEE Trans. Comput., C-24, pp. 101–117.

[365] S. CHEN, D. KUCK, AND A. SAMEH [1978]. *Practical parallel band triangular system solvers,* ACM Trans. Math. Softw., 4, pp. 270–77.

[366] S. CHEN AND A. SAMEH [1975]. *On parallel triangular solvers,* Proc. 1975 Sagamore Conf. Par. Proc., pp. 237–38.

[367] K. CHENG AND S. SAHNI [1987]. *VLSI systems for band matrix multiplication,* Parallel Computing, 4, pp. 239–258.

[368] T. CHENG AND O. JOHNSON [1982]. *3D vector forward modeling,* Seismics Acous. Lab. 5th year Prog. Rev., 10, pp. 210–228.

[369] H. CHEONG AND A. VEIDENBAUM [1987]. *The performance of software managed multiprocessor cache on parallel numerical algorithms,* Proc. Int. Conf. on Supercomputing, Athens, Springer-Verlag, June.

[370] M. CHERN AND T. MURATA [1983]. *Efficient matrix multiplication on a concurrent data-loading array processor,* Proc. 1983 Int. Conf. Par. Proc., pp. 90–94.

[371] M. CHERN AND T. MURATA [1983]. *A fast algorithm for concurrent LU decomposition and matrix inversion,* Proc. 1983 Int. Conf. Par. Proc., pp. 79–86.

[372] G. CHERRY [1984], *Parallel programming in ANSI standard Ada.* Reston.

[373] T. CHEUNG AND J. SMITH [1986]. *A simulation study of the CRAY X-MP memory system,* IEEE Trans. Comput., C-35, pp. 613–622.

[374] R. CHIMA AND G. JOHNSON [1983]. *Efficient solution of the Euler and Navier-Stokes equations with a vectorized multiple-grid algorithm,* Paper 83-1893, AIAA.

[375] R. CHIN, G. HEDSTROM, F. HOWES, AND J. McGRAW [1986]. *Parallel computation of multiple-scale problems,* in Wouk [1999], pp. 136–153.

[376] R. CHIN, G. HEDSTROM, F. HOWES, AND J. McGRAW [1986]. *Parallel computation of multiple-scale problems,* New Computing Environments: Parallel, Vector, and Systolic, Philadelphia, pp. 136–153.

[377] R. CHIN, G. HEDSTROM, J. SCROGGS, AND D. SORENSEN [1987]. *Parallel computation of a domain decomposition method,* Tech. Report 657, Center for Supercomputing Research and Development, University of Illinois at Urbana-Champaign, April.

[378] R. CHIN, G. HEDSTROM, AND C. SIEWERT [1986]. *On the use of the FN method for radiative transfer problems,* Tech. Report UCRL-94464, Lawrence Livermore National Laboratory.

[379] Y. CHOW AND W. KOHLER [1979]. *Models for dynamic load balancing in a heterogeneous multiple processor system,* IEEE Trans. Comput., C-28, pp. 354–.

[380] N. CHRIST AND A. TERRANO [1984]. *A very fast parallel processor,* IEEE Trans. Comput., 33, pp. 344–350.

[381] C. CHRISTARA [1988]. *Parallel Algorithms/Architectures for the Solution of Elliptic Partial Differential Equations,* PhD dissertation, Purdue University.

[382] C. CHRISTARA, E. HOUSTIS, AND J. RICE [1988]. *A parallel spline collocation-capacitance method for elliptic partial differential equations,* Tech. Report CSD-TR-735, Department of Computer Science, Purdue University.

[383] A. CHRONOPOULOS AND C. GEAR [1987]. *Implementation of preconditioned S-step conjugate gradient methods on a multi processor system with memory hierarchy,* Tech. Report 1346, Department of Computer Science, University of Illinois at Urbana-Champaign.

[384] E. CHU [1988]. *Orthogonal Decomposition of Dense and Sparse Matrices on Multiprocessors,* PhD dissertation, University of Waterloo.

[385] E. CHU AND A. GEORGE [1987]. *Gaussian elimination with partial pivoting and load balancing on a multiprocessor,* Parallel Computing, 5, pp. 65–74.

[386] E. CHU AND A. GEORGE [1987]. *QR factorization of a dense matrix on a shared memory multiprocessor,* Tech. Report ORNL/TM-10581, Oak Ridge National Laboratory, October.

[387] E. CHU AND A. GEORGE [1988]. *QR factorization of a dense matrix on a hypercube multiprocessor,* Tech. Report ORNL/TM-10691, Oak Ridge National Laboratory.

[388] M. CHU AND H. HAMILTON [1987]. *Parallel solution of ODE's by multiblock methods,* SIAM J. Sci. Statist. Comput., 8, pp. 342–353.

[389] H. CHUANG AND L. CHEN [1987]. *A fixed size systolic array for arbitrarily large eigenvalue problems,* Proc. 1987 Int. Conf. Par. Proc., pp. 550–556.

[390] J. CHUN, T. KAILATH, AND H. LEV-ARI [1987]. *Fast parallel algorithms for QR and triangular factorization,* SIAM J. Sci. Statist. Comput., 8, pp. 899–913.

[391] J. CLAUSING, R. HAGSTROM, E. LUSK, AND R. OVERBEEK [1985]. *A technique for achieving portability among multiprocessors: Implementation on the Lemur,* Parallel Computing, 2, pp. 137–162.

[392] A. CLEARY, D. HARRAR, AND J. ORTEGA [1986]. *Gaussian elimination and Choleski factorization on the FLEX/32,* Tech. Report RM-86-13, Department of Applied Mathematics,

The University of Virginia, December.

[393] A. CLEARY, E. POOLE, J. ORTEGA, O. STORAASLI, AND C. VAUGHAN [1988]. *Solution of structural analysis problems on a parallel computer*, Proceedings of the 29th AIAA Structures, Structural Dynamics and Materials Conference, pp. 596–605.

[394] T. CLEMANS-AUGUST AND U. TROTTENBERG [1988]. *A short note on standard parallel multigrid algorithms for 3D*, Appl. Math. & Comp., 27, pp. 101–116.

[395] E. CLEMENTI, J. DETRICH, S. CHIN, G. CORONGIU, D. FOLSOM, D. LOGAN, R. CALTABIANO, A. CARNEVALI, J. HELIN, M. RUSSO, A. GNUDI, AND P. PALAMIDESE [1987]. *Large-scale computations on a scalar, vector and parallel "supercomputer"*, Parallel Computing, 5, pp. 13–44.

[396] J. CLINARD AND A. GEIST [1987]. *Implementing fracture mechanics analysis on a distributed-memory parallel processor*, Tech. Report ORNL/TM-10367, Oak Ridge National Laboratory, March.

[397] M. CLINT, C. HOLT, R. PERROTT, AND A. STEWART [1984]. *Algorithms for the parallel computation of eigensystems*, in Feilmeier et al. [623], pp. 123–130.

[398] C. CLOS [1953]. *A study of non-blocking switching networks*, Bell System Tech. J., 32, pp. 406–424.

[399] D. COCHRANE AND D. TRUHLAR [1986]. *Strategies and performance norms for efficient utilization of vector pipeline computers as illustrated by the classical mechanical simulation of rotationally inelastic collisions*, Tech. Report 86-4, University of Minnesota Supercomputer Institute, January.

[400] J. COCKE AND D. SLOTNICK [1958]. *The use of parallelism in numerical calculations*, Research Memorandum RC-55, IBM.

[401] B. CODENOTTI [1988]. *Fast parallel algorithms for matrix inversion and linear systems solution*, Appl. Math. Letters, 1, pp. 33–36.

[402] B. CODENOTTI AND P. FAVATI [1987]. *Iterative methods for the parallel solution of linear systems*, I. J. Comp. & Math. Appl., 13, pp. 631–634.

[403] B. CODENOTTI AND P. FAVATI [1987]. *Low rank modification of Jacobi and JOR iterative methods*, Comp. Math. Appl., 13, pp. 617–621.

[404] E. COFFMAN AND R. GRAHAM [1972]. *Optimal scheduling for two-processor systems*, Acta Informatica, 1, pp. 200–213.

[405] T. COLEMAN [1988]. *A chordal preconditioner for large scale optimization*, Math. Prog., 40, pp. 265–288.

[406] W. COLLIER, C. MCCALLIEN, AND J. ENDERBY [1984]. *Tough problems in reactor design*, in Paddon [1512], pp. 91–106.

[407] P. CONCUS, G. GOLUB, AND G. MEURANT [1985]. *Block preconditioning for the conjugate gradient method*, SIAM J. Sci. Statist. Comput., 6, pp. 220–252.

[408] V. CONRAD AND Y. WALLACH [1977]. *Iterative solution of linear equations on a parallel processor system*, IEEE Trans. Comput., C-26, pp. 838–847.

[409] J. CONROY [1986]. *Parallel Direct Solution of Sparse Linear Systems of Equations*, PhD dissertation, University of Maryland. Also available as Computer Science Tech. Report No. 1714, October.

[410] CONTROL DATA CORPORATION [1979]. *Final report. Feasibility study for NASF*, Contractor Report NAS2-9896, NASA.

[411] CONTROL DATA CORPORATION [1982]. *Proceedings Symposium CYBER 205 Applications*, Ft. Collins, CO.

[412] M. COSNARD, M. MARRAKCHI, Y. ROBERT, AND D. TRYSTRAM [1988]. *Parallel Gaussian elimination on an MIMD computer*, Parallel Computing, 6, pp. 275–296.

[413] M. COSNARD, J. MULLER, AND Y. ROBERT [1986]. *Parallel QR-decomposition of a rectangular matrix*, Numer. Math., 48, pp. 239–249.

[414] M. COSNARD AND Y. ROBERT [1986]. *Complexity of parallel QR factorization*, J. ACM, 33, pp. 712–723.

[415] M. COSNARD, Y. ROBERT, P. QUINTON, AND M. TCHUENTE, eds. [1986]. *Parallel Algorithms and Architectures*, North-Holland, Amsterdam.

[416] M. COSNARD, Y. ROBERT, AND D. TRYSTRAM [1985]. *Comparison des méthodes parallèles de diagonalisation pour la résolution de systèmes linéaires denses*, C.R. Acad. Sci. Paris, I 301(16), pp. 781–784.

[417] M. COSNARD, Y. ROBERT, AND D. TRYSTRAM [1986]. *Résolution parallèle de systèmes linéaires denses par diagonalisation*, E.D.F. Bulletin de la Direction des Etudes et des Recherches, C(2), pp. 67–87.

[418] G. COTTI [1987]. *A parallel perturbed biharmonic solver*, I. J. Comp. & Math. Appl., 13, pp. 681–86.

[419] W. COWELL AND C. THOMPSON [1986]. *Transforming Fortran DO loops to improve performance on vector architectures*, ACM Trans. Math. Softw., 12, pp. 324–353.

[420] C. COX [1988]. *Implementation of a divide and conquer cyclic reduction algorithm on the FPS T-20 hypercube*, Tech. Report URI-037, Department of Mathematical Sciences, Clemson University, January.

[421] M. COX [1983]. *Ocean modeling on the Cyber 205 at GFDL*, in Gary [700], pp. 27–32.

[422] R. CRANE, M. MINKOFF, K. HILLSTROM, AND S. KING [1986]. *Performance modeling of large-grained parallelism*, Tech. Report ANL/MLS-TM-63, Argonne National Laboratory, March.

[423] CRAY RESEARCH, INC. [1982]. *Science, Engineering and the CRAY-1, Proceedings of a Cray Research Inc. Symposium*.

[424] T. CROCKETT [1987]. *Performance of Fortran floating-point operations on the Flex/32 multicomputer*, ICASE Interim Report 4, ICASE, NASA Langley Research Center, Hampton, VA.

[425] W. CROWTHER, J. GOODHUE, E. STARR, R. THOMAS, W. MILLIKEN, AND T. BLACKADAR [1985]. *Performance measurements on a 128-node Butterfly parallel processor*, Proc. 1985 Int. Conf. Par. Proc., pp. 531–540.

[426] B. CRUTCHFIELD [1987]. *A vectorizing C compiler*, Supercomputer, 19, pp. 27–36.

[427] L. CSANKY [1976]. *Fast parallel matrix inversion algorithms*, SIAM J. Comput., 5, pp. 618–623.

[428] M. CULLEN [1983]. *Current progress and prospects in numerical techniques for weather prediction models*, J. Comp. Phys., 50, pp. 1–37.

[429] J. CUPPEN [1981]. *A divide and conquer method for the symmetric tridiagonal eigenproblem*, Numer. Math., 36, pp. 177–195.

[430] Z. CVETANOVIC [1986]. *Performance analysis of the FFT algorithm on a shared memory parallel architecture*, Tech. Report RC11719(52739), IBM T. J. Watson Research Center.

[431] Z. CVETANOVIC [1987]. *The effects of problem partitioning allocation and granularity on the performance of multi-processor systems*, IEEE Trans. Comput., C-36, pp. 421–432.

[432] G. CYBENKO, D. KRUMME, AND K. VENKATARAMAN [1987]. *Fixed hypercube embedding*, Tech. Report, Department of Computer Science, Tufts University, August.

[433] W. CYRE, C. DAVIS, A. FRANK, L. JEDYNAK, M. REDMOND, AND V. RIDEOUT [1977]. *WISPAC: A parallel array computer for large scale system simulation*, Simulation, 11, pp. 165–172.

[434] C. DALY AND J. DUCROZ [1988]. *Performance of a subroutine library on vector processing machines*, Comput. Phys. Comm. To appear.

[435] K. DATTA [1985]. *Parallel complexities and computations of Cholesky's decomposition and QR factorization*, Int. J. Comput. Math., 15, pp. 67–82.

[436] A. DAVE AND I. DUFF [1987]. *Sparse matrix calculations on the CRAY-2*, Parallel Computing, 5, pp. 55–64.

[437] E. DAVIDSON, D. KUCK, D. LAWRIE, AND A. SAMEH [1986]. *Supercomputing trade-offs and the Cedar system*, Tech. Report 577, Center for Supercomputing Research and Development, University of Illinois at Urbana-Champaign, May.

[438] A. DAVIS [1983]. *Computer architecture*, IEEE Spectrum, 20(11), pp. 94–99.

[439] G. DAVIS [1986]. *Column LU factorization with pivoting on a hypercube multiprocessor*, SIAM J. Algebraic Discrete Methods, 7, pp. 538–550.

[440] G. DAVIS, R. FUNDERLIC, AND A. GEIST [1987]. *A hypercube implementation of the implicit double shift QR algorithm*, in Heath [860], pp. 619–626.

[441] T. DAVIS [1986]. *PSolve: A concurrent algorithm for solving sparse systems of linear equations*, Tech. Report 612, Center for Supercomputing Research and Development, University of Illinois at Urbana-Champaign, December.

[442] T. DAVIS AND E. DAVIDSON [1987]. *PSolve: A concurrent algorithm for solving sparse systems of linear equations*, Proc. 1987 Int. Conf. Par. Proc., pp. 483–490.

[443] W. DAVY AND W. REINHARDT [1975]. *Computation of shuttle non-equilibrium flow fields on a parallel processor*, Tech. Report NASA SP-347, NASA Ames Research Center.

[444] I. DAVYDOVA AND I. DAVYDOV [1985]. *Features characterizing the solution of computational problems on current and projected highly efficient computing systems*, Computational Processes and Systems, Izdatel'stvo Nauka, Moscow, pp. 162–172.

[445] S. DAY AND B. SHKOLLER [1982]. *A 3-D earthquake model*, in Control Data Corporation [411].

[446] M. DAYDE [1986]. *Parallelisation d'algorithmes d'optimisation pour des problèmes d'optimum design*, PhD dissertation, Institut National Polytechnique de Toulouse, France.

[447] P. DE RIJK [1986]. *A one-sided Jacobi algorithm for computing the singular value decomposition on a vector computer*, Tech. Report 86-21, Math. Inst., Univ. Amsterdam.

[448] C. DE VORE [1984]. *Vectorization and implementation of an efficient multigrid algorithm for the solution of elliptic partial differential equations*, Memorandum Report 5504, Naval Research Laboratory.

[449] G. DEIWERT AND H. ROTHMUND [1983]. *Three dimensional flow over a conical afterbody containing a centered propulsive jet: A numerical simulation*, AIAA 16th Fluid and Plasma Dynamics Conference. Also in Gary [700], pp. 187-200.

[450] E. DEKEL, D. NASSIMI, AND S. SAHNI [1981]. *Parallel matrix and graph algorithms*, SIAM J. Comput., 10, pp. 657-673.

[451] J.-M. DELOSME [1987]. *A processor for two-dimensional symmetric eigenvalue and singular value arrays*, Tech. Report YALEU/DCS/RR-540, Department of Computer Science, Yale University, May.

[452] J.-M. DELOSME AND I. IPSEN [1986]. *Parallel solution of symmetric positive definite systems with hyperbolic rotations*, Lin. Alg. & Appl., 77, pp. 75-111.

[453] J.-M. DELOSME AND I. IPSEN [1987]. *Efficient systolic arrays for the solution of Toeplitz systems: An illustration of a methodology for the construction of systolic architectures in VLSI*, Systolic Arrays, Adam Hilger, Ltd., Bristol, pp. 37-46.

[454] J.-M. DELOSME AND M. MORF [1981]. *Scattering arrays for matrix computations*, SPIE 25th Tech. Symp., San Diego, CA.

[455] P. DELSARTE, Y. GENIN, AND Y. KAMP [1980]. *A method of matrix inverse triangular decomposition based on contiguous principal submatrices*, Lin. Alg. & Appl., 31, pp. 194-212.

[456] L. DELVES, A. SAMBA, AND J. HENDRY [1984]. *Band matrices on the DAP*, in Paddon [1512], pp. 167-183.

[457] B. DEMBART AND K. NEVES [1977]. *Sparse triangular factorization on vector computers*, Exploring Applications of Parallel Processing to Power System Analysis, Report EE 566-SR, Electric Power Research Institute.

[458] J. DEMINET [1982]. *Experience with multiprocessor algorithms*, IEEE Trans. Comput., C-31, pp. 278-288.

[459] P. DENNING [1985]. *Parallel computation*, American Scientist, 73, pp. 322-323.

[460] P. DENNING [1987]. *Evaluating supercomputers*, Tech. Report TR-87.2, RIACS, NASA Ames Research Center, January.

[461] P. DENNING AND G. ADAMS [1987]. *Research questions for performance analysis of supercomputers*, Proceedings of the International Symposium on Large Scale Scientific Computation, Amsterdam, Netherlands, North-Holland.

[462] J. DENNIS [1980]. *Data flow supercomputers*, Computer, 13(11), pp. 48-56.

[463] J. DENNIS [1982]. *High speed data flow computer architecture for the solution of the Navier-Stokes equations*, Tech. Report, Massachusetts Institute of Technology Laboratory for Computer Science.

[464] J. DENNIS [1984]. *Data flow ideas for supercomputers*, Proc. COMPCON 84, IEEE Comp. Soc. Conf., pp. 15-20.

[465] J. DENNIS [1984]. *High speed data flow computer architecture for the solution of the Navier-Stokes equations*, Computation Structures Group Memo 225, Massachusetts Institute of Technology Laboratory for Computer Science.

[466] J. DENNIS, G. GAO, AND K. TODD [1984]. *Modeling the weather with a dataflow supercomputer*, IEEE Trans. Comput., C-33, pp. 592-603.

[467] J. DENNIS AND K. WENG [1977]. *Application of data flow computation to the weather problem*, in Kuck et al. [1133], pp. 143-157.

[468] J. DEUTSCH [1985]. *Algorithms and Architecture for Multiprocessor-Based Circuit Simulation*, PhD dissertation, University of California, Berkeley, Electronics Research Laboratory.

[469] J. DEUTSCH AND A. NEWTON [1984]. *MSLICE: A multiprocessor based circuit simulator*, Proc. 1984 Int. Conf. Par. Proc., pp. 207-214.

[470] J. DEUTSCH AND A. NEWTON [1984]. *A multiprocessor implementation of relaxation based electrical circuit simulation*, Proc. 21st Design Automation Conference.

[471] J. DEVREESE AND P. VAN CAMP, eds. [1985]. *Supercomputers in Theoretical and Experimental Science*, Plenum Publishing Corp., New York, NY.

[472] D. DEWEY AND A. PATERA [1987]. *Geometry-defining processors for partial differential equations*, Architecture and Performance of Specialized Computer Systems, B. Alder, ed., Academic Press.

[473] S. DHALL AND C. LIU [1978]. *On a real-time scheduling problem*, Oper. Res., 26, pp. 127-

140.

[474] M. DIAMOND [1975]. *The stability of a parallel algorithm for the solution of tridiagonal linear systems*, Proc. 1975 Sagamore Conf. Par. Proc., p. 235.

[475] J. DIAZ [1986]. *Calculating the block preconditioner on parallel multivector processors*, Proc. Workshop on Applied Computing in the Energy Field, Stillwater, OK.

[476] J. DIAZ, S. BETTE, W. JINES, AND T. STEIHANG [1985]. *Development and performance of a block pre-conditioned iterative solver for linear systems in thermal simulation*, Tech. Report OU-PPI-TR-85-05, School of Electrical Engineering and Computer Science, University of Oklahoma, January.

[477] J. DIAZ, W. JINES, A. MCDONALD, AND T. STEIHANG [1986]. *Block diagonal scaling for iterative methods — Thermal simulation*, Comm. Applied Numer. Methods. To appear.

[478] J. DIAZ, W. JINES, AND T. STEIHANG [1985]. *On a convergence criterion for linear (inner) iterative solvers for reservoir simulation*, Proc. SPE 1985 Res. Simul. Symp., Dallas, TX, February, pp. 41–47.

[479] R. DIEKKAMPER [1984]. *Vectorized finite element analysis of nonlinear problems in structural analysis*, in Feilmeier et al. [623], pp. 293–298.

[480] Q. DINH [1982]. *Simulation Numérique en Eléments Finis d'écoulements de Fluides Visqueux Incompressibles par Une Méthode de Décomposition de Domaines Sur Processeurs Vectoriels*, PhD dissertation, Univ. P. et M. Curie, Paris.

[481] Q. DINH, R. GLOWINSKI, B. MANTEL, J. PERIAUX, AND P. PERRIER [1981]. *Subdomain solutions of nonlinear problems in fluid dynamics on parallel processors*, 5th International Symposium on Computational Methods in Applied Sciences and Engineering, Versailles, France, North-Holland.

[482] L. DIXON, P. DUCKSBURY, AND P. SINGH [1982]. *A parallel version of the conjugate gradient algorithm for finite element problems*, Tech. Report 132, NOC, Hatfield, Herts.

[483] L. DIXON AND K. PATEL [1982]. *The place of parallel computing in numerical optimization: Four parallel algorithms for nonlinear optimization*, Tech. Report 125, NOC, Hatfield, Herts.

[484] D. DODSON [1981]. *Preliminary timing study for the CRAYPACK library*, Internal Memorandum G4550-CM-39, Boeing Computer Services.

[485] D. DODSON AND J. LEWIS [1982]. *Improving the performance of a sparse matrix solver on the CRAY-1*, in Cray Research, Inc. [423], pp. 13–15.

[486] D. DODSON AND J. LEWIS [1985]. *Issues relating to extension of the basic linear algebra subprograms*, ACM SIGNUM Newsletter, 20(1), pp. 2–18.

[487] S. DOI AND N. HARADA [1987]. *A preconditioning algorithm for solving nonsymmetric linear systems suitable for supercomputers*, in Kartashev and Kartashev [1055], pp. 503–509.

[488] J. DONGARRA [1978]. *Some LINPACK timings on the CRAY-1*, Proc. 1978 LASL Workshop on Vector and Parallel Processors, pp. 58–75.

[489] J. DONGARRA [1983]. *Redesigning linear algebra algorithms*, E.D.F. Bulletin de la Direction des Etudes et des Recherches, C(1), pp. 51–59.

[490] J. DONGARRA [1984]. *Increasing the performance of mathematical software through high-level modularity*, Proc. Sixth Int. Symp. Comp. Methods in Eng. & Applied Sciences, Versailles, France, North-Holland, pp. 239–248.

[491] J. DONGARRA [1985]. *Performance of various computers using standard linear equations software in a Fortran environment*, Tech. Report MCA-TM-23, Argonne National Laboratory.

[492] J. DONGARRA [1986]. *How do the mini-supers stack up?*, Computer, 19(3), p. 92.

[493] J. DONGARRA, ed. [1987]. *Experimental Parallel Computing Architectures*, North-Holland.

[494] J. DONGARRA, J. DUCROZ, I. DUFF, AND S. HAMMARLING [1987]. *A proposal for a set of level 3 basic linear algebra subprograms*, ACM SIGNUM Newsletter, 22(3), pp. 2–14.

[495] J. DONGARRA, J. DUCROZ, S. HAMMARLING, AND R. HANSON [1984]. *A proposal for an extended set of Fortran basic linear algebra subprograms*, Technical Memo 41, Mathematics and Computer Science Division, Argonne National Laboratory, December.

[496] J. DONGARRA, J. DUCROZ, S. HAMMARLING, AND R. HANSON [1986]. *An update notice on the extended BLAS*, ACM SIGNUM Newsletter, 21(4), pp. 2–4.

[497] J. DONGARRA, J. DUCROZ, S. HAMMARLING, AND R. HANSON [1988]. *An extended set of basic linear algebra subprograms*, ACM Trans. Math. Softw., 14, pp. 1–17.

[498] J. DONGARRA AND I. DUFF [1986]. *Performance of vector computers for direct and indirect addressing in Fortran*, Harwell Report, Harwell Laboratory.

[499] J. DONGARRA AND I. DUFF [1987]. *Advanced architecture computers*, Tech. Report ANL-MCS-TM-57 (Revision 1), Argonne National Laboratory.

[500] J. DONGARRA AND S. EISENSTAT [1984]. *Squeezing the most out of an algorithm in CRAY-*

FORTRAN, ACM Trans. Math. Softw., 10, pp. 221–230.

[501] J. DONGARRA, F. GUSTAVSON, AND A. KARP [1984]. *Implementing linear algebra algorithms for dense matrices on a vector pipeline machine*, SIAM Rev., 26, pp. 91–112.

[502] J. DONGARRA AND T. HEWITT [1986]. *Implementing dense linear algebra algorithms using multitasking on the CRAY X-MP-4 (or, Approaching the gigaflop)*, SIAM J. Sci. Statist. Comput., 7, pp. 347–350.

[503] J. DONGARRA AND A. HINDS [1979]. *Unrolling loops in FORTRAN*, Softw. Pract. Exper., 9, pp. 219–229.

[504] J. DONGARRA AND A. HINDS [1985]. *Comparison of the CRAY X-MP-4, Fujitsu VP-200 and Hitachi S-810/20. An Argonne perspective*, Tech. Report ANL-8579, Argonne National Laboratory, October.

[505] J. DONGARRA AND R. HIROMOTO [1983]. *A collection of parallel linear equations routines for the Denelcor HEP*, Tech. Report ANL/MCS-TM-15, Argonne National Laboratory, Argonne, IL, September.

[506] J. DONGARRA AND R. HIROMOTO [1984]. *A collection of parallel linear equation routines for the Denelcor HEP*, Parallel Computing, 1, pp. 133–142.

[507] J. DONGARRA AND L. JOHNSSON [1987]. *Solving banded systems on a parallel processor*, Parallel Computing, 5, pp. 219–246.

[508] J. DONGARRA, L. KAUFMAN, AND S. HAMMARLING [1986]. *Squeezing the most out of eigenvalue solvers on high performance computers*, Lin. Alg. & Appl., 77, pp. 113–136.

[509] J. DONGARRA AND A. SAMEH [1984]. *On some parallel banded system solvers*, Tech. Report ANL/MCS-TM-27, Argonne National Laboratory.

[510] J. DONGARRA, A. SAMEH, AND D. SORENSEN [1986]. *Implementation of some concurrent algorithms for matrix factorization*, Parallel Computing, 3, pp. 25–34.

[511] J. DONGARRA AND D. SORENSEN [1985]. *A fast algorithm for the symmetric eigenvalue problem*, IEEE Proceedings of the 7th Symposium on Computer Arithmetic, Urbana, pp. 338–342.

[512] J. DONGARRA AND D. SORENSEN [1986]. *Linear algebra on high performance computers*, Appl. Math. & Comp., 20, pp. 57–88.

[513] J. DONGARRA AND D. SORENSEN [1987]. *A fully parallel algorithm for the symmetric eigenvalue problem*, SIAM J. Sci. Statist. Comput., 8, pp. s139–s154.

[514] J. DONGARRA AND D. SORENSEN [1987]. *A portable environment for developing parallel FORTRAN programs*, Parallel Computing, 5, pp. 175–186.

[515] J. DONGARRA AND D. SORENSON [1984]. *A parallel linear algebra library for the Denelcor HEP*, Tech. Report ANL/MCS/TM-33, Argonne National Laboratory.

[516] C. DOUGLAS, M. HENDERSON, S. HORIGUCHI, W. MIRANKER, B. SMITH, AND A. WINKLER [1988]. *The interaction of numerics and machines*, Research Report RC13429, IBM T.J. Watson Research Center, Yorktown Heights, NY.

[517] C. DOUGLAS, S. MA, AND W. MIRANKER [1987]. *Generating parallel algorithms through multigrid and aggregation/disaggregation techniques*, Proc. First IMACS Symposium on Computational Acoustics, D. Lee, R. Sternberg, and M. Schultz, eds., Amsterdam-New York, North-Holland.

[518] C. DOUGLAS AND W. MIRANKER [1988]. *Constructive interference in parallel algorithms*, SIAM J. Numer. Anal., 25, pp. 376–398.

[519] C. DOUGLAS AND W. MIRANKER [1988]. *Generating parallel algorithms through multigrid and aggregation/disaggregation techniques*, in McCormick [1312].

[520] C. DOUGLAS AND W. MIRANKER [1988]. *Some non-telescoping parallel algorithms based on serial multigrid/aggregation/disaggregation techniques*, in McCormick [1312], pp. 167–176.

[521] C. DOUGLAS AND B. SMITH [1988]. *Using symmetries and antisymmetries to analyze a parallel multigrid method*, SIAM J. Numer. Anal. To appear.

[522] K. DOWERS, S. LAKSHMIVARAHAN, AND S. DHALL [1987]. *On the comparison of the performance of Alliant FX/8, VAX 11/780, and IBM 3081 in solving linear tri-diagonal systems*, Tech. Report, School of Electrical Engineering and Computer Science, University of Oklahoma, January.

[523] B. DRAKE, F. LUK, J. SPEISER, AND J. SYMANSKI [1987]. *SLAPP: A systolic linear algebra parallel processor*, Computer, 20(7), pp. 45–47.

[524] J. DRAKE, B. LAWKINS, B. CARRERAS, H. HICKS, AND V. LYNCH [1987]. *Implementation of a 3-D nonlinear MHD calculation on the Intel hypercube*, Tech. Report ORNL-6335, Oak Ridge National Laboratory.

[525] R. DRESSLER, S. ROBERTSON, AND L. SPRADLEY [1982]. *Effects of Rayleigh accelerations applied to an initially moving fluid*, Materials Processing in the Reduced Gravity Envi-

ronment of Space, G. Rindone, ed., Elsevier Science Publishing Co.

[526] J. DRUMMOND [1983]. *Numerical study of a ramjet dump combustor flow field*, Paper 83-0421, AIAA.

[527] J. DRUMMOND AND E. WEIDNER [1982]. *Numerical study of a scramjet engine flow field*, AIAA Journal, 20, pp. 1182–1187.

[528] M. DUBOIS [1987]. *Performance of S.O.R. algorithms in multiprocessors*, in Kartashev and Kartashev [1055], pp. 414–423.

[529] M. DUBOIS AND F. BRIGGS [1982]. *Performance of synchronized iterative processes in multiprocessor systems*, IEEE Trans. Softw. Eng., SE-8, pp. 419–431.

[530] P. DUBOIS [1982]. *Swimming upstream: Table lookups and the evaluation of piecewise defined functions on vector computers*, in Rodrigue [1643], pp. 129–151.

[531] P. DUBOIS, A. GREENBAUM, AND G. RODRIGUE [1979]. *Approximating the inverse of a matrix for use in iterative algorithms on vector processors*, Computing, 22, pp. 257–268.

[532] P. DUBOIS AND G. RODRIGUE [1977]. *An analysis of the recursive doubling algorithm*, in Kuck et al. [1133], pp. 299–305.

[533] P. DUBOIS AND G. RODRIGUE [1977]. *Operator splitting on the STAR without transposing*, Tech. Report UCID-17515, Lawrence Livermore National Laboratory.

[534] P. DUCKSBURY [1986], *Parallel Array Processing*, Wiley.

[535] J. DUCROZ AND J. WASNIEWSKI [1987]. *Basic linear algebra computations on the Sperry ISP*, Supercomputer, 20/21, pp. 45–54.

[536] I. DUFF [1982]. *The solution of sparse linear equations on the CRAY-1*, CRAY Channels, 4(3).

[537] I. DUFF [1982]. *The solution of sparse linear equations on the CRAY-1*, in Cray Research, Inc. [423], pp. 17–39.

[538] I. DUFF [1984]. *The solution of sparse linear equations on the CRAY-1*, in Kowalik [1116], pp. 293–309.

[539] I. DUFF [1986]. *The influence of vector and parallel processors on numerical analysis*, Tech. Report AERE-R 12329, Computer Science and Systems Division, Harwell Laboratory, Oxon, England.

[540] I. DUFF [1986]. *Parallel implementation of multifrontal schemes*, Parallel Computing, 3, pp. 193–204.

[541] I. DUFF [1986]. *The parallel solution of sparse linear equations*. Handler, Haupt, Jeltsch, Juling, and Lange.

[542] I. DUFF [1986]. *Use of vector and parallel computers in the solution of large sparse linear equations*, Tech. Report ANL/MCS-TM-84, Argonne National Laboratory.

[543] I. DUFF [1986]. *The use of vector and parallel computers in the solution of large sparse linear equations*, Tech. Report AERE-R 12393, Computer Science and Systems Division, Harwell Laboratory, Oxon, England.

[544] I. DUFF [1987]. *Multiprocessing a sparse matrix code on the Alliant FX/8*, Tech. Report CSS-210, Computer Science and Systems Division, Harwell Laboratory, Oxon, England.

[545] I. DUFF, N. GOULD, M. LESCRENIER, AND J. REID [1987]. *The multifrontal method in a parallel environment*, Tech. Report CSS-211, Computer Science and Systems Division, Harwell Laboratory, Oxon, England.

[546] I. DUFF AND L. JOHNSSON [1986]. *The effect of orderings on the parallelization of sparse code*, Technical Memorandum, Mathematics and Computer Science Division, Argonne National Laboratory, Argonne, IL.

[547] I. DUFF AND L. JOHNSSON [1986]. *Node orderings and concurrency in sparse problems: An experimental investigation*, Proc. Int. Conf. Vector and Parallel Computing, Loen, Norway, June 2-6.

[548] I. DUFF AND J. REID [1982]. *Experience of sparse matrix codes on the CRAY-1*, Comput. Phys. Comm., 76, pp. 293–302.

[549] I. DUFF AND J. REID, eds. [1985]. *Vector and Parallel Processors in Computational Science, Proc. 2nd Int. Conf., Oxford, August 1984*, North-Holland.

[550] R. DUGAN, I. DURHAM, AND S. TALUKDAR [1979]. *An algorithm for power system simulation by parallel processing*, Proc. IEEE Power Eng. Soc. Summer Meeting.

[551] A. DULLER AND D. PADDON [1984]. *Processor arrays and the finite element method*, in Feilmeier et al. [623], pp. 131–136.

[552] M. DUNGWORTH [1979]. *The CRAY-1 computer system*, in Jesshope and Hockney [976], pp. 51–76.

[553] T. DUNIGAN [1987]. *Hypercube performance*, in Heath [860], pp. 178–192.

[554] T. DUNIGAN [1987]. *Performance of three hypercubes*, Tech. Report ORNL/TM-10400, Oak Ridge National Laboratory, May.

[555] T. DUNIGAN [1988]. *Performance of a second generation hypercube*, Tech. Report ORNL/TM-10881, Oak Ridge National Laboratory, September.

[556] I. DURHAM, R. DUGAN, A. JONES, AND S. TALUKDAR [1979]. *Power system simulation on a multiprocessor*, Proc. IEEE Power Eng. Soc. Summer Meeting.

[557] J. EASTWOOD AND C. JESSHOPE [1977]. *The solution of elliptic partial differential equations using number theoretical transforms with applications to narrow or computer hardware*, Comput. Phys. Comm., 13, pp. 233–239.

[558] D. EBERHARDT, D. BAGANOFF, AND K. STEVENS [1984]. *Study of the mapping of Navier-Stokes algorithms onto multiple-instruction/multiple-data-stream computers*, Tech. Report TM-85945, NASA Ames Research Center.

[559] P. EBERLEIN [1987]. *On one-sided Jacobi methods for parallel computation*, SIAM J. Algebraic Discrete Methods, 8, pp. 790–796.

[560] P. EBERLEIN [1987]. *On the Schur decomposition of a matrix for parallel computation*, IEEE Trans. Comput., C-36, pp. 167–174.

[561] P. EBERLEIN [1987]. *On using the Jacobi method on the hypercube*, in Heath [860].

[562] J. ECKERT JR., J. MAUCHLY, H. GOLDSTEIN, AND J. BRAINERD [1945]. *Description of the ENIAC and comments on electronic digital computing machines*, Applied Mathematics Panel Report 171.2R, University of Pennsylvania.

[563] O. EGECIOGLU, E. GALLOPOULOS, AND C. KOC [1987]. *Parallel Hermite interpolation: An algebraic approach*, Tech. Report 671, Department of Computer Science, University of Illinois at Urbana-Champaign.

[564] L. EHRLICH [1986]. *The numerical Schwartz alternating procedure and SOR*, SIAM J. Sci. Statist. Comput., 7, pp. 989–993.

[565] V. EIJKHOUT [1985]. *Scalar recurrences on chainable pipeline architectures*, Tech. Report CNA-202, Center for Numerical Analysis, University of Texas at Austin, December.

[566] S. EISENSTAT, M. HEATH, C. HENKEL, AND C. ROMINE [1988]. *Modified cyclic algorithms for solving triangular systems on distributed-memory multiprocessors*, SIAM J. Sci. Statist. Comput., 9(3), pp. 589–600.

[567] S. EISENSTAT AND M. SCHULTZ [1981]. *Trends in elliptic problem solvers*, in Schultz [1752], pp. 99–114.

[568] K. EKANADHAM AND ARVIND [1987]. *SIMPLE: PART I — An exercise in future scientific programming*, Tech. Report RC-12686, IBM, Yorktown Heights, NY, April.

[569] M. EL TARAZI [1982]. *Some convergence results for asynchronous algorithms*, Numer. Math., 39, pp. 325–340.

[570] M. EL TARAZI [1985]. *Iterative methods for systems of first order differential equations*, IMAJNA, 5, pp. 29–40.

[571] L. ELDEN [1987]. *A parallel QR decomposition algorithm*, Tech. Report, Department of Scientific Computing, Uppsala University, and Department of Mathematics, Linkoping University.

[572] G. ELLIS AND L. WATSON [1984]. *A parallel algorithm for simple roots of polynomials*, Comp. & Math., 10, pp. 107–122.

[573] H. ELMAN [1986]. *Approximate Schur complement preconditioners for serial and parallel computers*, Tech. Report 1704, Department of Computer Science, University of Maryland, College Park, MD, September.

[574] H. ELMAN AND E. AGRON [1988]. *Ordering techniques for the preconditioned conjugate gradient method on parallel computers*, Tech. Report TR-88-53, Department of Computer Science, University of Maryland.

[575] A. EMMEN, ed. [1985]. *Supercomputer Applications*, North-Holland, Amsterdam.

[576] P. EMMEN [1987]. *ETA-10: A "poor man's" supercomputer for 1 million dollars*, Supercomputer, 22, pp. 4–6.

[577] M. ENSELME, C. FRABOUL, AND P. LECA [1984]. *An MIMD architecture system for PDE numerical simulation*, in Vichnevetsky and Stepleman [1920], pp. 502–509.

[578] P. ENSLOW [1977]. *Multiprocessor organization: A survey*, ACM Computing Surveys, 9, pp. 103–129.

[579] M. EREEGOVAC AND T. LANG [1986]. *Vector processing*, in Fernbach [630], pp. 29–57.

[580] J. ERHEL [1983]. *Parallelisation d'an algorithme de gradient conjugue preconditionne*, Tech. Report 189, INRIA.

[581] J. ERHEL, W. JALBY, A. LICHNEWSKY, AND F. THOMASETT [1983]. *Quelques progress en calcul parallèle et vectorièl*, Coll. Inf. sur des Méthodes de Calcul Scientifique et Technique.

[582] J. ERHEL, A. LICHNEWSKY, AND F. THOMASETT [1982], *Parallelism in finite element computations*. Presented at the IBM Symposium on Vector Computers and Scientific Com-

puting, Rome.

[583] J. ERICKSEN [1972]. *Iterative and direct methods for solving Poisson's equation and their adaptability to ILLIAC IV*, Tech. Report 60, Center for Advanced Computation, University of Illinois at Urbana-Champaign.

[584] J. ERICKSEN AND R. WILHELMSON [1976]. *Implementation of a convective problem requiring auxiliary storage*, ACM Trans. Math. Softw., 2, pp. 187–195.

[585] G. ERLEBACHER, S. BOKHARI, AND M. HUSSAINI [1987]. *An efficient parallel algorithm for the simulation of three-dimensional compressible transition on a 20 processor Flex/32 multicomputer*, Tech. Report 87-41, ICASE, NASA Langley Research Center, Hampton, VA.

[586] C. ETHRIDGE, J. MOORE, AND V. TRUJILLO [1983]. *Experimental parallel microprocessor system*, Tech. Report LA-UR-83-1676, Los Alamos National Laboratory.

[587] D. EVANS [1979]. *On the numerical solution of sparse systems of finite element equations*, The Mathematics of Finite Elements & Applications III, Mafelap 1978 Conference Proceedings, J. Whiteman, ed., New York, Academic Press, pp. 448–58.

[588] D. EVANS [1982]. *Parallel numerical algorithms for linear systems*, in Evans [589], pp. 357–384.

[589] D. EVANS, ed. [1982]. *Parallel Processing Systems*, Cambridge University Press.

[590] D. EVANS [1983]. *New parallel algorithms in linear algebra*, E.D.F. Bulletin de la Direction des Etudes et des Recherches, C(1), pp. 61–69.

[591] D. EVANS [1984]. *New parallel algorithms for partial differential equations*, in Feilmeier et al. [623], pp. 3–56.

[592] D. EVANS [1984]. *Parallel S.O.R. iterative methods*, Parallel Computing, 1, pp. 3–18.

[593] D. EVANS AND M. BEKAKOS [1988]. *The solution of linear systems by the QIF algorithm on a wavefront array processor*, Parallel Computing, 7, pp. 111–130.

[594] D. EVANS AND R. DUNBAR [1983]. *The parallel solution of triangular systems of equations*, IEEE Trans. Comput., C-32, pp. 201–204.

[595] D. EVANS AND A. HADJIDIMOS [1980]. *A modification of the Quadrant Interlocking Factorisation parallel method*, Int. J. Comput. Math., 8, pp. 149–166.

[596] D. EVANS AND A. HADJIDIMOS [1981]. *Parallel solution to certain banded symmetric and centro-symmetric systems by using the Quadrant Interlocking Factorization method*, Math. Comp. Simul., 23, pp. 180–187.

[597] D. EVANS, A. HADJIDIMOS, AND D. NOUTSOS [1981]. *The parallel solution of banded linear equations by the new Quadrant Interlocking Factorisation (Q.I.F.) method*, Int. J. Comput. Math., 9, pp. 151–62.

[598] D. EVANS AND M. HATZOPOLOUS [1979]. *A parallel linear systems solver*, Int. J. Comput. Math., 7, pp. 227–38.

[599] D. EVANS, S. JIANPING, AND K. LISHAN [1988]. *The convergence factor of the parallel Schwartz overrelaxation method for linear systems*, Parallel Computing, 6, pp. 313–324.

[600] D. EVANS AND K. MAGARITIS [1988]. *Optical processing of banded matrix algorithms using outer product concepts*, Parallel Computing, 6, pp. 119–126.

[601] D. EVANS AND G. MEGSON [1987]. *Construction of extrapolation tables by systolic arrays for solving ordinary differential equations*, Parallel Computing, 4, pp. 33–48.

[602] D. EVANS AND S. OKOLIE [1981]. *A recursive decoupling algorithm for solving banded linear systems*, Int. J. Comput. Math., 10, pp. 139–152.

[603] D. EVANS, J. SHANEHCHI, AND R. BARLOW [1984]. *Implementation of the conjugate gradient and Lanczos algorithms for large sparse banded matrices on the ICL DAP*, in Feilmeier et al. [623], pp. 143–151.

[604] D. EVANS AND R. SOJOODI-HAGHIGHI [1982]. *Parallel iterative methods for solving linear equations*, Int. J. Comput. Math., 11, pp. 247–284.

[605] L. EWERBRING, F. LUK, AND A. RUTTENBERT [1988]. *SVD computation on the Connection Machine*, 21st Annual Hawaii International Conf. on Sys. Sci.

[606] V. FABER [1981]. *Block relaxation strategies*, in Schultz [1752], pp. 271–275.

[607] V. FABER [1987]. *Global communication algorithms for hypercubes and other Cayley coset graphs*, Tech. Report LA-UR-87-3136, Los Alamos National Laboratory.

[608] V. FABER [1987]. *Latency and diameter in sparsely populated processor interconnection networks: A time and space analysis*, Tech. Report LA-UR-87-3635, Los Alamos National Laboratory.

[609] E. FADDEN [1980]. *The AD-10: A digital computer approach to time critical simulation*, Proc. 4th Power Plant Dynamics, Control, and Testing Symposium.

[610] V. FADEEVA AND D. FADEEV [1977]. *Parallel computations in linear algebra*, Kibernetica, 6, pp. 28–40.

[611] C. FARHAT [1986]. *Multiprocessors in Computational Mechanics*, PhD dissertation, University of California at Berkeley, Department of Civil Engineering.

[612] C. FARHAT AND E. WILSON [1987]. *Concurrent iterative solution of large finite element systems*, Comm. Appl. Numer. Meth., 3, pp. 319–326.

[613] C. FARHAT AND E. WILSON [1987]. *Modal superposition dynamic analysis on concurrent multiprocessors*, Eng. Computations.

[614] C. FARHAT AND E. WILSON [1987]. *Solution of finite element systems on concurrent processing computers*, Eng. Computers, 2, pp. 147–165.

[615] P. FARMWALD [1984]. *The S–1 Mark IIA supercomputer*, in Kowalik [1116], pp. 145–155.

[616] R. FATOOHI AND C. GROSCH [1987]. *Implementation of a four color cell relaxation scheme on the MPP, Flex/32 and CRAY-2*, Proc. 1987 Int. Conf. Par. Proc., pp. 424–426.

[617] R. FATOOHI AND C. GROSCH [1987]. *Implementation of an ADI method on parallel computers*, J. Sci. Comp., 2, pp. 175–193.

[618] R. FATOOHI AND C. GROSCH [1988]. *Implementation and analysis of a Navier-Stokes algorithm on parallel computers*, Tech. Report 88-5, ICASE, NASA Langley Research Center, Hampton, VA.

[619] R. FATOOHI AND G. GROSCH [1987]. *Solving the Cauchy-Riemann equations on parallel computers*, Tech. Report 87-34, ICASE, NASA Langley Research Center.

[620] G. FEIERBACH AND D. STEVENSON [1979]. *The ILLIAC IV*, in Jesshope and Hockney [976], pp. 77–92.

[621] M. FEILMEIER, ed. [1977]. *Parallel Computers — Parallel Mathematics, Proceedings of the IMACS Symposium*, Amsterdam, North-Holland.

[622] M. FEILMEIER [1982]. *Parallel numerical algorithms*, in Evans [589], pp. 285–338.

[623] M. FEILMEIER, G. JOUBERT, AND U. SCHENDEL, eds. [1984]. *Parallel Computing 83: Proceedings of the International Conference on Parallel Computing*, New York, North-Holland.

[624] M. FEILMEIER, G. JOUBERT, AND U. SCHENDEL, eds. [1986]. *Parallel Computing 85: Proceedings of the International Conference on Parallel Computing*, New York, North-Holland.

[625] M. FEILMEIER AND W. RÖNSCH [1982]. *Parallel nonlinear algorithms*, Comput. Phys. Comm., 76, pp. 335–348.

[626] C. FELIPPA [1981]. *Architecture of a distributed analysis network for computational mechanics*, Computers and Structures, 13, pp. 405–413.

[627] T. FENG [1981]. *A survey of interconnection networks*, Computer, 14(12), pp. 12–27.

[628] J. FEO [1988]. *An analysis of the computational and parallel complexity of the Livermore loops*, Parallel Computing, 7, pp. 163–186.

[629] E. FERNANDEZ AND B. BUSSEL [1973]. *Bounds on the number of processors and time for multiprocessor optimal schedules*, IEEE Trans. Comput., C-22, pp. 745–751.

[630] S. FERNBACH, ed. [1986]. *Supercomputers*, North-Holland.

[631] W. FICHTNER, L. NAGEL, R. PENUMALLI, W. PETERSON, AND J. D'ARCY [1984]. *The impact of supercomputers on IC technology development and design*, Proc. IEEE, 72, pp. 76–112.

[632] J. FIELD, A. KAPAUAN, AND L. SNYDER [1983]. *Pringle: A parallel processor to emulate chip computers*, Tech. Report CSD-TR-433, Department of Computer Science, Purdue University.

[633] A. FINN, F. LUK, AND C. POTTLE [1982]. *Systolic array computation of the singular value decomposition*, Proc. SPIE Symposium, Vol. 341 (Real Time Processing V), pp. 35–43.

[634] D. FISHER [1985]. *Matrix computation on processors in one, two and three dimensions*, Tech. Report 1556, Department of Computer Science, University of Maryland, August.

[635] D. FISHER [1988]. *Your favorite parallel algorithm may not be as fast as you think*, IEEE Trans. Comput., 37, pp. 211–214.

[636] P. FLANDERS, D. HUNT, S. REDDAWAY, AND D. PARKINSON [1977]. *Efficient high speed computing with the distributed array processor*, in Kuck et al. [1133], pp. 113–128.

[637] M. FLYNN [1966]. *Very high speed computing systems*, Proc. IEEE, 54, pp. 1901–1909.

[638] M. FLYNN [1972]. *Some computer organizations and their effectiveness*, IEEE Trans. Comput., C-21, pp. 948–960.

[639] H. FOERSTER, K. STEUBEN, AND U. TROTTENBERG [1981]. *Nonstandard multigrid techniques using checkered relaxation and intermediate grids*, in Schultz [1752], pp. 285–300.

[640] S. FOLLIN AND M. KASCIC [1986]. *A marching method for solving Poisson's equation on the ETA-10*, Comm. Appl. Numer. Meth., 2, pp. 239–243.

[641] K. FONG AND T. JORDAN [1977]. *Some linear algebraic algorithms and their performance on the CRAY-1*, Tech. Report LA-6774, Los Alamos National Laboratory.

[642] R. FONTECILLA [1987]. *A parallel nonlinear Jacobi algorithm for solving nonlinear equations*, Tech. Report 1807, Department of Computer Science, University of Maryland, March.

[643] B. FORNBERG [1981]. *A vector implementation of the fast Fourier transform algorithm*, Math. Comp., 36, pp. 189–191.

[644] B. FORNBERG [1983]. *Steady viscous flow past a circular cylinder*, in Gary [700], pp. 201–224.

[645] C. FOSTER [1976], *Content Addressable Parallel Processors*, van Nostrand Reinhold.

[646] D. FOULSER AND R. SCHREIBER [1987]. *The Saxpy Matrix-1: A general-purpose systolic computer*, Computer, 20(7), pp. 35–43.

[647] G. FOX [1984]. *Concurrent processing for scientific calculations*, Proc. COMPCON 84, IEEE Comp. Sci. Conf., pp. 70–73.

[648] G. FOX [1985]. *Square matrix decomposition — Symmetric, local, scattered*, CalTech Publication Hm-97, California Institute of Technology, Pasadena, CA.

[649] G. FOX [1987]. *The Caltech concurrent computation program*, in Heath [860], pp. 353–381.

[650] G. FOX AND W. FURMANSKI [1987]. *Communication algorithms for regular convolutions and matrix problems on the hypercube*, in Heath [860], pp. 223–238.

[651] G. FOX, M. JOHNSON, G. LYZENGA, S. OTTO, AND J. SALMON, eds. [1988]. *Solving Problems on Concurrent Processors, Volume I: General Techniques and Regular Problems*, Prentice-Hall, Inc. (To be published), Englewood Cliffs, NJ.

[652] G. FOX, A. KOWALA, AND R. WILLIAMS [1987]. *The implementation of a dynamic load balancer*, in Heath [860], pp. 114–121.

[653] G. FOX AND S. OTTO [1984]. *Algorithms for concurrent processors*, Physics Today, 37(5), pp. 50–59.

[654] G. FOX AND S. OTTO [1986]. *Concurrent computation and the theory of complex systems*, in Heath [858], pp. 244–268.

[655] G. FOX, S. OTTO, AND A. HEY [1987]. *Matrix algorithms on a hypercube I. Matrix multiplication*, Parallel Computing, 4, pp. 17–32.

[656] F. FRAILONG AND J. PAKLEZA [1979]. *Resolution of a general partial differential equation on a fixed size SIMD/MIMD large cellular processor*, Proceedings of the IMACS International Congress, Sorente.

[657] J. FRANCIONI AND J. JACKSON [1987]. *An implementation of a 2^d-section root finding method for the FPS T-series hypercube*, in Heath [860], pp. 495–500.

[658] M. FRANKLIN [1978]. *Parallel solution of ordinary differential equations*, IEEE Trans. Comput., C-25, pp. 413–470.

[659] M. FRANKLIN AND S. DHAR [1986]. *Interconnection networks: Physical design and performance analysis*, J. Par. Dist. Comp., 3, pp. 352–372.

[660] P. FREDERICKSON, R. HIROMOTO, AND J. LARSON [1987]. *A parallel Monte Carlo transport algorithm using a psuedo-random tree to guarantee reproducibility*, Parallel Computing, 4, pp. 281–290.

[661] P. FREDERICKSON AND O. MCBRYAN [1983]. *Parallel superconvergent multigrid*, in McCormick [1312], pp. 195–210.

[662] A. FRIEDMAN AND D. KERSHAW [1982]. *Vectorized incomplete Cholesky conjugate gradient (ICCG) package for the CRAY-1 computer*, Laser Program Annual Report UCRL-500021-81, Lawrence Livermore National Laboratory.

[663] S. FULLER, A. JONES, AND I. DURHAM [1980]. *CMU Cm* review*, Tech. Report AD-A050135, Department of Computer Science, Carnegie-Mellon University.

[664] S. FULLER AND P. OLEINICK [1976]. *Initial measurements of parallel programs on a multiminiprocessor*, Proc. 13th IEEE Computer Soc. Int. Conf., pp. 358–363.

[665] S. FULLER, J. OUSTERBOUT, L. RASKIN, P. RUBINFELD, P. SUNDHU, AND R. SWAN [1978]. *Multi-microprocessors: An overview and working example*, Proc. IEEE, 66(2), pp. 216–228.

[666] R. FULTON [1986]. *The impact of parallel computing on finite element computations*, Reliability of Methods for Engineering Analysis, Pineridge Press, Swansea, pp. 179–196.

[667] R. FUNDERLIC AND A. GEIST [1986]. *Torus data flow for parallel computation of missized matrix problems*, Lin. Alg. & Appl., 77, pp. 149–163.

[668] P. GADER [1988]. *Tridiagonal factorizations of Fourier matrices and application to parallel computations of discrete Fourier transforms*, Lin. Alg. & Appl., 102, pp. 169–210.

[669] D. GAJSKI [1979]. *Solving banded triangular systems on pipelined machines*, Proc. 1979 Int. Conf. Par. Proc., pp. 308–319.

[670] D. GAJSKI [1981]. *An algorithm for solving linear recurrence systems on parallel and pipelined machines*, IEEE Trans. Comput., C-30, pp. 190–206.

[671] D. GAJSKI, D. KUCK, D. LAWRIE, AND A. SAMEH [1983]. *Cedar — A large scale multiprocessor*, Proc. 1983 Int. Conf. Par. Proc., pp. 524–529.

[672] D. GAJSKI, D. LAWRIE, D. KUCK, AND A. SAMEH [1984]. *Cedar*, Proc. COMPCON 84, IEEE Comp. Soc. Conf., pp. 306–309.

[673] D. GAJSKI AND J.-K. PEIR [1985]. *Essential issues in multiprocessor systems*, Computer, 18(6), pp. 9–27.

[674] D. GAJSKI, A. SAMEH, AND J. WISNIENSKI [1982]. *Iterative algorithms for tridiagonal matrices on a WSI-multiprocessor*, Proc. 1982 Int. Conf. Par. Proc., pp. 82–89.

[675] Z. GALIL AND W. PAULI [1983]. *An efficient general-purpose parallel computer*, J. ACM, 30, pp. 286–299.

[676] K. GALLIVAN, W. JALBY, AND U. MEIER [1987]. *The use of BLAS3 in linear algebra on a parallel processor with a hierarchical memory*, SIAM J. Sci. Statist. Comput., 8, pp. 1079–1084.

[677] K. GALLIVAN, W. JALBY, U. MEIER, AND A. SAMEH [1987]. *The impact of hierarchical memory systems on linear algebra algorithm design*, CSRD Report 625, Center for Supercomputing Research and Development, University of Illinois at Urbana-Champaign.

[678] E. GALLOPOULOS [1984]. *The Massively Parallel Processor for problems in fluid dynamics*, Proc. Vector and Parallel Processors in Computational Science II Conference, Oxford, England.

[679] E. GALLOPOULOS [1985]. *Fluid dynamics modeling*, in Potter [1584], pp. 85–103.

[680] E. GALLOPOULOS AND S. MCEWAN [1983]. *Numerical experiments with the Massively Parallel Processor*, Proc. 1983 Int. Conf. Par. Proc., pp. 29–35.

[681] E. GALLOPOULOS AND Y. SAAD [1987]. *A parallel block cyclic reduction algorithm for the fast solution of elliptic equations*, Tech. Report 659, Center for Supercomputing Research and Development, University of Illinois at Urbana-Champaign, April. To appear in Proc. Int. Conf. Supercomputing, Athens, Greece.

[682] G. GAMBOLATI, G. PINI, AND G. ZILLI [1988]. *Comparison of preconditionings for large sparse finite element problems*, Numer. Meth. PDE, 4, pp. 139–157.

[683] D. GANNON [1980]. *A note on pipelining a mesh connected multiprocessor for finite element problems by nested dissection*, Proc. 1980 Int. Conf. Par. Proc., pp. 197–204.

[684] D. GANNON [1981]. *On mapping non-uniform PDE structures and algorithms onto uniform array architectures*, Proc. 1981 Int. Conf. Par. Proc., pp. 100–105.

[685] D. GANNON [1985]. *On the structure of parallelism in a highly concurrent PDE solver*, Proceedings of the 7th Symposium on Computer Arithmetic, H. Kai, ed., Urbana, IL, pp. 252–259.

[686] D. GANNON [1986]. *Restructuring nested loops on the Alliant Cedar cluster: A case study of Gaussian elimination of banded matrices*, Tech. Report 543, Center for Supercomputing Research and Development, University of Illinois at Urbana-Champaign, February.

[687] D. GANNON AND W. JALBY [1987]. *The influence of memory hierarchy on algorithm organization: Programming FFTs on a vector multiprocessor*, Tech. Report 663, Center for Supercomputing Research and Development, University of Illinois at Urbana-Champaign, May.

[688] D. GANNON AND J. PANETTA [1986]. *Restructuring SIMPLE for the CHiP architecture*, Parallel Computing, 3, pp. 305–326.

[689] D. GANNON, L. SNYDER, AND J. VAN ROSENDALE [1983]. *Programming substructure computations for elliptic problems on the CHiP system*, in Noor [1450], pp. 65–80.

[690] D. GANNON AND J. VAN ROSENDALE [1984]. *On the impact of communication complexity in the design of parallel numerical algorithms*, IEEE Trans. Comput., C-33, pp. 1180–1194.

[691] D. GANNON AND J. VAN ROSENDALE [1984]. *Parallel architectures for iterative methods on adaptive, block structured grids*, in Birkhoff and Schoenstadt [173], pp. 93–104.

[692] D. GANNON AND J. VAN ROSENDALE [1986]. *On the structure of parallelism in a highly concurrent PDE solver*, J. Par. Dist. Comp., 3, pp. 106–135.

[693] G. GAO [1986]. *A maximally pipelined tridiagonal linear equation solver*, J. Par. Dist. Comp., 3, pp. 215–235.

[694] G. GAO [1986]. *A pipelined solution method of tridiagonal linear equation systems*, Proc. 1986 Int. Conf. Par. Proc., pp. 84–91.

[695] G. GAO [1987]. *A stability classification method and its application to pipelined solution of linear recurrences*, Parallel Computing, 4, pp. 305–321.

[696] Q.-S. GAO AND R.-Q. WANG [1983]. *Vector computer for sparse matrix operations*, Proc. 1983 Int. Conf. Par. Proc., pp. 87–89.

[697] J. GARDINER AND A. LAUB [1987]. *Implementation of two control system design algorithms on a message-passing hypercube*, in Heath [860], pp. 512–519.

[698] M. GAREY, R. GRAHAM, AND D. JOHNSON [1978]. *Performance guarantees for scheduling algorithms*, Oper. Res., 26, pp. 3–21.

[699] J. GARY [1977]. *Analysis of applications programs and software requirements for high speed computers*, in Kuck et al. [1133], pp. 329–354.

[700] J. GARY, ed. [1984]. *CYBER 200 Applications Seminar, Proceedings of seminar held at NASA Goddard Space Flight Center, October, 1983. NASA-CP-2295.*

[701] J. GARY, S. MCCORMICK, AND R. SWEET [1983]. *Successive overrelaxation, multigrid, and preconditioned conjugate gradients algorithms for solving a diffusion problem on a vector computer*, Appl. Math. & Comp., 13(3-4), pp. 285–310. (Special Issue, Proceedings of the First Copper Mountain Conference on Multigrid Methods, Copper Mountain, CO, S. McCormick and U. Trottenberg, eds.).

[702] M. GAUTZSCH, G. WEILAND, AND D. MULLER-RICHARDS [1980]. *Possibilities and problems with the application of vector computers*, Tech. Report, German Research and Testing Establishment for Aerospace.

[703] T. GAYLORD AND E. VECRIEST [1987]. *Matrix triangularization using arrays of integrated optical Givens rotation devices*, Computer, 20(12), pp. 59–66.

[704] W. GEAR [1986]. *The potential for parallelism in ordinary differential equations*, Tech. Report R-86-1246, Department of Computer Science, University of Illinois at Urbana-Champaign, February.

[705] N. GEHANI [1984], *Ada Concurrent Programming*, Prentice-Hall, Inc., Englewood Cliffs, NJ.

[706] D. GEHRINGER, D. SIEWIOREK, AND Z. SEGALL [1987], *Parallel Processing: The Cm* Experience*, Digital Press, Digital Equipment Corp., Bedford, MA.

[707] E. GEHRINGER, A. JONES, AND Z. SEGALL [1982]. *The Cm* testbed*, Computer, 15(10), pp. 40–53.

[708] A. GEIST [1985]. *Efficient parallel LU factorization with pivoting on a hypercube multiprocessor*, Tech. Report ORNL-6211, Oak Ridge National Laboratory, October.

[709] A. GEIST [1987]. *Solving finite element problems with parallel multifrontal schemes*, in Heath [860], pp. 656–661.

[710] A. GEIST AND G. DAVIS [1988]. *Finding eigenvalues and eigenvectors of unsymmetric matrices using a hypercube multiprocessor*, Tech. Report ORNL/TM-10938, Oak Ridge National Laboratory, October.

[711] A. GEIST AND M. HEATH [1985]. *Parallel Cholesky factorization on a hypercube multiprocessor*, Tech. Report ORNL-6190, Oak Ridge National Laboratory, August.

[712] A. GEIST AND M. HEATH [1986]. *Matrix factorization on a hypercube multiprocessor*, in Heath [858], pp. 161–180.

[713] A. GEIST, M. HEATH, AND E. NG [1987]. *Parallel algorithms for matrix computations*, The Characteristics of Parallel Algorithms, R. Douglass, D. Gannon, and L. Jamieson, eds., MIT Press, Cambridge, pp. 233–251.

[714] A. GEIST AND E. NG [1988]. *A partitioning strategy for parallel sparse Cholesky factorization*, Tech. Report ORNL/TM-10937, Oak Ridge National Laboratory, September.

[715] A. GEIST AND C. ROMINE [1988]. *LU factorization algorithms on distributed-memory multiprocessor architectures*, SIAM J. Sci. Statist. Comput., 9(4), pp. 639–649.

[716] A. GEIST AND C. ROMINE [1989]. *LU factorization on distributed-memory multiprocessors*, Parallel Processing for Scientific Computing, Society for Industrial and Applied Mathematics, Philadelphia, ch. 3, pp. 15–18.

[717] A. GEIST, R. WARD, G. DAVIS, AND R. FUNDERLIC [1988]. *Finding eigenvalues and eigenvectors of unsymmetric matrices using a hypercube multiprocessor*, Proc. Third Conf. Hypercube Concurrent Comput. Appl., G. Fox, ed., New York, Association for Computing Machinery, pp. 1577–1582.

[718] E. GELENBE, A. LICHNEWSKY, AND A. STAPHYLOPATIS [1982]. *Experience with the parallel solution of partial differential equations on a distributed computing system*, IEEE Trans. Comput., C-31, pp. 1157–1165.

[719] W. GENTLEMAN [1975]. *Error analysis of the QR decomposition by Givens transformations*, Lin. Alg. & Appl., 10, pp. 189–197.

[720] W. GENTLEMAN [1978]. *Some complexity results for matrix computations on parallel processors*, J. ACM, 25, pp. 112–115.

[721] W. GENTLEMAN [1981], *Design of numerical algorithms for parallel processing*. Presented at the Parallel Processing Conference at Bergams, Italy.

[722] W. GENTLEMAN AND H. KUNG [1981]. *Matrix triangularization by systolic arrays*, Proc. SPIE 298, Real-time Signal Processing IV, pp. 19–26.

[723] W. GENTZSCH [1983]. *How to maintain the efficiency of highly serial algorithms involving recursions on vector computers*, Proc. Conf. Vector and Parallel Methods in Scientific Computing, Paris.

[724] W. GENTZSCH [1984]. *Benchmark results on physical flow problems*, in Kowalik [1116],

pp. 211–228.

[725] W. GENTZSCH [1984]. *Numerical algorithms in computational fluid dynamics on vector computers*, Parallel Computing, 1, pp. 19–33.

[726] W. GENTZSCH [1984], *Vectorization of Computer Programs with Applications to Computational Fluid Dynamics*, Heyden & Son, Philadelphia, PA.

[727] W. GENTZSCH [1987]. *A fully vectorizable SOR variant*, Parallel Computing, 4, pp. 349–354.

[728] W. GENTZSCH AND G. SCHAFER [1984]. *Solution of large linear systems on vector computers*, in Feilmeier et al. [623], pp. 159–166.

[729] A. GENZ AND D. SWAYNE [1984]. *Parallel implementation of ALOD methods for partial differential equations*, in Feilmeier et al. [623], pp. 167–172.

[730] A. GEORGE, M. HEATH, AND J. LIU [1986]. *Parallel Cholesky factorization on a shared memory multiprocessor*, Lin. Alg. & Appl., 77, pp. 165–187.

[731] A. GEORGE, M. HEATH, J. LIU, AND E. NG [1986]. *Solution of sparse positive definite systems on a shared memory multiprocessor*, Int. J. Par. Prog., 15, pp. 309–325.

[732] A. GEORGE, M. HEATH, J. LIU, AND E. NG [1988]. *Solution of sparse positive definite systems on a hypercube*, Tech. Report ORNL/TM-10865, Oak Ridge National Laboratory, October. (Submitted to J. Comput. Appl. Math.).

[733] A. GEORGE, M. HEATH, J. LIU, AND E. NG [1988]. *Sparse Cholesky factorization on a local memory multiprocessor*, SIAM J. Sci. Statist. Comput., 9, pp. 327–340.

[734] A. GEORGE, M. HEATH, E. NG, AND J. LIU [1987]. *Symbolic Cholesky factorization on a local-memory multiprocessor*, Parallel Computing, 5, pp. 85–96.

[735] A. GEORGE, J. LIU, AND E. NG [1987]. *Communication reduction in parallel sparse Cholesky factorization on a hypercube*, in Heath [860], pp. 576–586.

[736] A. GEORGE, J. LIU, AND E. NG [1988], *Communication results for parallel sparse Cholesky factorization on a hypercube*. Submitted to Parallel Computing.

[737] A. GEORGE AND E. NG [1988]. *Parallel sparse Gaussian elimination with partial pivoting*, Tech. Report ORNL/TM-10866, Oak Ridge National Laboratory. (To appear in Annals of Operations Research).

[738] A. GEORGE AND E. NG [1988]. *Some shared memory is desirable in parallel sparse matrix computations*, SIGNUM Newsletter, 23(2), pp. 9–13.

[739] A. GEORGE, W. POOLE, AND R. VOIGT [1978]. *Analysis of dissection algorithms for vector computers*, Comput. Math. Appl., 4, pp. 287–304.

[740] A. GEORGE, W. POOLE, AND R. VOIGT [1978]. *A variant of nested dissection for solving n by n grid problems*, SIAM J. Numer. Anal., 15, pp. 662–673.

[741] A. GERASOULIS, N. MISSIRILIS, I. NELKEN, AND R. PESKIN [1988]. *Implementing Gauss Jordan on a hypercube multicomputer*, Proc. 3rd Conf. on Hypercube Multiprocessors.

[742] I. GERTNER AND M. SHAMASH [1987]. *VLSI architectures for multidimensional Fourier transform processing*, IEEE Trans. Comput., C-36, pp. 1265–1274.

[743] A. GHOSH [1987]. *Realization of conjugate gradient algorithm on optical linear algebra processors*, Applied Optics, 26(2), pp. 611–613.

[744] H. GIETL [1987]. *The conjugate gradient method with vectorized preconditioning on the Siemens XP-200 vector processor*, Supercomputer, 19, pp. 43–51.

[745] E. GILBERT [1958]. *Gray codes and paths on the n-cube*, Bell System Tech. J., 37, pp. 815–826.

[746] E. GILBERT [1982]. *Algorithm partitioning tools for a high-performance multiprocessor*, Tech. Report UCRL-53401, Lawrence Livermore National Laboratory, Livermore, CA, December.

[747] J. GILBERT [1988]. *An efficient parallel sparse partial pivoting algorithm*, Tech. Report CMI 88/45052-1, Dept. of Science and Technology, Chr-Michelson Institute, August.

[748] J. GILBERT AND H. HAFSTEINSSON [1986]. *A parallel algorithm for finding fill in a sparse symmetric matrix*, Tech. Report TR 86-789, Department of Computer Science, Cornell University.

[749] J. GILBERT AND E. ZMIJEWSKI [1987]. *A parallel graph partitioning algorithm for a message-passing multiprocessor*, Tech. Report TR 87-803, Department of Computer Science, Cornell University.

[750] D. GILL AND E. TADMOR [1988]. *An $O(N^2)$ method for computing the eigensystem of $N \times N$ symmetric tridiagonal matrices by the divide and conquer approach*, Tech. Report 88-19, ICASE, NASA Langley Research Center, Hampton, VA.

[751] S. GILL [1968]. *Parallel programming*, Comput. J., 1, pp. 2–10.

[752] P. GILMORE [1968]. *Structuring of parallel algorithms*, J. ACM, 15, pp. 176–192.

[753] P. GILMORE [1971]. *Numerical solution of partial differential equations by associative pro-*

cessing, Proc. 1971 FJCC, AFIPS Press, Montvale, NJ, pp. 411–418.

[754] P. GILMORE [1971]. *Parallel relocation*, Tech. Report, Goodyear Aerospace Corporation, Akron, OH.

[755] R. GINOSAR AND D. HILL [1985]. *Design and implementation of switching systems for parallel processors*, Proc. 1985 Int. Conf. Par. Proc., pp. 674–680.

[756] M. GINSBURG [1982]. *Some observations on supercomputer computational environments*, Proc. 10th IMACS World Congress on Systems Simulation and Scientific Computation, vol. 1, IMACS, pp. 297–301.

[757] E. GIROUX [1977]. *A large mathematical model implementation on the STAR-100 computer*, in Kuck et al. [1133], pp. 287–298.

[758] B. GLICKFELD AND R. OVERBEEK [1985]. *Quasi-automatic parallelization: A simplied approach to multiprocessing*, Tech. Report ANL-85-70, Argonne National Laboratory, Argonne, IL.

[759] I. GLOUDEMAN [1984]. *The anticipated impact of supercomputers on finite element analysis*, Proc. IEEE, 72, pp. 80–84.

[760] J. GLOUDEMAN, C. HENNRICH, AND J. HODGE [1984]. *The evolution of MSC/NASTRAN and the supercomputer for enhanced performance*, in Kowalik [1116], pp. 393–402.

[761] J. GLOUDEMAN AND J. HODGE [1982]. *The adaption of MSC/NASTRAN to a supercomputer*, Proc. 10th IMACS World Congress on Systems Simulation and Scientific Computation, vol. 1, IMACS, pp. 302–304.

[762] R. GLOWINSKI, G. GOLUB, G. MEURANT, AND J. PERIAUX, eds. [1988]. *Proceedings of the First International Symposium on Domain Decomposition Methods for Partial Differential Equations*, Philadelphia, PA, Society for Industrial and Applied Mathematics.

[763] R. GLOWINSKI AND M. WHEELER [1988]. *Domain decomposition and mixed finite element methods for elliptic problems*, in Glowinski et al. [762], pp. 144–172.

[764] P. GNOFFO [1982]. *A vectorized, finite-volume, adaptive-grid algorithm for Navier-Stokes calculations*, Numerical Grid Generation, J. Thompson, ed., Elsevier Science Publishing Corp.

[765] I. GOHBERG, T. KAILATH, I. KOLTRACHT, AND P. LANCASTER [1987]. *Linear complexity parallel algorithms for linear systems of equations with recursive structure*, Lin. Alg. & Appl., 88, pp. 271–316.

[766] R. GOKE AND G. LIPOVSKI [1973]. *Banyan networks for partitioning on multiprocessor systems*, Proc. 1st Ann. Symp. Computer Arch., pp. 21–30.

[767] M. GOLDMANN [1988]. *Vectorization of the multiple shooting method for the nonlinear boundary value problem in ordinary differential equations*, Parallel Computing, 7, pp. 97–110.

[768] G. GOLUB AND D. MAYERS [1983]. *The use of preconditioning over irregular regions*, Proc. 6th Int. Conf. Computing Methods in Science and Engineering, Versailles, France.

[769] G. GOLUB, R. PLEMMONS, AND A. SAMEH [1986]. *Parallel block schemes for large scale least squares computations*, Tech. Report 574, Center for Supercomputing Research and Development, University of Illinois at Urbana-Champaign, April.

[770] G. GOLUB AND C. VAN LOAN [1989], *Matrix Computations*, The Johns Hopkins University Press, Baltimore. (in press).

[771] M. GONZALEZ [1977]. *Deterministic processor scheduling*, ACM Computing Surveys, 9, pp. 173–204.

[772] R. GONZALEZ [1986]. *Domain Decomposition for Two-Dimensional Elliptic Operators on Vector and Parallel Machines*, PhD dissertation, Rice University.

[773] R. GONZALEZ AND M. WHEELER [1987]. *Domain decomposition for elliptic partial differential equations with Neumann boundary conditions*, Parallel Computing, 5, pp. 257–263.

[774] GOODYEAR AEROSPACE CORP. [1974]. *Application of STARAN to fast Fourier transforms*, Tech. Report GER-16109, Goodyear Aerospace Corp., May.

[775] K. GOSTELOW AND R. THOMAS [1980]. *Performance of a simulated dataflow computer*, IEEE Trans. Comput., C-29, pp. 905–919.

[776] A. GOTTLIEB [1984]. *Avoiding serial bottlenecks in ultraparallel MIMD computers*, Proc. COMPCON 84, IEEE Comp. Soc. Conf., pp. 354–359.

[777] A. GOTTLIEB, R. GRISHMAN, C. KRUSKAL, K. McAULIFFE, L. RUDOLPH, AND M. SNIR [1983]. *The NYU Ultracomputer — Designing an MIMD shared memory parallel computer*, IEEE Trans. Comput., C-32, pp. 175–189.

[778] A. GOTTLIEB, B. LUBACHEVSKY, AND L. RUDOLPH [1983]. *Basic techniques for the efficient coordination of very large numbers of cooperating sequential processors*, ACM Trans. Program. Lang. Syst., 5, pp. 164–189.

[779] A. GOTTLIEB AND J. SCHWARTZ [1982]. *Networks and algorithms for very-large-scale parallel*

computation, Computer, 15(1), pp. 27–36.

[780] D. GOTTLIEB AND R. HIRSH [1988]. *Parallel pseudospectral domain decomposition techniques*, Tech. Report 88-15, ICASE, NASA Langley Research Center, Hampton, VA.

[781] D. GOTTLIEB, M. HUSSAINI, AND S. ORSZAG [1984]. *Theory and applications of spectral methods*, in Voigt et al. [1925], pp. 1–54.

[782] G. GOUDREAU, R. BAILEY, J. HALLQUIST, R. MURRAY, AND S. SACKETT [1983]. *Efficient large-scale finite element computations in a Cray environment*, in Noor [1450], pp. 141–154.

[783] W. GRAGG AND L. REICHEL [1987]. *A divide and conquer algorithm for the unitary eigenproblem*, in Heath [860], pp. 639–650.

[784] M. GRAHAM [1976]. *An Array Computer for the Class of Problems Typified by the General Circulation Model of the Atmosphere*, PhD dissertation, University of Illinois at Urbana-Champaign, Department of Computer Science.

[785] R. GRAHAM [1969]. *Bounds on multiprocessing timing anomalies*, SIAM J. Appl. Math., 17, pp. 416–429.

[786] R. GRAHAM, E. LAWLER, J. LENSTRA, AND A. RINNOOY KAN [1979]. *Optimization and approximation in deterministic sequencing and scheduling: A survey*, Ann. Discrete Math., 5, pp. 169–.

[787] R. GRAVES [1973]. *Partial implicitization*, J. Comp. Phys., 13, pp. 439–444.

[788] J. GRCAR AND A. SAMEH [1981]. *On certain parallel Toeplitz linear system solvers*, SIAM J. Sci. Statist. Comput., 2, pp. 238–256.

[789] A. GREENBAUM [1986]. *A multigrid method for multiprocessors*, Appl. Math. & Comp., 19(1-4), pp. 75–88. (Special Issue, Proceedings of the Second Copper Mountain Conference on Multigrid Methods, Copper Mountain, CO, S. McCormick, ed.).

[790] A. GREENBAUM [1986]. *Solving sparse triangular linear systems using Fortran with parallel extensions on the NYU Ultracomputer prototype*, Ultracomputer Note 99, New York University, April.

[791] A. GREENBAUM [1986]. *Synchronization costs on multiprocessors*, Ultracomputer Note 98, New York University, April.

[792] A. GREENBAUM AND G. RODRIGUE [1977]. *The incomplete Choleski conjugate gradient method for the STAR (5 point operator)*, Tech. Report, Lawrence Livermore National Laboratory.

[793] A. GREENBERG, R. LADNER, M. PATERSON, AND Z. GALIL [1982]. *Efficient parallel algorithms for linear recurrence computation*, Info. Proc. Letters, 15, pp. 31–35.

[794] D. GREENSPAN [1988]. *Particle modeling of cavity flow on a vector computer*, Comput. Meth. Appl. Mech. Engrg., 66, pp. 291–300.

[795] J. GRIFFIN AND H. WASSERMAN [1985]. *Parallel debugging: A preliminary proposal*, Tech. Report LA-UR-85-3967, Los Alamos National Laboratory.

[796] R. GRIMES [1988]. *Solving systems of large dense linear equations*, J. Supercomputing, 1, pp. 291–300.

[797] R. GRIMES AND H. SIMON [1987]. *Dynamic analysis with the Lanczos algorithm on the SCS-40*, Tech. Report ETA-TR-43, Boeing Computer Services, January.

[798] R. GRIMES AND H. SIMON [1987]. *Solution of large dense symmetric generalized eigenvalue problems using secondary storage*, Tech. Report ETA-TR-53, Boeing Computer Services, May.

[799] D. GRIT AND J. MCGRAW [1983]. *Programming divide and conquer on a multiprocessor*, Tech. Report UCRL-88710, Lawrence Livermore National Laboratory.

[800] W. GROPP [1986]. *Dynamic grid manipulation for PDE's on hypercube parallel processors*, Tech. Report YALEU/DCS/RR-458, Department of Computer Science, Yale University, March.

[801] W. GROPP [1987]. *Solving PDEs on loosely-coupled parallel processors*, Parallel Computing, 5, pp. 165–174.

[802] W. GROPP [1988]. *Local uniform mesh refinement on loosely-coupled parallel processors*, I. J. Comp. Math. Appl., 15, pp. 375–389.

[803] W. GROPP AND I. IPSEN [1988]. *Recursive mesh refinement on hypercubes*, Tech. Report RR-616, Department of Computer Science, Yale University.

[804] W. GROPP AND D. KEYES [1988]. *Complexity of parallel implementation of domain decomposition techniques for elliptic partial differential equations*, SIAM J. Sci. Statist. Comput., 9, pp. 312–327.

[805] W. GROPP AND E. SMITH [1987]. *Computational fluid dynamics on parallel processors*, Tech. Report YALEU/DCS/RR-570, Department of Computer Science, Yale University.

[806] C. GROSCH [1978]. *Poisson solvers on a large array computer*, Proc. 1978 LASL Workshop

on Vector and Parallel Processors, pp. 98–132.

[807] C. GROSCH [1979]. *Performance analysis of Poisson solvers on array computers*, in Jesshope and Hockney [976], pp. 147–181.

[808] C. GROSCH [1979]. *Performance analysis of tridiagonal equation solvers on array computers*, Tech. Report TR 79-4, Department of Mathematical and Computing Sciences, Old Dominion University, Norfolk, VA.

[809] C. GROSCH [1980], *The effect of the data transfer pattern of an array computer on the efficiency of some algorithms for the tridiagonal and Poisson problems*. Presented at the Conference on Array Architectures for Computing in the 80's and 90's.

[810] C. GROSCH [1987]. *Adapting a Navier-Stokes code to the ICL-DAP*, SIAM J. Sci. Statist. Comput., 8, pp. s96–s117.

[811] D. GRUNWALD AND D. REED [1987]. *Benchmarking hypercube hardware and software*, in Heath [860], pp. 169–177.

[812] R. GUILILAND [1981]. *Solution of the shallow water equations on the sphere*, J. Comp. Phys., 43, pp. 79–94.

[813] A. GUPTA, B. MOSSBERG, G. POPE, AND K. SEPEHRNOORI [1985]. *Application of vector processors to chemical enhanced oil recovery simulation*, Tech. Report 85-5, Center for Enhanced Oil & Gas Recovery Research, University of Texas at Austin.

[814] D. GUPTA, G. POPE, AND K. SEPEHRNOORI [1986]. *Application of vector processors to chemical-enhanced oil recovery simulation*, Comm. Appl. Numer. Meth., 2, pp. 297–303.

[815] J. GURD, C. KIRKHAM, AND I. WATSON [1985]. *The Manchester prototype dataflow computer*, Comm. ACM, 28, pp. 34–52.

[816] J. GURD AND I. WATSON [1982]. *Preliminary evaluation of a prototype dataflow computer*, Proc. IFIP World Computer Congress, North-Holland, pp. 545–551.

[817] J. GUSTAFSON [1986]. *Subdivision of PDE's on FPS scientific computers*, Comm. Appl. Numer. Meth., 2, pp. 305–310.

[818] J. GUSTAFSON [1988]. *Reevaluating Amdahl's law*, Comm. ACM., 31, pp. 532–533.

[819] J. GUSTAFSON, S. HAWKINSON, AND K. SCOTT [1986]. *The architecture of a homogeneous vector supercomputer*, Proc. 1986 Int. Conf. Par. Proc., pp. 649–652.

[820] J. GUSTAFSON, G. MONTRY, AND R. BENNER [1988]. *Development of parallel methods for a 1024-processor hypercube*, SIAM J. Sci. Statist. Comput., 9, pp. 609–638.

[821] J. HACK [1986]. *Peak vs. sustained performance in highly concurrent vector machines*, Computer, 19(9), pp. 11–19.

[822] W. HACKBUSCH [1978]. *On the multigrid method applied to difference equations*, Computing, 20, pp. 291–306.

[823] W. HACKBUSCH AND U. TROTTENBERG, eds. [1982]. *Multigrid Methods*, Springer-Verlag, Berlin.

[824] M. HAFEZ AND D. LOVELL [1983]. *Improved relaxation schemes for transonic potential calculations*, Paper 83-0372, AIAA.

[825] M. HAFEZ AND E. MURMAN [1978]. *Artificial compressibility methods for numerical solution of transonic full potential equation*, AIAA 11th Fluid and Plasma Dynamics Conference, Seattle, WA.

[826] M. HAFEZ AND J. SOUTH [1979]. *Vectorization of relaxation methods for solving transonic full potential equations*, Flow Research Report, Flow Research, Inc., Kent, WA.

[827] B. HAILPERN [1982]. *Concurrent processing*, Tech. Report RC 9582 (42314), IBM, San Jose, CA, September.

[828] L. HALADA [1980]. *A parallel algorithm for solving band systems of linear equations*, Proc. 1980 Int. Conf. Par. Proc., pp. 159–160.

[829] L. HALADA [1981]. *A parallel algorithm for solving band systems and matrix inversion*, CONPAR 81, Conf. Proc., Lecture Notes in Computer Science III, W. Händler, ed., Springer-Verlag, pp. 433–440.

[830] L. HALCOMB AND D. DIESTLER [1986]. *Integration of a large set of coupled differential equations on the Cyber 205 vector processor*, Comput. Phys. Comm., 39, pp. 27–36.

[831] H. HALIN, R. BUHRER, W. HALG, H. BENZ, B. BRON, H. BRUNDIERS, A. ISACCSON, AND M. TADIAN [1980]. *The ETHM multiprocessor project: Parallel simulation of continuous system*, Simulation, 35, pp. 109–123.

[832] S.-P. HAN AND G. LOU [1988]. *A parallel algorithm for a class of convex programs*, SIAM J. Control Optim., 26, pp. 345–355.

[833] W. HÄNDLER, E. HOFMANN, AND H. SCHNEIDER [1976]. *A general purpose array with a broad spectrum of applications*, Informatik-Fachbrichte, Springer-Verlag, Berlin-Heidelberg.

[834] W. HÄNDLER, E. MAEHLE, AND K. WIRL [1985]. *DIRMU multiprocessor configurations*, Proc. 1985 Int. Conf. Par. Proc., pp. 652–656.

[835] W. HANKEY AND J. SHANG [1982]. *Vector processors and CFD*, in Cray Research, Inc. [423], pp. 49–66.

[836] H. HAPP, C. POTTE, AND K. WIRGAN [1978]. *Parallel processing for large scale transient stability*, Proc. IEEE Can. Conf. Comm. Power, pp. 204–207.

[837] A. HARDING AND J. CARLING [1984]. *The three-dimensional solution of the equations of flow and heat transfer in glass-melting tank furnaces: Adapting to the DAP*, in Paddon [1512], pp. 115–133.

[838] U. HARMS AND H. LUTTERMAN [1988]. *Experiences in benchmarking the three supercomputers CRAY-1M, CRAY-X/MP, Fujitsu VP-200 compared with the CYBER 76*, Parallel Computing, 6, pp. 373–382.

[839] D. HARPER AND J. JUMP [1987]. *Vector access performance in parallel memories using a skewed storage scheme*, IEEE Trans. Comput., C-36, pp. 1440–1449.

[840] D. HARRAR AND J. ORTEGA [1988]. *Solution of three-dimensional generalized Poisson equations on vector computers*, Tech. Report RM-88-17, The University of Virginia, October.

[841] L. HART [1988]. *Asynchronous adaptive methods on parallel computers*, in McCormick [1312].

[842] L. HART, S. MCCORMICK, A. O'GALLAGHER, AND J. THOMAS [1986]. *The Fast Adaptive Composite-grid method (FAC): Algorithms for advanced computers*, Appl. Math. & Comp., 19(1-4), pp. 103–126. (Special Issue, Proceedings of the Second Copper Mountain Conference on Multigrid Methods, Copper Mountain, CO, S. McCormick, ed.).

[843] M. HATZOPOULOS [1982]. *Parallel linear system solvers for tridiagonal matrices*, in Evans [589], pp. 389–394.

[844] M. HATZOPOULOS [1983]. *A symmetric parallel linear system solver*, Int. J. Comput. Math., 13, pp. 133–141.

[845] M. HATZOPOULOS AND D. EVANS [1988]. *Comments on the paper "A short proof of the existence of the W-Z factorization"*, Parallel Computing, 6, p. 259.

[846] M. HATZOPOULOS AND N. MISSIRLIS [1985]. *Advantages for solving linear systems in an asynchronous environment*, J. Comput. Appl. Math., 12/13, pp. 331–340.

[847] R. HAY AND I. GLADWELL [1985]. *Solving almost block diagonal linear equations on the CDC Cyber 205*, Numerical Analysis Report 98, University of Manchester, January.

[848] J. HAYES, T. MUDGE, Q. STOUT, S. COLLEY, AND J. PALMER [1986]. *Architecture of a hypercube supercomputer*, Proc. 1986 Int. Conf. Par. Proc., pp. 653–660.

[849] L. HAYES [1974]. *Comparative analysis of iterative techniques for solving Laplace's equation on the unit square on a parallel processor*, Master's thesis, University of Texas at Austin, Department of Mathematics.

[850] L. HAYES [1984]. *Alternating Direction method on vector processors*, NASA/NSF Workshop on Parallel Computation in Heat Transfer and Fluid Flow, University of Maryland, November.

[851] L. HAYES [1985]. *A vectorized matrix vector multiply and overlapping block iterative method*, in Numrich [1469], pp. 91–100.

[852] L. HAYES AND P. DEVLOO [1984]. *An overlapping block iterative scheme for finite element methods*, Tech. Report, Department of Aerospace Engineering and Engineering Mechanics, University of Texas at Austin.

[853] L. HAYES AND P. DEVLOO [1986]. *A vectorized version of a sparse matrix-vector multiply*, Int. J. Num. Met. Eng., 23, pp. 1043–56.

[854] L. HAYNES, R. LAU, D. SIEWIOREK, AND D. MIZELL [1982]. *A survey of highly parallel computing*, Computer, 15(1), pp. 9–24.

[855] M. HEAD-GORDON AND P. PIELA [1986]. *Parallel algorithms for solving linear equations using Givens transformations*, Int. J. Comput. Math., 12A, pp. 987–990.

[856] L. HEATH, A. ROSENBERG, AND B. SMITH [1988]. *The physical mapping problem for parallel architectures*, J. ACM, 35, pp. 603–634.

[857] M. HEATH [1985]. *Parallel Cholesky factorization in message-passing multiprocessor environments*, Tech. Report ORNL-6150, Oak Ridge National Laboratory, May.

[858] M. HEATH, ed. [1986]. *Hypercube Multiprocessors, 1986*, Philadelphia, PA, Society for Industrial and Applied Mathematics.

[859] M. HEATH [1987]. *Hypercube applications at Oak Ridge National Laboratory*, in Heath [860], pp. 395–417.

[860] M. HEATH, ed. [1987]. *Hypercube Multiprocessors, 1987*, Philadelphia, Society for Industrial and Applied Mathematics.

[861] M. HEATH AND C. ROMINE [1988]. *Parallel solution of triangular systems on distributed-*

memory multiprocessors, SIAM J. Sci. Statist. Comput., 9(3), pp. 558–588.

[862] M. HEATH AND D. SORENSEN [1986]. *A pipelined Givens method for computing the QR factorization of a sparse matrix*, Lin. Alg. & Appl., 77, pp. 189–203.

[863] D. HELLER [1974]. *A determinant theorem with applications to parallel algorithms*, SIAM J. Numer. Anal., 11, pp. 559–568.

[864] D. HELLER [1976]. *Some aspects of the cyclic reduction algorithm for block tridiagonal linear systems*, SIAM J. Numer. Anal., 13, pp. 484–496.

[865] D. HELLER [1978]. *A survey of parallel algorithms in numerical linear algebra*, SIAM Rev., 20, pp. 740–777.

[866] D. HELLER AND I. IPSEN [1982]. *Systolic network for orthogonal equivalence transformations and their application*, Proc. Conference on Advanced Research in VLSI, Cambridge, MIT Press, pp. 113–122.

[867] D. HELLER AND I. IPSEN [1983]. *Systolic networks for orthogonal decompositions*, SIAM J. Sci. Statist. Comput., 4, pp. 261–269.

[868] D. HELLER, D. STEVENSON, AND J. TRAUB [1976]. *Accelerated iterative methods for the solution of tridiagonal linear systems on parallel computers*, J. ACM, 23, pp. 636–654.

[869] R. HELLIER [1982]. *DAP implementation of the WZ algorithm*, Comput. Phys. Comm., 26, pp. 321–323.

[870] P. HEMKER [1984]. *Performance of multigrid software on vector machines*, Supercomputer.

[871] P. HEMKER, R. KETTLER, P. WESSELING, AND P. DE ZEEUW [1983]. *Multigrid methods: Development of fast solvers*, Appl. Math. & Comp., 13(3-4), pp. 311–326. (Special Issue, Proceedings of the First Copper Mountain Conference on Multigrid Methods, Copper Mountain, CO, S. McCormick and U. Trottenberg, eds.).

[872] P. HEMKER, P. WESSELING, AND P. DE ZEEUW [1984]. *A portable vector code for autonomous multigrid modules*, PDE Software: Modules, Interfaces and Systems, B. Engquist and T. Smedsaas, eds., North-Holland, Amsterdam, pp. 29–40.

[873] R. HEMPEL [1988]. *Parallel multigrid algorithms for the biharmonic and the Stokes equations, implementation and performance*, in McCormick [1312].

[874] R. HEMPEL [1988]. *The Suprenum communications subroutine library for grid-oriented problems*, Tech. Report ANL-87-23, Argonne National Laboratory.

[875] J. HENDRY AND L. DELVES [1984]. *GEM calculations on the DAP*, in Paddon [1512], pp. 185–194.

[876] C. HENKEL, M. HEATH, AND R. PLEMMONS [1988]. *Cholesky downdating on a hypercube*, Proc. Third Conf. Hypercube Concurrent Comput. Appl., G. Fox, ed., New York, Association for Computing Machinery, pp. 1592–1598.

[877] L. HERTZBERGER, D. GOSMAN, G. KIEFT, G. POR, M. SCHOOREL, AND L. WIGGERS [1981]. *FAMP system*, Comput. Phys. Comm., 22, pp. 253–260.

[878] P. HIBBARD AND N. OSTLUND [1980]. *Numerical computation on Cm**, Proc. 1980 Int. Conf. Par. Proc., pp. 135–136.

[879] L. HIGBIE [1978]. *Speeding up FORTRAN (CFT) programs on the CRAY-1*, Pub. 2240207, CRAY Research Inc.

[880] N. HIGHAM [1989]. *Exploiting fast matrix multiplication within the level 3 BLAS*, Computer Science Tech. Report 89-984, Department of Computer Science, Cornell University.

[881] N. HIGHAM AND R. SCHREIBER [1988]. *Fast polar decomposition of an arbitrary matrix*, Computer Science Tech. Report 88-942, Department of Computer Science, Cornell University. (To appear in SIAM J. Sci. Statist. Comput.).

[882] W. HILLIS [1985], *The Connection Machine*, MIT Press, New Haven, CT.

[883] R. HINTZ AND D. TOTE [1972]. *Control Data STAR-100 processor design*, Proc. COMPCON 72, IEEE Comp. Soc. Conf., pp. 1–4.

[884] K. HIRAKI, T. SHIMADA, AND K. NISHIDA [1984]. *A hardware design of the SIGMA-1, a data flow computer for scientific computations*, Proc. 1984 Int. Conf. Par. Proc., pp. 524–531.

[885] R. HIROMOTO [1984]. *Experiences with the Denelcor HEP*, Parallel Computing, 1, pp. 197–206.

[886] R. HIROMOTO [1985]. *Parallel processing a plasma simulation problem using the particle-in-cell method*, Tech. Report LA-UR-85-2393, Los Alamos National Laboratory.

[887] C.-T. HO AND L. JOHNSSON [1986]. *Distributed routing algorithm for broadcasting and personalized communication in hypercubes*, Proc. 1986 Int. Conf. Par. Proc., pp. 640–648.

[888] C.-T. HO AND L. JOHNSSON [1987]. *Algorithms for matrix transposition on Boolean n-cube configured ensemble architectures*, Proc. 1987 Int. Conf. Par. Proc., pp. 621–629.

[889] C.-T. HO AND L. JOHNSSON [1987]. *On the embedding of arbitrary meshes in Boolean cubes with expansion two dilation two*, Proc. 1987 Int. Conf. Par. Proc., pp. 188–191.

[890] L. HOBBS, D. THEIS, J. TRIMBLE, H. TITUS, AND D. HIGHBERG [1970], *Parallel Processor Systems: Technologies and Applications*, Spartan Books.

[891] R. HOCKNEY [1965]. *A fast direct solution of Poisson's equation using Fourier analysis*, J. ACM, 12, pp. 95–113.

[892] R. HOCKNEY [1977]. *Super-computer architecture*, Proc. Infotech State of the Art Conf. on Future Systems.

[893] R. HOCKNEY [1979]. *The large parallel computer and university research*, Cont. Phys., 20, pp. 149–185.

[894] R. HOCKNEY [1982]. *Characterization of parallel computers and algorithms*, Comput. Phys. Comm., 26, pp. 285–291.

[895] R. HOCKNEY [1982]. *Optimizing the FACR (l) Poisson solver on parallel computers*, Proc. 1982 Int. Conf. Par. Proc., pp. 62–71.

[896] R. HOCKNEY [1982], *Poisson solving on parallel computers*. Presented at the IBM Symposium on Vector Computers and Scientific Computing, Rome.

[897] R. HOCKNEY [1983]. *Characterization of parallel computers*, Proceedings of World Congress on System Simulation and Scientific Computation, International Association for Mathematics and Computers in Simulation, vol. 1, pp. 269–271.

[898] R. HOCKNEY [1983]. *Characterizing computers and optimizing the FACR (l) Poisson solver on parallel unicomputers*, IEEE Trans. Comput., C-32, pp. 933–941.

[899] R. HOCKNEY [1984]. *The $n_{1/2}$ method of algorithm analysis*, PDE Software: Modules, Interfaces and Systems, B. Engquist and T. Smedsaas, eds., Elsevier, pp. 429–444.

[900] R. HOCKNEY [1984]. *Optimizing the FACR (l) Poisson-solver on parallel computers*, in Paddon [1512], pp. 45–65.

[901] R. HOCKNEY [1984]. *Performance of parallel computers*, in Kowalik [1116], pp. 159–176.

[902] R. HOCKNEY [1985]. *MIMD computing in the USA — 1984*, Parallel Computing, 2, pp. 119–136.

[903] R. HOCKNEY [1985]. *Performance characterization of the HEP*, in Parallel MIMD Computation: HEP Supercomputer and Its Applications [1117], pp. 59–90.

[904] R. HOCKNEY [1985]. *$(r_\infty, n_{1/2}, s_{1/2})$ measurements on the 2-CPU CRAY X-MP*, Parallel Computing, 2, pp. 1–14.

[905] R. HOCKNEY [1987]. *Parametrization of computer performance*, Parallel Computing, 5, pp. 97–104.

[906] R. HOCKNEY AND C. JESSHOPE [1981], *Parallel Computers: Architecture, Programming and Algorithms*, Adam Hilger, Ltd., Bristol, United Kingdom.

[907] R. HOCKNEY AND D. SNELLING [1984]. *Characterizing MIMD computers, e.g., the Denelcor HEP*, in Feilmeier et al. [623], pp. 521–526.

[908] C. HOHEISEL, M. SCHOEN, AND R. VOGELSANG [1984]. *Vectorized computation of correlation functions from phase space trajectories generated by molecular dynamic calculations*, Comput. Phys. Comm., 34, pp. 9–14.

[909] J. HOLLAND [1959]. *A universal computer capable of executing an arbitrary number of subprograms simultaneously*, Proc. European Joint Comp. Conf., pp. 108–113.

[910] R. HOLT, G. GRAHAM, E. LAZOWSKA, AND M. SCOTT [1978], *Structured Concurrent Programming*, Addison-Wesley, Reading, MA.

[911] B. HOLTER [1988]. *Vectorized multigrid solvers for the two-dimensional diffusion equation*, in McCormick [1312].

[912] W. HOLTER [1986]. *A vectorized multigrid solver for the three-dimensional Poisson equation*, Appl. Math. & Comp., 19(1-4), pp. 127–144. (Special Issue, Proceedings of the Second Copper Mountain Conference on Multigrid Methods, Copper Mountain, CO, S. McCormick, ed.).

[913] H.-C. HOPPE AND H. MUHLENBEIN [1986]. *Parallel adaptive full-multigrid methods on message-based multiprocessors*, Parallel Computing, 3, pp. 269–288.

[914] R. HORD [1982], *The Illiac IV: The First Supercomputer*, Computer Science Press.

[915] S. HORIGUCHI, Y. KAWAZOE, AND H. NARA [1984]. *A parallel algorithm for the integration of ordinary differential equations*, Proc. 1984 Int. Conf. Par. Proc., pp. 465–469.

[916] E. HOROWITZ [1986]. *Particle codes and the Cray-2*, Tech. Report UCRL-95055, Lawrence Livermore National Laboratory.

[917] E. HOROWITZ [1987]. *Vectorizing the interpolation routines of particle-in-cell codes*, J. Comp. Phys. To appear.

[918] T. HOSHINO, R. HIROMOTO, S. SEKIGUCHI, AND S. MAJIMA [1987]. *Mapping schemes of the particle-in-cell method implemented on the PAX computer*, Tech. Report LA-UR-87-2879, Los Alamos National Laboratory.

[919] T. HOSHINO, T. KAMIMURA, T. IIDA, AND T. SHIRAKAWA [1985]. *Parallelized ADI scheme*

using GECR (Gauss-Elimination-Cyclic Reduction) method and implementation of Navier-Stokes equation on the PAX computer, Proc. 1985 Int. Conf. Par. Proc., pp. 426–433.

[920] T. HOSHINO, T. KAWAI, T. SHIRAKAWA, J. HIGASHINO, A. YAMAOKA, H. ITO, T. SATO, AND K. SAWADA [1983]. *PACS: A parallel microprocessor array for scientific calculations*, ACM Trans. on Comp. Sys., 1, pp. 195–221.

[921] T. HOSHINO, S. MAJIMA, K. TAKENOUCHI, AND Y. OYANAGI [1984]. *Monte Carlo simulation of a spin model on the parallel computer PAX*, Comput. Phys. Comm., 34, pp. 31–38.

[922] T. HOSHINO, T. SHIRAKAWA, T. KAMIMURA, T. KAGEYAMA, K. TAKENOUOCHI, H. ABE, S. SEKIGUCHI, Y. OYANAGI, AND K. TOSHIO [1983]. *Highly parallel procesor array "PAX" for wide scientific applications*, Proc. 1983 Int. Conf. Par. Proc., pp. 95–105.

[923] T. HOSHINO AND K. TAKENOUCHI [1984]. *Processing of the molecular dynamic model by the parallel computer PAX*, Comput. Phys. Comm., 31, pp. 287–296.

[924] S. HOTOVY AND L. DICKSON [1979]. *Evaluation of a vectorizable 2-D transonic finite difference algorithm*, Paper 79-0276, AIAA.

[925] E. HOUSORS AND O. WING [1984]. *Pseudo-conjugate directions for the solution of the nonlinear unconstrained optimization problem on a parallel computer*, J. Optimization Theory and Applications, 42, pp. 169–180.

[926] C. HOUSTIS, E. HOUSTIS, AND J. RICE [1984]. *Partitioning and allocation of PDE computations in distributed systems*, PDE Software: Modules, Interfaces and Systems, B. Engquist and T. Smedsaas, eds., North-Holland, Amsterdam, pp. 67–87.

[927] C. HOUSTIS, E. HOUSTIS, AND J. RICE [1986]. *Performance evaluation models for distributed computing*, Tech. Report CSD-TR-576, Department of Computer Science, Purdue University, January.

[928] C. HOUSTIS, E. HOUSTIS, AND J. RICE [1987]. *Partitioning PDE computations: Methods and performance evaluation*, Parallel Computing, 5, pp. 141–164.

[929] C. HOUSTIS, E. HOUSTIS, J. RICE, AND M. SAMARTZIS [1987]. *Benchmarking of bus multiprocessor hardware on large scale scientific computing*, in Vichnevetsky and Stepleman [1921].

[930] E. HOUSTIS, J. RICE, AND E. VAVALIS [1987]. *Parallelization of a new class of cubic spline collocation methods*, in Vichnevetsky and Stepleman [1921], pp. 167–174.

[931] E. HOUSTIS, J. RICE, AND E. VAVALIS [1988]. *A Schwartz splitting variant of cubic spline collocation methods for elliptic PDEs*, Tech. Report CSD-TR-745, Department of Computer Science, Purdue University.

[932] T. HU [1961]. *Parallel sequencing and assembly line problem*, Oper. Res., 9, pp. 841–848.

[933] H.-M. HUANG [1974]. *A parallel algorithm for symmetric tridiagonal eigenvalue problems*, Tech. Report 109, Center for Advanced Computation, University of Illinois at Urbana-Champaign, February.

[934] J. HUANG AND O. WING [1978]. *On minimum completion time and optimal scheduling of parallel triangulation of a sparse matrix*, IEEE Power Engineering Society Summer Meeting, Los Angeles, Institute of Electrical and Electronics Engineers, Inc. (IEEE Pes Abstract No. A78-567-0).

[935] J. HUANG AND O. WING [1979]. *Optimal parallel triangulation of a sparse matrix*, IEEE Trans. Circuits and Syst., CAS-26, pp. 726–732.

[936] K. HUANG AND J. ABRAHAM [1982]. *Efficient parallel algorithms for processor arrays*, Proc. 1982 Int. Conf. Par. Proc., pp. 271–279.

[937] K. HUANG AND J. ABRAHAM [1984]. *Fault-tolerant algorithms and their application to solving Laplace equations*, Proc. 1984 Int. Conf. Par. Proc., pp. 117–122.

[938] R. HUFF, J. DAWSON, AND G. CULLER [1982]. *Plasma physics on an array processor*, in Rodrigue [1643], pp. 365–396.

[939] T. HUGHES AND R. FERENCZ [1988]. *Fully vectorized EBE preconditioners for nonlinear solid mechanics: Applications to large-scale three-dimensional continuum, shell and contact/impact problems*, in Glowinski et al. [762], pp. 261–280.

[940] T. HUGHES, R. FERENCZ, AND J. HALLQUIST [1987]. *Large scale vectorized implicit calculations in solid mechanics on a CRAY-X-MP/48 utilizing EBE preconditioned conjugate gradient*, Comput. Meth. Appl. Mech. Engrg., 61, pp. 215–248.

[941] D. HUNT [1979]. *Application techniques for parallel hardware*, in Jesshope and Hockney [976], pp. 205–219.

[942] D. HUNT, S. WEBB, AND A. WILSON [1981]. *Applications of a parallel processor to the solution of finite difference problems*, in Schultz [1752], pp. 339–344.

[943] C. HUSON, T. MACKE, J. DAVIES, M. WOLFE, AND B. LEASURE [1986]. *The KAP/205: An*

advanced source-to-source vectorizer for the Cyber 205 supercomputer, Proc. 1986 Int. Conf. Par. Proc., pp. 827–835.

[944] K. HWANG [1982]. *Partitioned matrix algorithms for VLSI arithmetic systems*, IEEE Trans. Comput., C-31, pp. 1215–1224.

[945] K. HWANG [1984], *Computer Architecture and Parallel Computing*, McGraw Hill, New York, NY.

[946] K. HWANG [1985]. *Multiprocessor supercomputers for scientific/engineering applications*, Computer, 18(6), pp. 57–73.

[947] K. HWANG AND F. BRIGGS [1984], *Computer Architecture and Parallel Processing*, McGraw Hill, New York, NY.

[948] K. HWANG AND Y.-H. CHENG [1980]. *VLSI computing structures for solving large scale linear systems of equations*, Proc. 1980 Int. Conf. Par. Proc., pp. 217–227.

[949] K. HWANG AND J. GHOSH [1987]. *Hypernet: A communication-efficient architecture for constructing massively parallel computers*, IEEE Trans. Comput., C-36, pp. 1450–1466.

[950] K. HWANG, S. JACOBS, AND E. SWARTZLANDER, eds. [1986]. *Parallel Processing*, North-Holland.

[951] K. HWANG, S. SU, AND L. NI [1981]. *Vector computer architecture and processing techniques*, Advances in Computers, 20, pp. 115–197.

[952] K. HWANG AND Z. XU [1985]. *Remps: A reconfigurable multiprocessor for scientific supercomputing*, Proc. 1985 Int. Conf. Par. Proc., pp. 102–111.

[953] L. HYAFIL AND H. KUNG [1974]. *Parallel algorithms for solving triangular linear systems with small parallelism*, Tech. Report, Department of Computer Science, Carnegie-Mellon University.

[954] L. HYAFIL AND H. KUNG [1975]. *Bounds on the speed-ups of parallel evaluation of recurrences*, Proc. Second USA — Japan Comp. Conf., pp. 178–182.

[955] L. HYAFIL AND H. KUNG [1977]. *The complexity of parallel evaluation of linear recurrences*, J. ACM, 24, pp. 513–521.

[956] M. INOUYE, ed. [1977]. *Future Computer Requirements for Computational Aerodynamics*, Workshop at NASA-Ames, Conf. Publ. No. 2032.

[957] I. IPSEN [1984]. *A parallel QR method using fast Givens' rotations*, Tech. Report YALEU/DCS/RR-299, Department of Computer Science, Yale University.

[958] I. IPSEN [1984]. *Singular value decomposition with systolic arrays*, Proc. Soc. Photo-Optical Eng., Bellingham, WA.

[959] I. IPSEN [1987]. *Systolic algorithms for the parallel solution of dense symmetric positive-definite Toeplitz systems*, Tech. Report YALEU/DCS/RR-539, Department of Computer Science, Yale University, May.

[960] I. IPSEN AND E. JESSUP [1987]. *Solving the symmetric tridiagonal eigenvalue problem on the hypercube*, Tech. Report YALEU/DCS/RR-548, Department of Computer Science, Yale University.

[961] I. IPSEN AND E. JESSUP [1987]. *Two methods for solving the symmetric tridiagonal eigenvalue problem on the hypercube*, in Heath [860], pp. 627–638.

[962] I. IPSEN AND Y. SAAD [1985]. *The impact of parallel architectures on the solution of eigenvalue problems*, Tech. Report YALEU/DCS/RR-444, Department of Computer Science, Yale University, December.

[963] I. IPSEN, Y. SAAD, AND M. SCHULTZ [1986]. *Complexity of dense linear system solution on a multiprocessor ring*, Lin. Alg. & Appl., 77, pp. 205–239.

[964] M. IQBAL, J. SALTZ, AND S. BOKHARI [1986]. *A comparative analysis of static and dynamic load balancing strategies*, Proc. 1986 Int. Conf. Par. Proc., pp. 1040–1047.

[965] M. ISHIGURO AND Y. KOSHI [1982]. *Vectorization for solving the neutron diffusion equations — Some numerical experiments*, Nuc. Sci. Eng., 80, pp. 322–328.

[966] W. JALBY AND U. MEIER [1986]. *Optimizing matrix operations on a parallel multiprocessor with a memory hierarchy*, Tech. Report 555, Center for Supercomputing Research and Development, University of Illinois at Urbana-Champaign, February.

[967] W. JALBY, U. MEIER, AND A. SAMEH [1986]. *The behaviour of conjugate gradient based algorithms on a multi-vector processor with a memory hierarchy*, Tech. Report 607, Center for Supercomputing Research and Development, University of Illinois at Urbana-Champaign, November.

[968] L. JAMIESON, D. GANNON, AND R. DOUGLAS, eds. [1987]. *The Characteristics of Parallel Algorithms*, MIT Press.

[969] L. JAMIESON, P. MUELLER, AND H. SIEGEL [1986]. *FFT algorithms for SIMD parallel processing systems*, J. Par. Dist. Comp., 3, pp. 48–71.

[970] D. JAYASIMHA AND M. LOUI [1987]. *The communication complexity of parallel algorithms*,

Tech. Report 629, Center for Supercomputing Research and Development, University of Illinois at Urbana-Champaign.

[971] J. JESS AND H. KEES [1982]. *A data structure for parallel L/U decomposition*, IEEE Trans. Comput., C-31, pp. 231–239.

[972] C. JESSHOPE [1977]. *Evaluation of Illiac: Overlap, non-overlap*, Institute for Advanced Computation Newsletter, 1, pp. 4–5.

[973] C. JESSHOPE [1980]. *The implementation of the fast radix 2 transforms on array processors*, IEEE Trans. Comput., C-29, pp. 20–27.

[974] C. JESSHOPE [1980]. *Some results concerning data routing in array processors*, IEEE Trans. Comput., C-29, pp. 659–662.

[975] C. JESSHOPE AND J. CRAIGIE [1979]. *Some principles of parallelism in particle and mesh modeling*, in Jesshope and Hockney [976], pp. 221–236.

[976] C. JESSHOPE AND R. HOCKNEY, eds. [1979]. *Infotech State of the Art Report: Supercomputers, vol. 1 & 2*, Maidenhead: Infotech Int. Ltd.

[977] S. JIANPING AND K. LISHAN [1987]. *An asynchonous parallel mixed algorithm for linear and nonlinear equations*, Parallel Computing, 5, pp. 313–321.

[978] G. JOHNSON [1987]. *Parallel processing in fluid dynamics*, Tech. Report 87003, Institute for Scientific Computing, Fort Collins, CO.

[979] G. JOHNSON AND J. SWISSHELM [1988]. *Multigrid for parallel-processing supercomputers*, in McCormick [1312].

[980] G. JOHNSON, J. SWISSHELM, AND S. KUMAR [1985]. *Concurrent processing adaptation of a multiple-grid algorithm*, AIAA J.

[981] G. JOHNSON, J. SWISSHELM, D. PRYOR, AND J. ZIEBARTH [1986]. *Multitasked embedded multigrid for three-dimensional flow simulation*, Lecture Notes in Physics, vol. 264, Springer-Verlag, Berlin, pp. 350–356.

[982] J. JOHNSON [1983]. *ETA leaves home*, Datamation, 29(10), pp. 74–86.

[983] O. JOHNSON [1981]. *Vector function chainer software for banded preconditioned conjugate gradient calculations*, Advances in Computer Methods for Partial Differential Equations - IX, Proc. 10th IMACS World Congress on Systems Simulation and Scientific Computation, vol. 1, IMACS, pp. 243–245.

[984] O. JOHNSON [1984]. *Three-dimensional wave equation computations on vector computers*, Proc. IEEE, 72, pp. 90–95.

[985] O. JOHNSON AND M. EDWARDS [1981]. *Progress on the 3D wave equation program for the CDC Cyber 205*, Fourth year Semi-Annual Prog. Rep. vol. 7, Seismic Acoustics Lab.

[986] O. JOHNSON AND M. LEWITT [1982]. *PPCG software for the CDC CYBER 205*, in Control Data Corporation [411].

[987] O. JOHNSON, C. MICCHELLI, AND G. PAUL [1983]. *Polynomial preconditioners for conjugate gradient calculations*, SIAM J. Numer. Anal., 20, pp. 362–376.

[988] O. JOHNSON AND G. PAUL [1981]. *Optimal parametrized incomplete inverse preconditioning for conjugate gradient calculations*, Tech. Report RC-8644, IBM, Yorktown Heights, NY.

[989] O. JOHNSON AND G. PAUL [1981]. *Vector algorithms for elliptic partial differential equations based on the Jacobi method*, in Schultz [1752], pp. 345–351.

[990] L. JOHNSSON [1981]. *Computational arrays for band matrix equations*, Tech. Report 4287:TR:81, Department of Computer Science, California Institute of Technology, May.

[991] L. JOHNSSON [1982]. *A computational array for the QR-method*, Proc. MIT Conf. on Advanced Res. in VLSI, P. Penfield, ed., Artech House, pp. 123–129.

[992] L. JOHNSSON [1982]. *Pipelined linear equation solvers and VLSI*, Proc. Microelectronics 1982, Australia, May, Institution of Electrical Engineers, pp. 42–46.

[993] L. JOHNSSON [1984]. *Highly concurrent algorithms for solving linear systems of equations*, in Birkhoff and Schoenstadt [173], pp. 105–126.

[994] L. JOHNSSON [1984]. *Odd-even cyclic reduction on ensemble architectures and the solution of tridiagonal systems of equations*, Tech. Report YALEU/DCS/RR-339, Department of Computer Science, Yale University.

[995] L. JOHNSSON [1985]. *Band matrix systems solvers on ensemble architectures*, Algorithms, Architectures and the Future of Scientific Computation, University of Texas Press, Austin, TX.

[996] L. JOHNSSON [1985]. *Cyclic reduction on a binary tree*, Comput. Phys. Comm., 37, pp. 195–203.

[997] L. JOHNSSON [1985]. *Data permutations and basic linear algebra computations on ensemble architectures*, Tech. Report YALEU/DCS/RR-367, Department of Computer Science, Yale University, February.

[998] L. JOHNSSON [1985]. *Solving narrow banded systems on ensemble architectures*, ACM Trans. Math. Softw., 11, pp. 271–288.

[999] L. JOHNSSON [1986]. *Band matrix systems solvers on ensemble architecture*, Supercomputers, F. Matsen and T. Tajima, eds., University of Texas Press, pp. 195–216.

[1000] L. JOHNSSON [1987]. *Communication efficient basic linear algebra computations on hypercube architectures*, J. Par. Dist. Comp., 4, pp. 133–172.

[1001] L. JOHNSSON [1987]. *Solving tridiagonal systems on ensemble architectures*, SIAM J. Sci. Statist. Comput., 8, pp. 354–392.

[1002] L. JOHNSSON [1988]. *Algorithms for matrix transposition on Boolean N-cube configured ensemble architectures*, SIAM J. Matrix Anal. Appl., 9, pp. 419–454.

[1003] L. JOHNSSON AND C.-T. HO [1987]. *Multiple tridiagonal systems, the Alternating Direction methods and Boolean cube configured multiprocessors*, Tech. Report YALEU/DCS/TR-532, Department of Computer Science, Yale University, June.

[1004] L. JOHNSSON, C.-T. HO, AND F. SAIED [1986]. *Solving multiple tridiagonal systems, the Alternating Direction method, and Boolean cube configured multiprocessors*, Tech. Report YALEU/DCS/RR-552, Department of Computer Science, Yale University.

[1005] L. JOHNSSON, C.-T. HO, AND F. SAIED [1987]. *Fast linear algebra routines on hypercubes*, Parallel Processing and Medium Scale Multiprocessors, A. Wouk, ed., Society for Industrial and Applied Mathematics. To appear.

[1006] L. JOHNSSON, Y. SAAD, AND M. SCHULTZ [1987]. *Alternating Direction methods on multiprocessors*, SIAM J. Sci. Statist. Comput., 8, pp. 686–700.

[1007] A. JONES, R. CHANSLER, I. DURHAM, P. FEILER, D. SCELZA, K. SCHWANS, AND S. VEGDAHL [1978]. *Programming issues raised by a multi-microprocessor*, Proc. IEEE, 66(2), pp. 229–237.

[1008] A. JONES AND E. GEHRINGER, eds. [1980]. *The Cm* multiprocessor project: A research review*, Tech. Report CMU-CS-80-131, Department of Computer Science, Carnegie-Mellon University.

[1009] A. JONES AND P. SCHWARTZ [1980]. *Experience using multiprocessor systems: A status report*, ACM Computing Surveys, 12, pp. 121–165.

[1010] H. JORDAN [1978]. *The Finite Element Machine programmer's reference manual*, Tech. Report CSDG 78-2, Department of Computer Science, University of Colorado, Boulder.

[1011] H. JORDAN [1978]. *A special purpose architecture for finite element analysis*, Proc. 1978 Int. Conf. Par. Proc., pp. 263–66.

[1012] H. JORDAN [1981]. *Parallelizing a sparse matrix package*, Tech. Report CSDG 81-1, Computer Systems Design Group, University of Colorado, Boulder.

[1013] H. JORDAN [1983]. *Performance measurements on HEP — A pipelined MIMD computer*, Proc. 10th Ann. Int. Symp. Comp. Arch.

[1014] H. JORDAN [1984]. *Experience with pipelined multiple instruction streams*, Proc. IEEE, 72, pp. 113–123.

[1015] H. JORDAN [1985]. *Parallel computation with the Force*, Tech. Report 85-45, ICASE, NASA Langley Research Center, Hampton, VA, October.

[1016] H. JORDAN [1986]. *The Force on the Flex: Global parallelism and portability*, Tech. Report 86-54, ICASE, NASA Langley Research Center, Hampton, VA, August.

[1017] H. JORDAN [1986]. *Structuring parallel algorithms in an MIMD, shared memory environment*, Parallel Computing, 3, pp. 93–110.

[1018] H. JORDAN [1987]. *The Force*, Tech. Report 87-1-1, Department of Electrical and Computer Engineering, University of Colorado, Boulder, January.

[1019] H. JORDAN [1987]. *Interpreting parallel processor performance measurements*, SIAM J. Sci. Statist. Comput., 8, pp. s220–s226.

[1020] H. JORDAN AND D. PODSIADLO [1980]. *A conjugate gradient program for the Finite Element Machine*, Tech. Report CSDG, Department of Computer Science, University of Colorado, Boulder.

[1021] H. JORDAN AND P. SAWYER [1979]. *A multimicroprocessor system for finite element structural analysis*, Trends in Computerized Structural Analysis and Synthesis, A. Noor and H. McComb, eds., Pergammon Press, New York, NY, pp. 21–29.

[1022] H. JORDAN, M. SCALABRIN, AND W. CALVERT [1979]. *A comparison of three types of multiprocessor algorithms*, Proc. 1979 Int. Conf. Par. Proc., pp. 231–238.

[1023] T. JORDAN [1974]. *A new parallel algorithm for diagonally dominant tri-diagonal matrices*, Tech. Report, Los Alamos National Laboratory.

[1024] T. JORDAN [1979]. *A performance evaluation of linear algebra software in parallel architectures*, Performance Evaluation of Numerical Software, L. Fosdick, ed., North-Holland, pp. 59–76.

[1025] T. JORDAN [1982]. *CALMATH: Some problems and applications*, in Cray Research, Inc. [423], pp. 5–8.

[1026] T. JORDAN [1982]. *A guide to parallel computation and some CRAY-1 experiences*, in Rodrigue [1643], pp. 1–50.

[1027] T. JORDAN [1984]. *Conjugate gradient preconditioners for vector and parallel processors*, in Birkhoff and Schoenstadt [173], pp. 127–139.

[1028] T. JORDAN AND K. FONG [1977]. *Some linear algebraic algorithms and their performance on the CRAY-1*, in Kuck et al. [1133], pp. 313–316.

[1029] G. JOUBERT AND E. CLOETH [1984]. *The solution of tridiagonal linear systems with an MIMD parallel computer*, Proc. 1984 GAMM Conference, Z. Angew. Math. Mech.

[1030] A. KAПAEV [1985]. *Multiprocessor supersystems with programmable architecture based on the data-stream principle*, Computational Processes and Systems, Izdatel'stvo Nauka, Moscow, pp. 140–153.

[1031] S. KAK [1988]. *A two-layered mesh array for matrix multiplication*, Parallel Computing, 6, pp. 383–385.

[1032] L. KALE [1985]. *Lattice Mesh: A multi-bus architecture*, Proc. 1985 Int. Conf. Par. Proc., pp. 700–702.

[1033] E. KALNAY AND L. TAKOCS [1982]. *A simple atmospheric model on the sphere with 100% parallelism*, Research Review [1980-81], NASA-Goddard Modeling and Simulation Facility.

[1034] E. KALNEY-RIVAS, A. BAYLISS, AND J. STORCH [1976]. *Experiments with the fourth order GISS model of the global atmosphere*, Proc. Conf. on Simulation of Large-Scale Atmospheric Processes, Hamsburg, Germany.

[1035] C. KAMATH [1986]. *Solution of nonsymmetric systems of equations on a multiprocessor*, Tech. Report 591, Center for Supercomputing Research and Development, University of Illinois at Urbana-Champaign, August.

[1036] C. KAMATH AND A. SAMEH [1984]. *The preconditioned conjugate gradient algorithm on a multiprocessor*, in Vichnevetsky and Stepleman [1920], pp. 210–217.

[1037] C. KAMATH AND A. SAMEH [1986]. *A projection method for solving nonsymmetric linear systems on multiprocessors*, Tech. Report 611, Center for Supercomputing Research and Development, University of Illinois at Urbana-Champaign, October.

[1038] C. KAMATH, A. SAMEH, G. YANG, AND D. KUCK [1985]. *Structural computations on the Cedar system*, Computers and Structures, 20, pp. 47–54.

[1039] E. KAMGNIA AND A. SAMEH [1985]. *A numerical conformal mapping method for simply connected domains*, Tech. Report 507, Center for Supercomputing Research and Development, University of Illinois at Urbana-Champaign, September.

[1040] T. KAMIMURA AND T. HOSHINO [1985]. *Processing of Alternating Direction Implicit (ADI) method by parallel computer PAX*, Trans. Info. Proc. Soc. Japan, 26, pp. 19–24.

[1041] D. KAMOWITZ [1987]. *SOR and MGR[v] experiments on the Crystal multicomputers*, Parallel Computing, 4, pp. 117–142.

[1042] D. KAMOWITZ [1988]. *Experimental results for multigrid and transport problems*, in McCormick [1312].

[1043] F. KAMPE AND T. NGUYEN [1988]. *Performance comparison of the CRAY-2 and CRAY X-MP on a class of seismic data processing algorithms*, Parallel Computing, 7, pp. 41–54.

[1044] Y. KANEDA AND M. KOHATA [1982]. *Highly parallel computing of linear equations on the matrix-broadcast memory connected array processor system*, Proc. 10th IMACS World Congress on Systems Simulation and Scientific Computation, vol. 1, IMACS, pp. 320–322.

[1045] R. KANT AND T. KIMURA [1978]. *Decentralized parallel algorithms for matrix computations*, Proc. 5th Annual Symp. Comp. Arch., pp. 96–100.

[1046] A. KAPAUAN, K. WANG, D. GANNON, J. CUNY, AND L. SNYDER [1984]. *The Pringle: An experimental system for parallel algorithm and software testing*, Proc. 1984 Int. Conf. Par. Proc., pp. 1–6.

[1047] H. KAPITZA AND D. EPPEL [1987]. *A 3-D Poisson solver based on conjugate gradients compared to standard iterative methods and its performance on vector computers*, J. Comp. Phys., 68, pp. 474–484.

[1048] M. KAPS AND M. SCHLEGL [1987]. *A short proof for the existence of the WZ-factorization*, Parallel Computing, 4, pp. 229–232.

[1049] R. KAPUR AND J. BROWNE [1981]. *Block tridiagonal linear systems on a reconfigurable array computer*, Proc. 1981 Int. Conf. Par. Proc., pp. 92–99.

[1050] R. KAPUR AND J. BROWNE [1984]. *Techniques for solving block tridiagonal systems on reconfigurable array computers*, SIAM J. Sci. Statist. Comput., 5, pp. 701–719.

[1051] A. KARP [1987]. *Programming for parallelism*, Computer, 20(5), pp. 43–57.

[1052] A. KARP AND J. GREENSTADT [1987]. *An improved parallel Jacobi method for diagonalizing a symmetric matrix*, Parallel Computing, 5, pp. 281–294.

[1053] R. KARP AND R. MILLER [1966]. *Properties of a model for parallel computations: Determinacy, termination, queuing*, SIAM J. Appl. Math., 14, pp. 1390–1411.

[1054] R. KARP AND W. MIRANKER [1968]. *Parallel minimax search for a maximum*, J. Combin. Theory, 4, pp. 19–35.

[1055] L. KARTASHEV AND S. KARTASHEV, eds. [1987]. *Supercomputing '87: Proceedings of the Second International Conference on Supercomputing*, St. Petersburg, International Supercomputing Institute, International Supercomputing Institute.

[1056] S. KARTASHEV AND S. KARTASHEV, eds. [1986]. *Supercomputing Systems*, North-Holland, New York.

[1057] A. KASAHARA [1984]. *Recent mathematical and computational developments in numerical weather prediction*, in Parter [1529], pp. 85–126.

[1058] H. KASAHARA AND S. NARITA [1984]. *Practical multiprocessor scheduling algorithms for efficient parallel processing*, IEEE Trans. Comput., C-33, pp. 1023–1029.

[1059] M. KASCIC [1978]. *A direct Poisson solver on STAR*, Proc. 1978 LASL Workshop on Vector and Parallel Processors.

[1060] M. KASCIC [1979]. *Vector processing on the CYBER 200*, in Jesshope and Hockney [976], pp. 237–270.

[1061] M. KASCIC [1979]. *Vector processing on the CYBER 200 and vector numerical linear algebra*, Proc. 3rd GAMM Conf. on Numeric Mathematics in Fluid Dynamics.

[1062] M. KASCIC [1983]. *Syntactic and semantic vectorization: Whence cometh intelligence in supercomputing?*, Proc. 1983 Summer Computer Simulation Conf., Vancouver.

[1063] M. KASCIC [1984]. *Anatomy of a Poisson solver*, in Feilmeier et al. [623], pp. 173–179.

[1064] M. KASCIC [1984]. *Interplay between computer methods and partial differential equations: Iterative methods as exemplar*, in Vichnevetsky and Stepleman [1920], pp. 379–382.

[1065] M. KASCIC [1984]. *A performance survey of the CYBER 205*, in Kowalik [1116], pp. 191–210.

[1066] M. KASCIC [1984]. *Vorton dynamics: A case study of developing a fluid dynamics model for a vector processor*, Parallel Computing, 1, pp. 35–44.

[1067] M. KASCIC [1986]. *Vectorization as intelligent processing*, in Fernbach [630], pp. 59–67.

[1068] H. KASHIWAGI [1984]. *Japanese super-speed computer project*, in Kowalik [1116], pp. 117–125.

[1069] I. KATZ AND M. FRANKLIN [1985]. *Two strategies for root finding on multiprocessor systems*, SIAM J. Sci. Statist. Comput., 6, pp. 314–333.

[1070] I. KATZ, M. FRANKLIN, AND A. SEN [1977]. *Optimally stable parallel predictors for Adams-Moulton correctors*, Comput. Math. Appl., 3, pp. 217–233.

[1071] L. KAUFMAN [1984]. *Banded eigenvalue solvers on vector machines*, ACM Trans. Math. Softw., 10, pp. 73–86.

[1072] L. KAUFMAN AND N. SCHRYER [1989]. *Solving two dimensional partial differential equations on vector and scalar machines*, Int. J. Supercomputer Appl., 3(1), pp. 10–33.

[1073] M. KAUFMAN [1974]. *An almost-optimal algorithm for the assembly line scheduling problem*, IEEE Trans. Comput., C-23, pp. 1169–1174.

[1074] S. KEELING [1987]. *On implicit Runge-Kutta methods for parallel computations*, Tech. Report 87-58, ICASE, NASA Langley Research Center, Hampton, VA.

[1075] J. KELLER AND A. JAMESON [1978]. *Preliminary study of the use of the STAR-100 computer for transonic flow calculations*, Paper 78-12, AIAA.

[1076] R. KENDALL, G. MORRELL, D. PEACEMAN, W. SILLIMAN, AND J. WATTS [1983]. *Development of a multiple application reservoir simulator for use on a vector computer*, Paper 11483, SPE. SPE Middle East Oil Tech. Conf., Bahrain.

[1077] R. KENDALL, J. NOLEN, AND P. STANAT [1984]. *The impact of vector processors on petroleum resevoir simulation*, Proc. IEEE, 72, pp. 85–89.

[1078] M. KENICHI [1981]. *A vector-oriented finite-difference scheme for calculating three-dimensional compressible laminar and turbulent boundary layers on practical wing configurations*, Paper 81-1020, AIAA.

[1079] E. KERCKECFFS [1986]. *Parallel algorithms for ordinary differential equations — An introductory review*, Proceedings of the 1986 Summer Simulation Conference, Society for Computer Simulation, pp. 947–952.

[1080] D. KERSHAW [1982]. *Solution of single tridiagonal linear systems and vectorization of the ICCG algorithm on the CRAY-1*, in Rodrigue [1643], pp. 85–89.

[1081] D. KEYES AND W. GROPP [1987]. *A comparison of domain decomposition techniques for elliptic partial differential equations and their parallel implementation*, SIAM J. Sci.

Statist. Comput., 8, pp. s166–s202.

[1082] D. KEYES AND D. SMOOKE [1987]. *Analysis of a parallelized nonlinear elliptic boundary value problem solver with application to reacting flows*, Tech. Report 87-21, ICASE, NASA Langley Research Center, Hampton, VA.

[1083] J. KIGHTLEY AND I. JONES [1985]. *A comparison of conjugate gradient preconditionings for three-dimensional problems in a CRAY-1*, Comput. Phys. Comm., 37, pp. 205–214.

[1084] J. KIGHTLEY AND C. THOMPSON [1987]. *On the performance of some rapid elliptic solvers on a vector processor*, SIAM J. Sci. Statist. Comput., 8, pp. 701–715.

[1085] J. KILLOUGH [1979]. *The use of vector processors in reservoir simulation*, Proc. SPE Symposium Resevoir Simulation, Denver.

[1086] J. KILLOUGH [1986]. *A multi-level domain decomposition algorithm suitable for the solution of three-dimensional elliptic partial differential equations*, Tech. Report TR86-7, Department of Mathematical Sciences, Rice University.

[1087] T. KIMURA [1979]. *Gauss-Jordan elimination by VLSI mesh-connected processors*, in Jesshope and Hockney [976], pp. 271–290.

[1088] D. KINCAID, G. CAREY, T. OPPE, K. SEPEHENOORI, AND D. YOUNG [1984]. *Combining finite element and iterative methods for solving partial differential equations on advanced computer architectures*, in Vichnevetsky and Stepleman [1920], pp. 375–378.

[1089] D. KINCAID AND T. OPPE [1983]. *ITPACK on supercomputers*, Numerical Methods, A. Dold and B. Eckman, eds., Springer-Verlag, New York, pp. 151–161.

[1090] D. KINCAID AND T. OPPE [1988]. *A parallel algorithm for the general LU factorization*, Comm. Appl. Numer. Meth., 4, pp. 349–360.

[1091] D. KINCAID, T. OPPE, AND D. YOUNG [1982]. *Adapting ITPACK routines for use on a vector computer*, in Control Data Corporation [411].

[1092] D. KINCAID, T. OPPE, AND D. YOUNG [1986]. *Vector computations for sparse linear systems*, SIAM J. Algebraic Discrete Methods, 7, pp. 99–112.

[1093] D. KINCAID, T. OPPE, AND D. YOUNG [1986]. *Vectorized iterative methods for partial differential equations*, Comm. Appl. Numer. Meth., 2, pp. 789–796.

[1094] D. KINCAID AND D. YOUNG [1984]. *Adapting iterative algorithms for solving large sparse linear systems for efficient use of the CDC CYBER 205*, in Gary [700], pp. 147–160.

[1095] D. KIRKPATRICK, M. KLAWE, AND N. PIPPENGER [1985]. *Some graph coloring theorems with application to generalized connection networks*, SIAM J. Algebraic Discrete Methods, 6, pp. 576–582.

[1096] D. KNIGHT [1983]. *A hybrid explicit-implicit numerical algorithm for the three-dimensional compressible Navier-Stokes equations*, Paper 83-0223, AIAA. AIAA 21st Aerospace Sciences Meeting, January, Reno, Nevada.

[1097] J. KNIGHT AND D. DUNLOP [1983]. *On the design of a special purpose scientific programming language*, Softw. Pract. Exp., 13, pp. 893–907.

[1098] J. KNIGHT, W. POOLE, AND R. VOIGT [1975]. *System balance analysis for vector computers*, Proc. 1975 ACM National Conference, pp. 163–168.

[1099] J. KNOTT [1983]. *A performance analysis of the PASLIB version 2.1 SEND and RECV routines on the Finite Element Machine*, Contractor Report 172205, NASA Langley Research Center.

[1100] R. KOBER AND C. KUZNIA [1978]. *SMS — A multiprocessor architecture for high speed numerical computations*, Proc. 1978 Int. Conf. Par. Proc., pp. 18–23.

[1101] U. KODRES [1984]. *Processing efficiency of a class of multicomputer systems*, Int. J. Mini Microprocessors, 5(2), pp. 28–33.

[1102] P. KOGGE [1973]. *Maximal rate pipelined solutions to recurrence problems*, Proc. First Ann. Symp. on Comp. Arch., pp. 71–76.

[1103] P. KOGGE [1974]. *Parallel solution of recurrence problems*, IBM J. Res. Dev., 18, pp. 138–148.

[1104] P. KOGGE [1981], *The Architecture of Pipelined Computers*, McGraw Hill Book Company, New York, NY.

[1105] P. KOGGE AND H. STONE [1973]. *A parallel algorithm for the efficient solution of a general class of recurrence equations*, IEEE Trans. Comput., C-22, pp. 786–793.

[1106] W. KOHLER [1975]. *A preliminary evaluation of the critical path method for scheduling tasks on multiprocessor systems*, IEEE Trans. Comput., C-24, pp. 1235–1238.

[1107] O. KOLP AND H. MIERENDORFF [1986]. *Efficient multigrid algorithms for locally constrained parallel systems*, Appl. Math. & Comp., 19(1-4), pp. 169–200. (Special Issue, Proceedings of the Second Copper Mountain Conference on Multigrid Methods, Copper Mountain, CO, S. McCormick, ed.).

[1108] A. KONIGES AND D. ANDERSON [1987]. *ILUBCG2: A preconditioned biconjugate gradient routine for the solution of linear asymmetric matrix equations arising from 9-point discretizations*, Comput. Phys. Comm., 43, pp. 297–.

[1109] A. KONIGES AND D. ANDERSON [1987]. *Optimized matrix solution packages for use in plasma physics codes*, Annual Controlled Fusion Theory Conference, San Diego, CA. Paper 2D12.

[1110] A. KONIGES AND D. ANDERSON [1987]. *Vectorized and multitasked software packages for solving asymmetric matrix equations*, in Vichnevetsky and Stepleman [1921], p. 118.

[1111] H. KOPP [1977]. *Numerical weather forecast with the multi-microprocessor system SMS201*, in Feilmeier [621], pp. 265–268.

[1112] D. KORN AND J. LAMBIOTTE [1979]. *Computing the fast Fourier transform on a vector computer*, Math. Comp., 33, pp. 977–992.

[1113] V. KOTOV [1984]. *Formal models of parallel computations*, in Miklosko and Kotov [1363], pp. 109–141.

[1114] V. KOTOV AND V. VALKOUSKII [1984]. *Automatic construction of parallel programs*, in Miklosko and Kotov [1363], pp. 65–107.

[1115] J. KOWALIK [1983]. *Preliminary experience with multiple-instruction multiple data computation*, in Noor [1450], pp. 49–54.

[1116] J. KOWALIK, ed. [1984]. *Proceedings of the NATO Workshop on High Speed Computations*, West Germany, NATO ASI Series, vol. F-7, Berlin, Springer-Verlag.

[1117] J. KOWALIK [1985], *Parallel MIMD Computation: HEP Supercomputer and Its Applications*, MIT Press, Cambridge, MA.

[1118] J. KOWALIK AND S. KUMAR [1982]. *An efficient parallel block conjugate gradient method for linear equations*, Proc. 1982 Int. Conf. Par. Proc., pp. 47–52.

[1119] J. KOWALIK, R. LORD, AND S. KUMAR [1984]. *Design and performance of algorithms for MIMD parallel computers*, in Kowalik [1116], pp. 257–276.

[1120] M. KRATZ [1984]. *Some aspects of using vector computers for finite element analyses*, in Feilmeier et al. [623], pp. 349–354.

[1121] M. KRATZ [1984]. *Vectorised finite-element stiffness generation: Tuning the Noor-Lambiotte algorithm*, Parallel Computing, 1, pp. 121–132.

[1122] S. KRIST AND T. ZANG [1987]. *Algorithm implementation on the Navier-Stokes computer*, Tech. Report NASA-TM-89119, NASA Langley Research Center, Hampton, VA.

[1123] L. KRONSJO [1986], *Computational Complexity of Sequential and Parallel Algorithms*, Wiley, New York, NY.

[1124] C. KRUSKAL [1983]. *Searching, merging and sorting in parallel computations*, IEEE Trans. Comput., C-32(10), pp. 942–946.

[1125] C. KRUSKAL AND M. SNIR [1983]. *The performance of multistage interconnection networks for multiprocessors*, IEEE Trans. Comput., C-32(12), pp. 1091–1098.

[1126] D. KUCK [1976]. *Parallel processing of ordinary programs*, Advances in Computers, vol. 15, Academic Press, NY, pp. 119–179.

[1127] D. KUCK [1977]. *A survey of parallel machine organization and programming*, ACM Computing Surveys, 9, pp. 29–59.

[1128] D. KUCK [1978], *The Structure of Computers and Computation*, John Wiley and Sons, New York, NY.

[1129] D. KUCK, P. BUDNICK, S. CHEN, E. DAVIS, J. HAN, P. KRASKA, D. LAWRIE, Y. MURAOKA, R. STREHENDT, AND R. TOWLE [1973]. *Measurement of parallelism in ordinary Fortran programs*, Proc. Sagamore Conf. Parallel Processing, pp. 23–36.

[1130] D. KUCK, E. DAVIDSON, D. LAWRIE, AND A. SAMEH [1986]. *Parallel supercomputing today and the Cedar approach*, Science, 231, pp. 967–974.

[1131] D. KUCK AND D. GAJSKI [1984]. *Parallel processing of sparse structures*, in Kowalik [1116], pp. 229–244.

[1132] D. KUCK, D. LAWRIE, R. CYTRON, A. SAMEH, AND D. GAJSKI [1986]. *Cedar project*, in Sharp et al. [1782], pp. 97–123.

[1133] D. KUCK, D. LAWRIE, AND A. SAMEH, eds. [1977]. *High Speed Computer and Algorithm Organization*, Academic Press, New York, NY.

[1134] D. KUCK, J. McGRAW, AND M. WOLFE [1984]. *A debate: Retire FORTRAN?*, Physics Today, 37(5), pp. 66–75.

[1135] D. KUCK AND A. SAMEH [1972]. *Parallel computation of eigenvalues of real matrices*, Information Processing '71, North-Holland, pp. 1266–1272.

[1136] D. KUCK, A. SAMEH, R. CYTRON, A. VEIDENBAUM, C. POLYCHRONOPOULOS, G. LEE, T. McDANIEL, B. LEASURE, C. BECKMAN, J. DAVIES, AND C. KRUSKAL [1984]. *The effects of program restructuring algorithm change and architecture choice on program performance*, Proc. 1984 Int. Conf. Par. Proc., pp. 129–138.

[1137] D. KUCK AND R. STOKES [1982]. *The Burroughs Scientific Processor (BSP)*, IEEE Trans. Comput., C-31, pp. 363–376.

[1138] R. KUHN AND D. PADUA [1981], *Parallel Processing*, IEEE Computer Society Press.

[1139] A. KUMAR, R. GRAVES, AND K. WEILMUENSTER [1980]. *User's guide for vectorized code EQUIL for calculating equilibrium chemistry on Control Data STAR-100 computer*, NASA Tech. Memo. 80192, NASA Langley Research Center.

[1140] A. KUMAR, D. RUDY, J. DRUMMOND, AND J. HARRIS [1982]. *Experiences with explicit finite difference schemes for complex fluid dynamics problems on STAR-100 and CYBER 203 computers*, in Control Data Corporation [411].

[1141] M. KUMAR [1988]. *Measuring parallelism in computation-intensive scientific/engineering applications*, IEEE Trans. Comput., 37(9), pp. 1088–1098.

[1142] S. KUMAR [1982]. *Parallel Algorithms for Solving Linear Equations on MIMD Computers*, PhD dissertation, Washington State University, Department of Computer Science.

[1143] S. KUMAR AND J. KOWALIK [1984]. *Parallel factorization of a positive definite matrix on an MIMD computer*, Proc. 1984 Int. Conf. Par. Proc., pp. 410–416.

[1144] S. KUMAR AND J. KOWALIK [1986]. *Triangularization of a positive definite matrix on a parallel computer*, J. Par. Dist. Comp., 3, pp. 450–460.

[1145] H. KUNG [1976]. *Synchronized and asynchronous parallel algorithms for multi-processors*, Algorithms and Complexity, J. Traub, ed., Academic Press, New York, pp. 153–200.

[1146] H. KUNG [1979]. *Let's design algorithms for VLSI systems*, Proc. Conf. Very Large Scale Integration, California Institute of Technology, pp. 65–90.

[1147] H. KUNG [1980]. *The structure of parallel algorithms*, Advances in Computers, M. Youvits, ed., vol. 19, Academic Press, pp. 65–112.

[1148] H. KUNG [1982]. *Why systolic architectures?*, Computer, 15(1), pp. 37–46.

[1149] H. KUNG [1984]. *Systolic algorithms*, in Parter [1529], pp. 127–140.

[1150] H. KUNG AND C. LEISERSON [1979]. *Systolic arrays (for VLSI)*, Sparse Matrix Proceedings (1978), I. Duff and G. Stewart, eds., Society for Industrial and Applied Mathematics, pp. 256–282.

[1151] H. KUNG, R. SPROULL, AND G. STEELE, eds. [1981]. *VLSI Systems and Computations*, Computer Science Press, Rockville, MD.

[1152] H. KUNG AND D. STEVENSON [1977]. *A software technique for reducing the routing time on a parallel computer with a fixed interconnection network*, in Kuck et al. [1133], pp. 423–433.

[1153] H. KUNG AND J. WEBB [1985]. *Global operations on the CMU Warp machine*, Proceedings of 1985 AIAA Computers in Aerospace V Conference, October, AIAA, pp. 209–218.

[1154] H. KUNG AND S. YU [1982], *Integrating high-performance special-purpose devices into a system*. Presented at the IBM Symposium on Vector Computers and Scientific Computing, Rome.

[1155] S. KUNG [1984]. *On supercomputing with systolic/wavefront array processors*, Proc. IEEE, 72, pp. 867–884.

[1156] S. KUNG AND R. GAL-EZAR [1982]. *Linear or sparse array for eigenvalue and singular value decompositions?*, Proc. USC Workshop on VLSI and Modern Signal Processing, Los Angeles, pp. 89–98.

[1157] S. KUNG AND R. GAL-EZAR [1985]. *Eigenvalue, singular value and least squares solvers via the wavefront array processor*, in Snyder et al. [1808], pp. 201–212.

[1158] S. KUNG, R. GAL-EZAR, K. ARUN, AND D. BHASKARRAO [1982]. *Wavefront array processor; Architecture, language and application*, IEEE Trans. Comput., C-31, pp. 1054–1066.

[1159] S. KUNG AND Y. HU [1981]. *Fast and parallel algorithms for solving Toeplitz systems*, Proc. Internat. Symp. on Mini- and Micro-computers in Control and Measurement, San Francisco, may, pp. 163–168.

[1160] S. KUNG AND Y. HU [1983]. *A highly concurrent algorithm and pipelined architecture for solving Toeplitz systems*, IEEE Trans. Acoustics, Speech and Signal Processing, ASSP-31, pp. 66–76.

[1161] S. KUNG, S. LO, S. JEAN, AND J. HWANG [1987]. *Wavefront array processors — Concept to implementation*, Computer, 20(7), pp. 18–33.

[1162] S. KUNKEL AND S. J. [1987]. *Solving linear recurrences on pipelined computers*, in Kartashev and Kartashev [1055], pp. 384–391.

[1163] C.-C. KUO AND T. CHAN [1988]. *Two-color Fourier analysis of iterative algorithms for elliptic problems with red/black ordering*, CAM Report 88-15, Department of Mathematics, UCLA.

[1164] H.-C. KUO AND S. KUMAR [1986]. *Solving positive definite linear systems on vector comput-*

ers, Proc. 1986 Int. Conf. Par. Proc., pp. 441–443.

[1165] J. Kuo, B. Levy, and B. Muskus [1987]. *A local relaxation method for solving elliptic PDEs on mesh connected arrays*, SIAM J. Sci. Statist. Comput., 8, pp. 550–573.

[1166] A. Kwok [1986]. *The multiprocessor modified Pease FFT algorithm*, Tech. Report, Center for Supercomputing Research and Development, University of Illinois at Urbana-Champaign.

[1167] A. Kwok [1987]. *A performance analysis of architectural scalability*, Tech. Report 679, Center for Supercomputing Research and Development, University of Illinois at Urbana-Champaign, August.

[1168] C. Lai and H. Liddell [1987]. *A review of parallel finite element methods on the DAP*, Appl. Numer. Mod., 11, pp. 330–341.

[1169] S. Lakshmivarahan and S. Dhall [1986]. *A new hierarchy of hypercube interconnection schemes for parallel computers: Theory and applications*, Tech. Report, University of Oklahoma, August.

[1170] S. Lakshmivarahan and S. Dhall [1987]. *A lower bound on the communication complexity in solving linear tridiagonal systems on cube architectures*, in Heath [860], pp. 560–588.

[1171] J. Lambiotte [1975]. *The Solution of Linear Systems of Equations on a Vector Computer*, PhD dissertation, The University of Virginia, Department of Applied Mathematics and Computer Science.

[1172] J. Lambiotte [1979]. *The development of a STAR-100 code to perform a 2-D FFT*, Proc. Lawrence Livermore Lab. Conf. Sci. Compt.

[1173] J. Lambiotte [1984]. *Efficient sparse matrix multiplication scheme for the CYBER 203*, in Gary [700], pp. 243–256.

[1174] J. Lambiotte and L. Howser [1974]. *Vectorization on the STAR computer of several numerical methods for a fluid flow problem*, Tech. Report NASA TN D-7545, NASA Langley Research Center.

[1175] J. Lambiotte and R. Voigt [1975]. *The solution of tridiagonal linear systems on the CDC STAR-100 computer*, ACM Trans. Math. Softw., 1, pp. 308–329.

[1176] L. Lamport [1974]. *The parallel execution of DO loops*, Comm. ACM, 17, pp. 83–93.

[1177] B. Lang, J. Miellou, and P. Spiteric [1986]. *Asynchronous relaxation algorithms for optimal control problems*, Math. Comp. Simul., 28, pp. 227–242.

[1178] A. Larrabee and R. Babb [1987]. *Adaptation of a large-scale computational chemistry program for the Intel iPSC concurrent computer*, in Heath [860], pp. 464–472.

[1179] J. Larson [1984]. *Multitasking on the CRAY X-MP-2 multiprocessor*, Computer, 17(7), pp. 62–69.

[1180] K. Law [1982]. *Systolic systems for finite element methods*, Tech. Report R-82-139, Department of Civil Engineering, Carnegie-Mellon University.

[1181] Lawrence Livermore National Laboratory [1979]. *The S-1 project*, Tech. Report UCID-18619, Lawrence Livermore National Laboratory.

[1182] D. Lawrie [1975]. *Access and alignment of data in an array processor*, IEEE Trans. Comput., C-24, pp. 1145–1155.

[1183] D. Lawrie, T. Layman, D. Baer, and J. Randall [1975]. *Glypnir — A programming language for Illiac IV*, Comm. ACM, 18, pp. 157–164.

[1184] D. Lawrie and A. Sameh [1983]. *Applications of structural mechanics on large-scale multiprocessor computers*, in Noor [1450], pp. 55–64.

[1185] D. Lawrie and A. Sameh [1984]. *The computation and communication complexity of a parallel banded system solver*, ACM Trans. Math. Softw., 10, pp. 185–195.

[1186] C. Lazou [1987]. *Supercomputers and Their Use*, Oxford University Press.

[1187] T. LeBlanc [1986]. *Shared memory versus message passing in a tightly coupled multiprocessor: A case study*, Tech. Report, Department of Computer Science, University of Rochester, January.

[1188] T. LeBlanc, M. Scott, and C. Brown [1988]. *Large-scale parallel programming: Experience with the BBN Butterfly parallel processor*, SIGPLAN Notices, 23(9), pp. 161–172.

[1189] P. Leca and P. Roy [1983]. *Simulation numerique de la turbulence sur un système multiprocessor*, First. Int. Coll. on Vector and Parallel Methods, Paris.

[1190] G. Lee, C. Kruskal, and D. Kuck [1985]. *An empirical study of automatic restructuring of nonnumerical programs for parallel processors*, IEEE Trans. Comput., C-34, pp. 927–933.

[1191] J. Lee [1980]. *Three-dimensional finite element analysis of layered fiber-reinforced composite materials*, Computers and Structures, 12, p. 319.

[1192] R. Lee [1977]. *Performance bounds in parallel processor organizations*, in Kuck et al. [1133], pp. 453–455.

[1193] T. LEGENDI, D. PARKINSON, R. VOLLMAN, AND G. WOLF, eds. [1986]. *Parallel Processing by Cellular Automata and Arrays*, North-Holland.

[1194] M. LEHMAN [1966]. *A survey of problems and preliminary results concerning parallel processing and parallel processors*, Proc. IEEE, 54, pp. 1889–1901.

[1195] C. LEISERSON [1985]. *Fat-trees: Universal networks for hardware-efficient supercomputing*, Proc. 1985 Int. Conf. Par. Proc., pp. 393–402.

[1196] C. LEISERSON [1985]. *Fat-trees: Universal networks for hardware-efficient supercomputing*, IEEE Trans. Comput., C-34, pp. 892–901.

[1197] C. LEISERSON AND J. LEWIS [1988]. *Orderings for parallel sparse symmetric factorization*, Tech. Report ETA-TR-85, Boeing Computer Services, March.

[1198] E. LELARASMEE, A. RUEHLI, AND A. SANGIOVANNI-VINCENTELLI [1982]. *The wavefront relaxation method for time-domain analysis of large scale integrated circuits*, IEEE Trans. Computer-Aided Design of Integrated Circuits and Systems, CAD-1, pp. 131–145.

[1199] M. LEMKE [1985]. *Experiments with a vectorized multigrid Poisson solver on the CDC CYBER 205, Cray X-MP and Fujitsu VP 200*. Arbeitspapiere der GMD, Nr. 179. Gesellschaft fur Mathematik und Datenverarbeitung, St. Augustin.

[1200] J. LENSTRA AND A. RINNOOY KAN [1978]. *Complexity of scheduling under precedence constraints*, Oper. Res., 26, pp. 22–35.

[1201] M. LEUZE [1981]. *Memory Access Patterns in Vector Computers with Application to Problems in Linear Algebra*, PhD dissertation, Duke University, Department of Computer Science.

[1202] M. LEUZE [1986]. *Parallel triangularization of substructured finite element problems*, Lin. Alg. & Appl., 77, pp. 241–258.

[1203] M. LEUZE [1988]. *Independent set orderings for parallel Gaussian elimination*, Parallel Computing (to appear).

[1204] M. LEUZE AND L. SAXTON [1983]. *On minimum parallel computing times for Gaussian elimination*, Congressus Numerantium, 40, pp. 169–179.

[1205] J. LEVESQUE AND J. WILLIAMSON [1989], *A Guidebook to Fortran on Supercomputers*, Academic Press, San Diego, CA.

[1206] E. LEVIN [1985]. *Suitability of a data flow architecture for problems involving simple operations on large arrays*, Proc. 1985 Int. Conf. Par. Proc., pp. 518–520.

[1207] R. LEVINE [1982]. *Supercomputers*, Sci. Amer., 246, pp. 118–135.

[1208] J. LEWIS AND B. PEYTON [1988]. *A fast implementation of the Jess and Kees algorithm*, Tech. Report ETA-TR-90, Boeing Computer Services, May.

[1209] J. LEWIS AND H. SIMON [1986]. *The impact of hardware gather/scatter on sparse Gaussian elimination*, Proc. 1986 Int. Conf. Par. Proc., pp. 366–368.

[1210] J. LEWIS AND H. SIMON [1988]. *The impact of hardware gather/scatter on sparse Gaussian elimination*, SIAM J. Sci. Statist. Comput., 9, pp. 304–311.

[1211] G. LI AND T. COLEMAN [1987]. *A new method for solving triangular systems on distributed memory message-passing multiprocessors*, Tech. Report TR 87-812, Department of Computer Science, Cornell University.

[1212] G. LI AND T. COLEMAN [1987]. *A parallel triangular solver for a hypercube multiprocessor*, in Heath [860], pp. 539–551.

[1213] G. LI AND T. COLEMAN [1988]. *A parallel triangular solver for a distributed-memory multiprocessor*, SIAM J. Sci. Statist. Comput., 9, pp. 485–502.

[1214] G. LI AND B. WAH [1985]. *The design of optimal systolic algorithms*, IEEE Trans. Comput., C-34, pp. 66–77.

[1215] G. LI AND B. WAH [1985]. *Systolic processing for dynamic programming problems*, Proc. 1985 Int. Conf. Par. Proc., pp. 434–441.

[1216] K. LI-SHAN AND D. EVANS [1988]. *The convergence rate of the Schwartz alternating procedure (V) — for more than two subdomains*, Int. J. Comput. Math., 23, pp. 295–314.

[1217] A. LICHNEWSKY [1982]. *Sur la résolution de systèmes linéaires issus de la méthode des éléments finis par une machine multiprocesseurs*, Tech. Report 119, INRIA.

[1218] A. LICHNEWSKY [1983], *Some vector and parallel implementations for linear systems arising in PDE problems*. Presented at the SIAM Conference on Parallel Processing for Scientific Computing, Norfolk, VA, November.

[1219] A. LICHNEWSKY [1984]. *Some vector and parallel implementations for preconditioned conjugate gradient algorithms*, in Kowalik [1116], pp. 343–359.

[1220] D. LILES, J. MAHAFFY, AND P. GIGUERE [1984]. *An approach to fluid mechanics calculations on serial and parallel computer architectures*, in Parter [1529], pp. 141–160.

[1221] D. LIM AND R. THANAKIJ [1987]. *A survey of ADI implementations on hypercubes*, in Heath [860], pp. 674–679.

[1222] A. LIN [1987]. *Parallel and supercomputing of elliptic problems*, in Kartashev and Kartashev [1055], pp. 497–502.

[1223] T.-C. LIN AND D. MOLDORAN [1985]. *Tradeoffs in mapping algorithms to array processors*, Proc. 1985 Int. Conf. Par. Proc., pp. 719–726.

[1224] N. LINCOLN [1982]. *Technology and design tradeoffs in the creation of a modern supercomputer*, IEEE Trans. Comput., C-31, pp. 349–362.

[1225] N. LINCOLN [1983]. *Supercomputers = colossal computations + enormous expectations + renowned risk*, Computer, 16(5), pp. 38–47.

[1226] B. LINT AND T. AGERWALA [1981]. *Communication issues in the design and analysis of parallel algorithms*, IEEE Trans. Softw. Eng., SE-7, pp. 174–188.

[1227] E. LIPITAKIS [1984]. *Solving elliptic boundary value problems on parallel processors by approximate inverse matrix semi-direct methods based on the multiple explicit Jacobi iteration*, Comp. & Math. Appl., 10, pp. 171–184.

[1228] E. LIPITAKIS AND D. EVANS [1987]. *Explicit semi-direct methods based on approximate inverse matrix techniques for solving boundary value problems on parallel processors*, Math. Comp. Simul., 29, pp. 1–18.

[1229] G. LIPOVSKI AND K. DOTY [1978]. *Developments and directions in computer architecture*, Computer, 11(8), pp. 54–67.

[1230] G. LIPOVSKI AND A. TRIPATHI [1977]. *A reconfigurable varistructure array processor*, Proc. 1977 Int. Conf. Par. Proc., pp. 165–174.

[1231] J. LIPOVSKI AND M. MALEK [1987], *Parallel Computing*, John Wiley and Sons, New York, NY.

[1232] C. LIU AND J. LAYLAND [1973]. *Scheduling algorithms for multiprogramming in a hard-real-time environment*, J. ACM, 20, pp. 46–61.

[1233] J. LIU [1978]. *The solution of mesh equations on a parallel computer*, Tech. Report CS-78-19, Department of Computer Science, Waterloo University.

[1234] J. LIU [1986]. *Computational models and task scheduling for parallel sparse Cholesky factorization*, Parallel Computing, 3, pp. 327–342.

[1235] J. LIU [1987]. *Reordering sparse matrices for parallel elimination*, Tech. Report CS-87-01, Department of Computer Science, York University, Ontario, Canada, January.

[1236] J. LIU AND A. MIRZAIAN [1987]. *A linear reordering algorithm for parallel pivoting of chordal graphs*, Tech. Report CS-87-02, Department of Computer Science, York University, Ontario, Canada, February.

[1237] R. LIVESLEY, J. MODI, AND T. SMITHERS [1985]. *The use of parallel computation for finite element calculations*, Tech. Report CUED/F-CAMS/TR.248, Cambridge University Engineering Department, Cambridge, UK.

[1238] S.-S. LO AND B. PHILLIPPE [1986]. *The symmetric eigenvalue problem on a multiprocessor*, Tech. Report 590, Center for Supercomputing Research and Development, University of Illinois at Urbana-Champaign, April.

[1239] S.-S. LO, B. PHILLIPPE, AND A. SAMEH [1987]. *A multiprocessor algorithm for the symmetric tridiagonal eigenvalue problem*, SIAM J. Sci. Statist. Comput., 8, pp. s155–s165.

[1240] D. LOENDORF [1985]. *Development and use of an asynchronous MIMD computer for finite element analysis*, in Snyder et al. [1808], pp. 213–222.

[1241] D. LOGAN, C. MAPLES, D. WEAVER, AND W. RATHBUN [1984]. *Adapting scientific programs to the MIDAS multiprocessor system*, Proc. 1984 Int. Conf. Par. Proc., pp. 15–24.

[1242] H. LOMAX [1981]. *Some prospects for the future of computational fluid dynamics*, AIAA Comp. Fluid Dyn. Conference, June.

[1243] H. LOMAX AND T. PULLIAM [1982]. *A fully implicit factored code for computing three dimensional flows on the Illiac IV*, in Rodrigue [1643], pp. 217–250.

[1244] F. LOOTSMA AND K. RAGSDELL [1988]. *State-of-the-art in parallel nonlinear optimization*, Parallel Computing, 6, pp. 133–156.

[1245] R. LORD, J. KOWALIK, AND S. KUMAR [1980]. *Solving linear algebraic equations on a MIMD computer*, Proc. 1980 Int. Conf. Par. Proc., pp. 205–210.

[1246] R. LORD, J. KOWALIK, AND S. KUMAR [1983]. *Solving linear algebraic equations on an MIMD computer*, J. ACM, 30, pp. 103–117.

[1247] H. LORIN [1972], *Parallelism in Hardware and Software*, Prentice-Hall, Inc., Englewood Cliffs, NJ.

[1248] M. LOUTER-NOOL [1987]. *Basic linear algebra subprograms (BLAS) on the CDC CYBER 205*, Parallel Computing, 4, pp. 143–166.

[1249] B. LUBACHEVSKY AND D. MITRA [1984]. *Chaotic parallel computations of fixed points of nonnegative matrices of unit spectral radius*, Proc. 1984 Int. Conf. Par. Proc., pp. 109–116.

[1250] B. LUBACHEVSKY AND D. MITRA [1986]. *A chaotic asynchronous algorithm for computing the fixed point of a nonnegative matrix of unit spectral radius*, J. ACM, 33, pp. 130–150.

[1251] O. LUBECK AND V. FABER [1987]. *Modeling the performance of hybercubes: A case study using the particle-in-cell application*, Tech. Report LA-UR-87-1522, Los Alamos National Laboratory.

[1252] O. LUBECK, J. MOORE, AND R. MENDEZ [1985]. *A benchmark comparison of three supercomputers: Fujitsu VP-200, Hitachi S810/20 and CRAY X-MP/2*, Computer, 18(12), pp. 10–24.

[1253] O. LUBECK, J. MOORE, AND R. MENDEZ [1986]. *A performance evaluation of three supercomputers, Fujitsu XP-200, Hitachi S810/20, CRAY X-MP/24*, Appl. Math. & Comp., 20, pp. 143–144.

[1254] R. LUCAS [1987]. *Solving Planar Systems of Equations on Distributed-Memory Multiprocessors*, PhD dissertation, Stanford University, Department of Electrical Engineering.

[1255] B. LUCIER AND R. OVERBEEK [1987]. *A parallel adaptive numerical scheme for hyberbolic systems of conservation laws*, SIAM J. Sci. Statist. Comput., 8, pp. s203–s219.

[1256] F. LUK [1980]. *Computing the singular value decomposition on the Illiac IV*, ACM Trans. Math. Softw., 6, pp. 524–539.

[1257] F. LUK [1985]. *Algorithm-based fault tolerance for parallel matrix equation solvers*, Tech. Report EE-CEG-85-2, Department of Electrical and Computer Engineering, Cornell University. To appear in Proc. SPIE, vol. 564; Real Time Signal Processing VIII.

[1258] F. LUK [1985]. *A parallel method for computing the generalized singular value decomposition*, J. Par. Dist. Comp., 2, pp. 250–260.

[1259] F. LUK [1986]. *Architectures for computing eigenvalues and SVDs*, Tech. Report EE-CEG-86-1, Department of Electrical and Computer Engineering, Cornell University, February. To appear in Proc. SPIE vol. 614: Highly Parallel Signal Processing Architectures.

[1260] F. LUK [1986]. *Fault-tolerant matrix triangularization on systolic arrays*, Tech. Report EE-CEG-86-2, Department of Electrical and Computer Engineering, Cornell University.

[1261] F. LUK [1986]. *A rotation method for computing the QR-decomposition*, SIAM J. Sci. Statist. Comput., 7, pp. 452–459.

[1262] F. LUK [1986]. *A triangular processor array for computing singular values*, Lin. Alg. & Appl., 77, pp. 259–273.

[1263] F. LUK AND H. PARK [1986]. *On parallel Jacobi orderings*, Tech. Report EE-CEG-86-5, Department of Electrical and Computer Engineering, Cornell University.

[1264] F. LUK AND S. QIAO [1986]. *Analysis of a recursive least squares signal processing algorithm*, Tech. Report EE-CEG-86-7, Department of Electrical and Computer Engineering, Cornell University.

[1265] F. LUK AND S. QIAO [1986]. *Computing the C–S decomposition on systolic arrays*, SIAM J. Sci. Statist. Comput., 7, pp. 1121–1125.

[1266] M. LUNDQUIST [1987]. *An implementation of the preconditioned conjugate gradient algorithm on the FPS T-20 hypercube*, Tech. Report URI-044, Department of Mathematical Sciences, Clemson University, December.

[1267] S. LUNDSTROM [1987]. *Applications considerations in the system design of highly concurrent multiprocessors*, IEEE Trans. Comput., C-36, pp. 1292–1309.

[1268] S. LUNDSTROM AND G. BARNES [1980]. *A controllable MIMD architecture*, Proc. 1980 Int. Conf. Par. Proc., pp. 19–27.

[1269] E. LUSK AND R. OVERBEEK [1983]. *Implementation of monitors with macros: A programming aid for the HEP and other parallel processors*, Tech. Report ANL-83-97, Argonne National Laboratory, December.

[1270] G. LYZENGA, A. RAEFSKY, AND B. HAGER [1988]. *Finite elements and the method of conjugate gradient on concurrent processors*, Solving Problems on Concurrent Processors, Volume II: Scientific and Engineering Applications, G. Fox and G. Lyzenga, eds., Prentice-Hall, Inc., Englewood Cliffs, NJ. To be published.

[1271] G. LYZENGA, A. RAEFSKY, AND G. HAGER [1985]. *Finite elements and the method of conjugate gradients on a concurrent processor*, Proc. ASME Int. Conf. Computers in Engineering, pp. 401–406.

[1272] R. MACCORMACK AND K. STEVENS [1976]. *Fluid dynamics applications of the ILLIAC IV computer*, Computational Methods and Problems in Aeronautical Fluid Dynamics, Academic Press, New York, pp. 448–465.

[1273] M. MACE AND R. WAGNER [1985]. *Globally optimum selection of memory storage patterns*, Proc. 1985 Int. Conf. Par. Proc., pp. 264–271.

[1274] N. MADSEN AND G. RODRIGUE [1975]. *Two notes on algorithm design for the CDC STAR-100*, Tech. Memo. 75-1, Lawrence Livermore National Laboratory.

[1275] N. MADSEN AND G. RODRIGUE [1976]. *A comparison of direct methods for tridiagonal systems on the CDC STAR-100*, Preprint UCRL-76993, Rev. 1, Lawrence Livermore National Laboratory.

[1276] N. MADSEN AND G. RODRIGUE [1977]. *Odd-even reduction for pentadiagonal matrices*, in Feilmeier [621], pp. 103–106.

[1277] N. MADSEN, G. RODRIGUE, AND J. KARUSH [1976]. *Matrix multiplication by diagonals on a vector/parallel processor*, Inf. Proc. Letts., 5, pp. 41–45.

[1278] G. MAGO [1979]. *A network of microprocessors to execute reduction languages*, Int. J. Comp. and Info. Sci., 8, pp. 349–385 and 435–471.

[1279] G. MAGO [1980]. *A cellular computer architecture for functional programming*, Proc. COMPCON Spring, IEEE Comp. Soc. Conf., pp. 179–187.

[1280] G. MAGO AND R. PARGAS [1982]. *Solving partial differential equations on a cellular tree machine*, Proc. 10th IMACS World Congress on Systems Simulation and Scientific Computation, vol. 1, IMACS, pp. 368–373.

[1281] A. MALONY [1986]. *Cedar performance measurements*, Tech. Report 579, Center for Supercomputing Research and Development, University of Illinois at Urbana-Champaign, June.

[1282] D. MANDELL [1987]. *Experiences and results multitasking a hydrodynamics code on global and local memory machines*, Proc. 1987 Int. Conf. Par. Proc., pp. 415–420.

[1283] P. MANHARDT, R. LEWIS, D. BOULDIN, AND A. BAKER [1982]. *Array processing of the 3-dimensional Navier-Stokes equations*, Phase I Final Reports, NSF SBIR, March.

[1284] C. MAPLES [1985]. *Pyramids, crossbars and thousands of processors*, Proc. 1985 Int. Conf. Par. Proc., pp. 681–688.

[1285] C. MAPLES, D. WEAVER, D. LOGAN, AND W. RATHBUN [1983]. *Performance of a modular interactive data analysis system (MIDAS)*, Proc. 1983 Int. Conf. Par. Proc., pp. 514–519.

[1286] C. MAPLES, D. WEAVER, W. RATHBUN, AND D. LOGAN [1984]. *The operation and utilization of the MIDAS multiprocessor architecture*, Proc. 1984 Int. Conf. Par. Proc., pp. 197–206.

[1287] D. MARINESCU AND C. LIN [1986], *Preliminary results on multiprocessor modeling and analysis using stochastic, high level Petri nets*. Presented at the Twenty-Fourth Allerton Conference on Communication, Control and Computing.

[1288] D. MARINESCU AND J. RICE [1987]. *Domain oriented analysis of PDE splitting algorithms*, J. Information Sciences, 43, pp. 3–24.

[1289] D. MARINESCU AND J. RICE [1987]. *Nonhomogeneous parallel computation I. Synchronization analysis of parallel algorithms*, Tech. Report TR-683, Department of Computer Science, Purdue University.

[1290] D. MARINESCU AND J. RICE [1987]. *Synchronization of nonhomogeneous parallel computations*, Proceedings of the SIAM Conference on Parallel Processing for Scientific Computing, December. Also Computer Science Tech. Report CSD-TR-683, Purdue University, May, 1987.

[1291] D. MARINESCU AND J. RICE [1988]. *On the effects of synchronization in parallel computing*, Tech. Report CS-TR-750, Department of Computer Science, Purdue University.

[1292] A. MARTIN [1980]. *A distributed implementation method for parallel programming*, Information Processing 80, S. H. Lavington, ed., North-Holland, Amsterdam, pp. 309–314.

[1293] H. MARTIN [1977]. *A discourse on a new supercomputer, PEPE*, in Kuck et al. [1133], pp. 101–112.

[1294] J. MARTIN AND D. MUELLER-WICHARDS [1987]. *Supercomputer performance evaluation: Status and directions*, J. Supercomputing, 1, pp. 87–104.

[1295] W. MARTIN, T.-C. WAN, D. POLAND, T. MUDGE, AND T. ABDEL-RAHMAN [1987]. *Monte Carlo photon transport on the NCUBE*, in Heath [860], pp. 454–463.

[1296] F. MATSEN AND T. TAJIMA, eds. [1986]. *Supercomputers: Algorithms, Architectures and Scientific Computation*, University of Texas Press.

[1297] O. MCBRYAN [1985]. *Computational methods for discontinuities in fluids*, Lectures in Applied Mathematics, vol. 22, American Mathematical Society, pp. 63–79.

[1298] O. MCBRYAN [1986]. *Numerical computation on massively parallel hypercubes*, Tech. Report LA-UR-86-4218, Los Alamos National Laboratory.

[1299] O. MCBRYAN [1986]. *Using supercomputers as attached processors*, Tech. Report LA-UR-86-3773, Los Alamos National Laboratory.

[1300] O. MCBRYAN [1987]. *The Connection Machine: PDE solution on 65,536 processors*, Research Report LA-UR-86-4219, Los Alamos National Laboratory.

[1301] O. MCBRYAN [1987]. *Numerical computation on massively parallel hypercubes*, in Heath

[860], pp. 706–719.

[1302] O. McBRYAN AND E. VAN DE VELDE [1985]. *Parallel algorithms for elliptic equation solution on the HEP computer*, Proceedings of the Conference on Parallel Processing using the Heterogeneous Element Processor, March 1985, University of Oklahoma.

[1303] O. McBRYAN AND E. VAN DE VELDE [1985]. *Parallel algorithms for elliptic equations*, Comm. Pure. & Appl. Math., 38, pp. 769–795.

[1304] O. McBRYAN AND E. VAN DE VELDE [1986]. *Elliptic equation algorithms on parallel computers*, Comm. Appl. Numer. Meth., 2, pp. 311–316.

[1305] O. McBRYAN AND E. VAN DE VELDE [1986]. *Hypercube programs for computational fluid dynamics*, in Heath [858], pp. 221–243.

[1306] O. McBRYAN AND E. VAN DE VELDE [1986]. *The multigrid method on parallel computers*, Multigrid Methods II, W. Hackbusch and U. Trottenberg, eds., vol. 1228 of Lecture Notes in Mathematics, Springer-Verlag, Berlin.

[1307] O. McBRYAN AND E. VAN DE VELDE [1987]. *Hypercube algorithms and implementations*, SIAM J. Sci. Statist. Comput., 8, pp. s227–s287.

[1308] O. McBRYAN AND E. VAN DE VELDE [1987]. *Matrix and vector operations on hypercube parallel processors*, Parallel Computing, 5, pp. 117–126.

[1309] J. McCLELLAN AND D. RUMELHART [1988], *Explorations in Parallel Distributed Processing*, MIT Press.

[1310] C. McCORMICK [1982]. *Performance of MSC/NASTRAN on the CRAY computer*, in Cray Research, Inc. [423], pp. 88–98.

[1311] S. McCORMICK [1988]. *Adaptive multilevel algorithms on advanced computers*, in McCormick [1312].

[1312] S. McCORMICK, ed. [1988]. *Multigrid Methods, Proceedings of the Third Copper Mountain Conference on Multigrid Methods, Copper Mountain, CO, April 6–10, 1987*, Marcel Dekker.

[1313] S. McCORMICK AND G. RODRIGUE [1979]. *Multigrid methods for multiprocessor computers*, Tech. Report, Lawrence Livermore Laboratory.

[1314] L. McCULLEY AND G. ZAHER [1974], *Heat shield response to conditions of planetary entry computed on the ILLIAC IV*. Unpublished manuscript under NASA Ames Research Center Contract No. 6911.

[1315] T. McDANIEL [1985]. *Non-linear recurrences and EISPACK*, Tech. Report 511, Center for Supercomputing Research and Development, University of Illinois at Urbana-Champaign, October.

[1316] B. McDONALD [1980]. *The Chebyshev method for solving non-self-adjoint elliptic equations on a vector computer*, J. Comp. Phys., 35, pp. 147–168.

[1317] H. McFADDIN AND J. RICE [1987]. *Parallel and vector problems on the FLEX/32*, Tech. Report CSD-TR-661, Department of Computer Science, Purdue University.

[1318] D. McGLYNN AND L. SCALES [1984]. *On making the NAG run faster*, in Paddon [1512], pp. 73–89.

[1319] J. McGRAW AND T. AXELROD [1984]. *Exploiting multiprocessors: Issues and options*, Tech. Report UCRL-91734, Lawrence Livermore National Laboratory, October.

[1320] J. McGREGOR AND M. SALANA [1983]. *Finite element computation with parallel VLSI*, Proc. 8th ASCE Conf. Elec. Comp., University of Houston, pp. 540–553.

[1321] C. MEAD AND L. CONWAY [1979], *Introduction to VLSI Systems*, Addison-Wesley, Reading, PA.

[1322] P. MEHROTRA AND T. PRATT [1982]. *Language concepts for distributed processing of large arrays*, Proc. of Symp. on Principles of Distributed Computing, Ottawa, Canada, pp. 19–28.

[1323] R. MEHROTRA AND E. GEHRINGER [1985]. *Superlinear speed-up through randomized algorithms*, Proc. 1985 Int. Conf. Par. Proc., pp. 291–300.

[1324] U. MEIER [1985]. *A parallel partition method for solving banded systems of linear equations*, Parallel Computing, 2, pp. 33–43.

[1325] U. MEIER [1986]. *Two parallel SOR variants of the Schwartz alternating procedure*, Parallel Computing, 3, pp. 205–215.

[1326] U. MEIER AND A. SAMEH [1987]. *Numerical linear algebra on the CEDAR multiprocessor*, Proc. SPIE, Vol. 826, Advanced Alg. and Arch. for Signal Processing.

[1327] R. MELHEM [1983]. *An abstract systolic model and its application to the design of finite element systems*, Tech. Report ICMA-83-66, Institute for Computational Mathematics and Applications, University of Pittsburgh.

[1328] R. MELHEM [1985]. *Formal analysis of a systolic system for finite element matrices*, J. Comput. System Sci., 31, pp. 1–27.

[1329] R. MELHEM [1985]. *On the design of a pipelined/systolic finite element system*, Computers and Structures, 20, pp. 67–76.

[1330] R. MELHEM [1986]. *Application of data driven networks to sparse matrix multiplication*, Proc. 1986 Int. Conf. Par. Proc., pp. 758–761.

[1331] R. MELHEM [1986]. *Toward efficient implementations of PCCG methods on vector super-computers*, Int. J. Supercomputer Appl., 1, pp. 70–98.

[1332] R. MELHEM [1987]. *Determination of stripe structures for finite element matrices*, SIAM J. Numer. Anal., 24(6), pp. 1419–1433.

[1333] R. MELHEM [1987]. *An efficient implementation of the SSOR/PCCG method on vector computers*, in Kartashev and Kartashev [1055], pp. 470–477.

[1334] R. MELHEM [1987]. *Iterative solution of sparse linear systems on systolic arrays*, Proc. 1987 Int. Conf. Par. Proc., pp. 560–563.

[1335] R. MELHEM [1987]. *Parallel Gauss-Jordan elimination for the solution of dense linear systems*, Parallel Computing, 4, pp. 339–344.

[1336] R. MELHEM [1987]. *A study of data interlock in computational networks for sparse matrix multiplication.*, IEEE Trans. Comput., 36, pp. 1101–1107.

[1337] R. MELHEM [1988]. *Iterative solutions of sparse linear systems on systolic arrays*, Tech. Report ICMA-87-105, University of Pittsburgh.

[1338] R. MELHEM [1988]. *A modified frontal technique suitable for parallel systems*, SIAM J. Sci. Statist. Comput., 9, pp. 289–304.

[1339] R. MELHEM [1988]. *Parallel solution of linear systems with striped sparse matrices*, Parallel Computing, 6, pp. 145–184.

[1340] R. MELHEM AND K. RAMARO [1988]. *Multicolor reordering of sparse matrices resulting from irregular grids*, ACM Trans. Math. Softw., 14, pp. 117–138.

[1341] R. MELHEM AND W. RHEINBOLDT [1984]. *A mathematical model for the verification of systolic networks*, SIAM J. Comput., 13, pp. 341–365.

[1342] L. MELKEMI AND M. TCHUENTE [1987]. *Complexity of matrix product on a class of orthogonally connected systolic arrays*, IEEE Trans. Comput., C-36, pp. 615–619.

[1343] D. MELSON AND J. KELLER [1983]. *Experiences in using the CYBER 203 and CYBER 205 for three-dimensional transonic flow calculations*, Paper 83-0500, AIAA. AIAA 21st Aerospace Sciences Meeting, January. Also in Control Data Corp. [411].

[1344] N. MELSON [1986]. *Vectorizable multigrid algorithms for transonic-flow calculations*, Appl. Math. & Comp., 19(1-4), pp. 217–238. (Special Issue, Proceedings of the Second Copper Mountain Conference on Multigrid Methods, Copper Mountain, CO, S. McCormick, ed.).

[1345] R. MENDEZ [1984]. *Benchmark on Japanese-American supercomputers — Preliminary results*, IEEE Trans. Comput., C-35, p. 374. An expanded version appeared in the SIAM News 17, No. 2, March, 1984, p. 3.

[1346] M. MERRIAM [1985]. *On the factorization of block-tridiagonals without storage constraints*, SIAM J. Sci. Statist. Comput., 6, pp. 182–192.

[1347] M. MERRIAM [1986]. *Application of data flow concepts to a multigrid solver for the Euler equations*, Appl. Math. & Comp., 19(1-4), pp. 239–264. (Special Issue, Proceedings of the Second Copper Mountain Conference on Multigrid Methods, Copper Mountain, CO, S. McCormick, ed.).

[1348] G. MEURANT [1984]. *The block preconditioned conjugate gradient method on vector computers*, BIT, 24, pp. 623–633.

[1349] G. MEURANT [1987]. *Multitasking the conjugate gradient method on the CRAY X-MP/48*, Parallel Computing, 5, pp. 267–280.

[1350] G. MEURANT [1988]. *Domain decomposition versus block preconditioning*, in Glowinski et al. [762], pp. 231–249.

[1351] G. MEYER [1977]. *Effectiveness of multiprocessor networks for solving the nonlinear Poisson equation*, in Kuck et al. [1133], pp. 323–326.

[1352] G. MEYER AND L. PODRAZIK [1987]. *A parallel first-order linear recurrence solver*, J. Par. Dist. Comp., 4, pp. 117–132.

[1353] G. MEYER AND L. PODRAZIK [1987]. *Parallel implementations of gradient based iterative algorithms for a class of discrete optimal control problems*, Proc. 1987 Int. Conf. Par. Proc., pp. 491–494.

[1354] R. MEYER [1986]. *Numerical algorithms on the Crystal multicomputer*, Comm. Appl. Numer. Meth., 2, pp. 251–254.

[1355] J. MEZO AND W. SYMES [1987]. *Domain decomposition algorithms for linear hyperbolic equations*, Tech. Report 87-20, Department of Mathematical Sciences, Rice University, August.

[1356] P. MICHIELSE [1987]. *Solution methods for bidiagonal and tridiagonal linear systems for parallel and vector computers*, Tech. Report 87-04, Delft University of Technology, Delft.

[1357] P. MICHIELSE AND H. VAN DER VORST [1986]. *Data transport in Wang's partition method*, Tech. Report 86-32, Delft University of Technology, Delft.

[1358] P. MICHIELSE AND H. VAN DER VORST [1988]. *Data transport in Wang's partition method*, Parallel Computing, 7, pp. 87–96.

[1359] H. MIERENDORFF [1988]. *Parallelization of multigrid methods with local refinements for a class of nonshared memory systems*, in McCormick [1312], pp. 449–465.

[1360] J. MIKLOSKO [1984]. *Complexity of parallel algorithms*, in Miklosko and Kotov [1363], pp. 45–63.

[1361] J. MIKLOSKO [1984]. *Correlation of algorithms, software and hardware of parallel computers*, in Miklosko and Kotov [1363], pp. 359–395.

[1362] J. MIKLOSKO [1984]. *Synthesis of parallel numerical algorithms*, in Miklosko and Kotov [1363], pp. 13–43.

[1363] J. MIKLOSKO AND V. KOTOV, eds. [1984]. *Algorithms, Software and Hardware of Parallel Systems*, Springer-Verlag, Berlin.

[1364] R. MILLER [1974]. *A comparison of some theoretical models of parallel computation*, IEEE Trans. Comput., C-22, pp. 710–717.

[1365] R. MILLER AND Q. STOUT [1985]. *Varying diameter and problem size in mesh-connected computers*, Proc. 1985 Int. Conf. Par. Proc., pp. 697–699.

[1366] R. MILLSTEIN [1973]. *Control structures in Illiac IV Fortran*, Comm. ACM, 16, pp. 622–627.

[1367] M. MINSKY [1970]. *Form and content in computer science*, J. ACM, 17, pp. 197–215.

[1368] M. MINSKY AND S. PAPERT [1971]. *On some associative, parallel and analog computations*, Associative Information Techniques, E. Jacks, ed., Elsevier, NY.

[1369] W. MIRANKER [1971]. *A survey of parallelism in numerical analysis*, SIAM Rev., 13, pp. 524–547.

[1370] W. MIRANKER [1978]. *Parallel methods for solving equations*, Math. Comp. Simul., 20, pp. 93–101.

[1371] W. MIRANKER [1979]. *Hierarchical relaxation*, Computing, 23, pp. 267–285.

[1372] W. MIRANKER AND W. LINIGER [1967]. *Parallel methods for the numerical integration of ordinary differential equations*, Math. Comp., 21, pp. 303–320.

[1373] W. MIRANKER AND A. WINKLER [1984]. *Spacetime representations of computational structures*, Computing, 32, pp. 93–114.

[1374] A. MIRIN [1987]. *Experiences parallelizing a 3-D MHD code*, Annual Controlled Fusion Theory Conference, San Diego, CA.

[1375] A. MIRIN [1987]. *Multiprocessing efficiency of 3-D MHD calculations on the NMFECC Cray-2*, American Physical Society Division of Plasma Physics Meeting, San Diego, CA. Paper 6S8.

[1376] A. MIRIN [1987]. *Predicting multitasking overlap on the NMFECC Cray-2*, Twelfth Conf. on Numerical Simulation of Plasmas, San Francisco, CA. Paper CM3.

[1377] A. MIRIN [1988]. *Predicting multiprocessing efficiency on the Cray multiprocessors in a time-sharing environment/application to a 3-D magnetohydrodynamics code*, Tech. Report UCRL-97580, Lawrence Livermore National Laboratory. Submitted to Computers in Phys.

[1378] N. MISSIRLIS [1984]. *A parallel iterative method for solving a class of linear systems*, in Feilmeier et al. [623], pp. 181–189.

[1379] N. MISSIRLIS [1985]. *A parallel iterative system solver*, Lin. Alg. & Appl., 65, pp. 25–44.

[1380] N. MISSIRLIS [1987]. *Scheduling parallel iterative methods on multiprocessor systems*, Parallel Computing, 5, pp. 295–302.

[1381] N. MISSIRLIS AND D. EVANS [1984]. *A second order iterative scheme suitable for parallel implementation*, in Vichnevetsky and Stepleman [1920], pp. 203–206.

[1382] N. MISSIRLIS AND F. TJAFERIS [1988]. *Parallel matrix factorizations on a shared memory MIMD computer*, Proc. Int. Conf. Supercomputing '87, Springer-Verlag.

[1383] D. MITRA [1987]. *Asynchronous relaxations for the numerical solution of differential equations by parallel processors*, SIAM J. Sci. Statist. Comput., 8, pp. s43–s58.

[1384] K. MIURA [1971]. *The block iterative method for Illiac IV*, Doc. 41, Center for Advanced Computation, University of Illinois at Urbana-Champaign.

[1385] K. MIURA AND K. UCHIDA [1984]. *FACOM vector processor VP-100/VP-200*, in Kowalik [1116], pp. 127–138.

[1386] J. MODI [1982]. *Jacobi Methods for Eigenvalue and Related Problems in a Parallel Computing Environment*, PhD dissertation, University of London.

[1387] J. MODI [1988], *Parallel Algorithms and Matrix Computation*, Oxford University Press, Oxford.

[1388] J. MODI AND G. BOWGEN [1984]. *Implementation of QR factorization on the DAP using Householder transformations*, Tech. Report CUED/F-CAMS/TR.241, Cambridge University Engineering Department, Cambridge, UK.

[1389] J. MODI AND G. BOWGEN [1984]. *QR factorization and singular value decomposition on the DAP*, in Paddon [1512], pp. 209–228.

[1390] J. MODI AND M. CLARKE [1984]. *An alternative Givens ordering*, Numer. Math., 43, pp. 83–90.

[1391] J. MODI, R. DAVIES, AND D. PARKINSON [1984]. *Extension of the parallel Jacobi method to the generalized eigenvalue problem*, in Feilmeier et al. [623], pp. 191–197.

[1392] J. MODI AND D. PARKINSON [1982]. *Study of Jacobi methods for eigenvalues and singular value decomposition on DAP*, Comput. Phys. Comm., 26, pp. 317–320.

[1393] J. MODI AND I. PRYCE [1984]. *Mobile Jacobi schemes for parallel computation*, Tech. Report CUED/F-CAMS/TR.242, Cambridge University Engineering Department, Cambridge, UK.

[1394] J. MODI AND I. PRYCE [1985]. *Efficient implementation of Jacobi's method on the DAP*, Numer. Math., 46, pp. 443–454.

[1395] D. MODIANO [1987]. *Performance of a common CFD loop on two parallel architectures*, Tech. Report CFDL-TR-87-11, Massachusetts Institute of Technology.

[1396] J. MOHAN [1984]. *Performance of parallel programs: Model and analyses*, Tech. Report CMU-CS-84-141, Department of Computer Science, Carnegie-Mellon University, Pittsburgh, PA.

[1397] I. MOLCHANOV [1985]. *Applications software of the ES multiprocessor computing complex*, Computational Processes and Systems, Izdatel'stvo Nauka, Moscow, pp. 99–108.

[1398] D. MOLDOVAN, C. WU, AND J. FORTES [1984]. *Mapping an arbitrarily large QR algorithm into a fixed size VLSI array*, Proc. 1984 Int. Conf. Par. Proc., pp. 365–373.

[1399] C. MOLER [1986]. *Matrix computation on distributed memory multiprocessors*, in Heath [858], pp. 181–195.

[1400] R. MONTOYE AND D. LAWRIE [1982]. *A practical algorithm for the solution of triangular systems on a parallel processing system*, IEEE Trans. Comput., C-31, pp. 1076–1082.

[1401] J. MOONEY [1986]. *Simulation of a reaction-diffusion system on large dimpled surfaces using a vector computer*, Math. Comp. Simul., 28, pp. 209–226.

[1402] M. MOORE, R. HIROMOTO, AND O. LUBECK [1984]. *Experiences with the Denelcor HEP*, Parallel Computing, 1, pp. 197–206.

[1403] W. MOORE AND K. STEIGLITZ [1984]. *Efficiency of parallel processing in the solution of Laplace's equation*, in Vichnevetsky and Stepleman [1920], pp. 252–257.

[1404] J.-M. MORF AND J.-M. DELOSME [1981]. *Matrix decompositions and inversions via elementary signature-orthogonal transformations*, ISSM Int. Symp. Mini & Microcomputers in Control and Measurements, San Francisco.

[1405] A. MORGAN AND L. WATSON [1987]. *Solving polynomial systems of equations on a hypercube*, in Heath [860], pp. 501–511.

[1406] K. MORIARTY, M. HARAGUCHI, AND C. PANGALI [1984]. *Efficient implementation of the SU(3) lattice gauge theory algorithm on the Fujitsu VP200 vector processor*, Comput. Phys. Comm., 34, pp. 1–8.

[1407] K. MORIARTY AND D. KUBA [1985]. *Efficient multi-tasking of the SU(3) lattice gauge theory algorithm on the CRAY-X-MP*, Comput. Phys. Comm., 36, pp. 351–362.

[1408] P. MORICE [1972]. *Calcul parallèle et décomposition dans la resolution d'equations aux derivées partialles de type elliptique*. IRIA, Rocquencourt, France.

[1409] R. MORISON AND S. OTTO [1988]. *The scattered decomposition for finite elements*, J. Sci. Comput., 2, pp. 59–76.

[1410] M. MORJARIA AND G. MAKINSON [1984]. *Unstructured sparse matrix vector multiplication on the DAP*, in Paddon [1512], pp. 157–166.

[1411] T. MOTO-OKA, ed. [1982]. *Fifth Generation Computer Systems*, North-Holland, New York.

[1412] T. MOTO-OKA [1984]. *Japanese project on fifth generation computer systems*, in Kowalik [1116], pp. 99–116.

[1413] H. MUHLENBEIN AND S. WARHANT [1985]. *Concurrent multigrid methods in an object-oriented environment*, Proc. 1985 Int. Conf. Par. Proc., pp. 143–146.

[1414] H. MUKAI [1981]. *Parallel algorithms for solving systems of nonlinear equations*, Comp. Math. Appl., 7, pp. 235–250.

[1415] H. MÜLLER, W. SCHÖNAUER, AND E. SCHNEPF [1985]. *Design considerations for the linear solver LINSOL on a CYBER 205*, Supercomputer Applications, A. Emmen, ed., North-Holland, Amsterdam, pp. 39–49.

[1416] H. MÜLLER, W. SCHÖNAUER, AND E. SCHNEPF [1985].   *Vergleich   verschiedener Lösungsverfahren für lineare Gleichungen mit Diagonalenspeicherung auf der CYBER 205*. Mitteilungen Nr. 3, Gesellschaft für Informatik, Parallel-algorithmen und -Rechnerstrukturen (PARS).

[1417] D. MULLER-WICHANDS AND W. GENTZSCH [1982]. *Performance comparisons among several parallel and vector computers on a set of fluid flow problems*, Tech. Report IB 262-82 RO1, DFVLR, Goettingen.

[1418] W. MYERS [1986]. *Getting the cycles out of a supercomputer*, Computer, 19(3), pp. 89–92.

[1419] K. NAGEL [1979]. *Weather simulation with the multi-microprocessor system SMS 701*, Military Electronics Defense EXPO 78, Proceedings of the Conference, Wiesbaden, West Germany, Oct. 3-5, Interario, S.A. Geneva, pp. 60–67.

[1420] V. NAIK AND M. PATRICK [1987]. *Analysis of communication requirements of sparse Cholesky factorization with nested dissection ordering*, Proc. of the Third SIAM Conference of Parallel Processing for Scientific Computing, Los Angeles.

[1421] V. NAIK AND M. PATRICK [1988]. *Data traffic reduction schemes for sparse Cholesky factorizations*, Tech. Report 88-14, ICASE, NASA Langley Research Center, Hampton, VA.

[1422] V. NAIK AND S. TA'ASAN [1987]. *Implementation of multigrid methods for solving Navier-Stokes equations on a multiprocessor system*, Tech. Report 87-37, ICASE, NASA Langley Research Center, Hampton, VA.

[1423] V. NAIK AND S. TA'ASAN [1987]. *Performance studies of the multigrid algorithms implemented on hypercube multiprocessor systems*, in Heath [860], pp. 720–729.

[1424] K. NAKAJIMA [1984]. *A graph theoretical approach to parallel triangulation of a sparse asymmetric matrix*, Proceedings of 1984 Conf. on Information Science and Systems.

[1425] N. NANDAKUMAR [1986]. *Polynomial preconditioning of symmetric indefinite systems*, Tech. Report 580, Center for Supercomputing Research and Development, University of Illinois at Urbana-Champaign, June.

[1426] J. NASH AND S. HANSEN [1988]. *Modified Fadeeva algorithm for concurrent execution of linear algebraic operations*, IEEE Trans. Comput., 37, pp. 129–137.

[1427] J. NAVARRO, J. LLABERIA, AND M. VALERO [1986]. *Solving matrix problems with no size restriction on a systolic array processor*, Proc. 1986 Int. Conf. Par. Proc., pp. 676–683.

[1428] J. NAVARRO, J. LLABERIA, AND M. VALERO [1987]. *Partitioning: An essential step in mapping algorithms*, Computer, 20(7), pp. 77–89.

[1429] I. NAVON, P. PHUA, AND M. RAMAMURTHY [1987].   *Vectorization of conjugate-gradient methods for large-scale minimization*, Tech. Report FSU-SCRI-87-43, Supercomputer Computations Research Institute, Florida State University, Tallahassee, FL, August.

[1430] B. NETA AND H.-M. TAI [1985]. *LU factorization on parallel computers*, Comput. Math. Appl., 11, pp. 573–580.

[1431] M. NEUMANN AND R. PLEMMONS [1987]. *Convergence of parallel multisplitting iterative methods for M-matrices*, Lin. Alg. & Appl., 88, pp. 559–575.

[1432] K. NEVES [1982]. *Mathematical libraries for vector computers*, Comput. Phys. Comm., 26, pp. 303–310.

[1433] K. NEVES [1984]. *Vectorization of scientific software*, in Kowalik [1116], pp. 277–291.

[1434] E. NG, S. THOMPSON, AND P. TUTTLE [1987]. *Experiments with method of lines solvers on a shared-memory parallel computer*, in Vichnevetsky and Stepleman [1921], pp. 161–166.

[1435] L. NI AND K. HWANG [1983]. *Pipelined evaluation of first-order recurrence systems*, Proc. 1983 Int. Conf. Par. Proc., pp. 537–544.

[1436] D. NICOL [1987]. *Mapping a battlefield simulation onto message-passing parallel architectures*, Tech. Report 87-51, ICASE, NASA Langley Research Center, Hampton, VA.

[1437] D. NICOL [1987]. *Performance issues for domain-oriented time-driven distributed simulations*, Tech. Report 87-50, ICASE, NASA Langley Research Center, Hampton, VA.

[1438] D. NICOL [1988]. *Parallel algorithms for mapping pipelined and parallel computations*, Tech. Report 88-2, ICASE, NASA Langley Research Center, Hampton, VA.

[1439] D. NICOL AND P. REYNOLDS [1987]. *Optimal dynamic remapping of parallel computations*, Tech. Report 87-49, ICASE, NASA Langley Research Center, Hampton, VA.

[1440] D. NICOL AND J. SALTZ [1987]. *Principles for problem aggregation and assignment in medium scale multiprocessors*, Tech. Report 87-39, ICASE, NASA Langley Research Center, Hampton, VA.

[1441] D. NICOL AND J. SALTZ [1987]. *Schedules for mapping irregular parallel computations*, Tech. Report 87-52, ICASE, NASA Langley Research Center, Hampton, VA, September.

[1442] D. NICOL AND J. SALTZ [1988]. *Dynamic remapping of parallel computations with varying resource demands*, IEEE Trans. Comput., 37(9), pp. 1073–1087.

[1443] D. NICOL AND F. WILLARD [1987]. *Problem size, parallel architecture and optimal speedup*, Proc. 1987 Int. Conf. Par. Proc., pp. 347–354.

[1444] J. NIEVERGELT [1964]. *Parallel methods for integrating ordinary differential equations*, Comm. ACM, 7, pp. 731–733.

[1445] A. NOBILE AND V. ROBERTO [1986]. *Efficient implementation of multidimensional and fast Fourier transforms on a CRAY X-MP*, Comput. Phys. Comm., 40, pp. 189–202.

[1446] J. NOCEPURENKO [1988]. *A polynomially stable fast parallel algorithm for tridiagonal systems*, USSR Comput. Math. & Math. Phys., 26.4, pp. 1–5.

[1447] T. NODERA [1984]. *PCG method for four color ordered finite difference schemes*, in Vichnevetsky and Stepleman [1920], pp. 222–228.

[1448] J. NOLEN, D. KUBA, AND M. KASCIC [1979]. *Application of vector processors to the solution of finite difference equations*, Fifth Symposium on Reservoir Simulation. Also in SPEJ., August 1981.

[1449] J. NOLEN AND P. STANAT [1981]. *Reservoir simulation on vector processing computers*, Paper 9649, SPE. SPE Middle East Oil Tech. Conf, Manama, Bahrain.

[1450] A. NOOR, ed. [1983]. *Impact of New Computing Systems on Computational Mechanics*, The American Society of Mechanical Engineers.

[1451] A. NOOR AND R. FULTON [1975]. *Impact of the CDC-STAR-100 computer on finite-element systems*, J. Structural Div., ASCE, 101(ST4), pp. 287–296.

[1452] A. NOOR AND S. HARTLEY [1978]. *Evaluation of element stiffness matrices on CDC STAR-100 computer*, Computers and Structures, 9, pp. 151–161.

[1453] A. NOOR, H. KAMEL, AND R. FULTON [1978]. *Substructuring techniques — Status and projections*, Computers and Structures, 8, pp. 621–632.

[1454] A. NOOR AND J. LAMBIOTTE [1978]. *Finite element dynamic analysis on the CDC STAR-100 computer*, Computers and Structures, 10, pp. 7–19.

[1455] A. NOOR AND J. PETERS [1986]. *Element stiffness computation on CDC Cyber 205 computer*, Comm. Appl. Numer. Meth., 2, pp. 317–328.

[1456] A. NOOR, O. STORAASLI, AND R. FULTON [1983]. *Impact of new computing systems on finite element computations*, in Noor [1450], pp. 1–32.

[1457] A. NOOR AND S. VOIGT [1975]. *Hypermatrix scheme for the STAR-100 computer*, Computers and Structures, 5, pp. 287–296.

[1458] C. NORRIE [1984]. *Supercomputers for superproblems: An architectural introduction*, Computer, 17(3), pp. 62–74.

[1459] D. NORRIE [1984]. *The finite element method and large scale computation*, Proc. 4th Int. Symp. on Finite Element Methods in Flow Problems, Tokyo, University of Tokyo Press, North-Holland Publishing Co., pp. 947–954.

[1460] A. NORTON AND G. PFISTER [1985]. *A methodology for predicting multiprocessor performance*, Proc. 1985 Int. Conf. Par. Proc., pp. 772–781.

[1461] A. NORTON AND A. SILBERGER [1987]. *Parallelization and performance analysis of the Cooley-Tukey FFT algorithm for shared-memory architectures*, IEEE Trans. Comput., C-36, pp. 581–591.

[1462] D. NOSENCHUCK, D. KRIST, AND T. ZANG [1988]. *On multigrid methods for the Navier-Stokes computer*, in McCormick [1312].

[1463] D. NOSENCHUCK AND M. LITTMAN [1986]. *The coming of age of the parallel processing supercomputer*, 23rd Annual Space Conf., Kennedy Space Center, Florida, April.

[1464] D. NOSENCHUCK AND M. LITTMAN [1986]. *The Navier-Stokes computer*, Symp. on Future Directions in Computational Mechanics, ASME Winter Meeting, December.

[1465] D. NOSENCHUCK, M. LITTMAN, AND W. FLANNERY [1986]. *Two-dimensional nonsteady viscous flow simulation on the Navier-Stokes computer mini-node*, J. Sci. Comput., 1, pp. 53–73.

[1466] B. NOUR-OMID AND K. PARK [1987]. *Solving structural mechanics problems on the Caltech hypercube*, Comput. Meth. Appl. Mech. Engrg., 61, pp. 161–176.

[1467] B. NOUR-OMID, B. PARLETT, AND A. RAEFSKY [1988]. *Comparison of Lanczos with conjugate gradient using element preconditioning*, in Glowinski et al. [762], pp. 250–260.

[1468] B. NOUR-OMID, A. RAEFSKY, AND G. LYZENGA [1987]. *Solving finite element equations on concurrent computers*, Proceedings of the ASME Symposium on Parallel Computations and their Impact on Mechanics, December 13-18.

[1469] R. NUMRICH, ed. [1985]. *Supercomputer Applications Symposium, Proceedings of Symposium at Purdue University, October 31 - November 1, 1984*.

[1470] W. OAKES AND R. BROWNING [1979]. *Experience running ADINA on CRAY-1*, Proc. ADINA Conf. Report 82448-9, Massachusetts Institute of Technology.

[1471] S. O'DONNELL, P. GEIGER, AND M. SCHULTZ [1983]. *Solving the Poisson equation on the*

FPS-164, Tech. Report YALEU/DCS/RR-292, Department of Computer Science, Yale University.

[1472] S. O'DONNELL AND V. ROKHLIN [1987]. *A fast algorithm for the numerical evaluation of conformal mappings*, Tech. Report YALEU/DCS/RR-554, Department of Computer Science, Yale University, July.

[1473] W. OED AND O. LANGE [1983]. *The solution of linear recurrence relations on pipelined processors*, Proc. 1983 Int. Conf. Par. Proc., pp. 545–547.

[1474] W. OED AND O. LANGE [1984]. *Transforming linear recurrence relations for vector processors*, in Feilmeier et al. [623], pp. 211–216.

[1475] W. OED AND O. LANGE [1985]. *On the effective bandwidth of interleaved memories in vector processor systems*, Proc. 1985 Int. Conf. Par. Proc., pp. 33–40.

[1476] W. OED AND O. LANGE [1985]. *On the effective bandwidth of interleaved memories in vector processor systems*, IEEE Trans. Comput., C-34, pp. 949–957.

[1477] W. OED AND O. LANGE [1986]. *Modeling, measurement, and simulation of memory interference in the CRAY X-MP*, Parallel Computing, 3, pp. 343–358.

[1478] M. OGURA, M. SHER, AND J. ERICKSEN [1972]. *A study of the efficiency of ILLIAC IV in hydrodynamic calculations*, Tech. Report 59, Center for Advanced Computation, University of Illinois at Urbana-Champaign.

[1479] D. O'LEARY [1984]. *Ordering schemes for parallel processing of certain mesh problems*, SIAM J. Sci. Statist. Comput., 5, pp. 620–632.

[1480] D. O'LEARY [1987]. *Parallel implementation of the block conjugate gradiant algorithm*, Parallel Computing, 5, pp. 127–140.

[1481] D. O'LEARY [1987]. *Systolic arrays for matrix transpose and other reorderings*, IEEE Trans. Comput., C-36, pp. 117–122.

[1482] D. O'LEARY AND G. STEWART [1985]. *Data-flow algorithms for parallel matrix computations*, Comm. ACM, 28, pp. 840–853.

[1483] D. O'LEARY AND G. STEWART [1986]. *Assignment and scheduling in parallel matrix factorization*, Lin. Alg. & Appl., 77, pp. 275–300.

[1484] D. O'LEARY AND G. STEWART [1987]. *From determinacy to systolic arrays*, IEEE Trans. Comput., C-36, pp. 1355–1359.

[1485] D. O'LEARY, G. STEWART, AND R. VAN DE GEIJN [1986]. *DOMINO: A message passing environment for parallel computations*, Tech. Report TR-1648, Department of Computer Science, University of Maryland, April.

[1486] D. O'LEARY AND R. WHITE [1985]. *Multi-splittings of matrices and parallel solution of linear systems*, SIAM J. Algebraic Discrete Methods, 6, pp. 630–640.

[1487] P. OLEINICK [1978]. *The Implementation of Parallel Algorithms on an Asynchronous Multiprocessor*, PhD dissertation, Carnegie-Mellon University, Department of Computer Science.

[1488] P. OLEINICK [1982], *Parallel Algorithms on a Multiprocessor*, UMI Research Press.

[1489] P. OLEINICK AND S. FULLER [1978]. *The implementation of a parallel algorithm on C.mmp*, Tech. Report CMU-CS-78-125, Department of Computer Science, Carnegie-Mellon University.

[1490] J. OLIGER [1986]. *Parallelism and uncertainty in scientific computations*, International Congress on Computational and Applied Mathematics, University of Leuven, Belgium.

[1491] K. ONAGA AND T. TAKECHI [1986]. *A wavefront algorithm for LU decomposition of a partitioned matrix on VLSI processor arrays*, J. Par. Dist. Comp., 3, pp. 137–157.

[1492] T. OPPE AND D. KINCAID [1987]. *Numerical experiments with a parallel conjugate gradient method*, Tech. Report CNA-208, Center for Numerical Analysis, University of Texas at Austin.

[1493] T. OPPE AND D. KINCAID [1987]. *The performance of ITPACK on vector computers for solving large sparse linear systems arising in sample oil reservoir simulation problems*, Comm. Appl. Numer. Meth., 3, pp. 23–30.

[1494] T. OPSAHL [1984]. *DAP-TRAC: A Practical Application of Parallel Processing to a Large Engineering Code*, PhD dissertation, University of London.

[1495] T. OPSAHL AND D. PARKINSON [1986]. *An algorithm for solving sparse sets of linear equations with an almost tridiagonal structure on SIMD computers*, Proc. 1986 Int. Conf. Par. Proc., pp. 369–374.

[1496] D. ORBITS [1978]. *A Cray-1 timing simulator*, Tech. Report 118, Systems Engineering Laboratory, University of Michigan.

[1497] D. ORBITS AND D. CALAHAN [1976]. *Data flow considerations in implementing a full matrix solver with backing store on the CRAY-1*, Tech. Report 98, Systems Engineering Laboratory, University of Michigan.

[1498] D. ORBITS AND D. CALAHAN [1978]. *A CRAY-1 simulator and its application to development of high performance codes*, Proc. LASL Workshop on Vector and Parallel Processors.

[1499] S. ORSZAG AND A. PATERA [1981]. *Calculation of Von Karman's constant for turbulent channel flow*, Phys. Rev. Lett., 47, pp. 832–835.

[1500] S. ORSZAG AND A. PATERA [1981]. *Subcritical transition to turbulence in planar shear flows*, Transition and Turbulence, R. Meyer, ed., Academic Press, New York, pp. 127–146.

[1501] S. ORSZAG AND A. PATERA [1983]. *Secondary instability of wall bounded shear flows*, J. Fluid Mech., 128, pp. 347–385.

[1502] J. ORTEGA [1987]. *The ijk forms of factorization methods I. Vector computers*, Parallel Computing, 7(2), pp. 135–148.

[1503] J. ORTEGA [1988], *Introduction to Parallel and Vector Solution of Linear Systems*, Plenum Press.

[1504] J. ORTEGA AND C. ROMINE [1988]. *The ijk forms of factorization II. Parallel systems*, Parallel Computing, 7(2), pp. 149–162.

[1505] J. ORTEGA AND R. VOIGT [1977]. *Solution of partial differential equations on vector computers*, Proc. 1977 Army Numerical Analysis and Computers Conference, pp. 475–525.

[1506] J. ORTEGA AND R. VOIGT [1985]. *Solution of partial differential equations on vector and parallel computers*, SIAM Rev., 27, pp. 149–240.

[1507] J. ORTEGA AND R. VOIGT [1987]. *A bibliography on parallel and vector numerical algorithms*, Tech. Report I-3, ICASE, NASA Langley Research Center, Hampton, VA.

[1508] N. OSTLUND [1985]. *Waterloop V2/64: A highly parallel machine for numerical computation*, Comput. Phys. Comm., 37, pp. 109–117.

[1509] N. OSTLUND, P. HIBBARD, AND R. WHITESIDE [1982]. *A case study in the application of a tightly coupled multi-processor to scientific computations*, in Rodrigue [1643], pp. 375–364.

[1510] G. OSTROUCHOV [1987]. *Parallel computing on a hypercube: An overview of the architecture and some applications*, Proc. 19th Symp. on the Interface of Computer Science and Statistics, M. Heiberger, ed., Washington, D.C., American Statistical Association, pp. 27–32.

[1511] Y. OYANGAI [1986]. *An incomplete LDU decomposition of lattice fermions and its application to conjugate residual methods*, Comput. Phys. Comm., 42, pp. 333–344.

[1512] D. PADDON, ed. [1984]. *Supercomputers and Parallel Computation*, Clarendon Press, Oxford.

[1513] Y. PAKER [1977]. *Application of microprocessor networks for the solution of diffusion equations*, Math. Comp. Simul., 19, pp. 23–27.

[1514] Y. PAKER [1983], *Multi-Microprocessor Systems*, Academic Press, New York, NY.

[1515] J. PALMER [1974]. *Conjugate Direction Methods and Parallel Computing*, PhD dissertation, Stanford University, Department of Computer Science.

[1516] V. PAN AND J. REIF [1985]. *Efficient parallel solution of linear systems*, Proc. 17th Annual ACM Symposium on Theory of Computing, pp. 143–152.

[1517] R. PARGAS [1982]. *Parallel Solution of Elliptic Partial Differential Equations on a Tree Machine*, PhD dissertation, University of North Carolina, Chapel Hill, Department of Computer Science.

[1518] D. PARKER [1980]. *Notes on shuffle/exchange type switching networks*, IEEE Trans. Comput., C-29, pp. 213–222.

[1519] D. PARKINSON [1976]. *The ICL Distributed Array Processor DAP*, Computational Methods in Classical and Quantum Physics, M. Hooper, ed., Adv. Pub. Ltd.

[1520] D. PARKINSON [1982]. *The Distributed Array Processor (DAP)*, Comput. Phys. Comm., 28, pp. 325–336.

[1521] D. PARKINSON [1982]. *Using the ICL DAP*, Comput. Phys. Comm., 26, pp. 227–232.

[1522] D. PARKINSON [1984]. *Experience in exploiting large scale parallelism*, in Kowalik [1116], pp. 247–256.

[1523] D. PARKINSON [1984]. *The solution of N linear equations using P processors*, in Feilmeier et al. [623], pp. 81–87.

[1524] D. PARKINSON [1986]. *Parallel efficiency can be greater than unity*, Parallel Computing, 3, pp. 261–262.

[1525] D. PARKINSON [1987]. *Organizational aspects of using parallel computers*, Parallel Computing, 5, pp. 75–84.

[1526] D. PARKINSON AND H. LIDDELL [1982]. *The measurement of performance on a highly parallel system*, IEEE Trans. Comput., C-31, pp. 32–37.

[1527] D. PARKINSON AND M. WUNDERLICH [1984]. *A compact algorithm for Gaussian elimination over GF(2) implemented on highly parallel computers*, Parallel Computing, 1, pp. 65–73.

[1528] B. PARLETT, B. NOUR-OMID, AND J. JATVIG [1985]. *Implementation of Lanczos algorithms on vector computers*, in Numrich [1469], pp. 1–18.

[1529] S. PARTER, ed. [1984]. *Large Scale Scientific Computation*, Academic Press, Orlando, FL.

[1530] S. PARTER AND M. STEUERWALT [1982]. *Block iterative methods for elliptic and parabolic difference equations*, SIAM J. Numer. Anal., 19, pp. 1173–1195.

[1531] S. PARTER AND M. STEUERWALT [1985]. *Block iterative methods for elliptic finite element equations*, SIAM J. Numer. Anal., 22, pp. 146–179.

[1532] S. PARTER AND S. STEUERWALT [1980]. *On k-line and k × k block iterative schemes for a problem arising in 3-D elliptic difference equations*, SIAM J. Numer. Anal., 17, pp. 823–839.

[1533] H. PARTRIDGE AND C. BAUSCHLICHER [1986]. *Algorithms vs. architectures for computational chemistry*, Tech. Report TR 86.3, RIACS, NASA Ames Research Center, January.

[1534] J. PASCIAK [1988]. *Domain decomposition preconditioners for elliptic problems in two and three dimensions: First approach*, in Glowinski et al. [762], pp. 62–72.

[1535] K. PATEL [1982]. *Parallel computation and numerical optimization*, Tech. Report 129, NOC, Hatfield, Herts.

[1536] K. PATEL [1984]. *Implementation of a parallel (SIMD) modified Newton algorithm on the ICL DAP*, in Paddon [1512], pp. 229–249.

[1537] N. PATEL [1983]. *A Fully Vectorized Numerical Solution of the Incompressible Navier-Stokes Equations*, PhD dissertation, Mississippi State University, December.

[1538] N. PATEL AND H. JORDAN [1984]. *A parallelized point rowwise successive over-relaxation method on a multiprocessor*, Parallel Computing, 1, pp. 207–222.

[1539] A. PATERA [1986]. *Fast direct Poisson solvers for high order finite element discretization in rectangularly decomposable domains*, J. Comp. Phys., 65, pp. 474–480.

[1540] M. PATRICK AND T. PRATT [1986]. *Communication oriented programming of parallel iterative solutions of sparse linear systems*, Comm. Appl. Numer. Meth., 2, pp. 255–261.

[1541] M. PATRICK, D. REED, AND R. VOIGT [1987]. *The impact of domain partitioning on the performance of a shared memory multiprocessor*, Parallel Computing, 5, pp. 211–218.

[1542] P. PATTON [1985]. *Multiprocessors: Architecture and applications*, Computer, 18(6), pp. 929–940.

[1543] G. PAUL AND W. WILSON [1978]. *An introduction to VECTRAN and its use in scientific applications programming*, Proc. of LASL Workshop on Vector and Parallel Processors.

[1544] G. PAWLEY AND G. THOMAS [1982]. *The implementation of lattice calculations on the DAP*, J. Comp. Phys., 47, pp. 165–178.

[1545] M. PEASE [1967]. *Matrix inversion using parallel processing*, J. ACM, 14, pp. 757–764.

[1546] M. PEASE [1968]. *An adaptation of the fast Fourier transform for parallel processing*, J. ACM, 15, pp. 252–264.

[1547] M. PEASE [1977]. *The indirect binary n-cube microprocessor array*, IEEE Trans. Comput., 26(5), pp. 458–473.

[1548] W. PELKA AND A. PETERS [1986]. *Finite element ground water models implemented on vector computers*, I. J. Num. Meth. Fluids, 6, pp. 913–926.

[1549] R. PERROTT [1979]. *A standard for supercomputer languages*, in Jesshope and Hockney [976], pp. 291–308.

[1550] R. PERROTT [1987]. *Language developments for supercomputers*, Supercomputer, 19, pp. 19–26.

[1551] C. PESKIN [1981]. *Ultracomputer implementation of odd-even cyclic reduction*, Ultracomputer Note 19, Department of Computer Science, New York University, January.

[1552] F. PETERS [1981]. *Tree machines and divide-and-conquer algorithms*, CONPAR 81, Lecture Notes in Computer Science 111, W. Händler, ed., Berlin, Springer-Verlag, pp. 25–36.

[1553] F. PETERS [1984]. *Parallel pivoting algorithms for sparse symmetric matrices*, Parallel Computing, 1, pp. 99–110.

[1554] F. PETERS [1985]. *Parallelism and sparse linear equations*, Sparsity and Its Applications, D. Evans, ed., Cambridge University Press, pp. 285–301.

[1555] J. PETERSON [1977]. *Petri nets*, ACM Computing Surveys, 9, pp. 223–252.

[1556] J. PETERSON, J. TUAZON, D. LIEBERMAN, AND M. DANIEL [1985]. *The Mark III hypercube-ensemble concurrent computer*, Proc. 1985 Int. Conf. Par. Proc., pp. 71–73.

[1557] V. PETERSON [1978]. *Computational aerodynamics and the NASF*, Tech. Report CR-2032, NASA Ames Research Center.

[1558] V. PETERSON [1984]. *Application of supercomputers to computational aerodynamics*, Tech. Report TM-85965, NASA Ames Research Center.

[1559] V. PETERSON [1984]. *Impact of computers on aerodynamics research and development*, Proc.

IEEE, 72, pp. 68–79.

[1560] W. PETERSON [1983]. *Vector Fortran for numerical problems on CRAY-1*, Comm. ACM, 26, pp. 1008–1021.

[1561] G. PFISTER, W. BRANTLEY, D. GEORGE, S. HARVEY, W. KLEINFELDER, K. MCAULIFFE, E. MELTON, V. NORTON, AND J. WEISS [1985]. *The IBM research parallel processor prototype (RP3): Introduction and architecture*, Proc. 1985 Int. Conf. Par. Proc., pp. 764–771.

[1562] G. PFISTER AND V. NORTON [1985]. *Hot spot contention and combining in multistage interconnection networks*, Proc. 1985 Int. Conf. Par. Proc., pp. 790–797.

[1563] B. PHILLIPPE [1987]. *An algorithm to improve nearly orthonormal sets of vectors on a vector processor*, SIAM J. Algebraic Discrete Methods, 8, pp. 396–403.

[1564] D. PIERCE [1987]. *Implementing domain decoupled incomplete factorizations and a parallel conjugate gradient method on the Sequent Balance 21000*, Tech. Report ETA-TR-61, Boeing Computer Services, August.

[1565] D. PIERRE [1973]. *A nongradient minimization algorithm having parallel structure, with implementation for an array processor*, Comput. Elect. Engrg., 1, pp. 3–21.

[1566] I. PLANDER [1984]. *Parallel processors and multicomputer systems*, in Miklosko and Kotov [1363], pp. 273–321.

[1567] G. PLATZMAN [1979]. *The ENIAC computations of 1950 — Gateway to numerical weather prediction*, Bull. Amer. Meteor. Soc., 60, pp. 302–312.

[1568] R. PLEMMONS [1986]. *A parallel block iterative scheme applied to computations in structural analysis*, SIAM J. Algebraic Discrete Methods, 7, pp. 337–347.

[1569] C. POLYCHRONOPOULOS [1986]. *On program restructuring, scheduling, and communication for parallel processor systems*, Tech. Report 595, Center for Supercomputing Research and Development, University of Illinois at Urbana-Champaign, August.

[1570] C. POLYCHRONOPOULOS AND U. BANERJEE [1986]. *Speedup bounds and processor allocation for parallel programs on multiprocessors*, Proc. 1986 Int. Conf. Par. Proc., pp. 961–968.

[1571] E. POOLE [1986]. *Multi-color Incomplete Cholesky Conjugate Gradient Methods on Vector Computers*, PhD dissertation, The University of Virginia, Department of Applied Mathematics.

[1572] E. POOLE AND J. ORTEGA [1984]. *Incomplete Choleski conjugate gradient on the CYBER 203/205*, in Numrich [1469], pp. 19–28.

[1573] E. POOLE AND J. ORTEGA [1987]. *Multicolor ICCG methods for vector computers*, SIAM J. Numer. Anal., 24, pp. 1394–1418.

[1574] W. POOLE AND R. VOIGT [1974]. *Numerical algorithms for parallel and vector computers: An annotated bibliography*, Comp. Rev., 15, pp. 379–388.

[1575] D. POPLAWSKI [1988]. *Mapping rings and grids onto the FPS T-series hypercube*, Parallel Computing, 7, pp. 1–10.

[1576] P. PORTA [1987]. *Implicit finite difference simulation of an internal flow in a nozzle: An example of a physical application on a hypercube*, Tech. Report YALEU/DCS/RR-553, Department of Computer Science, Yale University.

[1577] P. PORTA [1987]. *Implicit finite-difference simulation of an internal flow on a hypercube*, Tech. Report YALEU/DCS/RR-594, Department of Computer Science, Yale University.

[1578] T. PORTA [1987]. *A programmable systolic array for factorial data analysis part I. Matrix computations*, Tech. Report YALEU/DCS/RR-542, Department of Computer Science, Yale University.

[1579] T. PORTA [1987]. *A programmable systolic array for factorial data analysis part II. The symmetric eigenvalue problem*, Tech. Report YALEU/DCS/RR-543, Department of Computer Science, Yale University.

[1580] A. POTHEN [1988]. *Simplicial cliques, shortest elimination trees and supernodes in sparse Cholesky factorization*, Tech. Report CS-88-13, Department of Computer Science, Pennsylvania State University.

[1581] A. POTHEN AND P. RAGHAVAN [1987]. *Distributed orthogonal factorization: Givens and Householder algorithms*, Tech. Report CS-87-24, Department of Computer Science, Pennsylvania State University.

[1582] A. POTHEN, J. SOMESH, AND U. VEMULAPATI [1987]. *Orthogonal factorization on a distributed memory multiprocessor*, in Heath [860], pp. 587–596.

[1583] J. POTTER [1983]. *Image processing on the Massively Parallel Processor*, Computer, 16(1), pp. 62–67.

[1584] J. POTTER, ed. [1985]. *The Massively Parallel Processor*, MIT Press, Boston, MA.

[1585] C. POTTLE [1979]. *Solution of sparse linear equations arising from power system simulation on vector and parallel processors*, ISA Trans., 18(3), pp. 81–88.

[1586] F. PREPARATA AND D. SARWATE [1978]. *An improved parallel processor bound in fast matrix inversion*, Inf. Proc. Letts., 7, pp. 148–150.

[1587] F. PREPARATA AND J. VUILLEMIN [1980]. *Optimal integrated-circuit implementation of triangular matrix inversion*, Proc. 1980 Int. Conf. Par., pp. 211–216.

[1588] F. PREPARATA AND J. VUILLEMIN [1981]. *The cube-connected cycles: A versatile network for parallel computation*, Comm. ACM, 24, pp. 300–309.

[1589] H. PRICE AND K. COATS [1974]. *Direct methods in reservoir simulation*, J. Soc. Pet. Eng., 14, pp. 295–308.

[1590] D. PRYOR AND P. BURNS [1987]. *A parallel Monte Carlo model for radiative heat transfer*, Tech. Report 87001, Institute for Scientific Computing, Fort Collins, CO.

[1591] T. PULLIAM AND H. LOMAX [1979]. *Simulation of three-dimensional compressible viscous flow on the Illiac IV computer*, AIAA J., 18, pp. 159–167.

[1592] L. PYLE AND S. WHEAT [1984]. *A Kosloff/basal method 3D migration program implemented on the CYBER 205 supercomputer*, in Gary [700], pp. 327–358.

[1593] G. QING-SHI AND W. RONG-QUAN [1983]. *Vector computer for sparse matrix operations*, Proc. 1983 Int. Conf. Par. Proc., pp. 87–89.

[1594] A. QUARTERONI AND G. SACCHI-LANDRIANI [1988]. *Domain decomposition preconditioners for the spectral collocation method*, Tech. Report 88-11, ICASE, NASA Langley Research Center, Hampton, VA, January.

[1595] D. QUINLAN [1988]. *Multilevel load balancing for hyercubes*, in McCormick [1312].

[1596] M. QUINN [1987], *Designing Efficient Algorithms for Parallel Computers*, McGraw-Hill, New York.

[1597] C. RADEHAUS, M. WALDOWSKI, K. KARDELL, J. BERKEMEIER, M. WIESEMAN, AND H. PURVINS [1985]. *Special purpose computer for non-linear differential equations*, Comput. Phys. Comm., 36, pp. 345–350.

[1598] S. RAJAN [1972]. *A parallel algorithm for high-speed subsonic compressible flow over a circular cylinder*, J. Comp. Phys., 12, pp. 534–552.

[1599] I. RAJU AND J. CREWS [1982]. *Three-dimensional analysis of [0/90]$_s$ and [90/0]$_s$ laminates with a central circular hole*, Composite Tech. Rev., 4(4), pp. 116–124.

[1600] I. RAMAKRISHNAN AND P. VARMAN [1984]. *Modular matrix multiplication on a linear array*, IEEE Trans. Comput., C-33, pp. 952–958.

[1601] I. RAMAKRISHNAN AND P. VARMAN [1985]. *An optimal family of matrix multiplication algorithms on linear arrays*, Proc. 1985 Int. Conf. Par. Proc., pp. 376–383.

[1602] C. RAMAMOORTHY, K. CHANDY, AND M. GONZALEZ [1972]. *Optimal scheduling strategies in a multiprocessor system*, IEEE Trans. Comput., C-21, pp. 137–146.

[1603] C. RAMAMOORTHY AND H. LI [1977]. *Pipeline architecture*, ACM Computing Surveys, 9, pp. 61–102.

[1604] M. RAMAMURTHY [1987]. *Performance improvement beyond vectorization on the Cyber 205*, Supercomputer, 22, pp. 41–51.

[1605] A. RANADE [1985]. *Interconnection networks and parallel memory organizations for array processing*, Proc. 1985 Int. Conf. Par. Proc., pp. 41–47.

[1606] J. RANSON, O. STORAASLI, AND R. FULTON [1984]. *Application of concurrent processing to structural dynamic response computations*, Research in Structures and Dynamics — 1984, NASA, pp. 31–44. NASA CP 2335.

[1607] L. RASKIN [1978]. *Performance evaluation of multiple processor systems*, Tech. Report CMU-CS-78-141, Department of Computer Science, Carnegie-Mellon University.

[1608] J. RATTNER [1985]. *Concurrent processing: A new direction in scientific computing*, Conf. Proc. 1985 Nat. Comp. Conf., vol. 54, AFIPS, pp. 157–166.

[1609] W. RAY [1984], *Cyberplus: A multiparallel operating system*. Presented at the Los Alamos Workshop on Operating Systems and Environments for Parallel Processing, August 7-9, Los Alamos, NM.

[1610] G. REA [1983]. *A software debugging aid for the Finite Element Machine*, Tech. Report, Department of Computer Science, University of Colorado.

[1611] S. REDDAWAY [1979]. *The DAP approach*, in Jesshope and Hockney [976], pp. 309–329.

[1612] S. REDDAWAY [1984]. *Distributed array processor, architecture and performance*, in Kowalik [1116], pp. 89–98.

[1613] D. REDHED, A. CHEN, AND S. HOTOVY [1979]. *New approach to the 3D transonic flow analysis using the STAR-100 computer*, AIAA J., 17, pp. 98–99.

[1614] D. REED [1983]. *Performance Based Design and Analysis of Multimicrocomputer Networks*, PhD dissertation, Purdue University.

[1615] D. REED, L. ADAMS, AND M. PATRICK [1987]. *Stencils and problem partitionings: Their influence on the performance of multiple processor systems*, IEEE Trans. Comput., C-36, pp. 845–858.

[1616] D. REED AND M. PATRICK [1984]. *A model of asynchronous iterative algorithms for solving large sparse linear systems*, Proc. 1984 Int. Conf. Par. Proc., pp. 402–409.

[1617] D. REED AND M. PATRICK [1985]. *Iterative solution of large sparse linear systems on a static data flow architecture: Performance studies*, Proc. 1985 Int. Conf. Par. Proc., pp. 25–32.

[1618] D. REED AND M. PATRICK [1985]. *Iterative solution of large sparse linear systems on a static data flow architecture: Performance studies*, IEEE Trans. Comput., C-34, pp. 874–881.

[1619] D. REED AND M. PATRICK [1985]. *Parallel iterative solution of sparse linear systems: Models and architectures*, Parallel Computing, 2, pp. 45–67.

[1620] D. REHAK, W. KEIROUZ, C. HENDRICKSON, AND Z. CENDRES [1985]. *Evaluation of finite element system architectures*, Computers and Structures, 20, pp. 17–30.

[1621] L. REICHEL [1987]. *Parallel iterative methods for the solution of Fredholm integral equations of the second kind*, in Heath [860], pp. 520–529.

[1622] J. REID [1987]. *The exploitation of parallelism by using Fortran 8X features*, Supercomputer, 19, pp. 8–18.

[1623] G. REIJNS AND M. BARTON, eds. [1987]. *Highly Parallel Computers*, North-Holland, Amsterdam.

[1624] B. REILLY [1970]. *On implementing the Monte Carlo evaluation of the Boltzmann collision integral on ILLIAC IV*, Tech. Report I-140, Coordinated Science Laboratory, University of Illinois at Urbana-Champaign.

[1625] E. REITER AND G. RODRIGUE [1984]. *An incomplete Choleski factorization by a matrix partition algorithm*, in Birkhoff and Schoenstadt [173], pp. 161–173.

[1626] J. RICE [1985]. *Problems to test parallel and vector languages*, Tech. Report CSD-TR 516, Department of Computer Science, Purdue University, May.

[1627] J. RICE [1985]. *Using supercomputers today and tomorrow*, Proc. Third US Army Conf. on Applied Math and Computing, May.

[1628] J. RICE [1986]. *Multi-FLEX machines: Preliminary report*, Tech. Report CSD-TR-612, Department of Computer Science, Purdue University.

[1629] J. RICE [1986]. *Parallelism in solving PDE's*, Proceedings of the Fall Joint Computer Conference, Washington, DC, IEEE Computer Society Press, pp. 540–546.

[1630] J. RICE [1987]. *Parallel methods for PDE's*, Tech. Report.

[1631] J. RICE [1987]. *Supercomputing about physical objects*, Tech. Report TR-708, Department of Computer Science, Purdue University.

[1632] J. RICE AND D. MARINESCU [1987]. *Analysis and modeling of Schwartz splitting algorithms for elliptic PDE's*, in Vichnevetsky and Stepleman [1921].

[1633] C. RIEGER [1981]. *ZMOB: Hardware from a user's viewpoint*, Proc. IEEE Comput. Soc. Conf. Pattern Recognition and Image Processing, pp. 399–408.

[1634] J. RIGANATI AND P. SCHNECK [1984]. *Supercomputing*, Computer, 17(10), pp. 97–113.

[1635] A. RIZZI [1985]. *Vector coding the finite volume procedure for the Cyber 205*, Parallel Computing, 2, pp. 295–312.

[1636] A. RIZZI AND M. HODOUS [1985]. *Large scale flowfield simulation using the Cyber 205*, in Numrich [1469], pp. 159–177.

[1637] F. ROBERT [1970]. *Méthodes iteratives serie-parallèl*, C. R. Acad. Sci. Paris, 271, pp. 847–850.

[1638] F. ROBERT, M. CHARNAY, AND F. MUSY [1975]. *Iterations chaotiques serie-parallèl pour des equations non-linéares de point fixe*, Appl. Mate., 20, pp. 1–38.

[1639] Y. ROBERT [1985]. *Block LU decomposition of a band matrix on a systolic array*, Int. J. Comput. Math., 17, pp. 295–316.

[1640] Y. ROBERT AND M. TCHUENTE [1985]. *Systolic resolution of dense linear systems*, RAIRO-MMNA, 19, pp. 179–194 and 315–326.

[1641] J. ROBINSON [1979]. *Some analysis techniques for asynchronous multiprocessor algorithms*, IEEE Trans. Softw. Eng., SE-5, pp. 24–31.

[1642] J. ROBINSON, R. RILEY, AND R. HARTKA [1982]. *Evaluation of the SPAR thermal analyzer on the CYBER-203 computer*, Computational Aspects of Heat Transfer and Structures, H. Adelman, ed., NASA Langley Research Center, pp. 405–424. NASA-CP 2216.

[1643] G. RODRIGUE, ed. [1982]. *Parallel Computations*, Academic Press, New York.

[1644] G. RODRIGUE [1984]. *A parallel first-order method for parabolic partial differential equations*, in Kowalik [1116], pp. 329–342.

[1645] G. RODRIGUE [1985]. *Inner/outer iterative methods and numerical Schwartz algorithms*, Parallel Computing, 2, pp. 205–218.

[1646] G. RODRIGUE [1986]. *Parallel scientific computing: Philosophy and directions*, Tech. Report UCRL-93792, Lawrence Livermore National Laboratory.

[1647] G. RODRIGUE [1986]. *Some ideas for decomposing the domain of elliptic partial differential equations in the Schwartz process*, Comm. Appl. Numer. Meth., 2, pp. 245–249.

[1648] G. RODRIGUE [1986]. *Some new parallel methods for solving the heat equation*, Tech. Report UCRL-95278, Lawrence Livermore National Laboratory.

[1649] G. RODRIGUE, E. GIROUX, AND M. PRATT [1980]. *Perspectives on large-scale scientific computation*, Computer, 13(12), pp. 65–80.

[1650] G. RODRIGUE, C. HENDRICKSON, AND M. PRATT [1982]. *An implicit numerical solution of the two dimensional diffusion equation and vectorization experiments*, in Rodrigue [1643], pp. 101–128.

[1651] G. RODRIGUE, N. MADSEN, AND J. KARUSH [1976]. *Odd-even reduction for banded linear equations*, Tech. Report UCRL-78652, Lawrence Livermore National Laboratory.

[1652] G. RODRIGUE AND P. SAYLOR [1986]. *Domain decomposition and inner/outer iteration for elliptic partial differential equations II*, Tech. Report UCRL-92077-II, Lawrence Livermore National Laboratory.

[1653] G. RODRIGUE AND J. SIMON [1984]. *Jacobi splittings and the method of overlapping domains for elliptic PDEs*, in Vichnevetsky and Stepleman [1920], pp. 383–386.

[1654] G. RODRIGUE AND D. WOLITZER [1984]. *Incomplete block cyclic reduction*, Proc. 10th IMACS World Congress on Systems Simulation and Scientific Computation, vol. 1, IMACS, pp. 101–103.

[1655] G. RODRIGUE AND D. WOLITZER [1984]. *Preconditioning by incomplete block cyclic reduction*, Math. Comp., 42, pp. 549–565.

[1656] G. RODRIGUE AND D. WOLITZER [1986]. *A new class of explicit methods for parabolic partial differential equations*, Tech. Report UCRL-95669, Lawrence Livermore National Laboratory.

[1657] R. ROGALLO [1977]. *An Illiac program for the numerical simulation of homogeneous incompressible turbulence*, NASA Tech. Report TM-73203, NASA Ames Research Center.

[1658] C. ROMINE [1986]. *Factorization Methods for the Parallel Solution of Linear Systems*, PhD dissertation, The University of Virginia, Department of Applied Mathematics.

[1659] C. ROMINE [1987]. *Parallel solution of triangular systems on a hypercube*, in Heath [860], pp. 552–559.

[1660] C. ROMINE AND J. ORTEGA [1988]. *Parallel solution of triangular systems of equations*, Parallel Computing, 6, pp. 109–114.

[1661] W. RÖNSCH [1984]. *Stability aspects in using parallel algorithms*, Parallel Computing, 1, pp. 75–98.

[1662] W. RÖNSCH [1984]. *Timing and stability analysis of summation algorithms*, in Feilmeier et al. [623], pp. 225–231.

[1663] A. ROOZE [1988]. *An asynchronous iteration method of solving nonlinear equations using parallel approximation of an inverse operator*, USSR Comput. Math. & Math. Phys., 26.4, pp. 188–191.

[1664] J. ROSENFELD [1969]. *A case study in programming for parallel processors*, Comm. ACM, 12, pp. 645–655.

[1665] L. RUDINSKI AND G. PIEPER [1979]. *Evaluating computer program performance on the CRAY-1*, Tech. Report 79-9, Argonne National Laboratory.

[1666] J. RUDOLPH [1972]. *A production implementation of an associative array processor - STARAN*, Proc. Fall Joint Comp. Conf., Montvale, NJ, AFIPS Press, pp. 229–241.

[1667] T. RUDY [1980]. *Analysis of a 2-D code on the CRAY-1*, Tech. Report UCID-18549, Lawrence Livermore National Laboratory.

[1668] M. RUSCHITZKU, M. CHONTENSEN, M. AMES, AND R. VICHNEVETSKY, eds. [1984]. *Parallel and Large Scale Computers: Performance, Architecture, Applications*, North-Holland, Amsterdam.

[1669] R. RUSSELL [1978]. *The CRAY-1 computer system*, Comm. ACM, 21, pp. 63–72.

[1670] Y. SAAD [1983]. *Least squares polynomials in the complex plane with applications to solving sparse non-symmetric matrix problems*, Tech. Report YALEU/DCS/RR-276, Department of Computer Science, Yale University.

[1671] Y. SAAD [1985]. *Practical use of polynomial preconditionings for the conjugate gradient method*, SIAM J. Sci. Statist. Comput., 6, pp. 865–882.

[1672] Y. SAAD [1986]. *Communication complexity of the Gaussian elimination algorithm on multiprocessors*, Lin. Alg. & Appl., 77, pp. 315–340.

[1673] Y. SAAD [1986]. *Gaussian elimination on hypercubes*, in Cosnard et al. [415].

[1674] Y. SAAD [1987]. *On the design of parallel numerical methods in message passing and shared memory environments*, Proceedings of International Seminar on Scientific Supercomputers, Paris, France, February 2-6.

[1675] Y. SAAD AND A. SAMEH [1981]. *Iterative methods for the solution of elliptic difference equations on multiprocessors*, CONPAR 81, pp. 395–411.

[1676] Y. SAAD AND A. SAMEH [1981]. *A parallel block Stiefel method for solving positive definite systems*, in Schultz [1752], pp. 405–411.

[1677] Y. SAAD, A. SAMEH, AND P. SAYLOR [1985]. *Solving elliptic difference equations on a linear array of processors*, SIAM J. Sci. Statist. Comput., 6, pp. 1049–1063.

[1678] Y. SAAD AND M. SCHULTZ [1985]. *Alternating Direction methods on multiprocessors: An extended abstract*, Tech. Report YALEU/DCS/RR-381, Department of Computer Science, Yale University, April.

[1679] Y. SAAD AND M. SCHULTZ [1985]. *Data communication in hypercubes*, Tech. Report YALEU/DCS/RR-428, Department of Computer Science, Yale University, October.

[1680] Y. SAAD AND M. SCHULTZ [1985]. *Topological properties of hypercubes*, Tech. Report YALEU/DCS/RR-389, Department of Computer Science, Yale University, June.

[1681] Y. SAAD AND M. SCHULTZ [1986]. *Data communications in parallel architectures*, Tech. Report YALEU/DCS/RR-461, Department of Computer Science, Yale University, March.

[1682] Y. SAAD AND M. SCHULTZ [1986]. *Parallel implementations of preconditioned conjugate gradient methods*, Mathematical and Computational Methods in Seismic Exploration and Reservoir Modeling, W. Fitzgibbon, ed.

[1683] Y. SAAD AND M. SCHULTZ [1987]. *Parallel direct methods for solving banded linear systems*, Lin. Alg. & Appl., 88, pp. 623–650.

[1684] P. SADAYAPPAN AND F. ERCAL [1987]. *Nearest-neighbor mapping of finite element graphs onto processor meshes*, IEEE Trans. Comput., C-36, pp. 1408–1424.

[1685] P. SADAYAPPAN, F. ERCAL, AND S. MARTIN [1987]. *Mapping finite element graphs onto processor meshes*, Proc. 1987 Int. Conf. Par. Proc., pp. 192–195.

[1686] F. SAIED, C.-T. HO, L. JOHNSSON, AND M. SCHULTZ [1987]. *Solving Schrödinger's equation on the Intel iPSC by the Alternating Direction method*, in Heath [860], pp. 680–691.

[1687] M. SALAMA, S. UTKU, AND R. MELOSH [1983]. *Parallel solution of finite element equations*, Proceedings of the 8th Conference on Electronic Computation, ASCE, pp. 526–539.

[1688] J. SALTZ [1987]. *Analysis of parameterized methods for problem partitioning*, Tech. Report YALEU/DCS/RR-537, Department of Computer Science, Yale University, May.

[1689] J. SALTZ [1987]. *Automated problem scheduling and reduction of synchronization delay effects*, Tech. Report 87-22, ICASE, NASA Langley Research Center, Hampton, VA.

[1690] J. SALTZ AND M. CHEN [1987]. *Automated problem mapping: The Crystal run-time system*, in Heath [860], pp. 130–140.

[1691] J. SALTZ AND V. NAIK [1988]. *Towards developing robust algorithms for solving partial differential equations on MIMD machines*, Parallel Computing, 6, pp. 19–44.

[1692] J. SALTZ, V. NAIK, AND D. NICOL [1987]. *Reduction of the effects of the communication delays in scientific algorithms on message passing MIMD architectures*, SIAM J. Sci. Statist. Comput., 8, pp. s118–s138.

[1693] J. SALTZ AND D. NICOL [1986]. *Statistical methodologies for the control of dynamic remapping*, ICASE Report 86-46, NASA Langley Research Center, Hampton, VA, July.

[1694] A. SAMEH [1971]. *Illiac IV applications*, Proc. 9th Annual Allerton Conf. Circuit System Theory, pp. 1030–1038.

[1695] A. SAMEH [1971]. *On Jacobi and Jacobi-like algorithms for a parallel computer*, Math. Comp., 25, pp. 579–590.

[1696] A. SAMEH [1977]. *Numerical parallel algorithms — A survey*, in Kuck et al. [1133], pp. 207–228.

[1697] A. SAMEH [1981], *Parallel algorithms in numerical linear algebra*. Presented at the CREST Conference.

[1698] A. SAMEH [1983]. *An overview of parallel algorithms in numerical linear algebra*, E.D.F. Bulletin de la Direction des Etudes et des Recherches, C(1), pp. 129–134.

[1699] A. SAMEH [1984]. *A fast Poisson solver for multiprocessors*, in Birkhoff and Schoenstadt [173], pp. 175–186.

[1700] A. SAMEH [1984]. *On two numerical algorithms for multiprocessors*, in Kowalik [1116], pp. 311–328.

[1701] A. SAMEH [1985]. *On some parallel algorithms on a ring of processors*, Comm. Phys. Comm., 37, pp. 159–166.

[1702] A. SAMEH [1985]. *Solving the linear least squares problem on a linear array of processors*, in Snyder et al. [1808], pp. 191–200.

[1703] A. SAMEH AND R. BRENT [1977]. *Solving triangular systems on a parallel computer*, SIAM J. Numer. Anal., 14, pp. 1101–1113.

[1704] A. SAMEH, S. CHEN, AND D. KUCK [1976]. *Parallel Poisson and biharmonic solvers*, Computing, 17, pp. 219–230.

[1705] A. SAMEH AND D. KUCK [1977]. *Parallel direct linear system solvers — A survey*, in Feilmeier [621], pp. 25–30.

[1706] A. SAMEH AND D. KUCK [1977]. *A parallel QR algorithm for symmetric tridiagonal matrices*, IEEE Trans. Comput., C-26, pp. 147–153.

[1707] A. SAMEH AND D. KUCK [1978]. *On stable parallel linear system solvers*, J. ACM, 25, pp. 81–91.

[1708] A. SAMEH AND C. TAFT [1982], *Preconditioning strategies for the conjugate gradient algorithm on multiprocessors*. Presented at the 1982 Sparse Matrix Symposium.

[1709] J. SANGUINETTI [1986]. *Performance of a message based multiprocessor*, Computer, 19(9), pp. 47–55.

[1710] N. SARIGUL, M. JIN, R. KOLAR, AND H. KAMEL [1985]. *Design of array processor software for nonlinear structural analysis*, Computers and Structures, 20, pp. 963–974.

[1711] V. SAUNDERS AND M. GUEST [1982]. *Applications of the Cray-1 for quantum chemistry calculations*, Comput. Phys. Comm., 26, pp. 389–395.

[1712] J. SAVAGE [1984]. *Space-time tradeoffs for banded matrix problems*, J. ACM, 31, pp. 422–437.

[1713] A. SAWCHUK AND T. STRAND [1984]. *Digital optical computing*, Proc. IEEE, 72, pp. 758–779.

[1714] P. SAYLOR [1987]. *Leapfrog variants of iterative methods for linear algebraic equations*, Tech. Report R-87-1373, Department of Computer Science, University of Illinois at Urbana-Champaign.

[1715] M. SCHAEFER [1987]. *A polynomial based iterative method for linear parabolic equations*, Tech. Report 661, Center for Supercomputing Research and Development, University of Illinois at Urbana-Champaign, May.

[1716] U. SCHENDEL [1984], *Introduction to Numerical Methods for Parallel Computers*, John Wiley and Sons, New York. (Translator, B. W. Conolly).

[1717] U. SCHENDEL AND M. SCHYSKA [1984]. *Parallelle algorithmen in der nichtlinearen optimierung*, Preprint 161/84, Fachbereich Mathematik, Freie Universität Berlin.

[1718] D. SCHIMMEL AND F. LUK [1985]. *A new systolic array for the singular value decomposition*, Tech. Report EE-CEG-85-7, Department of Electrical and Computer Engineering, Cornell University, December.

[1719] R. SCHNABEL [1985]. *Parallel computing in optimization*, Computational Mathematical Programming, K. Schittkowski, ed., Springer-Verlag, Berlin, pp. 357–382.

[1720] R. SCHNABEL [1987]. *Concurrent function evaluations in local and global optimization*, Comput. Meth. Appl. Mech. Engrg., 64, pp. 537–552.

[1721] E. SCHNEPF AND W. SCHÖNAUER [1983]. *Parallelization of PDE software for vector computers*, in Feilmeier et al. [623].

[1722] E. SCHNEPF, W. SCHÖNAUER, AND H. MÜLLER [1985]. *Applications of the PDE solver FIDISOL on different vector computers*, Supercomputer, 10, pp. 21–28.

[1723] E. SCHNEPF, W. SCHÖNAUER, AND H. MÜLLER [1985]. *Performance of the PDE black box solver FIDISOL on a CYBER 205*, Supercomputer Applications, H. Emmen, ed., North-Holland, Amsterdam, pp. 51–59.

[1724] W. SCHÖNAUER [1983]. *The efficient solution of large linear systems resulting from the FDM for 3-D PDE's on vector computers*, Proc. First Intern. Coll. on Vector and Parallel Computing in Scientific Applications, A. Bassanut, ed., pp. 135–142. E.D.F. Bulletin de la Direction des Etudes et des Recherches, Ser. C., no. 1.

[1725] W. SCHÖNAUER [1983]. *Numerical experiments with instationary Jacobi-OR methods for the iterative solution of linear equations*, ZAMM, 63, pp. T380–T382.

[1726] W. SCHÖNAUER, ed. [1987]. *Scientific Computing on Vector Computers*, North-Holland.

[1727] W. SCHÖNAUER AND W. GENTZSCH, eds. [1986]. *The Efficient Use of Vector Computers with Emphasis on Computational Fluid Dynamics*, vol. 12 of Notes on Numerical Fluid Mechanics, John Wiley and Sons, New York, NY.

[1728] W. SCHÖNAUER, H. MÜLLER, AND E. SCHNEPF [1986]. *Pseudo-residual type methods for the iterative solution of large linear systems on vector computers*, Parallel Computing 85, M. Feilmeier, J. Joubert, and U. Schendel, eds., North-Holland, Amsterdam, pp. 193–198.

[1729] W. SCHÖNAUER AND K. RAITH [1982]. *A polyalgorithm with diagonal storing for the solution of very large indefinite linear banded systems on a vector computer*, Proc. 10th IMACS World Congress on Systems Simulation and Scientific Computation, vol. 1, IMACS, pp. 326–328.

[1730] W. SCHÖNAUER AND E. SCHNEPF [1986]. *Introduction to the workshop: Some bottlenecks and deficiencies of existing vector computers and their consequences for the develop-*

ment of general PDE software, The Efficient Use of Vector Computers with Emphasis to Computational Fluid Dynamics, W. Schönauer and W. Gentzsch, eds., Vieweg, Braunschweig, pp. 1–34.

[1731] W. SCHÖNAUER AND E. SCHNEPF [1987]. *Software considerations for the "black box" solver FIDISOL for partial diferential equations*, ACM Trans. Math. Softw., 13, pp. 333–349.

[1732] W. SCHÖNAUER AND E. SCHNEPF [1988]. *FIDISOL: A black box solver for partial differential equations*, Parallel Computing, 6, pp. 185–194.

[1733] W. SCHÖNAUER, E. SCHNEPF, AND H. MÜLLER [1984]. *PDE software for vector computers*, in Vichnevetsky and Stepleman [1920], pp. 258–267.

[1734] W. SCHÖNAUER, E. SCHNEPF, AND H. MÜLLER [1985]. *Designing PDE software for vector computers as a data flow algorithm*, Comp. Phy. Comm., 37, pp. 233–237.

[1735] W. SCHÖNAUER, E. SCHNEPF, AND K. RAITH [1983]. *The redesign and vectorization of the SLDGL-program package for the self-adaptive solution of nonlinear systems of elliptic and parabolic PDE's*, Conference of the IFIP Working Group 2.5 on Numerical Software, Sweden.

[1736] W. SCHÖNAUER, E. SCHNEPF, AND K. RAITH [1984]. *Modularization of PDE software for vector computers*, ZAMM, 64, pp. T309–T312.

[1737] W. SCHÖNAUER AND H. WIETSCHORKE [1987], *The questions of accuracy, geometrical flexibility and vectorability for the FDM*. Submitted to 1987 Meeting of ASME.

[1738] R. SCHREIBER [1982]. *Systolic arrays for eigenvalue computation*, Proc. SPIE Symp. East 1982, 341, Real Time Signal Processing V.

[1739] R. SCHREIBER [1983]. *Computing generalized inverses and eigenvalues of symmetric matrices using systolic arrays*, Proceedings of the Sixth International Conference on Computer Methods in Science and Engineering.

[1740] R. SCHREIBER [1983]. *On the systolic arrays of Brent, Luk and Van Loan for the symmetric eigenvalue and singular value problems*, Tech. Report TRITA-NA-8311, Department of Numerical Analysis and Computer Science, Royal Institute of Technology.

[1741] R. SCHREIBER [1983]. *A systolic architecture for singular value decomposition*, Proc. First Intern. College Vector and Parallel Computing in Scientific Appl., Paris, March.

[1742] R. SCHREIBER [1984]. *Systolic arrays: High performance parallel machines for matrix computation*, in Birkhoff and Schoenstadt [173], pp. 187–194.

[1743] R. SCHREIBER [1986]. *On systolic array methods for band matrix factorizations*, BIT, 26, pp. 303–316.

[1744] R. SCHREIBER [1986]. *Solving eigenvalue and singular value problems on an undersized systolic array*, SIAM J. Sci. Statist. Comput., 7, pp. 441–451.

[1745] R. SCHREIBER [1987]. *Cholesky factorization by systolic array*, Tech. Report 87-14, Department of Computer Science, Rensselaer Polytechnic Institute, May.

[1746] R. SCHREIBER [1987]. *Systolic linear algebra machines: A survey*, Signal Processing, S. Haykin, ed., Prentice-Hall, Inc., Englewood Cliffs, NJ.

[1747] R. SCHREIBER [1988]. *Block algorithms for parallel machines*, Numerical Algorithms for Modern Parallel Computer Architectures, M. Schultz, ed., vol. 13 of Volumes in Mathematics and its Applications, Springer-Verlag, Berlin, pp. 197–207.

[1748] R. SCHREIBER AND P. KUEKES [1982]. *Systolic linear algebra machines in digital signal processing*, Proc. USC Workshop on VLSI and Modern Signal Processing, Los Angeles, Englewood Cliffs, NJ, Prentice-Hall, Inc.

[1749] R. SCHREIBER AND B. PARLETT [1988]. *Block reflectors: Theory and computation*, SIAM J. Numer. Anal., 25, pp. 189–205.

[1750] R. SCHREIBER AND W. TANG [1982]. *Vectorizing the conjugate gradient method*, in Control Data Corporation [411].

[1751] R. SCHREIBER AND C. VAN LOAN [1989]. *A storage efficient WY representation for products of Householder transformations*, SIAM J. Sci. Statist. Comput., 10, pp. 53–57.

[1752] M. SCHULTZ, ed. [1981]. *Elliptic Problem Solvers*, Academic Press, New York, NY.

[1753] M. SCHULTZ [1984]. *Solving elliptic problems on an array processor system*, in Birkhoff and Schoenstadt [173], pp. 77–92.

[1754] M. SCHULTZ [1985]. *Multiple array processors for ocean acoustic problems*, Tech. Report YALEU/DCS/RR-363, Department of Computer Science, Yale University, February.

[1755] K. SCHWAN, W. BO, N. BAUMAN, P. SADAYAPPAN, AND F. ERCAL [1987]. *Mapping parallel applications to a hypercube*, in Heath [860], pp. 141–154.

[1756] H. SCHWANDT [1985]. *Newton-like interval methods for large nonlinear systems of equations on vector computers*, Comput. Phys. Comm., 37, pp. 223–232.

[1757] H. SCHWANDT [1987]. *Interval arithmetic block cyclic reduction on vector computers*, J. Par. Dist. Comp., 4, pp. 459–487.

[1758] H. SCHWANDT [1987]. *An interval arithmetic method for the solution of nonlinear systems of equations on a vector computer*, Parallel Computing, 4, pp. 323–338.

[1759] J. SCHWARTZ [1980]. *Ultracomputers*, ACM Trans. Program. Lang. Syst., 2, pp. 484–521.

[1760] J. SCHWARTZ [1983]. *A taxonomic table of parallel computers, based on 55 designs*, Ultracomputer Note 69, Courant Institute, New York University.

[1761] U. SCHWIEGELSHOHN AND L. THIELE [1987]. *A systolic array for cyclic-by-rows Jacobi algorithms*, J. Par. Dist. Comp., 4, pp. 334–340.

[1762] D. SCOTT [1986]. *Avoiding the square-root bottleneck in the Choleski factorization of a matrix on a parallel computer*, Lin. Alg. & Appl., 77, pp. 341–344.

[1763] D. SCOTT, M. HEATH, AND R. WARD [1986]. *Parallel block Jacobi eigenvalue algorithms using systolic arrays*, Lin. Alg. & Appl., 77, pp. 345–355.

[1764] M. SCOTT AND G. MONTRY [1988]. *Some experiments in multitasking on an ELXSI system 6400*, Appl. Math. & Comp., 26, pp. 135–150.

[1765] N. SCOTT, P. MILLIGAN, AND H. RILEY [1987]. *The parallel computation of Racah coefficients using transputers*, Comput. Phys. Comm., 46, pp. 83–98.

[1766] R. SCOTT [1981]. *On the choice of discretization for solving PDE's on a multi-processor*, in Schultz [1752], pp. 419–422.

[1767] R. SCOTT, J. BOYLE, AND B. BAGHERI [1987]. *Distributed data structures for scientific computation*, in Heath [860], pp. 55–66.

[1768] S. SCOTT, H. DEMUTH, AND J. HALEY [1988]. *Comparison of parallel SOR algorithms for solution of sparse matrix problems*, in Kartashev and Kartashev [1055], pp. 424–432.

[1769] M. SEAGER [1986]. *Overhead considerations for parallelizing conjugate gradient*, Comm. Appl. Numer. Meth., 2, pp. 273–279.

[1770] M. SEAGER [1986]. *Parallelizing conjugate gradient for the CRAY X-MP*, Parallel Computing, 3, pp. 35–48.

[1771] S. SEDUKEIN [1985]. *The computing structures of algorithms and VLSI-based computer architecture*, Computational Processes and Systems, Izdatel'stvo Nauka, Moscow, pp. 129–139.

[1772] C. SEITZ [1982]. *Ensemble architectures for VLSI — A survey and taxonomy*, Proc. MIT Conf. on Advanced Res. in VLSI, P. Penfield, ed., Artech House, pp. 130–135.

[1773] C. SEITZ [1984]. *Concurrent VLSI architectures*, IEEE Trans. Comput., C-33, pp. 1247–.

[1774] C. SEITZ [1984]. *Experiments with VLSI ensemble machines*, J. VLSI and Comp. Sys., 1(3).

[1775] C. SEITZ [1985]. *The cosmic cube*, Comm. ACM, 28, pp. 22–33.

[1776] C. SEITZ AND J. MATISOO [1984]. *Engineering limits on computer performance*, Physics Today, 37(5), pp. 38–45.

[1777] M. SEJNOWSKI, E. UPCHURCH, R. KAPUR, D. CHARLU, AND G. LIPOVSKI [1980]. *An overview of the Texas Reconfigurable Array Computer*, AFIPS Conf. Proc., NCC, pp. 631–641.

[1778] A. SHAH [1980]. *Group broadcast mode of interprocessor communications for the finite element machine*, Tech. Report CSDG-80-1, Department of Computer Science, University of Colorado.

[1779] J. SHANEHCHI AND D. EVANS [1981]. *New variants of the Quadrant Interlocking Factorization (QIF) method*, CONPAR 81 Conf. Proc. Lecture Notes in Computer Science III, W. Händler, ed., Springer-Verlag, pp. 493–507.

[1780] J. SHANEHCHI AND D. EVANS [1982]. *Further analysis of the QIF method*, Int. J. Comput. Math., 11, pp. 143–154.

[1781] J. SHANG, P. BUNING, W. HANKEY, AND M. WIRTH [1980]. *Performance of a vectorized three-dimensional Navier-Stokes code on the CRAY-1 computer*, AIAA J., 18, pp. 1073–1079.

[1782] D. SHARP, N. METROPOLIS, AND J. WORLTON, eds. [1986]. *Frontiers of Supercomputing*, University of California Press, Berkeley, CA.

[1783] J. SHARP [1987], *An Introduction to Distributed and Parallel Processing*, Blackwell Scientific Publications, London.

[1784] D. SHASHA AND M. SNIR [1986]. *Efficient and correct execution of parallel programs that share memory*, Tech. Report 206, Ultracomputer Laboratory, New York University, March.

[1785] D. SHAW [1984]. *SIMD and MSIMD variants of the NON-VON supercomputer*, Proc. COMPCON 84, IEEE Comp. Soc. Conf., pp. 360–363.

[1786] G. SHEDLER [1967]. *Parallel numerical methods for the solution of equations*, Comm. ACM, 10, pp. 286–291.

[1787] G. SHEDLER AND M. LEHMAN [1967]. *Evaluation of redundancy in a parallel algorithm*, IBM Systems J., 6, pp. 142–149.

[1788] M. SHELL, D. BOULDIN, AND P. MANHARDT [1985]. *Design and implementation of a VLSI systolic array for solving nonlinear parallel differential equations*, Proc. 1985 Int. Conf. Par. Proc., pp. 96–98.

[1789] S. SHEU, W. LIN, AND C. DAS [1987]. *An efficient parallel algorithm of conjugate gradient method*, in Kartashev and Kartashev [1055], pp. 488–496.

[1790] T. SHIMADA, K. HIRAKI, AND K. NISHIDA [1984]. *An architecture of a data flow computer and its evaluation*, Proc. COMPCON 84, IEEE Comp. Soc. Conf., pp. 486–490.

[1791] H. SIEGEL [1979]. *Interconnection networks for SIMD machines*, Computer, 12(6), pp. 57–65.

[1792] H. SIEGEL [1985], *Interconnection Networks for Large-Scale Parallel Processing: Theory and Case Studies*, Lexington Books.

[1793] H. SIEGEL AND R. MCMILLEN [1981]. *The multistage cube: A versatile interconnection network*, Computer, 14, pp. 65–76.

[1794] L. SIEGEL, H. SIEGEL, AND P. SWAIN [1982]. *Performance measurements for evaluating algorithms for SIMD machines*, IEEE Trans. Softw. Eng., SE-8, pp. 319–331.

[1795] D. SIEWIOREK [1983]. *State-of-the-art in parallel computing*, in Noor [1450], pp. 33–48.

[1796] D. SILVESTER [1988]. *Optimising finite element matrix calculations using the general technique of element vectorization*, Parallel Computing, 6, pp. 157–164.

[1797] M. SIMMONS AND O. LUBECK [1986]. *Benchmark of the Convex C-1 mini supercomputer*, Tech. Report LA-UR-86-2890, Los Alamos National Laboratory, August.

[1798] H. SIMON [1985]. *Incomplete LU preconditioners for conjugate gradient type iterative methods*, Proc. 8th SPE Symp. on Reservoir Simulation, Dallas, TX, February.

[1799] R. SKEEL [1987]. *Waveform iteration and the shifted Picard splitting*, Tech. Report 700, Department of Computer Science, University of Illinois at Urbana-Champaign, November.

[1800] D. SLOTNICK, W. BORCK, AND R. MCREYNOLDS [1962]. *The SOLOMON computer*, Proc. AFIPS, FJCC, 22, pp. 97–107.

[1801] L. SMARR [1985]. *An approach to complexity: Numerical computations*, Science, 228, pp. 403–408.

[1802] B. SMITH [1978]. *A pipelined, shared resource MIMD computer*, Proc. 1978 Int. Conf. Par. Proc., pp. 6–8.

[1803] R. SMITH AND J. PITTS [1979]. *The solution of the three-dimensional viscous compressible Navier-Stokes equations on a vector computer*, Advances in Computer Methods for Partial Differential Equations-III, IMACS, pp. 245–252.

[1804] R. SMITH, J. PITTS, AND J. LAMBIOTTE [1978]. *A vectorization of the Jameson-Caughey NYU transonic swept-wing computer program FLO-22-VI for the STAR-100 computer*, NASA Tech. Rept. TM-78665, NASA Langley Research Center.

[1805] L. SNYDER [1982]. *Introduction to the configurable highly parallel computer*, Computer, 15(1), pp. 47–56.

[1806] L. SNYDER [1985]. *An inquiry into the benefits of multigauge parallel computation*, Proc. 1985 Int. Conf. Par. Proc., pp. 488–497.

[1807] L. SNYDER [1986], *Type architectures, shared memory and the corollary of modest potential*. Preprint.

[1808] L. SNYDER, L. JAMIESON, D. GANNON, AND H. SIEGEL, eds. [1985]. *Algorithmically Specialized Parallel Computers*, Academic Press, Orlando, FL.

[1809] J. SOLEM [1984]. *MECA: A supercomputer for Monte Carlo*, Tech. Report LA-10005, Los Alamos National Laboratory.

[1810] P. SOLL, N. HABRA, AND G. RUSSELL [1977]. *Experience with a vectorized general circulation climate model on STAR-100*, in Kuck et al. [1133], pp. 311–312.

[1811] M. SOLOMON AND R. FINKEL [1979]. *The Roscoe operating system*, Proc. 7th Symp. Op. Sys. Princ., pp. 108–114.

[1812] D. SORENSEN [1984]. *Buffering for vector performance on a pipelined MIMD machine*, Parallel Computing, 1, pp. 143–164.

[1813] D. SORENSEN [1985]. *Analysis of pairwise pivoting in Gaussian elimination*, IEEE Trans. Comput., C-34, pp. 274–278.

[1814] J. SOUTH [1985]. *Recent advances in computational aerodynamics*, Paper 85-0366, AIAA. 23rd Aerospace Sciences Meeting, Reno, NV.

[1815] J. SOUTH, J. KELLER, AND M. HAFEZ [1980]. *Computational transonics on a vector computer*, ARO Report 80-3, U. S. Army Numerical Analysis and Computers Conference, August.

[1816] J. SOUTH, J. KELLER, AND M. HAFEZ [1980]. *Vector processor algorithms for transonic flow calculations*, AIAA J., 18, pp. 786–792.

[1817] M. SRINIVAS [1983]. *Optimal parallel scheduling of Gaussian elimination DAG's*, IEEE Trans. Comput., C-32, pp. 1109–1117.

[1818] P. STANAT AND J. NOLEN [1982]. *Performance comparisons for reservoir simulation problems on three supercomputers*, 6th SPE Symposium Reservoir Simulation. Also in Control Data Corp. [411].

[1819] B. STEFFEN [1988]. *Implementation of a resonant cavity package on MIMD computers*, Parallel Computing, 7, pp. 55–64.

[1820] B. STEFFEN [1988]. *Multigrid methods for calculation of electromagnets and their implementation on MIMD computers*, in McCormick [1312].

[1821] K. STEVENS [1975]. *CFD — A Fortran-like language for the Illiac IV*, Sigplan Notices, pp. 72–80.

[1822] K. STEVENS [1979]. *Numerical aerodynamics simulation facility project*, in Jesshope and Hockney [976], pp. 331–342.

[1823] G. STEWART [1987]. *A parallel implementation of the QR-algorithm*, Parallel Computing, 5, pp. 187–196.

[1824] H. STONE [1971]. *Parallel processing with the perfect shuffle*, IEEE Trans. Comput., C-20, pp. 153–161.

[1825] H. STONE [1973]. *An efficient parallel algorithm for the solution of a tridiagonal linear system of equations*, J. ACM, 20, pp. 27–38.

[1826] H. STONE [1975]. *Parallel tridiagonal equation solvers*, ACM Trans. Math. Softw., 1, pp. 289–307.

[1827] H. STONE [1977]. *Multiprocessor scheduling with the aid of network flow algorithms*, IEEE Trans. Softw. Eng., SE-3, pp. 85–94.

[1828] H. STONE [1980]. *Parallel computation*, Introduction to Computer Architecture, H. Stone, ed., Science Research Associates, Inc., second ed., pp. 363–425.

[1829] H. STONE [1987], *High Performance Computer Architecture*, Addison-Wesley, New York.

[1830] O. STORAASLI, S. PEEBLES, T. CROCKETT, J. KNOTT, AND L. ADAMS [1982]. *The Finite Element Machine: An experiment in parallel processing*, Proc. of Conf. on Res. in Structures and Solid Mech., pp. 201–217. NASA Conf. Pub. 2245, NASA Langley Research Center, Hampton, VA.

[1831] O. STORAASLI, J. RANSON, AND R. FULTON [1984]. *Structural dynamic analysis on a parallel computer: The Finite Element Machine*, 25th AIAA Structures, Structural Dynamics and Materials Conf., Palm Springs, CA. 84-0966-CP.

[1832] P. STOTTS [1982]. *A comparative survey of concurrent programming languages*, SIGPLAN Notices, 17(9), pp. 76–87.

[1833] T. STRAETER [1973]. *A parallel variable metric optimization algorithm*, NASA Technical Note D-7329, NASA Langley Research Center, Hampton, VA.

[1834] T. STRAETER AND A. MARKOS [1975]. *A parallel Jacobson-Oksman optimization algorithm*, NASA Technical Note D-8020, NASA Langley Research Center, Hampton, VA.

[1835] J. STRIKWERDA [1982]. *A time split difference scheme for the compressible Navier-Stokes equations with applications to flows in slotted nozzles*, in Rodrigue [1643], pp. 251–267.

[1836] J. STRINGER [1982]. *Efficiency of D4 Gaussian elimination on a vector computer*, in Cray Research, Inc. [423], pp. 115–121.

[1837] S. SU AND A. THAKORE [1987]. *Matrix operations on a multicomputer system with switchable main memory modules and dynamic control*, IEEE Trans. Comput., C-36, pp. 1467–1484.

[1838] R. SUGARMAN [1980]. *Superpower computers*, IEEE Spectrum, pp. 28–34.

[1839] H. SULLIVAN AND T. BASHKOW [1977]. *A large scale homogeneous fully distributed parallel machine*, Proc. 4th Annual Symp. Comp. Arch., pp. 105–117.

[1840] H. SULLIVAN AND T. BASHKOW [1977]. *A large scale, homogeneous, fully distributed parallel machine*, Comput. Arch. News, 5, pp. 105–117.

[1841] C. SUTTI [1983]. *Nongradient minimization methods for parallel processing computers*, J. Optim. Theory Appl., 39, pp. 465–488.

[1842] R. SWAN, S. FULLER, AND D. SIEWIOREK [1977]. *Cm* — A modular multi-microprocessor*, Proc. AFIPS Nat. Computer Conf., Montvale, NJ, AFIPS Press, pp. 637–644.

[1843] P. SWARZTRAUBER [1979]. *A parallel algorithm for solving general tridiagonal equations*, Math. Comp., 33, pp. 185–199.

[1844] P. SWARZTRAUBER [1979]. *The solution of tridiagonal systems on the CRAY-1*, in Jesshope and Hockney [976], pp. 343–358.

[1845] P. SWARZTRAUBER [1982]. *Vectorizing the FFTs*, in Rodrigue [1643], pp. 51–83.

[1846] P. SWARZTRAUBER [1983]. *Efficient algorithms for pipeline and parallel computers*, in Noor [1450], pp. 89–104.

[1847] P. SWARZTRAUBER [1984]. *FFT algorithms for vector computers*, Parallel Computing, 1, pp. 45–63.

[1848] P. SWARZTRAUBER [1987]. *Multiprocessor FFTs*, Parallel Computing, 5, pp. 197–210.

[1849] R. SWEET [1987]. *A parallel and vector variant of the cyclic reduction algorithm*, Supercomputer, 22, pp. 18–25.

[1850] R. SWEET [1988]. *A parallel and vector variant of the cyclic reduction algorithm*, SIAM J. Sci. Statist. Comput., 9, pp. 761–765.

[1851] J. SWISSHELM AND G. JOHNSON [1985]. *Numerical simulation of three dimensional flowfields using the Cyber 205*, in Numrich [1469], pp. 179–195.

[1852] J. SWISSHELM, G. JOHNSON, AND S. KUMAR [1986]. *Parallel computation of Euler and Navier-Stokes flows*, Appl. Math. & Comp., 19(1-4), pp. 321–332. (Special Issue, Proceedings of the Second Copper Mountain Conference on Multigrid Methods, Copper Mountain, CO, S. McCormick, ed.).

[1853] C. TAFT [1982]. *Preconditioning strategies for solving elliptic equations on a multiprocessor*, Tech. Report, Department of Computer Science, University of Illinois at Urbana-Champaign.

[1854] H.-M. TAI AND R. SAEKS [1984]. *Parallel system simulation*, IEEE Trans. Syst. Man. Cybern., SMC-14, pp. 177–183.

[1855] Y. TAKAHASHI [1982]. *Partitioning and allocation in parallel computation of partial differential equations*, Proc. 10th IMACS World Congress on Systems Simulation and Scientific Computation, vol. 1, pp. 311–313.

[1856] W. TANG [1986]. *Schwartz Splitting, A Model for Parallel Computations*, PhD dissertation, Stanford University, Department of Computer Science.

[1857] O. TELEMAN AND B. JONSON [1986]. *Vectorizing a general-purpose molecular dynamics simulation program*, J. Comp. Chem., 7, pp. 58–66.

[1858] C. TEMPERTON [1979]. *Direct methods for the solution of the discrete Poisson equation: Some comparisons*, J. Comp. Phys., 31, pp. 1–20.

[1859] C. TEMPERTON [1979]. *Fast Fourier transforms and Poisson solvers on CRAY-1*, in Jesshope and Hockney [976], pp. 359–379.

[1860] C. TEMPERTON [1979]. *Fast Fourier transforms on CRAY-1*, Tech. Report 21, European Center for Median Range Weather Forecasts.

[1861] C. TEMPERTON [1980]. *On the FACR (l) algorithm for the discrete Poisson equation*, J. Comp. Phys., 34, pp. 314–329.

[1862] C. TEMPERTON [1984]. *Fast Fourier transforms on the CYBER 205*, in Kowalik [1116], pp. 403–416.

[1863] C. TEMPERTON [1988]. *Implementation of a prime factor FFT algorithm on CRAY-1*, Parallel Computing, 6, pp. 99–108.

[1864] G. TENNILLE [1982]. *Development of a one-dimensional stratospheric analysis program for the CYBER 203*, in Control Data Corporation [411].

[1865] A. THAKORE AND S. SU [1987]. *Matrix inversion and LU decomposition on a multicomputer system with dynamic control*, in Kartashev and Kartashev [1055], pp. 291–301.

[1866] C. THOLE [1988]. *Parallel multigrid algorithms on a message-based MIMD system*, in McCormick [1312].

[1867] C. THOLE [1988]. *The SUPRENUM approach: MIMD architecture for multigrid algorithms*, in McCormick [1312].

[1868] W. THOMAS AND E. LEWIS [1983]. *Two vectorized algorithms for the solution of three dimensional neutron diffusion equations*, Nuc. Sci. Eng., 84, pp. 67–71.

[1869] W. THOMPKINS AND R. HAIMES [1983]. *A minicomputer/array processor/memory system for large-scale fluid dynamic calculations*, in Noor [1450], pp. 117–126.

[1870] K. THURBER [1976], *Large Scale Computer Architectures: Parallel and Associative Processors*, Hayden Book Co.

[1871] K. THURBER AND L. WALD [1975]. *Associative and parallel processors*, ACM Computing Surveys, 7, pp. 215–245.

[1872] G. THURSTON [1987]. *A parallel solution for the symmetric eigenproblem*, Tech. Report NASA-TM-89082, NASA Langley Research Center, Hampton, VA.

[1873] J. TIBERGHIEN, ed. [1984]. *New Computer Architectures*, Academic Press, Orlando, FL.

[1874] D. TOLLE AND W. SIDDALL [1981]. *On the complexity of vector computations in binary tree machines*, Inform. Process. Lett., 13, pp. 120–124.

[1875] S. TOMBOULIAN, T. CROCKETT, AND D. MIDDLETON [1988]. *A visual programming environment for the Navier-Stokes computer*, ICASE Report 88-6, NASA Langley Research Center, Hampton, VA.

[1876] J. TRAUB, ed. [1974]. *Complexity of Sequential and Parallel Numerical Algorithms*, Academic Press.

[1877] J. TRAUB [1974]. *Iterative solution of tridiagonal systems on parallel or vector computers*, in Traub [1876], pp. 49–82.

[1878] R. TRAVASSOS AND H. KAUFMAN [1980]. *Parallel algorithms for solving nonlinear two-point boundary-value problems which arise in optimal control*, J. Optim. Theory Appl., 30, pp. 53–71.

[1879] P. TRELEAVEN [1979]. *Exploiting program concurrency in computing systems*, Computer, 12(1), pp. 42–50.

[1880] P. TRELEAVEN [1984]. *Decentralised computer architecture*, in Tiberghien [1873].

[1881] S. TRIPATHI, S. KAISLER, S. CHANDRAN, AND A. AGRAWALA [1986]. *Report of the workshop on design and performance issues in parallel architectures*, Tech. Report CS-TR-1705, Department of Computer Science, University of Maryland, September.

[1882] J. TUAZON, J. PETERSON, M. PNIEL, AND D. LIEBERMAN [1985]. *Caltech/JPL Mark II hypercube concurrent processor*, Proc. 1985 Int. Conf. Par. Proc., pp. 666–673.

[1883] L. TUCKER AND G. ROBINSON [1988]. *Architecture and applications of the Connection Machine*, Computer, 21(8), pp. 26–38.

[1884] L. UHR [1984], *Algorithm Structured Computer Arrays and Networks*, Academic Press, Orlando, FL.

[1885] J. ULLMAN [1983]. *Some thoughts about supercomputer organization*, Tech. Report STAN-CS-83-987, Department of Computer Science, Stanford University, October.

[1886] S. UNGER [1958]. *A computer oriented towards spatial problems*, Proc. IRE, 46, pp. 1744–1750.

[1887] S. UTKU, Y. CHANG, M. SALAMA, AND D. RAPP [1986]. *Simultaneous iterations algorithm for generalized eigenvalue problems on parallel processors*, Proc. 1986 Int. Conf. Par. Proc., pp. 59–66.

[1888] S. UTKU, M. SALAMA, AND R. MELOSH [1986]. *Concurrent Cholesky factorization of positive definite banded Hermitian matrices*, Int. J. Num. Meth. Eng., 23, pp. 2137–2152.

[1889] M. VAJTERSIC [1979]. *A fast parallel method for solving the biharmonic boundary value problem on a rectangle*, Proc. First European Conference on Parallel Distributed Processing, Toulouse, pp. 136–141.

[1890] M. VAJTERSIC [1981]. *Solving two modified discrete Poisson equations in $7\log n$ steps on n^2 processors*, CONPAR 81, pp. 473–432.

[1891] M. VAJTERSIC [1982]. *Parallel Poisson and biharmonic solvers implemented on the EGPA multiprocessor*, Proc. 1982 Int. Conf. Par. Proc., pp. 72–81.

[1892] M. VAJTERSIC [1984]. *Parallel marching Poisson solvers*, Parallel Computing, 1, pp. 325–330.

[1893] R. VAN DE GEIJN [1987]. *Implementing the QR-Algorithm on an Array of Processors*, PhD dissertation, University of Maryland, Department of Computer Science. Also Tech. Report TR-1897, Department of Computer Science, University of Maryland, August.

[1894] E. VAN DE VELDE AND H. KELLER [1987]. *The design of a parallel multigrid algorithm*, in Kartashev and Kartashev [1055], pp. 76–83.

[1895] H. VAN DER VORST [1982]. *A vectorizable variant of some ICCG methods*, SIAM J. Sci. Statist. Comput., 3, pp. 350–356.

[1896] H. VAN DER VORST [1983]. *On the vectorization of some simple ICCG methods*, First Int. Conf. Vector and Parallel Computation in Scientific Applications, Paris.

[1897] H. VAN DER VORST [1985]. *Comparative performance tests of Fortran codes on the CRAY-1 and CYBER 205*, Parallel Computers and Computations, J. van Leeuwen and J. Lenstra, eds., CWI, Amsterdam. CWI Syllabus 9.

[1898] H. VAN DER VORST [1986]. *Analysis of a parallel solution method for tridiagonal systems*, Tech. Report 86-06, Department of Mathematics and Information, Delft University of Technology.

[1899] H. VAN DER VORST [1986]. *(M)ICCG for 2D problems on vector computers*, Tech. Report 86-55, Department of Mathematics and Information, Delft University of Technology.

[1900] H. VAN DER VORST [1986]. *The performance of Fortran implementations for preconditioned conjugate gradients on vector computers*, Parallel Computing, 3, pp. 49–58.

[1901] H. VAN DER VORST [1987]. *Analysis of a parallel solution method for tridiagonal linear systems*, Parallel Computing, 5, pp. 303–311.

[1902] H. VAN DER VORST [1987]. *ICCG and related methods for 3D problems on vectorcomputers*, Tech. Report A-18, Data Processing Center, Kyoto University, Japan.

[1903] H. VAN DER VORST [1987]. *Large tridiagonal and block tridiagonal linear systems on vector and parallel computers*, Parallel Computing, 5, pp. 45–54.

[1904] H. VAN DER VORST AND J. VAN KATS [1983], *Comparative performance tests on the CRAY-1 and Cyber 205*. Preprint, May.

[1905] P. VAN LARHOVEN [1985]. *Parallel variable metric algorithms for unconstrained optimiza-*

tion, Math. Programming, 33, pp. 68–81.

[1906] C. VAN LOAN [1986]. *The block Jacobi method for computing the singular value decomposition*, Computational and Combinatorial Methods in Systems Theory, C. Byrnes and A. Lindquist, eds., Elsevier Science Publishers B.V. (North-Holland), Amsterdam, pp. 245–255.

[1907] C. VAN LOAN [1988]. *A block QR factorization scheme for loosely coupled systems of array processors*, Numerical Algorithms for Modern Parallel Computer Architectures, M. Schultz, ed., vol. 13 of IMA Volumes in Mathematics and its Applications, Springer-Verlag, Berlin, pp. 217–232.

[1908] R. VAN LUCHENE, R. LEE, AND V. MEYERS [1986]. *Large scale finite element analysis on a vector processor*, Computers and Structures, 24, pp. 625–635.

[1909] J. VAN ROSENDALE [1983]. *Algorithms and data structures for adaptive multigrid elliptic solvers*, Appl. Math. & Comp., 13(3-4), pp. 453–470. (Special Issue, Proceedings of the First Copper Mountain Conference on Multigrid Methods, Copper Mountain, CO, S. McCormick and U. Trottenberg, eds.).

[1910] J. VAN ROSENDALE [1983]. *Minimizing inner product data dependencies in conjugate gradient iteration*, Proc. 1983 Int. Conf. Par. Proc., pp. 44–46.

[1911] J. VAN ROSENDALE AND P. MEHROTRA [1985]. *The BLAZE language: A parallel language for scientific programming*, ICASE Report 85-29, NASA Langley Research Center, Hampton, VA.

[1912] F. VAN SCOY [1977]. *Some parallel cellular matrix algorithms*, Proc. ACM Comp. Sci. Conf.

[1913] E. VAN WEZENBECK AND W. RAVENEK [1987]. *Vectorization of the natural logarithm on the Cyber 205*, Supercomputer, 19, pp. 37–42.

[1914] S. VANKA [1987]. *Vectorized multigrid fluid flow calculations on a CRAY X-MP/48*, I. J. Num. Meth. Fluids, 7, pp. 635–648.

[1915] C. VAUGHAN AND J. ORTEGA [1987]. *SSOR preconditioned conjugate gradient on a hypercube*, in Heath [860], pp. 692–705.

[1916] S. VAVASIS [1986]. *Parallel Gaussian elimination*, Tech. Report CS 367A, Department of Computer Science, Stanford University, Stanford, CA.

[1917] A. VEEN [1986]. *Dataflow machine architecture*, ACM Computing Surveys, 18, pp. 365–396.

[1918] V. VENKAYYA, D. CALAHAN, P. SUMMERS, AND V. TISCHLER [1983]. *Structural optimization on vector processors*, in Noor [1450], pp. 155–190.

[1919] C. VERBER [1985]. *Integrated optical architecture for matrix multiplication*, Optical Engineering, 24, pp. 19–25.

[1920] R. VICHNEVETSKY AND R. STEPLEMAN, eds. [1984]. *Advances in Computer Methods for Partial Differential Equations - V*, Proceedings of the Fifth IMACS International Symposium, New Brunswick, Canada.

[1921] R. VICHNEVETSKY AND R. STEPLEMAN, eds. [1987]. *Advances in Computational Methods for Partial Differential Equations - VI*, Proceedings of the Sixth IMACS International Symposium, New Brunswick, Canada.

[1922] V. VOEVODIN [1985]. *Mathematical problems in the development of supercomputers*, Computational Processes and Systems, Izdatel'stvo Nauka, Moscow, pp. 3–12.

[1923] V. VOEVODIN [1986], *Mathematical Models and Methods for Parallel Processes*, Izdatel'stvo Nauka, Moscow.

[1924] R. VOIGT [1977]. *The influence of vector computer architecture on numerical algorithms*, in Kuck et al. [1133], pp. 229–244.

[1925] R. VOIGT, D. GOTTLIEB, AND M. HUSSAINI, eds. [1984]. *Spectral Methods for Partial Differential Equations*, Society for Industrial and Applied Mathematics, Philadelphia, PA.

[1926] R. VOITUS [1981]. *A multiple process software package for the Finite Element Machine*, Tech. Report, Department of Computer Science, University of Colorado.

[1927] J. VOLKERT AND W. HENNING [1986]. *Multigrid algorithms implemented on EGPA multiprocessor*, Proc. 1986 Int. Conf. Par. Proc., pp. 799–805.

[1928] J. VON NEUMANN [1966]. *A system of 29 states with a general transition rule*, Theory of Self-Reproducing Automata, A. Burks, ed., University of Illinois Press, pp. 305–317.

[1929] D. VRSALOVIC, D. SIEWIOREK, A. SEGALL, AND E. GEHRINGER [1984]. *Performance prediction for multiprocessor systems*, Proc. 1984 Int. Conf. Par. Proc., pp. 139–146.

[1930] D. VU AND C. YANG [1988]. *Comparing tridiagonal solvers on the CRAY X-MP /416 system*, CRAY Channels, 9(4), pp. 22–25.

[1931] E. WACHSPRESS [1984]. *Navier-Stokes pressure equation iteration*, in Birkhoff and Schoenstadt [173], pp. 315–322.

[1932] R. WAGNER [1983]. *The Boolean vector machine*, 1983 IEEE Conference Proc. 10th Annual Int. Symp. Comp. Arch., pp. 59–66.

[1933] R. WAGNER [1984]. *Parallel solution of arbitrarily sparse linear systems*, Tech. Report CS-1984-13, Department of Computer Science, Duke University.

[1934] R. WAGNER AND M. PATRICK [1988]. *A sparse matrix algorithm on the Boolean vector machine*, Parallel Computing, 6, pp. 359–372.

[1935] D. WALKER, G. FOX, A. HO, AND G. MONTRY [1987]. *A comparison of the performance of the Caltech Mark II hypercube and the Elxsi 6400*, in Heath [860].

[1936] Y. WALLACH [1982]. *Alternating sequential-parallel calculation of eigenvalues for symmetric matrices*, Computing, 28, pp. 1–16.

[1937] Y. WALLACH [1984]. *On two more eigenvalue methods for an alternating sequential parallel system*, Computing, 32, pp. 33–42.

[1938] Y. WALLACH AND V. CONRAD [1976]. *Parallel solution of load flow problems*, Arch. Elektrotechnik, 57, pp. 345–354.

[1939] Y. WALLACH AND V. CONRAD [1980]. *On block parallel methods for solving linear equations*, IEEE Trans. Comput., C-29, pp. 354–359.

[1940] J. WALLIS AND J. GRISHAM [1982]. *Petroleum reservoir simulation on the CRAY-1 and on the FPS-164*, Proc. 10th IMACS World Congress on Systems Simulation and Scientific Computation, vol. 1, pp. 308–310.

[1941] J. WALLIS AND J. GRISHAM [1982]. *Reservoir simulation on the CRAY-1*, in Cray Research, Inc. [423], pp. 122–139.

[1942] A. WALLQVIST, B. BERNE, AND C. PANGALI [1987]. *Exploiting physical parallelism using supercomputers: Two examples from chemical physics*, Computer, 20(5), pp. 9–21.

[1943] S. WALTON [1987]. *Performance of the one-dimensional fast Fourier transform on the hypercube*, in Heath [860], pp. 530–538.

[1944] H. WANG [1981]. *A parallel method for tridiagonal equations*, ACM Trans. Math. Softw., 7, pp. 170–183.

[1945] H. WANG [1982]. *On vectorizing the fast Fourier transform*, BIT, 20, pp. 233–243.

[1946] H. WANG [1982]. *Vectorization of a class of preconditioned conjugate gradient methods for elliptic difference equations*, Tech. Report, IBM Scientific Center, Palo Alto, CA.

[1947] W. WARE [1973]. *The ultimate computer*, IEEE Spectrum, 10(3), pp. 89–91.

[1948] H. WASSERMAN, M. SIMMONS, AND A. HAYES [1987]. *A benchmark of the SCS-40 computer: A mini-supercomputer compatible with the Cray X-MP/24*, Tech. Report LA-UR-87-659, Los Alamos National Laboratory, May.

[1949] P. WATANABE, J. FLOOD, AND S. YEN [1974]. *Implementation of finite difference schemes for solving fluid dynamic problems on Illiac IV*, Tech. Report T-11, Coordinated Science Laboratory, University of Illinois at Urbana-Champaign.

[1950] T. WATANABE [1987]. *Architecture and performance of NEC supercomputer SC system*, Parallel Computing, 5, pp. 247–256.

[1951] I. WATSON AND J. GURD [1982]. *A practical data flow computer*, Computer, 15(2), pp. 51–57.

[1952] W. WATSON [1972]. *The TI-ASC, a highly modular and flexible super computer architecture*, Proc. AFIPS, 41, pt. 1, pp. 221–228.

[1953] J. WATTS [1979]. *A conjugate gradient truncated direct method for the iterative solution of the reservoir simulation pressure equation*, Proc. SPE 54th Annual Fall Technical Conference and Exhibition, Las Vegas.

[1954] S. WEBB [1980]. *Solution of partial differential equations on the ICL distributed array processor*, ICL Technical Journal, pp. 175–190.

[1955] S. WEBB, J. MCKEONN, AND D. HUNT [1982]. *The solution of linear equations on a SIMD computer using a parallel iterative algorithm*, Comput. Phys. Comm., 26, pp. 325–329.

[1956] R. WEED, L. CARLSON, AND W. ANDERSON [1984]. *A combined direct/inverse three-dimensional transonic wing design method for vector computers*, Tech. Report 84-2156, AIAA, Seattle, WA, August.

[1957] E. WEIDNER AND J. DRUMMOND [1982]. *Numerical study of staged fuel injection for supersonic combustion*, AIAA Journal, 20, pp. 1426–1431.

[1958] J. WEILMUNSTER AND L. HOWSER [1976]. *Solution of a large hydrodynamic problem using the STAR-100 computer*, Tech. Report TM X-73904, NASA Langley Research Center.

[1959] J. WELSH [1982]. *Geophysical fluid simulation on a parallel computer*, in Rodrigue [1643], pp. 269–277.

[1960] P. WHITE [1985]. *Vectorization of weather and climate models for the Cyber 205*, in Numrich [1469], pp. 135–144.

[1961] R. WHITE [1985]. *Inversion of positive definite matrices on the MPP*, in Potter [1584], pp. 7–30.

[1962] R. WHITE [1986]. *A nonlinear parallel algorithm with application to the Stefan problem*,

SIAM J. Numer. Anal., 23, pp. 639–652.

[1963] R. WHITE [1986]. *Parallel algorithms for nonlinear problems*, SIAM J. Algebraic Discrete Methods, 7, pp. 137–149.

[1964] R. WHITE [1987]. *Multisplittings of a symmetric positive definite matrix*, Comput. Meth. Appl. Mech. Engrg., 64, pp. 567–578.

[1965] R. WHITESIDE, N. OSTLUND, AND P. HIBBARD [1984]. *A parallel Jacobi diagonalization algorithm for a loop multiple processor system*, IEEE Trans. Comput., C-33, pp. 409–413.

[1966] O. WIDLUND [1984]. *Iterative methods for elliptic problems on regions partitioned into substructures and the biharmonic dirichlet problem*, Tech. Report 101, Department of Computer Science, Courant Institute, New York.

[1967] O. WIDLUND [1988]. *Iterative substructuring methods: Algorithms and theory for elliptic problems in the plane*, Tech. Report 265, Department of Computer Science, New York University.

[1968] B. WIENKE AND R. HIROMOTO [1985]. *Chaotic iteration and parallel divergence*, Tech. Report LA-UR-85-3597, Los Alamos National Laboratory.

[1969] B. WIENKE AND R. HIROMOTO [1986]. *Parallel S_n iteration schemes*, Supercomputers, F. Matsen and T. Tajima, eds., University of Texas Press, pp. 399–414.

[1970] R. WILHELMSON [1974]. *Solving partial differential equations using ILLIAC IV*, Constructive and Computational Methods for Differential and Integral Equations, A. Dold and B. Eckmann, eds., Springer-Verlag, New York, pp. 453–476.

[1971] J. WILKINSON [1954]. *The calculation of the latent roots and vectors of matrices on the Pilot model of the ACE*, Proc. Camb. Phil. Soc., 50, Pt. 4, pp. 536–566.

[1972] E. WILLIAMS AND F. BOBROWICZ [1985]. *Speedup predictions for large scientific parallel programs on CRAY-XM-P-like architectures*, Proc. 1985 Int. Conf. Par. Proc., pp. 541–543.

[1973] S. WILLIAMS [1979]. *The portability of programs and languages for vector and array processors*, in Jesshope and Hockney [976], pp. 381–94.

[1974] D. WILLIAMSON [1983]. *Computational aspects of numerical weather prediction on the Cray computer*, in Noor [1450], pp. 127–140.

[1975] D. WILLIAMSON AND P. SWARZTRAUBER [1984]. *A numerical weather prediction model — Computational aspects*, Proc. IEEE, 72, pp. 56–67.

[1976] E. WILSON [1976]. *Special numerical and computer techniques for finite element analysis*, Formulation and Computational Algorithms in Finite Element Analysis, MIT Press, Cambridge, MA, pp. 2–25.

[1977] E. WILSON [1983]. *Finite element analysis on microcomputers*, in Noor [1450], pp. 105–116.

[1978] E. WILSON AND C. FARHAT [1988]. *Linear and nonlinear finite element analysis on multiprocessor computer systems*, Comm. Appl. Numer. Meth., 4, pp. 425–434.

[1979] K. WILSON [1982]. *Experience with an FPS array processor*, in Rodrigue [1643], pp. 279–314.

[1980] O. WING [1985]. *A content addressable systolic array for sparse matrix computation*, J. Par. Dist. Comp., 2, pp. 170–181.

[1981] O. WING AND J. HUANG [1977]. *A parallel triangulation process of sparse matrices*, Proc. 1977 Int. Conf. Par. Proc., pp. 207–214.

[1982] O. WING AND J. HUANG [1980]. *A computational model of parallel solutions of linear equations*, IEEE Trans. Comput., C-29, pp. 632–638.

[1983] A. WINKLER [1987]. *A parallel variational method for certain elliptic spectral problems*, Research Report RC12878, IBM.

[1984] N. WINSOR [1981]. *Vectorization of fluid codes*, in Book [203], pp. 152–163.

[1985] D. WISE [1985]. *Representing matrices as quadtrees for parallel processing*, Inf. Proc. Lettrs., 20, pp. 195–199.

[1986] D. WISE [1986]. *Parallel decomposition of matrix inversion using quadtrees*, Proc. 1986 Int. Conf. Par. Proc., pp. 92–99.

[1987] L. WITTIE [1980]. *Architectures for large networks of microcomputers*, Workshop in Interconnection Networks for Parallel and Distributed Processing, April, pp. 31–40.

[1988] L. WITTIE AND A. VAN TILBOUG [1980]. *Micros, a distributed operating system for Micronet, a reconfigurable network computer*, IEEE Trans. Comput., C-29, pp. 1133–44.

[1989] Y. WONG [1987]. *Approximate polynomial preconditioning applied to biharmonic equations on vector supercomputers*, Tech. Report NASA TM100217, NASA Lewis Research Center.

[1990] Y. WONG [1988]. *Solving large elliptic difference equations on Cyber 205*, Parallel Computing, 6, pp. 195–208.

[1991] Y. WONG AND J.-M. DELOSME [1987]. *Transformation of broadcasting into pipelining*, Tech. Report YALEU/DCS/RR-544, Department of Computer Science, Yale University.

[1992] P. WOO AND J. LEVEQUE [1982]. *Benchmarking a sparse elimination routine on the Cyber*

           205 and the CRAY-1, Proc. 6th SPE Symposium on Reservoir Simulation.

[1993] P. WOODWARD [1982]. *Trade-offs in designing explicit hydrodynamic schemes for vector computers*, in Rodrigue [1643], pp. 153–171.

[1994] P. WORLEY [1988]. *Information Requirements and the Implications for Parallel Computation*, PhD dissertation, Stanford University, Department of Computer Science. Also published as STAN-CS-88-1212, Department of Computer Science, Stanford University.

[1995] P. WORLEY [1988]. *Limits on parallelism in the numerical solution of linear PDEs*, Tech. Report ORNL/TM-10945, Oak Ridge National Laboratory, October.

[1996] P. WORLEY AND R. SCHREIBER [1986]. *Nested dissection on a mesh-connected processor array*, New Computing Environments: Parallel, Vector and Systolic, A. Wouk, ed., Society for Industrial and Applied Mathematics, Philadelphia, pp. 8–38.

[1997] J. WORLTON [1981]. *A philosophy of supercomputing*, Tech. Report LA-8849-MS, Los Alamos National Laboratory.

[1998] J. WORLTON [1984]. *Understanding supercomputer benchmarks*, Datamation, 30(14), pp. 121–130.

[1999] A. WOUK, ed. [1986]. *New Computing Environments: Parallel, Vector, and Systolic*, Society for Industrial and Applied Mathematics, Philadelphia, PA.

[2000] C. WU, J. FERZIGER, D. CHAPMAN, AND R. ROGALLO [1984]. *Navier-Stokes simulation of homogeneous turbulence on the CYBER 205*, in Gary [700], pp. 227–239.

[2001] W. WULF AND C. BELL [1972]. *C.mmp — A multiminiprocessor*, Proc. AFIPS Fall Joint Comp. Conf., Reston, VA, AFIPS Press, pp. 765–777.

[2002] W. WULF AND S. HARBISON [1978]. *Reflections in a pool of processors*, Tech. Report, Department of Computer Science, Carnegie-Mellon University.

[2003] M. WUNDERLICH [1985]. *Implementing the continued fraction factoring algorithm on parallel machines*, Math. Comp., 44, pp. 251–260.

[2004] M. YASUMURA, Y. TANAKA, AND Y. KANADA [1984]. *Compiling algorithms and techniques for the S-810 vector processor*, Proc. 1984 Int. Conf. Par. Proc., pp. 285–290.

[2005] P.-C. YEW [1986]. *Architecture of the Cedar parallel supercomputer*, Tech. Report 609, Center for Supercomputing Research and Development, University of Illinois at Urbana-Champaign, August.

[2006] D. YOUNG [1971], *Iterative Solution of Large Linear Systems*, Academic Press, New York.

[2007] D. YOUNG, T. OPPE, D. KINCAID, AND L. HAYES [1985]. *On the use of vector computers for solving large sparse linear systems*, Tech. Report CNA-199, Center for Numerical Analysis, University of Texas at Austin.

[2008] N. YOUSIF [1983]. *Parallel Algorithms for Asynchronous Multiprocessors*, PhD dissertation, Loughborough University.

[2009] N. YU AND P. RUBBERT [1982]. *Transonic flow simulations for 3D complex configurations*, in Cray Research, Inc. [423], pp. 41–47.

[2010] C.-P. YUAN [1987]. *Implementation of capacitance calculation program CAP2D on iPSC*, in Heath [860], pp. 485–494.

[2011] V. ZAKHAROV [1984]. *Parallelism and array processing*, IEEE Trans. Comput., C-33, pp. 45–78.

[2012] P. ZAVE AND G. COLE [1983]. *A quantitative evaluation of the feasibility of and suitable hardware structures for an adaptive parallel finite element system*, ACM Trans. Math. Softw., 9, pp. 271–292.

[2013] P. ZAVE AND W. RHEINBOLDT [1979]. *Design of an adaptive parallel finite element system*, ACM Trans. Math. Softw., 5, pp. 1–17.

[2014] E. ZMIJEWSKI [1987]. *Sparse Cholesky Factorization on a Multiprocessor*, PhD dissertation, Cornell University, Department of Computer Science, August.

[2015] E. ZMIJEWSKI AND J. GILBERT [1987]. *A parallel algorithm for sparse symbolic Cholesky factorization on a multiprocessor*, Parallel Computing, 7(2), pp. 199–210.

[2016] D. ZOIS [1988]. *Parallel processing techniques for FE analysis I. Stiffness loads and stresses evaluation. II System solution*, Computers and Structures, 28, pp. 247–274.